SWINDOLL'S

NEW TESTAMENT

INSIGHTS

INSIGHTS ON
REVELATION

CHARLES R. SWINDOLL

SWINDOLL'S

NEW TESTAMENT

INSIGHTS

INSIGHTS ON

REVELATION

ZONDERVAN®

ZONDERVAN.com/
AUTHORTRACKER
follow your favorite authors

ZONDERVAN

Insights on Revelation
Copyright © 2011 by Charles R. Swindoll

This title is also available as a Zondervan ebook. Visit www.zondervan.com/ebooks.

Requests for information should be addressed to:

Zondervan, *Grand Rapids, Michigan 49530*

Library of Congress Cataloging-in-Publication Data
    Swindoll, Charles R.
        Insights on Revelation / Charles R. Swindoll
            p. cm. (Swindoll's New Testament insights)
        ISBN 978-0-310-28434-5 (hardcover printed)
        1. Bible. N.T. Revelation—Commentaries. I. Title.
    BS2825.53.S95 2011
    228'.07—dc22
                                2010038228

Scripture taken from the *New American Standard Bible*. Copyright © 1960, 1962, 1963, 1968, 1971, 1972, 1973, 1975, 1977, 1995 by The Lockman Foundation. Used by permission.

Maps by International Mapping. Copyright © 2011 by Zondervan. All rights reserved.

Published in association with Yates & Yates, www.yates2.com.

Cover design: Rob Monacelli
Cover photography: PixelWorks Photography
Interior design: Sherri Hoffman

Printed in the United States of America

11 12 13 14 15 16 17 18 19 20 21 /DCI/ 23 22 21 20 19 18 17 16 15 14 13 12 11 10 9 8 7 6 5 4 3 2 1

CONTENTS

AUTHOR'S PREFACE

For almost sixty years I have loved the Bible. It was that love for the Scriptures, mixed with a clear call into the gospel ministry during my tour of duty in the Marine Corps, that resulted in my going to Dallas Theological Seminary to prepare for a lifetime of ministry. During those four great years I had the privilege of studying under outstanding men of God, who also loved God's Word. They not only held the inerrant Word of God in high esteem; they taught it carefully, preached it passionately, and modeled it consistently. A week never passes without my giving thanks to God for the grand heritage that has been mine to claim! I am forever indebted to those fine theologians and mentors, who cultivated in me a strong commitment to the understanding, exposition, and application of God's truth.

For more than forty-five years I have been engaged in doing just that—*and how I love it!* I confess without hesitation that I am addicted to the examination and the proclamation of the Scriptures. Because of this, books have played a major role in my life for as long as I have been in ministry—especially those volumes that explain the truths and enhance my understanding of what God has written. Through these many years I have collected a large personal library, which has proven invaluable as I have sought to remain a faithful student of the Bible. To the end of my days, my major goal in life is to communicate the Word with accuracy, insight, clarity, and practicality. Without resourceful and reliable books to turn to, I would have "run dry" decades ago.

Among my favorite and most well-worn volumes are those that have enabled me to get a better grasp of the biblical text. Like most expositors, I am forever searching for literary tools that I can use to hone my gifts and sharpen my skills. For me, this goal means finding resources that make the complicated simple and easy to understand, that offer insightful comments and word pictures that enable me to see the relevance of sacred truth in light of my twenty-first-century world, and that drive those truths home to my heart in ways I do not easily forget. When I come across such books, they wind up in my hands as I devour them and then place them in my library for further reference ... and, believe me, I often return to them. What a relief it is to have these resourceful works to turn to when I lack fresh insight, or when I need just the right story or illustration, or when I get stuck in the tangled text and cannot find my way out. For the serious expositor, a library is essential. As a mentor of mine once said, *"Where else can you have 10,000 professors at your fingertips?"*

In recent years I have discovered there are not nearly enough resources like those I just described. It was such a discovery that prompted me to consider becoming a part of the answer instead of lamenting the problem. But the solution would result in a huge undertaking. A writing project that covers all of the books and letters of the New Testament seemed overwhelming and intimidating. A rush of relief came when I realized that during the past forty-five-plus years I've taught and preached through most of the New Testament. In my files were folders filled with notes from those messages that were just lying there, waiting to be brought out of hiding, given a fresh and relevant touch in light of today's needs, and applied to fit into the lives of men and women who long for a fresh word from the Lord. *That did it!* I began to pursue the best publisher to turn my dream into reality.

Thanks to the hard work of my literary agents, Sealy and Matt Yates, I located a publisher interested in taking on a project this extensive. I thank the fine people at Zondervan Publishing House for their enthusiastic support of this multivolume venture that will require over ten years to complete. Having met most of them over the years through other written works I've authored, I knew they were qualified to handle such an undertaking and would be good stewards of my material, staying with the task of getting all of it into print. I am grateful for the confidence and encouragement of both Stan Gundry and Paul Engle, who have remained loyal and helpful from the beginning. It is also a pleasure to work alongside Verlyn Verbrugge; I sincerely appreciate his seasoned wisdom and keen-eyed assistance.

It has also been especially delightful to work, again, with my longtime friend and former editor, John Sloan. He has provided invaluable counsel as my general editor. Best of all has been John's enthusiastic support. I must also express my gratitude to both Mark Gaither and Mike Svigel for their tireless and devoted efforts, serving as my hands-on, day-to-day editors. They have done superb work as we have walked our way through the verses and chapters of all twenty-seven New Testament books. It has been a pleasure to see how they have taken my original material and helped me shape it into a style that remains true to the text of the Scriptures, at the same time interestingly and creatively developed, and all the while allowing my voice to come through in a natural and easy-to-read manner.

I need to add sincere words of appreciation to the congregations I have served in various parts of these United States for almost five decades. It has been my good fortune to be the recipient of their love, support, encouragement, patience, and frequent words of affirmation as I have fulfilled my calling to stand and deliver God's message year after year. The sheep from all those flocks have endeared themselves to this shepherd in more ways than I can put into words ... and none more than those I currently serve with delight at Stonebriar Community Church in Frisco, Texas.

Finally, I must thank my wife, Cynthia, for her understanding of my addiction to studying, to preaching, and to writing. Never has she discouraged me from staying at it. Never has she failed to urge me in the pursuit of doing my very best. On the contrary, her affectionate support personally, and her own commitment to excellence in leading *Insight for Living* for more than three decades, have combined to keep me faithful to my calling "in season and out of season." Without her devotion to me and apart from our mutual partnership throughout our lifetime of ministry together, *Swindoll's New Testament Insights* would never have been undertaken.

I am grateful that it has now found its way into your hands and, ultimately, onto the shelves of your library. My continued hope and prayer is that you will find these volumes helpful in your own study and personal application of the Bible. May they help you come to realize, as I have over these many years, that God's Word is as timeless as it is true.

The grass withers, the flower fades,
But the word of our God stands forever. (Isaiah 40:8)

Chuck Swindoll
Frisco, Texas

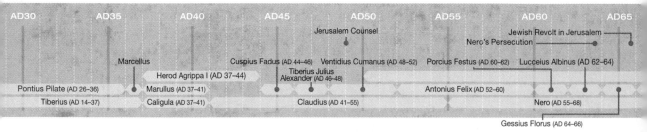

Jerusalem Counsel

Jewish Revolt in Jerusalem

Nero's Persecution

Marcellus

Cuspius Fadus (AD 44–46)   Ventidius Cumanus (AD 48–52)   Porcius Festus (AD 60–62)   Lucceius Albinus (AD 62–64)

Herod Agrippa I (AD 37–44)   Tiberius Julius Alexander (AD 46–48)

Pontius Pilate (AD 26–36)   Marullus (AD 37–41)   Antonius Felix (AD 52–60)

Tiberius (AD 14–37)   Caligula (AD 37–41)   Claudius (AD 41–55)   Nero (AD 55–68)

Gessius Florus (AD 64–66)

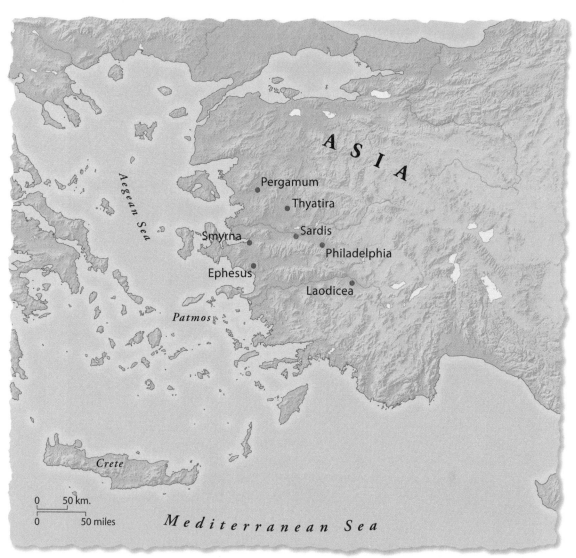

Western Asia Minor (modern Turkey), indicating the seven churches of Asia Minor and the island of Patmos

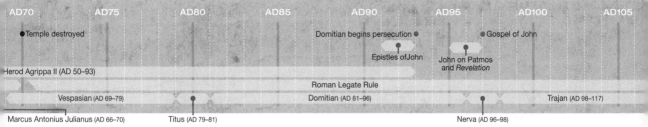

| AD70 | AD75 | AD80 | AD85 | AD90 | AD95 | AD100 | AD105 |

● Temple destroyed

Domitian begins persecution ●

● Gospel of John

Epistles of John

John on Patmos
and *Revelation*

Herod Agrippa II (AD 50–93)

Roman Legate Rule

Vespasian (AD 69–79)   Domitian (AD 81–96)   Trajan (AD 98–117)

Marcus Antonius Julianus (AD 66–70)   Titus (AD 79–81)   Nerva (AD 96–98)

REVELATION

Introduction

Lights dimmed and darkness enveloped audiences around the world. Chatter faded as an eerie musical score drowned out the whispers. In that darkness, the first syllables of an elvish tongue filled the theatre, and within minutes filmgoers around the globe found themselves caught up in a fantasy world so intricate that whole books have been written to interpret its complex mythology of hobbits, wizards, elves, and dwarves. The film adaptation of the literary classic *The Lord of the Rings* hurled viewers into an imaginary but vivid world filled with dark towers, dark lands, and dark lords. Epic battles against seemingly impossible foes culminated in the ultimate triumph of good over evil and the return of the long-awaited king.

Yet for all its absorbing intrigue, J. R. R. Tolkien's trilogy never came close to garnering the intense fascination that continues to surround the last book of the Bible—the book of Revelation. Its fast-paced barrage of images rivals anything Hollywood magic has mustered. Revelation describes the divinely inspired scene of the ultimate clash between good and evil, pointing us to the long-awaited King of kings, who will defeat the world's dark lord and his armies and usher in a new world of divine justice and eternal peace. No wonder curious Christians and serious scholars alike have marveled at its content and felt captivated by its imagery.

No book of the Bible has evoked greater fascination—or has led to more controversy—than Revelation. Its profound mysteries, elusive symbolism, powerful predictions, and colorful language are unparalleled in the rest of Scripture.

Thematic Outline of the Book of Revelation

Section	Messages of the Majestic Savior	Worship of the Worthy Lamb	Judgments of the Righteous Redeemer
Themes	Vision of the glorified throne Warnings to the wicked and rewards for the righteous Messages to the seven churches Jesus, our majestic messenger	Vision of the heavenly throne Splendor of heavenly worship and salvation of earthly remnants Breaking of the seven seals Jesus, our worthy Lamb	Visions of the beginning of the Tribulation Demonic deception, tragic death, and wicked defiance in the midst of judgment First blasts of the seven trumpets Jesus, our righteous Judge
	"The **Revelation** of Jesus Christ . . . "Blessed is he who reads . . . "I saw one **like** a son of man "Fear God, and give him glory . . .		
Key Terms	Repent Church Overcome	Worthy Seal Glory Honor	Trumpet Star Woe
Passage	1:1–3:22	4:1–7:17	8:1–10:11

Rivals of the Sovereign Lord	Real Faith Produces Genuine Humility	Real Faith Produces Genuine Patience
Visions of the middle of the Tribulation	Vision of the end of the Tribulation	Visions of Christ's reign
Trials of two witnesses, war of two armies, and reign of two beasts	Deliverance, death, and destruction in the last days	Final destinations of all humanity
Blowing of the seventh trumpet	Pouring of the seven bowls	End of the seventh age
Jesus, our sovereign Lord	Jesus, our great shepherd	Jesus, our coming king

the things which must **soon** take place (1:1)
the words of the **prophecy** . . . for the time is **near**." (1:3)
clothed in a robe reaching to the feet." (1:13)
Worship Him who made the heaven and the earth." (14:7)

Sign	Bowl	Justice
Authority	Wrath	Second Death
Testimony	Plague	New
	Hallelujah	

| 11:1–13:18 | 14:1–19:10 | 19:11–22:21 |

KEY TERMS

ἀποκάλυψις [*apokalypsis*] (602) "unveiling, disclosure, revelation"

Although this word appears only once in the book of Revelation (1:1), the Greek term *apokalypsis* functions as the title of the entire book. The word simply means the uncovering of something that has been hidden. In the New Testament the term can refer to (1) a development in God's plan of redemption that had been kept secret in the past (Rom. 16:25; Eph. 3:3); (2) a spiritual truth revealed in the present (1 Cor. 14:6; Eph. 1:17); or (3) future events in which God will break into human history (Rom. 2:5; 8:19; 1 Cor. 1:7; 2 Thess. 1:7). Interestingly, the book of Revelation involves all three aspects of this "unveiling" as it sheds light on Old Testament prophecies, reveals vital spiritual truths, and points to the ultimate revelation of God through Christ at the end of time.

ἐν τάχει [*en tachei*] (1722 + 5034), "soon," and ἐγγύς [*engys*] (1451) "near"

When Revelation says Christ will come "soon" (*en tachei*) (1:1) or that his return is "near" (*engys*) (1:3), these terms express Christ's coming as *impending*, not *immediate*. They reflect the suddenness of Christ's coming, not a short lapse of time before His coming. If Scripture meant to indicate that Christ's coming would be in a short amount of time after His ascension, it would likely have used *oligos*, used by John in Rev. 12:12 and 17:10 to indicate a short span of time. The terms *engys* and *en tachei* support the doctrine of *imminency* — that Christ could return at any moment.

ὅμοιος [*homoios*] (3664) "like, resembling, similar to"

The term *homoios* is used to draw out similarities between two things. It usually involves a symbolic correspondence — one thing *representing* or *resembling* another. Jesus repeatedly used the word in His parables when He likened the kingdom of heaven to various, everyday items (Matt. 13:31, 33). The book of Revelation uses the term twenty-one times, especially in passages using highly symbolic language (Rev. 9:10; 13:2). Readers of Revelation must keep this in mind. In many cases, John saw symbolic representations of future events and tried to put into words things that essentially were indescribable.

προσκυνέω [*proskyneō*] (4352) "bow down before, show reverence to, worship"

Worship runs like a golden thread throughout the book of Revelation. The common word for the outward manifestation of worship, *proskyneō*, occurs twenty-four times. Those in heaven worship God (4:10; 5:14; 7:11; 11:16; 19:4), but the wicked worship demons, Satan, the Antichrist, or idols (9:20; 13:4, 8, 15). The clear question for readers of Revelation is simple: to whom will you bow down, show reverence, and direct your worship — to God or Satan? In 14:7, an angel preaching the "eternal gospel" called all people on earth to "fear God, and give Him glory ... worship Him who made the heaven and the earth."

προφητεία [*prophēteia*] (4394) "prophecy"

The New Testament speaks of two types of "prophecy." *Predictions* point to future events (Matt. 13:14; 1 Tim. 1:18), whereas *proclamations* announce spiritual truths often gained through special revelation (1 Cor. 13:2). Many scholars regard the book of Revelation as belonging to the ancient genre called *apocalyptic*. In that literary style, the main purpose of the book would be to proclaim hidden spiritual truths about God, the world, Satan, and humanity, but not necessarily to predict future events. Revelation, however, describes itself as primarily a predictive "prophecy" (1:3; 22:18–19), that is, a revelation of "things which must soon take place" (1:1).

Attempts to interpret its details have spanned the extremes from the sublime to the ridiculous. Throughout my life of ministry, I've seen the book of Revelation drive fanatics to set dates for the return of Christ, frighten believers who find themselves overwhelmed by its judgment and wrath, and turn off skeptics who already think the Bible is filled with indecipherable nonsense.

How wrong! God promises great blessing to those who study the book of Revelation and heed its message. In fact, in the midst of the sometimes perplexing details of its visions, God's final message to humanity remains clear: in the end, good will triumph over evil, wickedness will be judged, and the righteous will receive their rewards.

Before we shine a spotlight on the big picture and sort out many of those complicated details, let's take some time to cover some foundational information about the book of Revelation. Let's also establish some necessary guidelines for understanding it. These things will help keep us balanced during our journey. Later, we'll get a glimpse of the book as a whole, which will help us keep an eye on our ultimate destination.

FOUNDATIONAL INFORMATION TO HELP US UNDERSTAND

More than sixty years had ticked away since the day a youthful, wide-eyed fisherman by the name of John, along with his brother, James, literally dropped his nets to follow Jesus (Matt. 4:21). During Jesus' three-year public ministry, John witnessed things most other disciples didn't. With Peter and James, John received a front row seat to the resurrection of a young girl from the dead (Mark 5:37–42). The same select three experienced the remarkable transfiguration of Jesus on Mount Hermon (Matt. 17:1–2). It may be this closeness with Jesus that led James and John—nicknamed the "Sons of Thunder" (Mark 3:17)—to try presumptuously to schmooze their way into the highest places of glory whenever Christ would take His throne and begin to reign (Mark 10:35–37). Yet this same special relationship gave them access to teachings of Jesus that went beyond those of His normal public ministry (Mark 13:3). We should also remember that Jesus called on Peter, James, and John to keep watch and pray with Him that night in the Garden of Gethsemane when Jesus was betrayed (Mark 14:33–34).

At the climax of Jesus' earthly ministry, that young disciple witnessed epochal events that would literally change the course of human history. He witnessed the Lord's crucifixion, where he received the unique responsibility to comfort and care for Jesus' mother, Mary (John 19:26–27). After Jesus' resurrection, John and Peter were the first to rush to the tomb. Though Peter entered the tomb before him, John was the first of the eleven remaining disciples to size up the empty tomb and believe that Jesus had risen (John 20:8).

In his old age—after nearly sixty years of preaching and teaching, primarily in Asia Minor (modern-day Turkey) near the city of Ephesus—John recounted his own memories of Christ's earthly ministry. In his gospel, John snuffed out a rumor spreading among the early Christians that he would not die before the coming of Christ (John 21:20–23).

In a certain sense, however, that disciple *would* live to "see" the return of Christ from heaven in glory. In the 90s, the apostle John had been exiled for his faith by Emperor Domitian to a penal colony on the island of Patmos, about forty miles from Ephesus in the Aegean Sea. As he was worshiping the Lord one Sunday morning, the veil between heaven and earth tore asunder and once again John was invited into the presence of the risen, glorified Jesus. This time Jesus commissioned John, "Write in a book what you see, and send it to the seven churches: to Ephesus and to Smyrna and to Pergamum and to Thyatira and to Sardis and to Philadelphia and to Laodicea" (1:11). What unfolded before John's eyes was a dramatic and often frightening series of God-given visions and voices portraying "the things which must soon take place" (1:1).

The Five "W"s of Revelation

WHO?	John, the disciple of Jesus and author of the gospel of John, as well as 1, 2, and 3 John
WHAT?	A written record of messages, prophecies, and visions that John personally saw and heard
WHERE?	The tiny island of Patmos, about forty miles off the coast of Asia Minor, where John had been exiled for his faith
WHEN?	About AD 95 or 96, making Revelation one of the last books of the Bible to be written
WHY?	To show believers the things that will take place in the end times, with a view toward exhorting them to repentance and faithfulness

The book of Revelation is the result of this encounter with the risen Lord. The title of the book comes from the Greek word *apokalypsis*, meaning "unveiling" or "disclosure." It means bringing something to light that formerly was hidden or kept secret. Today the term *apocalypse* conveys the idea of an imminent cosmic cataclysm or disaster. Though the apocalypse of John includes some of these catastrophic elements, the term is much broader. It refers to any kind of unveiling. In this case, God revealed the future to John in order to inform His people what will take place (1:1).

With this unveiling comes a blessing. Revelation 1:3 says, "Blessed is he who reads and those who hear the words of the prophecy, and heed the things which are written in it; for the time is near." Like a second bookend bracketing John's visions, 22:7 conveys Christ's words: "And behold, I am coming quickly. Blessed is he who heeds the words of the prophecy of this book."

GUIDELINES TO KEEP US FROM EXTREMES

We noted that the book of Revelation promises a blessing for those who read it, hear it, and heed its lessons (1:3). Many people, however, can miss the blessing by reading it wrongly, hearing things it doesn't say, or failing to put its big-picture principles into practice. We must all study this book with humility, seeking to balance careful reading, restrained and reasonable interpretation, and practical application. In the spirit of balance, let me suggest a few basic guidelines that can help keep us from going to extremes and missing out on the benefits of studying this book.

First, we should prepare to expect the unusual. The book of Revelation is not like any other book of the Bible. Though some books in the Old Testament, such as Daniel and Zechariah, contain similar and even complementary visions and symbols, Revelation has no equal in the New Testament. As we read John's description of what he saw and heard, we are bombarded with language, symbols, and images in a style like nothing we read elsewhere. Initial confusion is normal. Failure to catch the big picture in the midst of the details is common. In fact, misunderstanding can become a chronic condition. *That's okay!* Revelation doesn't package wisdom living into memorable verses like Proverbs or construct a logical argument like Romans. Rather, Revelation paints pictures and presents dramas that snare not only our minds, but also our hearts and imaginations. All this leads to the next guideline.

Second, we must restrain our imaginations. Because of the symbolic nature of many of the visions, some people try to bleed every little detail to produce specific, profound meaning. The result is often a complex scheme for the end times built more on speculation and conjecture than on the clear teachings of Scripture. In order to resist this overly creative approach to Revelation, we must emphasize the things that *are* clearly interpreted for us — either in the book of Revelation itself or in clear parallel passages from the Old or New Testaments. At the same time, we need to content ourselves with tentative conclusions or suspended judgment with regard to uncertain details. One seasoned expositor puts the situation well: "If we were to err, it would be better to err on the side of interpretive restraint than on the side of interpretive excess."[1]

Third, ask four questions. A tried and true method of biblical interpretation follows a path through (1) *observation* ("What does it say?"); (2) *interpretation* ("What does it mean?"); (3) *correlation* ("How does it fit?"); and (4) *application* ("How does it work?").[2] This four-step method of Bible study works well for Revelation — with a few stipulations. When it comes to Revelation, sometimes we need to suppress our curiosity and settle for the results of observation. That's because the apostle John himself didn't fully understand everything in his God-given visions (see 7:13 – 14). Much of the time, though, we can feel confident in our interpretations based on the

KNOWING WHAT THE BIBLE
TEACHES ABOUT THE FUTURE…

… *Communicates the full CHARACTER OF GOD, balancing our theology.*

… *Gives us HOPE for today and alleviates UNNECESSARY FEARS about the future.*

… *Compels us to live GODLY LIVES in view of FUTURE REWARDS.*

… *Moves us to WORSHIP GOD who will ultimately TRIUMPH OVER EVIL.*

context, an interpretation within the book of Revelation itself, or parallel passages in the rest of Scripture.

For the book of Revelation, the step of *correlation*—how the passage fits with other parts of the Bible—often becomes necessary for our *interpretation*. Once we understand the meaning of a passage, vision, or prophecy, we can move to the important step of *application*. Most of the time our applications will be concrete and personal. Occasionally the application will be general or theological. In either case, our goal must be more than satisfying curiosities or gathering facts. The purpose of Revelation is to *change* us, not simply to *inform* us.

OVERVIEW OF THE BOOK TO KEEP US FOCUSED

Like an epic drama, the book of Revelation takes a number of twists and turns, complete with characters, conflicts, and climaxes. It builds intensity as its plot moves toward an explosive conclusion, culminating in a stunning resolution that relieves the excruciating tensions of the story. Throughout the drama, we'll observe flashbacks and foreshadowing, repetition and contrast, zooming and panning, and enough interludes to give us opportunities to ponder and absorb what God is revealing about His glorious plan. As a sort of "preview" or "teaser trailer" of this divinely inspired, multimedia production, let me walk through its major movements. As we go deeper into the book, we'll return periodically to the big picture, keeping the major movements in mind in the midst of our scene-by-scene examination.

In 1:19, we find an inspired outline of the book. Jesus tells John explicitly what to write: "Write the things which you have seen, and the things which are, and the things which will take place after these things." Consider that threefold command. The *past* ("the things which you have seen") likely refers to the startling vision of Christ that John witnessed in 1:10–16. This reminds us that the central theme of the book is the majestic King Himself, Jesus. The *present* ("the things which are") refers to the messages Jesus dictates for the seven churches in Asia Minor in Revelation 2–3. Though these messages address specific situations in those first-century churches, Jesus Himself reminds us that they have application to every believer— "He who has an ear, let him hear what the Spirit says to the churches" (2:7, 11, 17, 29; 3:6, 13, 22). Taken literally, even if you have just one ear, these messages are for you ... today! The *future* ("the things which will take place after these things") refers to those events that will take place in coming years as the time grows nearer for the second coming of Christ and the ushering in of His promised kingdom (4:1–22:1).

The book of Revelation can also be described by focusing on its star Actor and major movements, or "episodes." None other than Jesus Christ occupies center stage throughout the inspired drama. All the episodes and scenes ultimately point to Him and His second coming as Judge and King. In a sense, Jesus Christ Himself is the One who is revealed through the series of visions, for "the testimony of Jesus is the spirit of prophecy" (19:10). So, the drama of Revelation portrays Jesus performing a variety of roles. I find it helpful to describe the flow of the book with six distinct but interconnected episodes centered on Christ. Let's briefly examine each of these in order.

Episode I: *Messages of the Majestic Savior* (1:1–3:22). This first episode includes John's own introduction to the book of Revelation (1:1–8), followed by a startling vision of Jesus' glorious majesty, in which He instructs John to write everything he sees and hears (1:9–20). Jesus then addresses the leaders of seven hand-picked churches in Asia Minor: Ephesus (2:1–7), Smyrna (2:8–11), Pergamum (2:12–17), Thyatira (2:18–29), Sardis (3:1–6), Philadelphia (3:7–13), and Laodicea (3:14–22). Christ functions as the exalted Head of the church, who is responsible for the church's present discipline and future reward.

Episode II: *Worship of the Worthy Lamb* (4:1–7:17). The first scene of this episode begins when the apostle John gets abruptly caught up into the spiritual realm—to the very throne room of heaven (4:1–2). There he witnesses the worship of God the Father and God the Son—the "Lamb of God" who is worthy to reveal events of the future through the ceremonial breaking of a seven-sealed scroll (4:3–5:14). Through symbolic visions, the "scroll judgments" begin to reveal the first stages of divine wrath upon the earth (6:1–6:17). In the midst of these judgments, however, John sees a vision of the redeemed from Israel and the nations, reminding us that even in the midst of judgment, God's grace and mercy prevail (7:1–17).

Episode III: *Judgments of the Righteous Redeemer* (8:1–10:11). After a half-hour respite at the breaking of the seventh seal, the second series of seven judgments commences—the seven trumpets (8:1–5). These trumpet blasts announce the next stage in divine wrath: a more intense display of God's righteous judgments against stubborn, unrepentant sinners (8:6–9:21). Just as the trumpet blasts approach a deafening crescendo, the soundings cease and John experiences another hiatus, in which he is recommissioned to prophesy concerning "peoples and nations and tongues and kings" (10:1–11).

Episode IV: *Rivals of the Sovereign Lord* (11:1–13:18). With John's recommissioning, the perspective of the great drama shifts from heavenly wrath to the conditions on earth, specifically events in the Promised Land. A conflict between two chosen witnesses prophesying in Jerusalem ends in their martyrdom and resurrection (11:1–14). After the seventh trumpet is blown in heaven to declare the arrival of Christ's kingdom (11:15 – 19), John witnesses a series of visions that describe in detail the final forms of the spiritual and earthly kingdom set up in opposition to Christ and the Kingdom of Heaven. In this dramatic portrayal, John sees the rise of two future political and religious tyrants energized by Satan, who are permitted to rule the world virtually unchecked for three and a half years (12:1 – 13:18).

Episode V: *Vengeance of the Glorious Deliverer* (14:1 – 19:10). The blasphemous exploits of Christ's wicked contenders give way to a series of visions that proclaim the final gathering of the earth for deliverance and harvesting in judgment (14:1 – 20). This, in turn, dissolves into a new vision of the most severe plagues of the end times — the seven bowls of wrath (15:1 – 16:21). At the brink of observing the final fate of the wicked armies of the earth, the action pauses and a great angel appears. He takes John aside to explain some of the symbols and events in the book of Revelation. These include a detailed description of the wicked empire's judgments and the victory of God's people (17:1 – 19:10).

Episode VI: *Reign of the Coming King* (19:11 – 22:21). Following a description of the final fate of earth's wicked rulers, the action of Revelation resumes. John witnesses a brilliant portrayal of the second coming of Christ with His armies (19:11 – 21), after which Christ and His resurrected saints commence their thousand-year reign of peace, which culminates in the final destruction not only of Satan, but of evil, pain, and death itself (20:1 – 15). The great drama of redemption comes to a close after John witnesses an astounding portrayal of the eternal state of ultimate peace and perfection in the new heavens and earth (21:1 – 22:5). Finally, like credits rolling during a closing score, the concluding words of Revelation remind us that Jesus is indeed coming again (22:6 – 21).

This book was not written to confuse, frighten, or entertain. Rather, it was given to believers to read, understand, and apply. Through this mile-high overview of the book, we have had a chance to catch a glimpse of Christ's power and glory. In the following pages, we'll embark on a journey through Revelation that focuses on the principles we need to read, comprehend, and ultimately obey. I pray with all my heart that this adventure through the book of Revelation will result in countless blessings in the life of every reader and bear fruit in the present age — and in the age to come.

Application

Practical Lessons before the Launch

Before we launch our vessel into the majestic waters of Revelation, let's review a few practical lessons to keep at the forefront of our minds throughout our voyage.

When we get distracted by waves of uncertainty, disturbed by storms of judgment, or merely start drifting through the doldrums of details, we can use these principles to enliven and enrich our journey.

First, *God's inerrant Word is a reliable map.* No matter how difficult it becomes to comprehend the mind-blowing visions in Revelation, we can have confidence that God's Word will accomplish its purpose in our lives, whether we feel it or not. In Isaiah 55:10 – 11 God says:

> For as the rain and the snow come down from heaven,
> And do not return there without watering the earth
> And making it bear and sprout,
> And furnishing seed to the sower and bread to the eater;
> So will My word be which goes forth from My mouth;
> It will not return to Me empty,
> Without accomplishing what I desire,
> And without succeeding in the matter for which I sent it.

This is why we can rely on the promise of God's blessing associated with reading and heeding the book of Revelation. We don't need to understand *everything* for God to accomplish His purpose in us through this magnificent book. If we comprehend at least the big picture of the book, we will have enough to guide us throughout life.

Second, *God's sovereign plan replaces fear with hope.* People all over the world live in bondage to superstition, fear of the unknown, and anxiety about the future. Not only do they question their personal path forward into the years to come, but many have an overwhelming feeling that the whole world and all of humanity are spinning out of control. Wars, famines, diseases, natural disasters — these tragedies make it look as though chaos reigns. The book of Revelation demonstrates, however, that no matter how bad things appear to be, God is working out His sovereign plan. This book assures us that in the end, God will win! Knowing this basic truth and ruminating on how that will happen will replace unnecessary fears with hope and confidence — not in us or in other people, but in God Himself.

Third, *God's glorious Son is worthy of worship.* The book of Revelation consistently and repeatedly points us to Jesus Christ as the center of prophecy (19:10). We praise Christ for what He *has done* for us on the cross by taking away our sins, and we praise Him for what He *is doing* for us by interceding for us in heaven. Revelation gives us another reason to praise Him — what He *will do* for us in the future. As such, Christ remains the center of our worship, the focus of our obedience, and the source of our blessing — both now and in eternity to come.

NOTES: Swindoll's New Testament Insights

1. Earl F. Palmer, *1, 2, 3 John, Revelation* (The Communicator's Commentary, vol. 12; gen. ed. Lloyd J. Ogilvie; Waco, TX: Word, 1982), 107.
2. See Howard G. Hendricks and William D. Hendricks, *Living by the Book: The Art and Science of Reading the Bible* (Chicago: Moody Press, 2007).

MESSAGES OF THE MAJESTIC SAVIOR (REVELATION 1:1–3:22)

Think before answering this question: If Jesus Christ Himself were to show up in your church unannounced, evaluate your worship, and carefully investigate the interpersonal relationships in your congregation, how would He react? Be honest, now. Would He sit down with your leadership, pat them on the back, and say how proud He was of them and encourage them to keep up the good work? Or would the Lord sit across from them, stare in their eyes, and shake His head in disappointment?

It's a frightening prospect to be evaluated directly by the One who knows every dark secret, concealed fact, longstanding grudge, embarrassing mistake, and less-than-pure motive. Yet this is exactly what Christ did, according to the first three chapters of the book of Revelation. Much to the surprise of the apostle John, who didn't expect to see the Lord again until his own death or the second coming, Christ appeared in majestic glory to deliver visions of the future and to dictate timely messages to seven specific churches. As would be expected if Jesus were to explore our personal lives or the lives of our churches, He gives varied diagnoses. From unimpeachable to despicable, from praiseworthy to pathetic, Christ would hold back neither encouragement nor rebuke. He called all the believers in the seven churches to examine their own lives and ministries to see if they measured up to His standards of faith, hope, and love.

The first major section of Revelation includes John's own introduction to the book (1:1–8), followed by a startling vision of Jesus' glorious majesty in which He instructed John to write everything he saw and heard (1:9–20). Jesus then addressed the leaders of seven hand-picked churches in Asia Minor: Ephesus (2:1–7), Smyrna (2:8–11), Pergamum (2:12–17), Thyatira (2:18–29), Sardis (3:1–6), Philadelphia (3:7–13), and Laodicea (3:14–22). Here we see Christ functioning as the exalted Head of the church, who is responsible for the church's discipline and reward at His coming. As the veil is lifted between earth and heaven and we hear the messages of the majestic Savior, let's allow His words to pierce the veil of our own hearts, fortifying our strengths and correcting our flaws.

The Messenger in His Majesty (Revelation 1:1–20)

¹The Revelation of Jesus Christ, which God gave Him to show to His bond-servants, the things which must soon take place; and He sent and

KEY TERMS

ἐκκλησία [*ekklēsia*] (1577) "assembly, church"

This word refers to the New Testament people of God who have been saved by faith in Christ and indwelt by the Holy Spirit. It includes all living and departed believers from Pentecost (Acts 2) to the resurrection and rapture of the church (1 Thess. 4:17). Though *ekklēsia* occurs twenty times in the book of Revelation, nineteen of those references are in the messages to the seven churches (Rev. 1–3). The last mention comes in the final words of the book, addressing those same churches (22:16). The "church" is not mentioned at all in chapters 4 through 21, which lends support to the view that the church will be raptured before the tribulation.

μετανοέω [*metanoeō*] (3340) "change one's mind, repent"

The biblical teaching of repentance starts with a genuine "change of mind" — an internal reversal of one's thoughts, attitudes, values, and emotions. It would be misleading, however, to conclude that authentic repentance is limited only to the invisibles of life. True repentance also leads to a change in actions. Thus, believers are called to "repent" by doing the things they did at first (2:5). Unbelievers also are called to "repent of the works of their hands, so as not to worship demons" (9:20).

νικάω [*nikaō*] (3528) "conquer, overpower, overcome"

In Revelation 2–3, Jesus extends promises to the one who "overcomes" (*nikaō*). The word has a wide range of meanings, from overpowering an enemy (Luke 11:22) to overcoming evil with good (Rom. 12:21). The meaning in John's writings, however, relates to overcoming Satan and the world by faith in the finished work of Jesus Christ, who overcame on our behalf (John 16:33; 1 John 4:4). The key to understanding what it means for believers to "overcome" is found in 1 John 5:4–5: "This is the victory that has overcome the world — our faith. Who is the one who overcomes the world, but he who believes that Jesus is the Son of God?"

communicated *it* by His angel to His bond-servant John, [2]who testified to the word of God and to the testimony of Jesus Christ, *even* to all that he saw. [3]Blessed is he who reads and those who hear the words of the prophecy, and heed the things which are written in it; for the time is near.

[4]John to the seven churches that are in Asia: Grace to you and peace, from Him who is and who was and who is to come, and from the seven Spirits who are before His throne, [5]and from Jesus Christ, the faithful witness, the firstborn of the dead, and the ruler of the kings of the earth. To Him who loves us and released us from our sins by His blood — [6]and He has made us *to be* a kingdom, priests to His God and Father — to Him *be*

the glory and the dominion forever and ever. Amen. [7]Behold, He is coming with the clouds, and every eye will see Him, even those who pierced Him; and all the tribes of the earth will mourn over Him. So it is to be. Amen.

[8]"I am the Alpha and the Omega," says the Lord God, "who is and who was and who is to come, the Almighty."

[9]I, John, your brother and fellow partaker in the tribulation and kingdom and perseverance *which are* in Jesus, was on the island called Patmos because of the word of God and the testimony of Jesus. [10]I was in the Spirit on the Lord's day, and I heard behind me a loud voice like *the sound* of a trumpet, [11]saying, "Write in a book what you see, and send *it* to the seven churches: to Ephesus and to Smyrna and to Pergamum and to Thyatira and to Sardis and to Philadelphia and to Laodicea." [12]Then I turned to see the voice that was speaking with me. And having turned I saw seven golden lampstands; [13]and in the middle of the lampstands *I saw* one like a son of man, clothed in a robe reaching to the feet, and girded across His chest with a golden sash. [14]His head and His hair were white like white wool, like snow; and His eyes were like a flame of fire. [15]His feet *were* like burnished bronze, when it has been made to glow in a furnace, and His voice *was* like the sound of many waters. [16]In His right hand He held seven stars, and out of His mouth came a sharp two-edged sword; and His face was like the sun shining in its strength. [17]When I saw Him, I fell at His feet like a dead man. And He placed His right hand on me, saying, "Do not be afraid; I am the first and the last, [18]and the living One; and I was dead, and behold, I am alive forevermore, and I have the keys of death and of Hades. [19]"Therefore write the things which you have seen, and the things which are, and the things which will take place after these things. [20]"As for the mystery of the seven stars which you saw in My right hand, and the seven golden lampstands: the seven stars are the angels of the seven churches, and the seven lampstands are the seven churches.

From psychics to seers, from statisticians to scientists — people from every nation and every generation have been trying to discover what the future might hold for them. Occasionally these forecasters get it right and things turn out the way they predicted. Far more often, however, these secular or religious prophets miss the mark. In your own lifetime, just think about some of the false forecasts that have let people down:

- A political analyst calls an election ... but the other candidate wins.
- An army general predicts a swift victory ... then the war drags on for years.
- A Bible scholar dates the return of Christ ... but Jesus doesn't appear.
- A financial expert banks on a bull market ... then Wall Street crashes.

Prophecies about the future are only as reliable as the wisdom, knowledge, and insight of their sources. When the source of information is limited to our human perspectives on the past and present, the most intelligent "expert" can offer only an educated guess. If, however, the source is the all-knowing, sovereign God, we can be certain that what He speaks will surely come to pass.

Before He gives us a glimpse of future events, however, God reveals the reliable source of this information. These visions of the future do not come to us from the pen of a crazed quack or wild-eyed fanatic. The prophecies of the book of Revelation come from our omniscient, sovereign God, through Jesus Christ Himself. They are therefore a reliable and relevant source of information concerning the future of the world.

—1:1–3—

The book of Revelation wasn't written to confuse, frighten, frustrate, or entertain us. The opening verse of this incredible book reveals its own purpose in no uncertain terms: "to show to His bond-servants, the things which must soon take place." Though the book reveals the unfolding of future events, don't let its portrayal of the end times distract you from the real heart of the book: the *Author* of those events. The title, "the Revelation of Jesus Christ" (1:1), can mean either the revelation *from* Jesus Christ or the revelation *concerning* Jesus Christ; in fact, it may mean both. As we witness the unfolding of events leading up to Christ's coming kingdom, our mental picture of the person of Jesus becomes clearer. This is true because "the testimony of Jesus Christ" mentioned in verse 2 is itself "the spirit [or inner heart] of prophecy" (19:10). The person and work of Christ is the blueprint that holds together all the pieces of the prophetic puzzle.

The Greek phrase translated "soon" or "quickly" in 1:1 is *en tachei*. The same phrase is used in Luke 18:8 in reference to the judgment of God and in Romans 16:20 in a description of the future destruction of Satan. The other common Greek term for impending fulfillment is found in Revelation 1:3, where the Greek word *engys* appears, meaning "near." These two terms, *en tachei* and *engys*, communicate that the fulfillment of future events could begin at any moment. It's as if Christ now stands at the very door of our world, ready to enter at any moment. We should not expect the return of Christ at a particular time, but rather be ready for His return no matter *when* it occurs.

In verse 3 John wrote that those who read, hear, and heed the words of the prophecy of Revelation would be "blessed." What does it mean to be "blessed" in a biblical sense? One commentator notes that the underlying Greek word "does not express superficial sentiment but instead the rugged and tested assurance that it is a good thing to be walking in the pathway of God's will."[1] The same Greek term

THE SEVEN "BEATITUDES" OF REVELATION

Blessed are those who:

- read, hear, and heed the prophecy (1:3). *They will grow through its life-changing message.*
- die in the Lord (14:13). *They will rest from labors and receive a reward.*
- stay alert and keep their clothes (16:15). *They will not be ashamed for their lack of reward.*
- are invited to the wedding feast of Christ (19:9). *They will experience everlasting celebration.*
- have a part in the first resurrection (20:6). *They will never suffer or die again.*
- heed the words of the prophecy of this book (22:7). *They will be ready for Christ's coming.*
- wash their robes (22:14). *They will receive reward for their deeds.*

is used repeatedly by Jesus in the famous "beatitudes" passage in the Sermon on the Mount (Matt. 5:3–11). We often think of Revelation as containing nothing but death, destruction, and suffering. In reality, Revelation contains seven "beatitudes" for believers, designed to provide hope and encouragement in the midst of trials.

— 1:4–8 —

John began by greeting the churches in Asia Minor with "grace ... and peace" (1:4).[2] When sinners come to Christ through simple faith, accepting Him as God in the flesh whose death on the cross paid the penalty for their sins, they receive eternal salvation through *grace*— unmerited, unearned, undeserved favor. God doesn't save us because of any good thing we have done, or will do, or even promise to do. God saves us solely by His grace through faith (Eph. 2:8–9). Salvation is God's gift to undeserving sinners— we must never forget that! The result of this precious grace is a relationship that offers us true peace that overcomes any trials and tribulations the world can bring. What a reassuring greeting to the members of the persecuted church! Though John will later describe *judgment* and *distress* that in the future will overtake wicked unbelievers, God's own people receive *grace* and *peace*.

This present peace and the future fulfillment of our salvation come from the Father, Son, and Holy Spirit. Drawing on several images he saw in the visions, John presented an "elaborate triadic formula for the Trinity."[3] He called the Father the One "who is and who was and who is to come" (1:4). We see this same description in the song of the four living creatures in 4:8. As an allusion to the divine name "I AM" in Exodus 3:14, it indicates God's complete transcendence over all history— past, present, and future.[4] God is just as much in control of our unknown future and unnerving present as He is of our unpleasant past.

The names John used for "Jesus Christ" are also drawn from Old and New Testament language. The titles "faithful witness," "firstborn," and "ruler of the kings of the earth" are drawn from Psalm 89:27 and 37; these refer to Christ's authority and kingship as the promised descendant of David. These phrases also appear in Colossians 1:18 and Revelation 3:14, possibly referring to Christ's authority to rule as the promised king from the line of David.

Finally, the Holy Spirit is described as "the seven Spirits who are before His throne" (1:4). John isn't describing seven distinct Holy Spirits; there's only one Holy Spirit (1 Cor. 12:13; Eph. 4:4). In a vision of the heavenly throne room described in Revelation 4, John saw the Holy Spirit symbolically represented by "seven lamps of fire burning before the throne" (4:5). The image of the "sevenfold Spirit" is also drawn from a similar image in Zechariah 4:2–7 and the seven qualities of the Holy Spirit in Isaiah 11:2–3: the Spirit (1) of the Lord, (2) of wisdom, (3) of understanding, (4) of counsel, (5) of strength, (6) of knowledge, and (7) of the fear of the Lord.[5]

In light of this glorious truth about the Triune God, John responded with a grand doxology or song of praise (1:5–6). He drew the attention of his readers back to the cross where he had once stood as an eyewitness to the sufferings of his Savior (John 19:26–27, 35). By shedding His blood, Christ paid the debt in full for the sins of the world and thereby released believers from the guilt and penalty of their sins. On our behalf He conquered death and gave new life to all who believe. We can therefore share with Christ His authority as Priest and coming King through a supernatural union with Him by the indwelling power of the Holy Spirit (Eph. 2:4–7; Rev. 5:10; 20:6). Such glorious news is worthy of a grand doxology!

Ultimately, the book of Revelation tells the story about Jesus Christ Himself. As John concluded the opening greeting, he broke into a prophetic description of the coming King in all His glory. When the true Sovereign steps foot on the Mount of Olives, no applause will erupt from those who have rejected Him. No marching band will play His anthem. No red carpet will mark His way. No massive banner will greet Him displaying a bold "Welcome Home!" Instead, His coming will be accompanied by mourning because He comes as Judge (1:7). Using biblical images common in his day, John previewed the glorious descent of Christ at the final battle of Armageddon. Every eye will see Him, even those who did not believe in Him, and all who see Him will mourn greatly.

Jolting us to attention, John interjected a direct quote from God Almighty Himself: "I am the Alpha and the Omega ... who is and who was and who is to come, the Almighty" (1:8). "Alpha" and "Omega," the first and last letters of the Greek alphabet, mark God as the One who has both creation and re-creation in His hands. It would be a terrible misunderstanding, however, if we were to assume God cares nothing about what comes between the "A" and "Z." This is why He reminds us that not only is He the God of the past and the future, but of the present as well. As "Almighty" God, the Lord exercises control over all time.

—**1:9–11**—

After a powerful introduction that climaxed in a quotation from the Almighty Himself (1:1–8), John transitioned abruptly to the setting of his first vision (1:9–11). As if he were going out of his way to keep the spotlight on Jesus, the apostle John introduced himself and his circumstances with succinct simplicity and humility: "I, John" (1:9). Having been banished to the penal colony on Patmos by the cruel Emperor Domitian for refusing to confess the emperor as "lord and god," John wasn't about to turn attention away from the only true Lord and God, Jesus Christ.

Though John could have pointed out items in his résumé that no one then alive could equal, he didn't. Instead, he described himself in ways that emphasized the common experiences he shared with fellow believers: "your brother and fellow partaker" (1:9). The term translated "partaker" is related to the concept of "fellowship." It's hard for most Christians today to imagine fellowship in the church without the three so-called essentials—*food*, *folks*, and *fun*. Yet John verified that fellowship in the early church centered on an altogether different threesome—*perseverance* through *tribulation* in light of the coming *kingdom*.

The Greek word *thlipsis* ("tribulation") can refer to the coming great tribulation of the end times, leading up to Christ's physical return (Matt. 24:21, 29). More commonly, though, it refers to general trials and persecutions experienced by Christians of every age (13:21; 24:9; John 16:33; Rom. 5:3).

The term *kingdom* refers to a future earthly kingdom that will be established at the return of Christ (Matt. 19:28; Acts 1:6–7; 2 Tim. 4:1; Rev. 20:4). In light of their common destiny as co-regents with Christ at His coming, believers are occasionally referred to as God's "kingdom" in a spiritual sense (1 Cor. 4:20; Col. 1:13).

In the context of shared suffering and in light of the promise of future glory, the Spirit enables believers to share in *perseverance*. The noun *hypomonē* (along with the cognate verb *hypomenō*) implies endurance under extreme difficulty, as a beast of burden might endure under a heavy load. God Himself gives believers the ability to endure hardship (Rom. 15:5; Col. 1:11).

In these three things—perseverance, tribulation, and the kingdom—Jesus Christ drew believers in John's day together by giving them purpose and perspective in the midst of suffering. If Christ the coming King could suffer unjustly for them, they could certainly endure persecution for Him.

During Domitian's reign, John was exiled to Patmos because of "the word of God and the testimony of Jesus" (1:9). Because of its unpleasant conditions, Rome had established the tiny, remote island of Patmos as a penal colony in the first century. According to the earliest historical records of the ancient church, the apostle John was exiled to Patmos for eighteen months beginning in AD 95.[6] Even in exile

DOMITIAN'S PERSECUTION IN HISTORICAL PERSPECTIVE

Throughout the history of the church, Christianity has suffered various degrees of persecution. Historians identify two major worldwide, official attacks on the church by the Roman Empire: the first by Emperor Decius in the AD 250s, the second about fifty years later under Diocletian. This latter, brutal persecution ended with the Edict of Milan of 313, in which Emperor Constantine put an end to official Roman persecution of Christianity. The following chart indicates major and minor persecutions in the early church, with a general indication of their intensity.

Local persecutions, however, both preceded and followed those major upheavals. In fact, in the years immediately following the resurrection and ascension of Christ, the church suffered opposition and persecution by both local synagogue leaders as well as Gentile authorities. In the late 60s, Nero persecuted the church in Rome, executing Peter and Paul as well as many other Christians. Thirty years later, a persecution arose under Domitian, in which a primary target was one of the last known surviving apostles, John.

Tradition has it that Roman authorities attempted to boil him in oil, but he was miraculously preserved, which baffled and frightened the superstitious officials. John was then exiled to Patmos because of his testimony of Jesus Christ. Domitian, afraid of the kingdom of God and wanting to rid the world of any threats to his own power, sought out the known descendants of King David. He called in two grandsons of Jesus' brother Jude for questioning regarding the nature of Christ's kingdom and whether they were heirs to the throne. To Domitian's surprise, however, these Jewish Christian relatives of Jesus explained that the kingdom they believed in and proclaimed was not earthly but heavenly, and it was to be established at the end of the world. Additionally, the two had little monetary worth. After showing the emperor their empty pockets, he released them from custody. John soon returned from exile and directed the churches of Asia until his death after the crowning of Emperor Trajan in AD 98.[7]

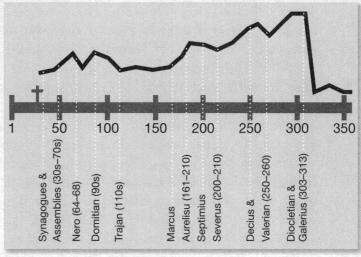

Persecutions in the early church

for his faith, dwelling in the uncertain surroundings of a rocky penal colony, the elderly apostle set aside time on "the Lord's day" (Sunday) to worship and pray. That's what I call devotion! Perhaps he was kneeling in prayer or reciting Psalms when something supernatural took hold of him and ripped him out of the sphere of this world and transported into the spiritual realm.[8]

Immediately upon finding himself "in the Spirit," John heard behind him the clear, penetrating voice of Christ calling to his beloved disciple "like a trumpet" (1:10). He gave a simple instruction: "Write in a book what you see, and send it to the seven churches: to Ephesus and to Smyrna and to Pergamum and to Thyatira and to Sardis and to Philadelphia and to Laodicea." Christ selected these seven churches because their situations represented conditions applicable to churches of every age, including our own. Ephesus, the first of the seven churches and John's own home church, was nearest to Patmos. The rest of the churches were on a natural overland route in the specific order given by Christ (see map in the introduction, page 10).

—1:12–20—

With the booming, majestic voice of the Savior still echoing in his ears, John slowly turned to see who was speaking to him. He noticed first not a man, but seven golden lampstands, each holding an oil-burning lamp (1:12). Then his eyes settled on the source of the voice—"one like a son of man" standing in the midst of the seven lampstands. This was Jesus, no doubt, but not the kind of Jesus John remembered from earlier years—preaching to the multitudes, healing the sick, suffering on the cross, or even ascending into heaven. No, the message from this Jesus sent John's memories racing backward in time more than sixty years to a powerful experience on the Mount of Transfiguration (Matt. 17:1–8; Mark 9:2–8; Luke 9:28–36). There Peter, James, and John had witnessed Christ transformed before their eyes as He briefly unveiled His glory. Now, near the end of his life, John saw a vision of the risen Lord in all His splendor.

John used the best descriptive terms he could muster to put into words what was essentially indescribable. The initial image resembled a human form, but He was clearly more than a man. The vision of the long robe, golden sash, white hair, flaming gaze, bronze feet, bellowing voice, and brilliant features (1:13–16) all point to one thing: Jesus Christ is God! From His mouth shot a two-edged sword—a symbol for the word of God (Heb. 4:12) as well as an instrument of judgment (Rev. 19:11–15). In his hands He held seven stars (1:16). In a brief glimpse of unveiled deity shrouded in mysterious symbols that surpassed even John's experience on the Mount of Transfiguration, that beloved disciple quickly learned his place in the universe. Saint John—evangelist, theologian, elder, apostle, and elite member of Christ's inner circle—was instantly reduced to a trembling sinner lying powerless before the King of kings and Lord of lords. In a word, the vision terrified him.

Yet in the midst of the apostle's heart-stopping terror, the unsurpassable Son of God stooped down, reached out with His nail-pierced hand, and comforted His old friend. Helping the elderly disciple to his feet, He told John not to fear. Then Jesus described himself in exalted terms: "I am the first and the last, and the living One; and I was dead, and behold, I am alive forevermore, and I have the keys of death and of Hades" (1:17–18).

Immediately the Lord reiterated his command for John to write everything he saw (1:19; cf. 1:11). Yet this time he outlined the divine information into three distinct units that can be broken down into past, present, and future.

Inspired Outline in Revelation 1:19		
Therefore write …		
(1) the things which you have seen,	(2) and the things which are,	(3) and the things which will take place after these things.
The Vision of Christ in Revelation 1	The Messages to the Churches in Revelation 2–3	The Visions of Future Things in Revelation 4–22.
"Then I turned to see the voice that was speaking with me" (1:12)	"To the angel of the church … write" (2:1, 8, 12, 18; 3:1, 7, 14)	"Come up here, and I will show you what must take place after these things" (4:1)

Like a reporter in the midst of a historic event, John began frantically recording the vision of Jesus still impressed upon his mind ("the things which you have seen"). Then Jesus helped all of us by interpreting two symbols from that vision: the stars and the lampstands. The seven stars in His right hand are the "angels" (or human messengers) of the seven churches mentioned in 1:11. The seven golden lampstands are the seven churches themselves (1:20). The charge is clear: John was to write everything he saw and heard and send it to the seven churches through each church's pastor. This wide distribution of the book guaranteed that the revelation from Jesus Christ would address not only believers in John's own day, but it would continue to inform and encourage believers of every age.

Application

Falling on Our Faces before the Glorious Lord

As I reflect on John's breath-taking experience on Patmos, I'm struck by two principles.

First, *the better our understanding of who Christ really is, the quicker we'll respond in submission and obedience.* Revelation 1:17 says, "And when I saw Him, I fell at His feet like a dead man." We sometimes hear people talk about meeting Jesus face-to-face, giving Him a hug, sitting on his lap, and asking Him all those theological and biblical questions that have been nagging them throughout their lives. In light of John's response to his brief glimpse of Christ's unveiled glory, such a view fails to measure up. As we ponder John's awesome encounter with the risen Lord, we should ask ourselves a couple of questions:

- Do I know and adore the awesome, glorious, powerful Jesus portrayed in the Bible, or have I adopted a culturally appropriate, mild-mannered, user-friendly Jesus after my own imaginations?

WHO ARE THE "ANGELS" IN REVELATION 2 – 3?

When we hear the word "angel" in the twenty-first century, we immediately picture heavenly messengers — sometimes appearing in human form, other times in brilliant attire. We may even imagine the six-winged creatures of Isaiah 6. If you lived in the first century and heard the Greek word *angelos*, however, white-clad and winged messengers may not be the first things to come to mind.

In fact, in both the Greek translation of the Old Testament and the New Testament, the word sometimes refers to a human messenger or herald, one who represents a king or carries an important message (Gen. 16:7–12; 1 Sam. 19:11–20; Mal. 3:1; Matt. 11:10; Luke 7:24, 27). One early Christian writing (c. AD 95–100) describes the pastor of Rome as the one whose job it was to send correspondence to the churches abroad, functioning in the role of a human *angelos*.[9] Context must determine whether the word refers to angelic heavenly beings or to human beings functioning as messengers.

The context of the word *angelos*, first mentioned in 1:20 and repeated throughout chapters 2 and 3, suggests that the *angelos* in each of the seven churches in Asia Minor were the head elders or "pastors" of the churches. In fact, several times the "messenger" of each church is addressed in the singular "you," and the "messenger" is also charged with bad behavior (as in 2:4, 14, 20). Heavenly, angelic beings cannot be charged with wrongdoing and be asked to repent.[10]

Therefore, we should understand that when Jesus told John to write his messages to each *angelos* of the seven churches, he referred to what we call today the "pastors" of the churches — men with whom John was probably familiar. We must also realize, however, that though the primary recipient was the pastor of each church, 1:11 reminds us that these messages were intended for the churches under each pastor's care.

- How should John's portrayal of Jesus affect my attitude in prayer? In worship? In obedience? Does my life reflect a response to the Jesus of Revelation 1:17? In what specific ways have I been too flippant or casual in my approach to my Master and Lord, Jesus Christ?

Second, *the greater our willingness to submit to Christ, the deeper will be the truths He reveals to us.* No, you won't receive divine visions of the future. No, Jesus Himself won't give you a message for your pastor. John's profound perception of the person of Christ, however, led him to a complete submission to His authority. In turn, this led to a deepening understanding of Christ and His plans for the future. As we open God's Word and encounter Christ, our attitudes of humility and submission will lead us into a deeper relationship with Him. Let me suggest what you can do to drive this principle home.

Read Psalm 111:10; Proverbs 1:7; and Proverbs 9:10. Look closely at these texts. According to them, what one thing is essential for deepening our understanding of obedience to God's revealed truth? Then ask yourself, "Do I open God's Word with this attitude? Do I show the kind of respect and reverence necessary to have true wisdom and understanding?" Why not pause and reread these verses? Consider committing them to memory.

Ephesus: The Church with Everything but the Greatest Thing (Revelation 2:1–7)

---

¹"To the angel of the church in Ephesus write:
The One who holds the seven stars in His right hand, the One who walks among the seven golden lampstands, says this:
²'I know your deeds and your toil and perseverance, and that you cannot tolerate evil men, and you put to the test those who call themselves apostles, and they are not, and you found them *to be* false; ³and you have perseverance and have endured for My name's sake, and have not grown weary. ⁴But I have *this* against you, that you have left your first love. ⁵Therefore remember from where you have fallen, and repent and do the deeds you did at first; or else I am coming to you and will remove your lampstand out of its place — unless you repent. ⁶Yet this you do have, that you hate the deeds of the Nicolaitans, which I also hate. ⁷He who has an ear, let him hear what the Spirit says to the churches. To him who overcomes, I will grant to eat of the tree of life which is in the Paradise of God.'"

Having followed the Lord's command to "write the things which you have seen" (the vision of Christ in Rev. 1), John turned to "the things which are" (the messages

Common Elements of Each Message in Revelation 2–3	
To	"To the angel of the church in …"
From	"Thus says …"
Contents	"I know …"
Commendation	"I am pleased about this …"
Concern	"I have this against you …"
Correction	"Repent! But if you don't …"

to the churches in Revelation 2–3). In these chapters, Christ evaluated each local assembly of believers mentioned in 1:11, beginning with the church in Ephesus and ending with the church in Laodicea. These messages count as Christ's "performance evaluations"—reviews of their faith and works, including points of encouragement and rebuke. Before we focus on the church in Ephesus, let's observe the overall pattern repeated as each church comes under the Lord's scrutinizing gaze.

As we read through each of the seven letters in chapters 2–3, we will notice certain similarities. Each one opens with an address to the representative of each church (the "angel" or pastor), which includes an initial identification of Christ. Then the content of the message follows (observations from Christ about each church). This includes any commendation, concern, correction, or counsel He may have. Finally, Christ ends with a call to action for those who have their ears attuned to hear what the Spirit of God is saying to the churches (2:7).

Although Christ followed this general outline for each of His messages, we can make some unique observations as we compare and contrast the individual performance evaluations. First, all of the letters include strengths and commendations, except for the letter to Laodicea. That church was in such woeful condition that Jesus expressed only concern, correction, and counsel. Second, each letter includes some kind of rebuke, except for Smyrna and Philadelphia. Those two churches appeared to have it all together. Finally, each letter has some remarkably relevant applications for churches and individuals of every age—and especially for believers today.

— 2:1 —

At the start of this message, Christ described Himself as "the One who holds the seven stars in His right hand, the One who walks among the seven golden lampstands." We should immediately recognize this description from the initial vision of the majestic Savior recorded in 1:12–16. In fact, as we explore the seven messages to the churches in Asia Minor, we will see that each introductory self-description draws on language and images from the first chapter, tying together the ultimate Messenger and His messages. We will also see that Christ applies the personal title for each message in the content of the message itself.

The lampstands symbolize the seven churches of Asia Minor, while the seven stars represent the "angels [messengers]," or pastoral leaders, of those churches (1:20). Christ's presence among these churches communicates that He knows everything about them. He doesn't merely stand in the midst of the churches; rather, He "walks among" them. He examines them from every angle. No praiseworthy quality or embarrassing imperfection can escape His notice. He's aware of their every thought, intention, and motive, caring enough for their present and future well-being that He will both encourage and correct them.

WELCOME TO EPHESUS

Although today the uninhabited city of Ephesus boasts impressive ruins, at the end of the first century Ephesus was the most important city of western Asia Minor and a major center of political, economic, and religious activity.[11] In the political sphere, the proconsul of Asia conducted most of his affairs in Ephesus.[12] In the economic arena, it was the first port of entry for seafaring vessels and therefore a strategic location for major trade routes. This granted Ephesus a robust market and a large, diverse population.[13] In its religious life, the city boasted one of the wonders of the ancient world — a grand temple dedicated to the fertility goddess, Artemis, also known as Diana. Besides this, Ephesus had a rigorous emperor cult with several temples dedicated to his worship.[14]

Paul founded the church at Ephesus around AD 52 (Acts 18–19). After that time, in approximately AD 65, Timothy became pastor of the Ephesian church (1 Tim. 1:3), followed perhaps by John the apostle.[15] At the time of the visions of the book of Revelation, while John was exiled to Patmos, the leadership of Ephesus may have temporarily passed to Onesimus, who, after John's death, carried on the pastorate.[16] It is possible, though uncertain, that the messenger ("angel") at Ephesus addressed in Revelation 2:1 was Onesimus.

Ruins of Ephesus

— 2:2-6 —

After a thorough examination of the pastor and church in Ephesus, Christ offered His diagnosis. He noted three commendations (2:2–3, 6) and one serious concern (2:4). He then offered a prescription for recovery, including His correction and counsel (2:5).

Christ complemented the church in Ephesus for toiling in good deeds (2:2), for enduring patiently in trials (2:2–3), and for standing against false doctrine (2:2, 6). Christ began by acknowledging the hard work of believers there in the service of the King. He coupled the general word for "work" (*ergon*) with the more specific term for "difficult labor" or "toil" (*kopos*). The resulting picture reveals a diligent, conscientious, industrious, and involved congregation. No sloth or indifference. No procrastination. No empty promises. The church in Ephesus kept busy caring for the sick, sheltering the homeless, feeding the hungry, visiting the prisoners, and clothing widows and orphans.

Christ also commended them for their patient endurance through trials (2:2–3). The Greek term *hypomonē*, used already in 1:9, implies endurance under extreme hardship, in the face of life-threatening challenges or against seemingly impossible odds. The Ephesian Christians faced special challenges. Because they refused to bow the knee to the goddess Diana or the images of the emperor, they found themselves maligned, slandered, boycotted, and abused. Not unlike Jewish merchants in Berlin in the 1930s, Christians in Ephesus would have been the objects of physical violence, social ostracism, and economic repression. Yet they endured. They bore up under the load. Clearly, Ephesus had been taught well by its predecessors, Paul, Timothy, and John.

Christ's third commendation relates to their doctrinal discernment (2:2, 6). The Ephesians sniffed out and rejected wicked men and they put so-called "apostles" to the test. Christ also praised them for taking a stand against a specific group of false teachers active in Asia Minor in the late first century. The sect of the Nicolaitans is mentioned as active in Ephesus and Pergamum only in 2:6 and 2:15. Their practices apparently related to participation in idolatry and sexual immorality, perhaps combining their worship of God with pagan temple worship. Nothing certain is known about them except that early Christians of the second and third centuries mentioned the Nicolaitans as a sect that some speculated were errant followers of Nicolas of Antioch, mentioned in Acts 6:5.[17] Another possibility is that "Nicolaitans" is itself a code name for those who like to "lord it over" others (cf. 2 Cor. 1:24; 3 John 9–10), combining two Greek words: *nikaō* ("to conquer") and *laos* ("people").

Regardless of the identity of the Nicolaitans, it's important to note that Christ said He hated their deeds (2:6) and that He praised the church in Ephesus for taking a firm stand against them. Today our world is drowning in a culture of blind tolerance of sin. Christians often have responded with a mandate to "love the sinner, but hate the sin." There seems to be biblical support for such a position, because Christ didn't say He hated the Nicolaitans themselves, but the *deeds* of the Nicolaitans (2:6). Nevertheless, this doesn't detract from the seriousness of their wickedness. Christ *does* call such people to repentance; He *does not* call Christians to tolerate their sins. This glimpse of Christ's stand against the sin and embrace of the sinner should give us confidence to speak the truth in love (Eph. 4:15), while letting God alone judge the world (1 Cor. 5:9–12).

Like an unexpected twist in the road during a pleasant drive through the countryside, Christ interrupted His commendation of the Ephesians with one abrupt word: "but" (2:4). The small Greek word *alla* indicates a sharp contrast, and in the case of Ephesus, it's very significant: "But ... you have left your first love" (2:4). The church in Ephesus had everything but the greatest thing. The erosion of the love they had at the beginning didn't happen overnight. No one suddenly wakes up one morning and says, "I don't love Jesus anymore. I'm tired of Jesus and I'm finished with all this Christianity stuff." It doesn't happen like that. It happens over the years—after hardship, questions you can't get answered, trials that don't seem to have reason, loss of health, loss of hope, loss of a loved one.

In the midst of the Ephesians' hard work and endurance for Jesus, their love for Him began to wane. Thirty-five years earlier, Paul had written to the church in Ephesus, commending them for their love (Eph. 1:15–16; 6:23–24). Now the love that had characterized their life and energized their faith had lost its original vigor. It wasn't enough that they continued to go through the motions. Jesus wanted more than their righteous, doctrinally discerning deeds. He wanted the devotion and adoration of their hearts. Over and over again the New Testament emphasizes the primary place of love in the Christian faith. In fact, 1 Corinthians 13:13 tells us the golden virtue is love—beating out the silver and bronze winners, faith and hope, every time. "The greatest of these is love."

After charging the Ephesians with abandon-

Condition of the Church in Ephesus

1st Love Lost

Though the church in Ephesus had maintained works, faith, and hope, they had lost their heartfelt personal affection for God and others.

ing their first love, Christ pointed out three simple ways to swing a U-turn and reestablish their walks in the right direction—*remember*, *repent*, and *repeat* (2:5). First, they were to *remember* from where they had fallen. The Ephesians had wandered far from their roots of love, and Christ was calling them to come to their senses and return home. As believers, remembering the way life used to be the first step on our way back to our first love for God and a vibrant love for others.

Second, the Ephesians needed to *repent*. The Greek word translated "repent" means a genuine change of heart and mind. A new attitude must be the first step in any authentic change of actions. Repentance is a true inward change, not a fake reformation of life or a mere outward modification of behavior. It's a work powerfully wrought by the grace of God in our innermost being, which involves a deeply personal decision.

Third, the Ephesians were expected to *repeat* the deeds they did at first. After remembering and repenting, believers who have lost their first love must do the things they did when they first came to know and love Jesus. This is not simply a change in actions, but a complete renewal of our attitudes that naturally leads to right behavior. If we have truly remembered and repented, the deeds revealing authentic change will unavoidably follow.

— **2:7** —

After commending the church at Ephesus for their strengths and expressing concern over their weaknesses, Jesus extended a promise to "him who overcomes" (2:7). Before we look at the specific promise, I must clear up a common misunderstanding of the recipients of the promise. Some have read the phrase "to him who overcomes" as referring to supersaints—outstanding believers who have somehow achieved a greater victory than other believers over the world, the flesh, and the devil. In this case, only those who have worked harder and persevered longer will receive the promises offered by Christ at the end of each message. Let me set the record straight; or better, let the apostle John set the record straight: "For whatever is born of God overcomes the world; and this is the victory that has overcome the world—our faith. Who is the one who overcomes the world, but he who believes that Jesus is the Son of God?" (1 John 5:4–5).

In other words, those who have been born again by faith alone in Christ alone are the ones who "overcome." This means that the promises in Revelation 2–3 addressed to those who overcome are meant for all believers. It is true that believers will also receive rewards proportionate to their works at the judgment seat of Christ (1 Cor. 3:10–15; 2 Cor. 5:10). The promises in Revelation, however, relate to all believers who have overcome death, sin, the world, and the devil by faith in Christ alone.

The promise in 2:7 refers back to the book of Genesis, tying together the all-but-forgotten original creation and the always-longed-for new creation. Jesus said, "I will grant to eat of the tree of life which is in the Paradise of God." The fruit will come from the same tree that stood in the midst of the garden of Eden when Adam and Eve were created innocent (Gen. 2:9). After the fall, sinful humans were not permitted to eat from this tree, which would have continued to provide eternal life (3:24). Christ promises, however, that believers in Him will have the right to eat again from the tree of life, when they have unfettered fellowship with God (Rev. 22:2).

What a glorious future we look forward to! Enriching fellowship ... intimacy with the Almighty ... enduring love.

Application

"Because He First Loved Us ..."

Christ's words to the church in Ephesus had direct application to their specific circumstances at the end of the first century. Yet Christ says that through these letters the Spirit of God speaks to anybody with ears to hear (2:7). That includes you and me! As I think about the content of this first message, I see one major theme jump to the surface: *love.*

Just as He walked around and examined the lampstands, so Christ is walking around and examining whether our own lights of love have dimmed. How common it is for believers who were once ablaze with love for God and love for others to slowly soften to smoldering embers! Christ wants to fan the flame so we'll become brilliant beacons of love in a loveless world. Stop and think. Has *your* love grown cold?

Reflect on your own love for the Lord and for others when you first came to Christ. Would you say your current attitudes and actions reflect a greater, lesser, or similar love? If you feel your love has lessened, what specific unloving behaviors have developed?

The kind of love God wants us to have toward Him and others is illustrated in the love Christ had for His Father and all humanity. Christ perfectly obeyed the Father throughout His earthly life. He humbled Himself, becoming obedient even to death on the cross (Phil. 2:8). Christ expressed His love for us in the same act, as He gave His life for us (Gal. 2:20; Eph. 5:2).

Let me challenge you to do something concrete in light of the importance of maintaining your love. Would you consider memorizing 1 John 4:19–21? Take time right now to commit this short passage to memory so you can always be reminded of the need for growing in love.

> We love, because He first loved us. If someone says, "I love God," and hates his brother, he is a liar; for the one who does not love his brother whom he has seen, cannot love God whom he has not seen. And this commandment we have from Him, that the one who loves God should love his brother also.

Smyrna: The Suffering Church under Attack (Revelation 2:8–11)

> [8]"And to the angel of the church in Smyrna write:
> The first and the last, who was dead, and has come to life, says this:
> [9]'I know your tribulation and your poverty (but you are rich), and the blasphemy by those who say they are Jews and are not, but are a synagogue of Satan. [10]Do not fear what you are about to suffer. Behold, the devil is about to cast some of you into prison, so that you will be tested, and you will have tribulation for ten days. Be faithful until death, and I will give you the crown of life. [11]He who has an ear, let him hear what the Spirit says to the churches. He who overcomes will not be hurt by the second death.'"

Regardless of race, nationality, ethnicity, gender, social status, age, or religion, all people share the "language" of suffering. We may not be able to relate to another culture's music. We may not enjoy a country's exotic taste in food, and we may fail to understand a particular people's humor. Yet for every human being, pain is pain. Anguish is anguish. We're all united by experiences of hardship, heartache, suffering, sadness, and grief.

For Christians, the language of suffering has a unique and profound dialect, often misunderstood by foreigners to the faith. Christians believe that all suffering has a specific purpose in God's sovereign plan; under the surface of its apparent meaninglessness, suffering speaks to the soul like nothing else. This isn't intended to make the claim that persecution is a thing of beauty or that wicked people are actually good. Rather, Christians know that in spite of their experiences of suffering in this world, God can turn around the intended or natural outcome and bring about blessings. Nevertheless, the benefits of suffering can be easily overlooked as pain intensifies or as fear and uncertainty set in.

Suffering and hardship often seem unbearable, but they have a way of purifying God's people. Perhaps this is why we're never far from life's trials. When the overwhelming tide of hardship rises, we must stand firm on the foundation of Christ rather than be washed away by the floodwaters of despair and hopelessness.

At the time of John's writing, the church in Smyrna had endured the fires of pain and the suffering of persecution, and their sorrows would soon increase. Their future looked bleak. Yet it's noteworthy that the church received no criticism from the One who knew them best. Not one negative word! The Smyrneans weren't suffering hardship because of any wrong they had done. Quite the opposite! In spite of their poverty due to persecution, they were spiritually rich.

— 2:8 —

In the midst of their suffering, the Lord Jesus Christ came to the church in Smyrna with a message of hope. The Master's timely message reminded them that God

NEXT STOP: SMYRNA

Just thirty-five miles north of Ephesus, the ancient city of Smyrna today goes by another name: Izmir. In John's day, the thriving city had a famous stadium, library, and theater, and it had a diverse population of perhaps a half-million people. As a vital port city, it boasted the second largest number of exports in Asia Minor.

Two forces would have put pressure on Christians in Smyrna. On the one hand, the Gentiles in Smyrna devoted themselves to the cult of emperor worship.[18] On the other hand, the city also had a large Jewish population committed to their Old Testament religion. This mixture of Roman patriots and Jewish zealots created a thorny environment for dedicated Christians. Believers refused to worship Emperor Domitian, and Jewish synagogues rejected them for worshiping Jesus as the Son of God.[19]

Though Jews in the Roman Empire were legally excused from sacrificing to the emperor, Christians enjoyed no such exemption after the synagogues cast them out. Therefore, believers in Smyrna faced physical, emotional, and economic pressures from both Jews and Gentiles.

Ancient ruins of Smyrna (in modern Izmir)

© Dr. Leen Ritmeyer

gives strength to those who suffer, and He also rewards those who endure. The benefits of perseverance not only ring out in this life, but also in the life to come.

Christ introduced Himself in a manner that highlights His majesty. Jesus had called Himself "the first and the last" at the beginning of John's vision (1:17). The name recalls a title used exclusively for the God of Israel in Isaiah 44:6 and 48:12.

> Thus says the LORD, the King of Israel and his Redeemer, the LORD of hosts: "I am the first and I am the last, and there is no God besides Me." (Isa. 44:6)

> Listen to Me, O Jacob, even Israel whom I called;
> I am He, I am the first, I am also the last.
> Surely My hand founded the earth,
> And My right hand spread out the heavens;
> When I call to them, they stand together. (Isa. 48:12–13)

The implication is clear. As "the first and the last," Christ claimed to be not only the Lord of hosts, the King of Israel, and the Redeemer, but also the Creator of heaven and earth, equal in power and majesty to God the Father Himself. Echoing almost exactly the same self-description in Revelation 1:17, Christ also describes Himself as the One "who was dead, and has come to life" (2:8).

The unity of Christ's deity and humanity are summed up in this brief title. As "the first," God the Son existed before there was a Smyrna, Asia Minor, Roman Empire, or anything at all. As "the last," Christ will outlive modern-day Izmir, Turkey, Europe, or this entire world system. Christ is the eternal, transcendent One, whose plan and work reach to those extremes of eternity, past and future. At the same time, Christ is fully human. He *has* to be human if He truly died and rose again.

The ancient Definition of Chalcedon (AD 451) says that Jesus Christ is properly understood by Christians as "perfect both in deity and also in humanness … actually God and actually man."[20] This careful statement reflects the beliefs of orthodox Christians all the way from the time of the apostles to the present day (see John 1:1–3, 14; Rom. 1:3–4; Phil. 2:6–8). As such, we must understand and embrace the doctrine of the two natures of Christ. He is both God *and* man.

Think about it. If Christ were only God, He would have been unable to die in the place of sinful humanity in order to pay the price for salvation. If He were only a man, the death He died would not have had an eternal benefit for the saved. Because He died in His incarnate humanity as the perfect sacrifice for sin, however, and because He was raised to live forever in the power of His indestructible life, He has authority to give eternal life to all who believe in Him. This doctrine of the incarnation is no mere theological conjecture; rather, it forms the very bedrock of our salvation.

Yet the truth of the deity and humanity of Christ also has an impact on our Christian life, as it did for the Smyrneans nearly two thousand years ago. If Christ were only God, we might perceive Him as aloof, separated from our human experiences of suffering and unable to understand or relate to our desperate plight. If Christ were only man, His death would have been just another martyrdom of a good man, nothing more. He would have been a weak victim of human tragedy, unable to conquer death and powerless to triumph over the grave.

But praise be to God that Christ is both "the first and the last" and the one "who was dead, and has come to life"! He is fully God and fully man — undiminished deity and true humanity. For this reason we can take comfort in the fact that the Eternal One dwells in time, that the infinite and untouchable God can be touched by finite beings, and that he *shares in* our pain, not simply *stares at* our suffering. The writer of Hebrews puts it beautifully:

> Therefore, since we have a great high priest who has passed through the heavens, Jesus the Son of God, let us hold fast our confession. For we do not have a high priest who cannot sympathize with our weaknesses, but One who has been tempted in all things as we are, yet without sin. Therefore let us draw near with confidence to the throne of grace, so that we may receive mercy and find grace to help in time of need. (Heb. 4:14–16)

— **2:9** —

Imagine yourself sitting among the gathering of God's people in Smyrna on a cold morning before sunrise. A small, lamp-lit room houses the remnant of beaten and beleaguered church members. The once-lively crowd of Christians now displays obvious gaps where men and women once sat. Some have fallen away under the persecution. Others are simply gone — arrested, exiled, or executed. Some of you risked your lives just to meet this morning to pray, to sing hymns to God, and to read from Holy Scripture. All of you are outcasts, desperate for a word of encouragement from the messenger sitting in your midst. In the dim light the pastor unrolls a scroll and begins to read with a calm, quiet confidence. Whispering and shuffling in the room ceases when you hear from whom the message comes — the risen Lord Himself. The entire group seems to hold its breath when Christ begins His commendation: "I know your tribulation and your poverty (but you are rich)" (2:9).

The message begins with "I know." In this case, Christ's knowledge of their plight was more than theoretical head knowledge. He knew firsthand the kind of suffering and pain they endured as rejected outcasts. The Christians in Smyrna were experiencing *tribulation*, which could include physical, economic, social, or religious persecution that causes distress.[21] Christians in that ancient city were

Condition of the Church in Smyrna

The church in Smyrna, though devoid of earthly wealth, was spiritually rich.

ostracized, verbally assaulted, boycotted, and mistreated.

The Smyrneans also suffered economic *poverty*. Their refusal to worship the emperor would have entailed severe financial repercussions. Imperial patriots would have at least avoided businesses owned by Christians, if they didn't also vandalize and loot their shops. Yet in the midst of this pressure, Christ told the church, "You are rich!" Their spiritual riches far outweighed their material poverty (2 Cor. 8:9; James 2:5).

Besides the ongoing physical and financial abuse, the church in Smyrna also endured verbal assault, or *blasphemy*. The word *blasphēmia* means "railing" or "slander." Although the Christian church had once been a part of the Jewish synagogue in many cities, when opposition grew from Jews who didn't accept Jesus as the Messiah, synagogues eventually rejected Jews who accepted the Messiah and ejected the Jewish Christians from their fellowship. The Jews in Smyrna were possibly calling any Jewish believers in Christ "false Jews." In His message to Smyrna, Jesus encouraged those same believers, pointing out that the Jews who accepted the Messiah were actually following the true fulfillment of Judaism (see Rom. 2:28–29). Of course, Jesus didn't say that *every* Jewish synagogue is a hate-filled gathering, but apparently the synagogue of Smyrna in the first century abused the Christians there.

— 2:10 —

I suppose that after the Smyrnean Christians heard Christ's sympathetic words regarding the reality of suffering, they felt ready to hear some good news, like "It's over!" ... "Relax! You made it!" ... "It's payback time!" Instead, Jesus warned of more suffering about to come. He knew that the normal human reaction to persecution, poverty, and blasphemy is fear. Trauma can result in paralysis, weakness, shying away—and can ultimately lead to a complete defection.

Christ targeted the real menace behind the persecution of the church. Similar to His own arrest, trial, and execution decades earlier, the ultimate perpetrator was not the Jews, nor the Romans, nor the inevitable wheels of fate. The real enemy was Satan, whose relentless attacks would continue. Yet Christ also encouraged the Christians that although the coming persecution would be severe, it would also be limited

From My Journal

Don't Let the Missed Shots Hurt

Winston Churchill reportedly said, "Nothing is more exciting in life than being shot at without result." Well, when you're a fulltime statesman who breathes the air of politics, I suppose you get used to potshots, mudslinging, and outright slander. But when you're just a simple believer sharing the truth in love and the verbal bullets fly, those missed shots still come as a surprise.

Personally, I made it all the way through most of my years in seminary before I really understood what it felt like to be "blasphemed" as a Christian. You know—to become the target of fiery obscenities, snide remarks, ugly insults. During my final year I worked with a campus ministry to secular universities. Actually, I barreled head-long into it. Before I knew it, I found myself standing on a "free speech platform"—a place on a secular campus where anybody could stand up and declare anything. So I stood up and passionately preached Christ.

Then it happened. A tomato hit me! I thought maybe it was meant for the guy on the other side of campus who was preaching communism. The guy next to me encouraged me to keep going: "Stay at it," he said, "That's part of it." So I raised my voice and pressed on. Before long the veggies changed to venom—verbal hand grenades screamed at the tops of their lungs. Strange as it may sound, I found something invigorating about that.

Don't get me wrong. That kind of minor persecution didn't make me a martyr, but never before had I experienced being shouted at by an angry crowd. (It wasn't the last!) The feeling was new to me. Yet one thing is true about wicked words, which isn't true about financial or physical hardship: Hostile words stay with you. They may not injure and they may not cause any permanent damage, but they sting, they linger. And if you don't let them bounce off or slide away like a ripe tomato, they can rob you of your boldness to proclaim the truth.

THE FIVE CROWNS FOR BELIEVERS

The New Testament mentions five heavenly "crowns" for believers — future rewards for faithfulness in this life.

1. Crown of Exultation	1 Thessalonians 2:19	For those who win others to Christ
2. Crown of Righteousness	2 Timothy 4:8	For those who live in the expectation of Christ's coming
3. Crown of Life	James 1:12; Revelation 2:10; 3:11	For those who endure persecution unto death
4. Crown of Imperishability	1 Corinthians 9:25	For those who run the race of life in purity and self control
5. Crown of Glory	1 Peter 5:4	For those who lead the church with humility

in scope and temporary in duration. *Some* (not all) would be cast into prison. *All* would be tested through tribulation—but only for ten days. Satan may be permitted to persecute the church, but as in the case of Job's suffering, God-appointed limits constrain what Satan can do.

Please notice that Jesus didn't leave the church with a general warning of trials and then just say, "Deal with it!" He's not a distant Deity who doesn't care. He's a faithful companion who responds to us in love. So He told the Smyrneans that even if they had to endure persecution unto physical death, they would receive "the crown of life." It's interesting that one of the last books of the Bible echoes a promise first given in one of the first. Those spiritually war-ravaged believers in Smyrna needed to hear this truth again: "Blessed is a man who perseveres under trial; for once he has been approved, he will receive the crown of life which the Lord has promised to those who love Him" (James 1:12).

— 2:11 —

After His words of encouragement and comfort, Christ ended His timely message to the church of Smyrna with a promise. It's a word of reassurance for that ancient church and for all believers in every era. Those who overcome—true believers in Christ—will not be hurt by the second death.

This is the first use of the phrase "second death" in Scripture, but the concept of future judgment for unbelievers finds clear expression in the Old Testament. The "second death" is associated with the destination of the unsaved after their bodily resurrection. Daniel 12:2 says that in the final days of earth's history, "many of those who sleep in the dust of the ground will awake, these to everlasting life, but the others to disgrace and everlasting contempt." Believers who have died physically will be raised in their immortal bodies to experience eternal life in glory (Dan. 12:3; Rev. 20:6). By contrast, unbelievers will suffer a second death as they are cast into the lake of fire in their resurrection bodies (Rev. 20:14; 21:8).

This promise of eternal life in glory with no possibility of experiencing death and damnation was meant to instill concrete hope in the Smyrnean believers. No matter how severe the persecution would grow and no matter what the church had to endure, Christ's promises would give them strength to persevere. The same promises remain true for us today.

Application

Help for Those Who Hurt

Do you ever fear pain and hardship? Are you wondering if your struggles will ever end? Do you feel anxious about what tragedies or trials may be just around the corner, ready to shatter the comfort of your relatively stable and predictable life? In this life of uncertainty, we can be sure of one thing — trials and suffering are unavoidable. But the good news is that through Christ we can overcome (John 16:33). In Christ's timely message to the first-century Christians in Smyrna, I see two timeless reminders that apply to Christians of every age. Let me personalize these for us.

First, *our Lord knows every detail of our circumstances.* As the "first and the last," who died and rose again (2:8), Christ knows us inside and out, from beginning to end. He knows every tragedy and triumph, each death and life. He knows all about the stress of tribulation. He knows all about the destitution of poverty. He knows all about the slander of blasphemy. He can relate to our circumstances ... *and He does!* Be encouraged. Read and reread Hebrews 4:14–15. Inscribe them on your heart.

Second, *if our hurtful situations remain or intensify, we have no reason to fear or flee.* The church in Smyrna would like to have heard that their tribulations had ended, that the worst had come and gone. Instead, Christ warned them that the worst was yet to come (2:10). Regardless of the journey, Christ will be with us through our trials. He won't abandon us, even unto death. In fact, death is but a doorway to a glorious life, free from all suffering, poverty, and slander. Be strengthened. Embrace the promises of Hebrews 13:5–6. Don't let them slip your mind.

Whatever your personal experience of pain, suffering, trial, or hardship, you can have confidence that Christ is with you through it all, and that His presence strengthens you with supernatural endurance. The words of the classic hymn "How Firm a Foundation" always encourage me, but especially in times of hardship. They can do the same for you.

> Fear not, I am with thee, oh, be not dismayed,
> For I am thy God, and will still give thee aid;
> I'll strengthen thee, help thee, and cause thee to stand,
> Upheld by My gracious, omnipotent hand.[22]

Pergamum: The Church That Compromised the Truth (Revelation 2:12 – 17)

> [12]"And to the angel of the church in Pergamum write:
> The One who has the sharp two-edged sword says this:
> [13]'I know where you dwell, where Satan's throne is; and you hold fast My name, and did not deny My faith even in the days of Antipas, My witness, My faithful one, who was killed among you, where Satan dwells. [14]But I have a few things against you, because you have there some who hold the teaching of Balaam, who kept teaching Balak to put a stumbling block before the sons of Israel, to eat things sacrificed to idols and to commit *acts of* immorality. [15]So you also have some who in the same way hold the teaching of the Nicolaitans. [16]Therefore repent; or else I am coming to you quickly, and I will make war against them with the sword of My mouth. [17]He who has an ear, let him hear what the Spirit says to the churches. To him who overcomes, to him I will give *some* of the hidden manna, and I will give him a white stone, and a new name written on the stone which no one knows but he who receives it.'"

Compromise. What feelings come to mind when you hear that word? I'll be honest. I often think of squirrelly politicians, closed-door deals, or caving to power or popularity. Yet a lifetime of ministry reminds me of the healthy side of compromise — meeting two parties halfway or coming to a workable consensus among competing interests. So, what does it really mean to compromise? To agree or appease? To cooperate or concede? To find common ground or give up ground? To bargain, barter, or bury the axe?

Because Christians believe in absolute truth, they sometimes feel that any form of compromise betrays their principles. The fact is that depending on the circumstances, the people involved, or the anticipated results, compromise can be good or bad, wise or worldly. *Wise compromise* means coming to an agreement "by mutual concession … to find or follow a way between extremes."[23] It holds together friendships, marriages, and churches. Wise compromise gives up personal preferences and selfish desires for the sake of unity and peace. It doesn't mean we throw in the towel on fundamental doctrines or morality. That would fall under the category of *worldly compromise*, which can be defined as "a shameful or disreputable concession."[24] That kind of compromise backs away from moral principles and easily surrenders truth to a lie. Worldly compromise is founded on selfish or impure motives. It divides people, breaks hearts, and damages relationships.

Like erosion, worldly compromise can slowly, silently, and subtly eat away at the truth. It begins as we turn a deaf ear to the corruption and falsehood around us. Eventually, we not only put up with these sins, we also become used to seeing them all around us. Even worse, we come to expect and accept them. From there, it isn't long before we embrace them. Biblical truth and morality cannot exist in a culture of compromise.

This is the heart of Christ's message to the Christians at Pergamum. The church in that worldly and wicked city found itself caught up in the swelling tide of false doctrine and questionable morality. The One who objectively examined that compromising church speaks to all churches trying to row against the strong current of a corrupting culture.

— **2:12** —

Like a cancerous tumor that penetrates and spreads through healthy flesh, compromise allows the sinews of falsehood to invade the truth, ultimately destroying it. Only a sharp scalpel in the hands of a precise surgeon can remove the cancer without killing the patient. Likewise, Christ, the Great Physician, is qualified not only to diagnose, but also to successfully treat the insidious disease of compromise.

Christ began His letter to the messenger of Pergamum by establishing Himself as the Judge who will make war against His enemies at the second coming and defeat them with His words (2:12, 16). As the Judge, He wields a sharp, double-edged sword. The type of sword mentioned here is the *rhomphaia*, a weapon similar to the sword used by the Romans in battle. This image, as seen in John's initial vision of Christ in Revelation 1:16, deliberately points us back to the Greek translation of Isaiah 11:4, where the Messiah is seen as the Judge who comes to "strike the earth with the rod of His mouth," that is, "with the breath [Gk. *pneuma*, or "Spirit"] of His lips He will slay the wicked."[25]

photobucket

Model of a rhomphaia

The "sword" from His mouth thus symbolizes the verbal pronouncement of judgment. Christ's adversaries, who gather against Him with an arsenal of weapons, will be felled simply by the words of His mouth. Paul used the same type of imagery to refer to the "sword of the Spirit, which is the word of God" (Eph. 6:17). Likewise, in Hebrews 4:12, the "word of God" is described as more powerful than a "two-edged sword." Though referring to a different type of sword than the *rhomphaia*, the point is clear: Christ's warfare against error and evil will be swift and decisive.

— 2:13–15 —

After His ominous self-description as the sword-wielding Judge, Christ began to evaluate the church's strengths and weaknesses—the commendations and concerns. In verse 13, Christ acknowledged the difficulties involved in living in Pergamum. The Greek word for "dwell" implies a permanent residence, perhaps even a commitment to stay.[26] Even though Pergamum was characterized as the seat of Satan's authority, the church didn't try to escape the extreme pressures. Instead,

THE CITY OF SATAN'S THRONE

Built only a couple miles inland from the ancient location of the historical city of Troy, Pergamum became one of the great cities of Asia Minor. By the first century AD, it was the official center of the imperial cult, having built its first great temple in 29 BC in honor of the goddess Roma and the emperor Augustus.[27] Besides being a major center for the worship of the gods Athena, Dionysus, and Asklepios, Pergamum's acropolis was crowned by a forty-foot tall altar to Zeus, to which Christ may have referred when He spoke of "Satan's throne" in Revelation 2:13.[28]

Though Pergamum had once been known for its immense library, which held nearly 200,000 volumes, in John's day the city became famous for its medicine. Galen, one of the founders of ancient medicine, had lived in Pergamum. The city also boasted a large gymnasium as well as a grand theater.[29]

Pergamon Altar, 180-159 BC/Pergamon Museum, Berlin, Germany/The Bridgeman Art Library

Altar of Zeus in Pergamum

the congregation chose to endure the hardship of their environment.

Let me illustrate this with a modern analogy. While everybody else was moving to the suburbs, the Christians in Pergamum were committed to remaining in the inner city. They decided to stay put in the midst of the noise, the violence, the corruption, and the temptations, to shine as a light in the darkness of the city. In fact, as we see in the case of the martyr Antipas, things had gotten bad. His martyrdom seemed so astounding that Christ called Antipas by the same name He calls Himself in Revelation 3:14—"faithful witness." The remnant of the church refused to deny Jesus, even in the face of such turmoil. What resolute strength! When it would have been expedient to stop claiming the name "Christian," the faithful Pergamum believers held onto Christ's name. When softening the fundamentals could have saved them from suffering and death, the faithful Christians of Pergamum refused to deny even one article of the faith.

Condition of the Church in Pergamum

The church in Pergamum harbored Balaamites and Nicolaitans, compromising their otherwise positive reputation as faithful Christians.

Even today, certain places are especially tough for Christians to live. Yet those who remain steadfast are "faithful witnesses." They refuse to deny Christ's name, even when Satan moves in next door or sets up shop across the street. Instead, they dig in and hold their ground, regardless of the personal cost. That's commendable faith!

Yet not all was well in Pergamum. Though a faithful remnant had stayed true to Christ, several matters remained unresolved, tarnishing the image of the faithful. The church had taken a route of compromise on key issues, giving both Balaamites and Nicolaitans safe haven.

Christ's reference to Balaam reaches back to events recorded in Numbers 22–25, in which that quintessential "prophet for pay" tried to lead Israel astray. He endorsed the Israelites in the wilderness marrying idol-worshiping pagans from the surrounding nations and then worshiping those foreign gods through idolatrous immorality. In a similar manner, the followers of Balaam in Pergamum encouraged idolatry and sexual immorality, fueled by selfishness, greed, and lust. The issue wasn't simply that such false teachers sprang up in their midst; every church experiences sin and rebellion. Yet Christ directed His rebuke toward the *faithful* believers in the church who failed to take action against the Balaamites.

It doesn't take long for the *practice* of compromise to become the *pattern* of compromise. Not only did the church in Pergamum put up with Balaamites without rebuke, they also accepted the Nicolaitans. Remember them? Christ mentioned those false teachers earlier in His letter to the church in Ephesus (2:6). Whereas the Ephesians received praise for hating the deeds of the Nicolaitans, the leadership and membership of Pergamum accepted them (2:15). While Ephesus understood how to love the sinner and *reject* the sin, Pergamum chose to love the sinner and *accept* the sin! They compromised doctrine and morality for the sake of peace and unity in the church. They took Christian love and grace to an extreme. Jesus' sword of rebuke was quick and decisive — "Enough! Repent!"

— **2:16–17** —

As He did for Ephesus, Christ offered the church in Pergamum an opportunity to get back on the right track. He called them to repent — to change their hearts and minds, leading to a change in behavior. In concrete terms, Christ demanded that the Pergamum Christians amend their attitudes regarding the Balaamites and the Nicolaitans, that they take the necessary actions to remove those false teachings from their midst. The compromise had to end. Christ's call for repentance included a warning for those who refused. If the faithful remnant refused to change their lackadaisical policies and if the wicked minority continued their libertine practices, Christ would discipline them. He would come swiftly, waging war against them with the double-edged sword — His just discipline as the righteous Judge.

Along with His warning, Christ included a threefold promise for those who would demonstrate their genuine nature as true believers, those who "overcome" (2:17). They would receive *divine food* ("hidden manna"), *special favor* ("white stone"), and a *new character* ("new name"). The "hidden manna" could refer to Christ Himself, the spiritual nourishment for believers, both now and for eternity. In John 6:48–51 Christ symbolically likened Himself to the "bread from heaven," the manna that came down from heaven and nourished the ancient Israelites during their wilderness wanderings.[30]

The reference to the "white stone" inscribed with a new name is less certain. It may symbolize special access to God because of their new identity in Christ, perhaps alluding to a white stone "ticket" used for admission into the theatre at Pergamum. Or it may refer to believers' verdict of "not guilty" because of their relationship with Christ, their substitute and advocate. In the ancient world either black or white stones were sometimes cast to indicate a decree of guilt or innocence.[31] Regardless of how the Christians in Pergamum understood these symbols, we can understand the big picture: if you remain faithful and take a stand for truth and morality, the result will be great reward from Christ upon His return.

Application

Overcoming a Culture of Compromise

Our culture demands equal rights for "alternative lifestyles," redefines and rejects traditional values, winks at sin, and glorifies rebellion; thus, Christ's attitude toward compromise should cause us to sit up and take notice. We must constantly remember four practical principles regarding worldly compromise as we consider our own attitudes, not only toward the evil that surrounds us, but also the evil that penetrates the church.

First, *compromise never occurs quickly.* Ships accidentally drift off course—but it's usually not because someone suddenly pulls the wheel to starboard or port. Most often, invisible waves, currents, and winds gradually move the ship in the wrong direction. Before the ship's crew knows it, the jagged rocks of the shoreline are ripping holes in its hull. Hebrews 2:1 presents a clear cure for the subtle drift: "For this reason we must pay much closer attention to what we have heard, so that we do not drift away from it." The need for shoring up the fundamentals has never been greater. We need to shed ourselves of the "been there, done that" attitude when it comes to the simple truth of Scripture and the Christian faith. Like ancient sailors fixed on the northern star, we must keep our eyes on the unmoving norms of the Christian faith.

Second, *compromise always lowers the original standard.* Compromise often begins when we try to replace God's perfect standard of truth with our own man-made rules and regulations. Throughout history we've seen churches and denominations compromise on issues ranging from the inspiration of God's Word to the deity of Christ for the sake of keeping their members or gaining larger numbers. Such compromises are never worth it! Hebrews 10:23 teaches just the opposite: "Let us hold fast the confession of our hope without wavering, for He who promised is faithful." Likewise, Jude, the brother of Jesus, exhorts believers to "contend earnestly for the faith which was once for all handed down to the saints" (Jude 3). Commit yourself neither to adding your own "truths" nor to subtracting from God's truth. Maintain the one standard of truth and godliness.

Third, *compromise is seldom offensive.* People who compromise regularly tend to be great politicians and excellent people-pleasers. While wise compromise over "gray" issues can prevent unnecessary offense and conflict (see 1 Cor. 10:32), worldly compromise on the truth offends the God who saved us (2 Tim. 2:12–13).

Too often I see Christians walk on eggshells when they're around sensitive believers, or they bend over backward to avoid offending others with the Christian faith. Yes, we should share the truth *in love* (Eph. 4:15), but we should still share *the truth*. John 15:19 should clear up the matter for us: "If you were of the world, the world would love its own; but because you are not of the world, but I chose you out of the world, because of this the world hates you." Don't expect to be loved by the general public when you refuse to compromise.

Finally, *compromise is often the first step toward total disobedience.* David's sins of adultery and murder did not happen because of one weak moment. Much earlier, he had begun to compromise his responsibilities as a king (2 Sam. 11:1), compromise what he allowed himself to see (11:2), and compromise how he used his servants (11:3–4). These small steps, which in themselves didn't appear important, led to a total collapse of his integrity. What small areas of compromises are you currently

THE SMALL TOWN WITH A BIG PROBLEM

You've heard of Dallas, Texas ... but probably not Sachse. You may have visited Paris, France ... but not Trainel. You can probably picture the great opera house in Sydney, Australia ... but when I talk about the Sea Cliff Bridge in Clifton, your mind probably draws a blank.

The city of Thyatira falls into that category of smaller towns caught in the shadows of their larger, more famous neighbors. Thyatira was originally founded as a shrine to the sun god Tyrimnus, whose description generally echoed that of Christ in Revelation 2:18.[33] Though not well-known in ancient history, Thyatira gained a reputation as a blue-collar town, where the trade guilds stood at the center of social and religious life.[34] This situation created a serious problem for the Christian in Thyatira. Membership in

a trade guild came with pagan religious obligations, and refusing to join a guild could mean giving up one's livelihood.[35]

In light of the dilemma in which the Christians of Thyatira found themselves, the woman "Jezebel" mentioned in 2:20 may have represented a group that advocated Christian participation in the pagan rituals of the trade guilds. This would have included idolatry and ritual immorality in temple worship.

Todd Bolen/www.BiblePlaces.com

Ruins of the ancient city of Thyatira

involved in? White lies on your taxes? Slight exaggerations on your résumé? Secret peeks at Internet pornography? Just a little harmless gossip now and then? Review these four principles of compromise, then ask yourself: What is keeping me today from heeding Christ's warning and turning from compromise?

Thyatira: The Church Where Tolerance Went to Seed (Revelation 2:18–29)

---

[18]"And to the angel of the church in Thyatira write:

The Son of God, who has eyes like a flame of fire, and His feet are like burnished bronze, says this:

[19]'I know your deeds, and your love and faith and service and perseverance, and that your deeds of late are greater than at first. [20]But I have *this* against you, that you tolerate the woman Jezebel, who calls herself a prophetess, and she teaches and leads My bond-servants astray so that they commit *acts of* immorality and eat things sacrificed to idols. [21]I gave her time to repent, and she does not want to repent of her immorality. [22]Behold, I will throw her on a bed *of sickness*, and those who commit adultery with her into great tribulation, unless they repent of her deeds. [23]And I will kill her children with pestilence, and all the churches will know that I am He who searches the minds and hearts; and I will give to each one of you according to your deeds. [24]But I say to you, the rest who are in Thyatira, who do not hold this teaching, who have not known the deep things of Satan, as they call them — I place no other burden on you. [25]Nevertheless what you have, hold fast until I come. [26]He who overcomes, and he who keeps My deeds until the end, to him I will give authority over the nations; [27]and he shall rule them with a rod of iron, as the vessels of the potter are broken to pieces, as I also have received *authority* from My Father; [28]and I will give him the morning star. [29]He who has an ear, let him hear what the Spirit says to the churches.'"

On January 11, 1999, the cover of *Christianity Today* asked the following question: "Are you tolerant? (Should you be?)"[32] Over the last several decades, tolerationism has become one of the greatest "virtues" of our increasingly secular society. Now, I'm not talking about old-fashioned tolerance, a principle on which all good societies are built. Old tolerance meant that even though you outright disagreed and disapproved of somebody's beliefs, values, and lifestyle, you stuck to your own point of view and accepted the rights of others to believe and live as they chose. In other words, you didn't revive the Dark Ages—grabbing your pitchforks and rioting against people with different opinions. As long as they were acting within the

Condition of the Church in Thyatira

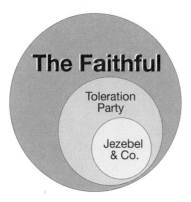

Though a strong remnant kept themselves pure, other believers in the church of Thyatira tolerated the wicked words of "Jezebel" and her followers.

confines of the law, their views—as strange as they may have been—were tolerated.

What I'm calling *tolerationism* is a different creature altogether. Now, instead of putting up with attitudes and actions with which we strongly disagree, society is increasingly expecting everybody to accept, approve, and validate *everybody's* beliefs, values, and lifestyles. Every strange idea and deviant behavior seeks to be affirmed as a normal alternative. In such a society, absolute truth in the realms of religion and ethics loses ground. How could there be such a thing as "truth" if everybody's contradictory opinions are accorded equal value? Once again, I'm not in favor of pummeling people with whom I disagree, but I also don't want to be pummeled simply *because* I disagree.

If you pay close attention to television programs or movies, you'll observe that much of the "virtue" of tolerance has been skewed. A culture that tolerates evil calls disagreement "phobia." Taking a stand is considered "hate." Conviction is seen as bigoted "fanaticism." Centuries-old Christian doctrine is regarded as "discrimination." As in many doctrinally weak churches today, this situation also prevailed in the ancient church of Thyatira. In His letter to that church, Christ addressed the issue of big sins in a small church—and the even bigger issue of tolerating them.

— 2:18–23 —

As He did in all His messages to the seven church of Asia Minor, Christ introduced Himself to the church in Thyatira in terms relevant to the church's specific situation. The description refers to John's initial vision of Christ in chapter 1, where Christ was seen with eyes of fire and feet glimmering like fired bronze (1:14–15). The imagery recalls other heavenly beings (Ezek. 1:7; Dan. 7:9), especially the angelic being described in Daniel 10:5–6. These elements indicate that Christ had broken into John's world from the heavenly realm and that He carried all the power and authority of the divine Son of God.[36]

As such, Christ could see the church's deepest, darkest secrets with eyes like flames of fire, as Hebrews 4:13 says: "And there is no creature hidden from His sight, but all things are open and laid bare to the eyes of Him with whom we have to do." What did His probing eyes see in Thyatira? He pierced the outer shell of faithful believers characterized by love, faith, service, and perseverance (Rev. 2:19). Hiding behind that commendable group thriving in their spiritual lives, Christ saw a dark spot of cancerous sin eating away from the inside.

After praising the faithful in Thyatira, Christ identified two more distinct groups in that church (2:20). Besides the group that excelled in good deeds, others were actively engaged in wickedness — and a third group tolerated that evil. These three groups coexisted in the church: the *Faithful, Toleration Party*, and the *Jezebel & Company*. They constituted the good, the bad, and the ugly of the church in Thyatira.

Jezebel & Company followed a false prophetess. Her real name probably wasn't "Jezebel." She likely had characteristics similar to the Jezebel of the Old Testament mentioned in 1 Kings 16–21. The original Jezebel corrupted the kingdom of Israel when she married King Ahab, leading the people into idolatry and sin (1 Kings 16:31–33). Jezebel was deceptive, idolatrous, domineering, scheming, and vicious. Similarly, the "Jezebel" of Thyatira led many in the church into similar sins, perhaps using similar methods. Though she had no official authority, she bullied people and introduced teachings contrary to what the established leadership taught.

It may be that Jezebel & Company represents one of the earliest gnostic groups, which flourished later in the second century. Gnosticism taught that matter (the body) and spirit (the soul) were completely separate from each other, and that the body was unable to be redeemed. Salvation concerned only the spirit. Some forms of Gnosticism reasoned in this manner: since the spirit is unaffected by the body, we can indulge the lusts of our flesh without doing damage to our spirits. That is, because God is concerned only with the condition of our souls, He doesn't care what we do with our bodies. What's worse than this kind of nasty false teaching? Many true Christians in Thyatira let her get away with it!

Thyatira's "Jezebel" is long gone. We don't even know her real name, much less where she's buried. Her style of false teaching, however, is alive and well today under a variety of names; and when faithful Christians put these modern heresies to sleep, the doctrines keep leaping back out of the grave! That's because it's so alluring to justify immorality in the name of grace. These false teachers — then and now — push the freedom we have in Christ to extremes, using grace as a license for sin. They have usurped the established authority of the church with their own haughtiness and have led many down the same path. Some have caused church splits within otherwise healthy congregations. All these rebellious actions are defended with twisted "do-it-yourself" doctrines. This was the standard operating procedure for Jezebel & Company.

Though Christ gave Jezebel enough time to repent of her wickedness, she refused (2:21). The result? Christ threw the book at her! Verses 22 and 23 contain some of the harshest words of judgment in these seven letters. The judgment includes sickness and death—not only for the false teacher, but also for her deceived followers. Does this mean all these people were unbelievers? Is it possible that some of them—perhaps even Jezebel herself—were real believers, although self-deceived? The Bible clearly teaches that true believers can fall into sin (Gal. 6:1). Such carnality can lead to severe discipline (Heb. 12:6–11). This discipline can lead even to sickness and death (1 Cor. 11:30–32; 1 John 5:16).

It's more likely, however, that Jezebel and many of her followers were false believers attempting to plant seeds of deception and bring destruction (2 Peter 2:1; Jude 1:4; 1 John 2:18–19). In either case, Christ's judgment would be swift and certain. Though *salvation* is always provided by grace through faith (Eph. 2:8–9), the *rewards* of believers will be given or taken away according to the quality of their work (1 Cor. 3:12–15; 2 Cor. 5:10). In a similar way, the *punishment* of the unsaved will be based on their wicked deeds (Rev. 20:12–15). So, whether she and her followers were severely errant saints or deceptive sinners, Jezebel & Company would be held accountable for their actions.

—2:24–29—

We might expect that after such a strong condemnation, the promises of Christ to those who overcome might be terse and tenuous. Not so! In fact, Christ had a rich, robust exhortation and encouragement to the "rest" in Thyatira—those among the *Faithful* party who were not caught up in Jezebel's charade and who refused to tolerate it (2:24). They were simply to "hold fast" to what they had, refuse to accommodate her wickedness, and stand against the deception at any cost (2:25). I'm sure it wasn't an easy position to maintain. Keeping the peace by holding our tongues is always easier than standing our ground and confronting wickedness. This is why Christ placed no further burden on them. Remaining faithful to Him in that culture of toleration was difficult enough!

Along with this encouragement to persevere, Christ offered the faithful in Thyatira a powerful promise for overcoming—they could look forward to reigning with Christ, the morning star (2:26–29; cf. 22:16). This promise is based on the Old Testament prophecy that God would send a king from the line of David to rule over the kings of the earth (Ps. 2:8–9). We know today that Jesus Christ ultimately will fulfill this prophecy when He returns (Luke 1:32–33; Rom. 1:3–4). Yet as we read on in Scripture, we discover that Christ didn't intend to fulfill this promise alone. He would exalt His hand-picked disciples as fellow rulers. In Matthew 19:28, Jesus told His disciples, "Truly I say to you, that you who have followed Me, in the regeneration when the Son of Man will sit on His glorious throne, you also shall sit upon twelve thrones, judging the twelve tribes of Israel."

In His promise to those who overcome in Thyatira, Christ quoted Psalm 2:8–9 and applies the prophecy to all faithful Christians. We, too, will reign with Him and will be involved in judging the nations (Rev. 2:26–27). In fact, His promise to give them "the morning star" (2:28) draws on similar images of the rule of the Davidic king from Numbers 24:17–18 and is mentioned again in Revelation 22:16.[37] The final fulfillment of this promise, now extended to all believers (2:29), will be seen in the second coming of Christ (19:11–16), where Psalm 2 is quoted again. The saints will reign with Christ for a thousand years (Rev. 20:4–6).

Application

Defeating Jezebel & Company

Jezebel & Company is still in business today … and it's thriving. Those who put up with her false teachings can be found in most churches. The sad reality is that tolerating sin is always easier than exposing and confronting it. As I step back and think about the troubling conditions in Thyatira and Christ's words of concern and correction, three practical implications come to mind.

First, the events in Thyatira teach us that *big problems can occur in small places.* Don't be surprised when trouble breaks loose! I know that most people reading these words don't come from giant churches that broadcast their services on national television. Those churches may be well-known, but compared to the majority of churches in the world, megachurches with media popularity are few. When bad things happen in big churches, everybody hears about it. This can sometimes lead smaller churches to think that they can fly under Satan's radar, that they don't factor into the enemy's strategic attacks on the global church. In fact, that kind of "it'll-never-happen-to-us" attitude is just what Satan wants us to think. It's a set-up for a sudden attack. Instead, we need to be ever on the alert, sober-minded, prepared. Read and reread Acts 20:28–31 and 1 Peter 5:8–9. Large or small, we must never think that we're immune to major upheavals in our churches.

Second, *bad teaching can come from gifted people.* Don't be misled! Jezebel of Thyatira was clearly gifted, perhaps even wealthy and influential. Maybe choosing to exercise biblical discipline against her would have meant losing not only Jezebel but all her followers, reducing the already small, blue-collar church to a tiny remnant. Today, we must be on the alert for teachers who, by their winsome charisma or worldly positions, can cause whopping problems. We can't let ourselves be mystified by a person's charisma or blinded by financial contributions. To let our guards down for a moment can lead to doctrinal deception and ruined lives.

Finally, *tolerance of bad teaching has no place in the church.* Take a stand! This section began with the questions, "Are you tolerant? Should you be?" Let me put the question another way: Should Christians ever judge others? That simple question often elicits an immediate "No!" After all, Jesus said, "Do not judge, and you will not be judged" (Luke 6:37). It seems pretty clear, doesn't it? Even Paul said, "Therefore you have no excuse, every one of you who passes judgment, for in that which you judge another, you condemn yourself" (Rom. 2:1). Yet in another passage Paul instructed the Corinthians to avoid judging sinners of the world around them. Instead, they were to judge those within the church by rebuking sin and

THE CITY WITH A FAÇADE OF FAME

In the early 1900s, store owners in the western United States designed the fronts of their buildings to look like three-story structures. They decorated these storefronts with fancy, intricate woodworking and vibrant colors. Upon entering the building, however, customers often found a drab, one-room shop and unattractive merchandise.

In the first century, the city of Sardis had a similar problem. Once a prominent and wealthy city in Lydia, an earthquake devastated Sardis in AD 17.[39] It continued to exist, but instead of prospering, its residents chose to dwell on its dead past, never regaining their former wealth and power.[40] Like a store with a false front, the city of Sardis had a reputation for being on top of the world, but that position had ceased to be a reality. The city seemed to have life, but in fact it was merely a shell of its former self.

The church of Sardis took its cues from the city. It had all of the external marks of a busy, productive congregation, but decay was taking its toll internally. The church left its glory days in the memory of what had been. Unfortunately, like the city that surrounded it, the reputation of the church's former glory no longer matched the current reality.

Ruins of Sardis

© William D. Mounce

correcting false teaching. This often meant removing the wicked person from the church through proper church discipline (1 Cor. 5:9–13). The purpose is not just the purity of the church, but also the repentance and restoration of the sinning believer. In other words, the biblical approach to toleration is, "Don't judge the world; God will judge them. Instead, hold the church of Christ to its own standards of doctrinal and moral purity."

Because Christ knows the deepest secrets of our hearts, we can't fool Him with a fancy façade. Christ's stinging rebuke of Thyatira left little room for indecision. If we're tolerating sin in our own lives or in the lives of those brothers and sisters closest to us, we need to come to terms with it. *Now!*

Sardis: Autopsy of a Dead Church (Revelation 3:1–6)

---

¹"To the angel of the church in Sardis write:

He who has the seven Spirits of God and the seven stars, says this:

'I know your deeds, that you have a name that you are alive, but you are dead. ²Wake up, and strengthen the things that remain, which were about to die; for I have not found your deeds completed in the sight of My God. ³So remember what you have received and heard; and keep *it*, and repent. Therefore if you do not wake up, I will come like a thief, and you will not know at what hour I will come to you. ⁴But you have a few people in Sardis who have not soiled their garments; and they will walk with Me in white, for they are worthy. ⁵He who overcomes will thus be clothed in white garments; and I will not erase his name from the book of life, and I will confess his name before My Father and before His angels. ⁶He who has an ear, let him hear what the Spirit says to the churches.'"

Ever been to a dead church? I hear that description from people a lot:

- "I grew up in a dead church."
- "Our church used to be dynamic; now it's dead."
- "Don't go to that church. It's dead."

What exactly does that mean?

Maybe it means their sanctuary is a morgue with a steeple. It's a congregation of corpses with undertakers for ushers, embalmers for elders, and morticians for ministers. Their pastor graduated from a theological cemetery. The choir director is the local coroner. They sing "Embalmed in Gilead" and "Amazing Grave, How Sweet the Ground." You might describe their worship as stiff. At the Rapture, they'll be the first churches taken up because the Bible says, "The dead in Christ shall rise first." They drive to church in one long line with their headlights on. Whenever someone joins their membership, the church office immediately notifies the next of kin. Each week they put an ad in the obituaries. The church van is a black hearse and the church sign is a tombstone. Their motto is, "Many are cold and a few are frozen."[38]

I wish that a dead church would be as obvious as that macabre description! In fact, however, most churches (even dead ones) look alive on the outside. What appears alive from our human perspective may be "dead" in the eyes of God. A dead church meets regularly to utter prayers, mouth lyrics, and collect enough cash to pay the bills. They may be growing in number. They may be buying land and constructing buildings. They may have well-staffed programs and all the latest slick technology. Yes, dead churches may have all these things—but are still dead.

Deceptively dead churches aren't a phenomenon only of the modern world. They existed all the way back in the first century. This is clear in the message to the church in Sardis, where Christ, the Great Physician, conducted an autopsy. Yet as the One who is "the resurrection and the life" (John 11:25), He turned an autopsy of death into an offer of life.

— 3:1 —

Christ introduced Himself to the church in Sardis in terms directly related to their situation: "He who has the seven Spirits of God and the seven stars." The seven spirits in 3:1 symbolize the sevenfold ministry of the Spirit,[41] and the seven stars represent the seven messengers (pastors) of the churches (1:4, 16, 20). How does this image relate to Sardis's condition as a "dead" church? Jesus seems to have emphasized that He holds in His hands the power of life for the churches through the work of the Holy Spirit.

The ancient Creed of Constantinople (381) describes the Holy Spirit as "the Lord and giver of life." Both the Old and New Testaments affirm this work of the Holy Spirit. Job 33:4 says, "The Spirit of God has made me, and the breath of the Almighty gives me life." In John 6:63 Jesus says, "It is the Spirit who gives life; the flesh profits nothing." And the apostle Paul famously writes, "The letter kills, but the Spirit gives life" (2 Cor. 3:6).

Christ held both the Holy Spirit and the messengers of the seven churches in His hands. He alone has the power to give life to the churches through the life-giving Spirit. Even though the church in Sardis had a reputation for life, most believers in that church lived with the constant reality of death. For many, rigor mortis had set in. They were apathetic, without the will to change. While some could have been candidates for resuscitation, most remained buried in "dead works." Few people made up the tiny, living remnant. Only Christ's penetrating inspection could lead to this diagnosis, for to the casual observer with an undiscerning eye, the church in Sardis appeared to be well.

What did it mean that the church in Sardis was, in large part, dead? Today we almost exclusively think of death in physical terms—when a person's heart stops beating or lungs stop breathing. The Bible's notion of death, however, includes both material and immaterial aspects. The Bible often speaks of physical death as the end of one's personal presence on earth (Gen. 23:13; Deut. 17:6; Josh. 1:2; Eccl. 9:5–6; John 11:14; James 2:26). But "dead" (Gk. *nekros*) can also refer metaphorically to the low moral quality of one's life, or spiritually to a person's position of condemnation, regardless of whether a person is physically alive (Matt. 8:22; Luke 15:24).[42]

When referring to inanimate things, *dead* means "of poor quality" or "useless." Therefore, in Hebrews 6:1 and 9:14, the works of a person prior to his or her new life in Christ were simply "dead" (cf. Col. 2:13; 1 Tim. 5:6). Christ used the same concept when He spoke of the church in Sardis as "dead" (Rev. 3:1). Although the believers were physically alive, their works and faith were useless and of poor quality (James 2:20, 26). To reverse this trend, they needed an awakening that could come only from the hand of Christ through the Spirit of life.

— 3:2-3 —

As we read the opening words of Christ's exhortation in verse 2, we might picture Him rushing into the church of Sardis like an emergency room physician bursting into a triage unit, finding people in different levels of "death." He didn't, however, start hauling out the corpses or finishing off the ones on their last leg. Rather, Christ sought to breathe new life into that comatose congregation. He wanted to revive and restore as many to health as would respond to His words. Like the doctor in charge of a trauma unit, He began shouting five orders in rapid succession (3:2–3). These five are Christ's prescription for the dying church in Sardis.

First, He called them to "wake up" (3:2). As if shaking somebody just before he or she loses consciousness, Christ took the church in Sardis into His arms and shouted, "Stay with Me!" A lack of vigilance will cause believers to drift off into the slumber of a dying culture, rendering their deeds ineffective and useless.

Second, Christ told the church in Sardis to "strengthen the things that remain" (3:2). For many in Sardis, a flicker of life shimmered with hope. It's likely that every dead church or denomination has at least a remnant of the living. Dwelling in the environment of a dead church week after week, however, takes its toll. In

From My Journal

Dead or Alive?

In November, 2009, news outlets reported a story out of Brussels, Belgium, concerning a man who had been diagnosed as remaining in a vegetative state for twenty-three years, after falling into a coma following an automobile accident. He had all the signs of unconsciousness—paralysis, unresponsiveness to stimuli, and brain scans that suggested a lack of awareness. Upon closer examination using a state-of-the-art brain scan, however, doctors hypothesized that the man was conscious for twenty-three years! Having the appearance of being practically "dead," tests suggested that he may have been quite alive.[43] Whether the conclusions of the physicians and scientists are to be believed, this story does bring up an important point as it relates to the issue of "dead" versus "living" churches.

The misdiagnosis of a church can go in both directions. Just as a dead church can appear "alive" to a person using unbiblical standards, a living church may appear "dead" to people applying worldly criteria. At first glance, a growing, healthy church may appear to be withering, weak, and dying. If we focus on impressive numbers, glitzy on-stage productions, or media "buzz" as our criteria for a "living" church, we can mistakenly regard a small church that lacks these external qualities as "dead." The truth is, when a church faithfully proclaims Christ and preaches the Word, and when growing believers serve in effective evangelistic and discipleship ministries, it lives, regardless of its size.

Looks can deceive. More than ever, we need to avoid the error of misdiagnosis. We can't afford to embrace a dead church because of an impressive external façade. Nor can we reject a truly living church because it fails to catch our attention by a flashy exterior and fleshly hype. We need to remember the easily-forgotten truth: "Man looks at the outward appearance, but the Lord looks at the heart" (1 Sam. 16:7).

time, those few warm bodies begin to cool to room temperature, along with the majority. In Sardis, even good deeds were done halfheartedly.

Third, Christ ordered His spiritual patients to "remember what you have received and heard" (3:3). The present tense of the verb "remember" means they were to keep bringing to mind the salvation and gifts of the Spirit they had received, and to keep at the forefront of their minds the good news of the gospel they had heard. To this day every true church's worship features a constant reminder: the Lord's Supper, or Communion. When this ordinance is practiced correctly, the church comes together to remember the death of Christ as payment for sins (Luke 22:19; 1 Cor. 11:24). Other ways of remembering include reading God's written Word and listening to the passionate proclamation of God's truth.

Fourth, Christ commanded the church in Sardis to "keep" the truth they received and heard (3:3). According to Scripture, remembering is more than just thinking; it involves doing. Christ tells us that physically doing things to help us remember will keep us from drifting into the death of spiritual fog and forgetfulness. Merely reading and hearing God's Word isn't enough. We must let it transform us. We must be as committed to *obedience* as we are to *orthodoxy*.

Finally, Christ instructed the church in Sardis to "repent" (3:3). He calls for a decisive change of mind and attitude that would set them on the right course toward recovery. He didn't whisper about their condition or try to smooth over the negatives of their past and present. The Great Physician quickly explained the seriousness of their spiritual state and wrote them a clear prescription: "No more playing around with spiritual things. No more talking about doing what's right. The time has come to do it! Start today!"

A stern warning accompanies Christ's strong commands. If the church in Sardis did not take His advice and repent, He would come to them "like a thief" (3:3). This threat would have been especially significant for the church in Sardis. At two points in its history, the defenses of that city, which appeared impenetrable, were breached. Enemies managed to locate a secret path on the cliff leading up to the city and to sneak in by cover of night.[44] Similarly, if Sardis refused to repent, Christ would pierce the hypocritical façade that church was presenting and expose them to His hand of discipline. Serious words designed to awaken the dead!

— **3:4–6** —

No matter how badly His people deteriorate, God always preserves a remnant to carry out His will and to bring forth fruit (2 Kings 19:30–31; Isa. 10:20–21; Rom. 11:5). This remnant can also serve as the seed for a bountiful revival. The same

Condition of the Church in Sardis

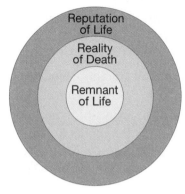

Though the church in Sardis had a reputation of spiritual vitality, all but a small remnant had become "dead" in their spiritual life.

was true in Sardis. Christ addressed this faithful remnant at the close of His message to that troubled church. Even members of the remnant, however, were in danger of being influenced by the spiritual stupor of the dead congregation surrounding them. So Jesus extended three promises to the few who had remained loyal.

The first promise Christ mentioned twice: "they will walk with Me in white" (3:4–5). In a later vision of the book of Revelation, John will see a large multitude of saints gathered in heaven who "have washed their robes and made them white in the blood of the Lamb" (7:14). The white robes represent the cleansing from sin received by faith in Christ. The image of "walking in white" is a promise of eternal, unblemished righteousness.

Christ's second promise is stated in the negative: "I will not erase his name from the book of life" (3:5). If a person is clothed with eternal righteousness, make no mistake: he or she has an eternally secure future. Obviously, God has no need of a literal book to remind Him of our standing before Him. The *biblos*, or "scroll of life," is a symbol of permanent security. Our future blessings are certain, as if God has written our names in a great registry of the citizens of heaven.

Finally, the third promise reveals the positive side of the second: "I will confess his name before My Father and before His angels" (3:5). This links two similar promises Christ made during His earthly ministry. Matthew 10:32 says, "Therefore everyone who confesses Me before men, I will also confess him before My Father who is in heaven." Similarly, Luke 12:8 says, "Everyone who confesses Me before men, the Son of Man will confess him also before the angels of God." In other words, on the day of judgment, Christ will vouch for those who belong to Him.

Throughout the letter to Sardis, Jesus played on the Greek word *onoma*, which can mean either "name" or "reputation." In 3:1 the church in Sardis had a "reputation" or "name" (*onoma*) for being alive, while in reality they were dead. In 3:4, Christ literally said, "You have a few names [*onoma*] in Sardis who have not soiled their garments." In 3:5, He promised that He would not remove their names (*onoma*) from the book of life and that He would confess their names (*onoma*) before God. All of this points to a profound truth. In Christ we have an eternal acceptance and identity. He will one day stand beside believers who have been clothed in white by the grace of God, whose names are written with permanent ink in the book of life, and He will announce, "This one's mine! His/her name is _____, and he/she is a child of the King!" *What an incredible thought*!

While many names in Sardis already had been etched onto the tombstone of that dead church, a few were missing. Those faithful few had a different destiny, a future with the One whose name was above all names, Jesus Christ their Lord and Life-giver.

Application

Five Marks of a Dead Church

Over the years as I've studied Scripture, reflected on the history of the church, and drawn on my decades of personal ministry experience, I've come up with five marks of sick and dying churches. One or two of these elements may be present in many (if not most) churches to some degree, but when I find them together, I know I'm dealing with a church in desperate need of healing and revival. As I present these observations, ask yourself, "Do any of these describe me? Am I contributing to the life of my church ... or to its death?"

First, *a dead church worships its past*. It's always about the way they were—amazing stories of conversions, remarkable revivals, and great former pastors. In contrast, living churches diligently build on their past and intentionally work toward the future.

Second, *a dead church is inflexible and resistant to change*. New approaches to ministry are met with skepticism, resistance, and/or fear. In contrast, living churches are open to changing methods so long as they accurately and effectively communicate the unchanging message.

Third, *a dead church often has carnal and lazy leadership*. Shot through with sins of pride, complacency, and entitlement, pastors and staff members are complacently riding the ship into the harbor of retirement. In contrast, the leadership at living churches is enthusiastically engaged in ministry because of devotion to their calling, not clipping the coupons of their career.

Fourth, *a dead church neglects children and youth*. Because of a combination of the first marks, children, teens, and young families are either turned off or driven away since their needs are ignored. In contrast, living churches invest in the lives of children and young people, knowing they are valuable to God and will shape the future of the church.

Finally, *a dead church lacks evangelistic and missionary zeal.* Turned inward on their own needs, preferences, and comfort, unhealthy churches give halfhearted attention to the conversion of the lost. In contrast, living churches devote time, resources, and energy to both local evangelism and worldwide missions.

In the message to Sardis, we saw Christ revealed as the Life-giver. He alone grants spiritual vitality to those with a comatose or dying faith. In light of His urgent alarm to Sardis, all of us who tend toward spiritual stupor must turn from stale religious routine and embrace the abundant life only Jesus Christ can provide. He extends a sincere invitation to you right now. If you feel the stiffness of spiritual rigor mortis setting in, take Christ's words to heart: wake up and declare your devotion.

Philadelphia: Little Strength, Open Door, Awesome God (Revelation 3:7–13)

> [7]"And to the angel of the church in Philadelphia write:
> He who is holy, who is true, who has the key of David, who opens and no one will shut, and who shuts and no one opens, says this:
> [8]'I know your deeds. Behold, I have put before you an open door which no one can shut, because you have a little power, and have kept My word, and have not denied My name. [9]Behold, I will cause *those* of the syna-gogue of Satan, who say that they are Jews and are not, but lie — I will make them come and bow down at your feet, and *make them* know that I have loved you. [10]Because you have kept the word of My perseverance, I also will keep you from the hour of testing, that *hour* which is about to come upon the whole world, to test those who dwell on the earth. [11]I am coming quickly; hold fast what you have, so that no one will take your crown. [12]He who overcomes, I will make him a pillar in the temple of My God, and he will not go out from it anymore; and I will write on him the name of My God, and the name of the city of My God, the new Jerusalem, which comes down out of heaven from My God, and My new name. [13]He who has an ear, let him hear what the Spirit says to the churches.'"

The size of a congregation, the limitations of its location, or the restrictions of its budget should never determine its vision. Instead, churches should set their vision based on the power of their God. God is infinite, magnificent, awesome, and mighty—beyond description or comprehension! When He chooses to open opportunities, the possibilities are endless. All we need to do is trust and follow Him wherever He leads.

God opens and closes doors according to His sovereign will and guided by His infinite wisdom. When He closes doors of opportunity, He doesn't do it to toy with us, spite us, or frustrate us. Instead, He closes doors to open others. This truth reassures me because I can trust in a God who knows what He's doing and why He's doing it, even though I rarely understand. At the same time, I know this seemingly endless closing and opening of doors can make us feel like laboratory mice running through a maze, trying to find that elusive "will" of God around the next corner. We can become aggravated as paths we really want to take suddenly get blocked, and we get pulled through other doors, kicking and screaming in protest. It's difficult to stay patient and trust God to reveal His plan to us, one step at a time.

During moments of honesty, though, most of us will admit that we like being in charge of our own lives. We want to make solid decisions and to accomplish the tasks we set out to do. If we do God's work, we sometimes want to plan and execute it in our own way on our terms. But only Christ is qualified to make decisions regarding His work. We're sinful; He's holy. We're deceitful; He's true. We're weak and inadequate; He's strong and all-powerful. So, when it comes to the course of our lives, God alone is in charge.

The church in the ancient city of Philadelphia provides a classic example of this. Even though it was the youngest of the seven churches and, quite likely, the smallest in size, this church received nothing but commendation from Christ. The believers there understood that the greatness of God far outweighed their humble circumstances. They also knew they had a simple responsibility: acknowledge the open door of opportunity set before them and move through it with confidence.

— **3:7** —

Christ is holy and true—perfectly pure in His righteousness and completely trustworthy in His character. He is also the One "who has the key of David, who opens and no one will shut, and who shuts and no one opens." This description echoes imagery from Isaiah 22, written during the reign of the righteous King Hezekiah. Under Hezekiah, a man named Eliakim served as the royal treasurer, with the authority and responsibility of guarding that treasure entrusted to his care. He was given a key that opened the vault, and he alone possessed the authority to access those vast riches. Isaiah 22:22 says, "Then I will set the key of the house of David on his shoulder, when he opens no one will shut, when he shuts no one will open."

In a similar way, the Father has handed the keys of authority over God's heavenly blessings to Christ alone. He controls access to the Father's spiritual treasury, turning difficult situations into wonderful opportunities. Here Jesus claims unrivaled sovereignty over the church, the storehouse of God's wisdom and the pillar and support of the truth (1 Tim. 3:15).

—3:8—

The church in Philadelphia was rich in good works, loyal to God's Word, and unashamed of their faith. What a stark contrast to their neighboring church in Sardis! Though coping with similar conditions, the Philadelphian believers responded in faithfulness, refusing to compromise the truth. Yet they continued to suffer persecution, hardship, and the frustrations of their apparently small size and limited influence. Yet in this situation Christ pointed out that they had tremendous opportunities despite their circumstantial setbacks.

THE ORIGINAL CITY OF BROTHERLY LOVE

Like its neighbor city of Sardis, in AD 17 a massive earthquake demolished the city of Philadelphia. In response, many Philadelphians moved out to surrounding areas to avoid future devastation and find lasting stability.[47] Those who stayed requested help from the emperor, Tiberius Caesar, who relieved the city of its tax burden long enough for the city to be rebuilt. As a result, the city took the name "Neocaesarea" in honor of the emperor.[48]

Another source of instability came not from geological tremors but from social and religious upheaval. Though the city was small at the end of the first century, it was home to a strong Jewish community. While it's likely that a large percentage of the Christians in Philadelphia were Jewish, this fact caused severe conflict between the church and members of the synagogue, who refused to accept Jesus as the Messiah.[49] In fact, so strong was this Jewish influence that within a couple decades the church in Philadelphia would find itself battling a false teaching in which the Old Testament law was exalted above the New Testament gospel.[50]

In light of the historical background of Philadelphia's disastrous earthquake, it's significant that Jesus promised that they would be made pillars in the temple of God, never to go out from it again (3:12). Similarly, the new name Jesus promised them may reflect the fact that Philadelphia itself was renamed after receiving aid from the emperor. Finally, the mention of the "synagogue of Satan" may relate to the attacks by local Jewish leaders on Jewish Christians' true "Jewishness," which resulted in the rejection of Jewish believers in Jesus. It could also refer to dangerous Judaizing heresies that eventually would work their way into the church of Philadelphia itself.

© Konstantin Yolshin/www.BigStockPhoto.com

Ruins of ancient Philadelphia

Commentators disagree on the meaning of the phrase "I have put before you an open door." Some say it refers to the "open door to heaven," reaffirming Christ's promise of salvation to the faithful Philadelphian church.[45] In this view, the phrase could tie in with the promise of rescue from the "hour of testing" by the Rapture of the church in 3:10; or it would fit with John's own removal to heaven in 4:1 through an open door.

Other scholars believe it speaks of an "open door for ministry," a platform for far-reaching evangelism.[46] If we allow the New Testament to interpret itself, this second option is more likely. A similar Greek phrase occurs in 2 Corinthians 2:12 in reference to an opportunity for ministry (see also Acts 14:27; 1 Cor. 16:9; Col. 4:3). If this is the meaning, Christ encouraged the church in Philadelphia with opportunities for ministry in the midst of their trials. That church didn't realize the "open door" they had. As the geographic gateway to the East, Philadelphia sat at the crossroads of several languages, cultures, and people groups. From an evangelistic and missionary perspective, this dynamic, diminutive church had great opportunities for ministry.

At the same time, the church of Philadelphia had only "a little power" (3:8). The Greek words used here indicate a small amount of resources and ability. It had nothing like the riches and influence of its neighbor, Laodicea. Nor did it have a rich history and heritage like Ephesus. It had neither the great reputation of Sardis nor the fame of faithfulness like Smyrna. Small, insignificant, poor, and often overlooked, the church in Philadelphia would have concluded that it had a small capacity for ministry. How wrong they were! Christians should never think that a big church is always an effective church. God often uses the limitations of individuals and churches as a platform from which to launch ambitious plans. He can do wondrous works even through the weak and foolish, the meek and humble — including you and me (1 Cor. 1:26–29).

The Philadelphians looked at the "little power" they had and emphasized the "little." Christ wanted to point them to that same condition and emphasize the "power." They had forgotten the words of Christ to His disciples: "If you have faith the size of a mustard seed, you will say to this mountain, 'Move from here to there,' and it will move; and nothing will be impossible to you" (Matt. 17:20).

— **3:9–13** —

The church in Philadelphia had a little power with great potential — not because of its size, resources, or influence, but because of the holiness, faithfulness, and sovereign authority of the Lord. Because they had kept His Word and refused to deny their Master, they were poised for great accomplishments through the open door of opportunity Christ had placed before them. Along with their unimpeachable spiritual condition, Christ relayed four encouraging promises.

First, He promised that He would cause their adversaries to be humiliated before them (3:9). The false teachers who fiercely contended with these Christians would be defeated. The promise doesn't say how this would happen, but perhaps several of them would be converted, as in the example of the apostle Paul. Though he was originally a severe persecutor of the church as the rabid Pharisee, Saul of Tarsus, the Lord Jesus humbled and temporarily blinded him on the road to Damascus, transforming him into Paul the apostle and sending him as a missionary to the Gentiles (Acts 9).[51] Regardless of how it would be accomplished, the attack on the church in Philadelphia by the unbelieving Jewish communities would soon be brought to an end.

Second, Christ promised that He would keep them—and all believers—from the coming worldwide tribulation. Although there are several possible interpretations of what it means to "keep" the believers from "the hour of testing" (3:10), it is most commonly understood as a reference to the expected period of coming wrath that God will send to judge the world in preparation for the return of Christ. Similarly, Paul said that Christians are waiting for Christ to come from heaven to rescue them "from the wrath to come" (1 Thess. 1:10).

What is the *means* by which believers are kept from this coming wrath? Of course, God has many options. He could choose to supernaturally protect us from His judgment, as He did for the Israelites during the plagues in Egypt. Or He could completely remove us from the place of His wrath, as He did with Lot before judging Sodom. God isn't limited to just one way of protecting His people, and He has used a variety of methods in the past. In 1 Thessalonians, however, Paul indicates the specific way in which God will save the church from the coming tribulation:

> For the Lord Himself will descend from heaven with a shout, with the voice of the archangel and with the trumpet of God, and the dead in Christ will rise first. Then we who are alive and remain will be caught up together with them in the clouds to meet the Lord in the air, and so we shall always be with the Lord. (1 Thess. 4:16–17).

This "catching up" or rapture of living believers is directly tied to being saved from wrath several verses later, when Paul wrote, "God has not destined us for wrath, but for obtaining salvation through our Lord Jesus Christ, who died for us, so that whether we are awake or asleep, we will live together with Him" (1 Thess. 5:9–10). Given this biblical background regarding rescue from wrath, it seems best to understand Revelation 3:10 as describing the promise of rescue from the time of tribulation by "catching up" true Christians from the earth.

Some object that because these events didn't occur in the first century, the original readers in Philadelphia never received this promise of protection from the coming tribulation. We must not forget, however, that immediately preceding the catching up of living Christians before the tribulation, those who had died from every generation of the church will be raised in new bodies and also will be caught up together with the church as one complete body of Christ (1 Thess. 4:16–17). So, even though the original recipients of this promise died in Christ before being rescued, they will still experience this promised rescue when their remains are snatched from the grave, transformed into immortal bodies, and caught up together with all believers of every age, not to experience wrath or tribulation, but to receive heavenly salvation and reward.

Condition of the Church in Philadelphia

Holy & True

Though it suffered from persecution, the church in Philadelphia was holy and true, having no marks or blemishes.

Third, Christ promised the church in Philadelphia that it would remain strong and secure (3:11–12). He reminded them that His coming will be sudden, unexpected, and quick; this would motivate them to continue to hold their confidence firmly so nobody would rob them of their heavenly reward (3:11). With this comes a great promise of permanence. Those who overcome would be like pillars in God's temple. Unlike the city of Philadelphia, which collapsed when the ground shook in the earthquake of AD 17, the church of Philadelphia would enter into the protection of God's unshakable heavenly temple, unable to be removed. What a tremendous image of our eternal security in Christ!

Finally, Christ gave the Philadelphians a promise of new ownership (3:12). In the ancient world, when a slave was freed, he often kept the household name of his master and was even granted his master's social status. Though born into bondage, a benevolent owner could give that servant a new identity.[52] Similarly, the spiritual marking of believers with God's name indicates a new citizenship and new identity. They no longer belonged to themselves; they had been bought for a price (1 Cor. 6:19–20). The city of Philadelphia itself had changed names and allegiances several times in its history, so it was important that the church be reminded that their citizenship was in heaven and that their allegiance was to God above all earthly things.

Application

Taking on "Insurmountable Opportunities"

Most of us spend too much time staring at closed doors. Dejected and disappointed, we wonder why in the world a certain plan of ours didn't unfold. As I think about those doors that are so rudely slammed in our faces throughout life, my mind goes back years ago to the words of cartoonist Walt Kelly in his *Pogo* comic strip: "We are confronted with insurmountable opportunities." The truth is that when God closes doors to passageways that seemed so obvious and easy, He opens other doors that may appear, well, less desirable and more difficult to enter. Insurmountable opportunities.

Are you in a place where sharing your faith is beset with difficulties, or where living your faith has unique challenges? By "place" I don't necessarily mean your physical location, though that can play a significant role. Sometimes our "place" in life can feel limiting. You may work at a job where your boss puts the kibosh on anything "religious." Or you attend a school where every perspective is tolerated — except yours. You may be a stay-at-home mom with a talkative toddler running around your feet all day. Or you may feel limited by physical disabilities, financial constraints, or a tyrannical schedule. Whatever the circumstances that appear to limit your opportunities and close the door on your prospects for fruitful ministry, Christ's words to the church in Philadelphia have something to say to you today. Let me focus on two applications regarding "insurmountable opportunities."

First, remember that "insurmountable opportunities" turn our attention away from ourselves and back to our God. That ignites a new vision that transcends our circumstances and stretches the imagination beyond our limitations. We don't want to limit God or miss His plan because we're seeing things only from our limited perspective. He has some things for us that are beyond our comprehension. We need to turn our attention away from our own "little power" to His all-sufficient provision. Then we'll begin to see how God can use "small" and "insignificant" people to accomplish great things for Him.

Second, don't forget that "insurmountable opportunities" force us to trust completely in the Lord our God. That prompts a firm faith that can overcome any obstacle. Walking by faith isn't just a nice idea or one of several options. It's *the* plan for God's people. We don't want to question Him or doubt His promise. When we remain faithful to Him and commit to follow Him wherever He leads, He will not only open doors of unbelievable opportunity for us, but He will also give us the strength to overcome the challenges that come our way.

So, as you look beyond your own current "limitations" and the doors that God has closed in your life, what other opportunities could you be overlooking? You might think through this question by asking yourself, "What *could* I have done for Christ last year?" Come up with five answers, then five more. As you think through this, pray that God will help you see the opportunities He's placing before you; then trust in Him to help answer the question, "What *can* I do for Christ next year?" Are you ready to step through an open door of opportunity in God's strength?

Laodicea: The Church That Nauseates God (Revelation 3:14–22)

---

¹⁴"To the angel of the church in Laodicea write:

The Amen, the faithful and true Witness, the Beginning of the creation of God, says this:

¹⁵'I know your deeds, that you are neither cold nor hot; I wish that you were cold or hot. ¹⁶So because you are lukewarm, and neither hot nor cold, I will spit you out of My mouth. ¹⁷Because you say, "I am rich, and have become wealthy, and have need of nothing," and you do not know that you are wretched and miserable and poor and blind and naked, ¹⁸I advise you to buy from Me gold refined by fire so that you may become rich, and white garments so that you may clothe yourself, and *that* the shame of your nakedness will not be revealed; and eye salve to anoint your eyes so that you may see. ¹⁹Those whom I love, I reprove and discipline; therefore be zealous and repent. ²⁰Behold, I stand at the door and knock; if anyone hears My voice and opens the door, I will come in to him and will dine with him, and he with Me. ²¹He who overcomes, I will grant to him to sit down with Me on My throne, as I also overcame and sat down with My Father on His throne. ²²He who has an ear, let him hear what the Spirit says to the churches.'"

Do these lines sound familiar?

- God helps those who help themselves.
- Pull yourself together.
- If you want something done right, do it yourself.
- Believe in yourself.
- Look out for number one.

While ancient pagans had hundreds of false gods to choose from, modern pagans have one false god that controls their lives: self. Self-expression, self-confidence, self-worth, self-reliance—these concepts all revolve around the myth that human beings have an inexhaustible source of strength within themselves.

Such worthy people, of course, have trouble attributing all worth to God, which is the very definition of worship!

Sadly, Christians aren't immune to the disease of self-reliance. When believers in Christ rely on their own strength for good works, operating by the power of the flesh rather than by the power of the Spirit (Gal. 3:3), they produce useless and insincere works. When believers think they're sufficient in their own resources, they glow with pride. And when believers look to themselves to provide for their own needs, they shine with self-sufficiency.

Christ's messages to the seven churches in Asia come to a close with a tragic letter

THE SELF-MADE CITY

Devastated by an earthquake in AD 60, the city of Laodicea chose to "pull itself up by its bootstraps" rather than seek imperial assistance like its neighbor, Philadelphia, had done earlier. Because of its location on important Asia trade routes, Laodicea quickly became one of the wealthiest cities in the region, a condition reflected in the membership of its Christian church (Rev. 3:17).[53]

Not unlike Wall Street, Laodicea was a major banking center of Asia Minor. This meant it attracted people of means. Money flowed freely through its streets, reflected in its buildings, in its businesses, and, yes, in its church. It boasted a thriving textile trade, with coveted garments woven from a special wool found only in Laodicea. Besides these things that pumped money into Laodicea's economy, the city also was famous for its medicine. In fact, some of their coins were minted with the faces of famous physicians from their city. They were especially known for Phrygian powder, a substance mixed with water and used as a salve to treat ailments of the eye. It's no surprise that Christ's message to Laodicea refers to their wealth, their clothing, and their healing ointment (3:17–18).

Yet Laodicea had one major problem. It lacked a supply of good water, which eventually led to the city's abandonment. One scholar writes: "For all its wealth, it could produce neither the healing power of hot water, like its neighbor Hierapolis, nor the refreshing power of cold water to be found at Colossae, but merely lukewarm water, useful only as an emetic."[54] Jesus rebuked the believers in Laodicea because they were neither cold nor hot. He intended to spit them out of His mouth — unless they repented (3:15–16).

Ruins of Laodicea

Todd Bolen/www.BiblePlaces.com

to the self-sufficient, self-righteous, self-serving church in Laodicea. In their inexhaustible wealth and independent spirit, the Laodiceans were severely rebuked by the One who knew them better than they knew themselves. In fact, the Lord didn't state a single word of commendation as He delivered His stinging reproof. That church suffered from pervasive self-reliance, hypocritical works done in their own strength, and an apathetic attitude toward the authority of Christ. Sadly, His hard words for Laodicea resonate with relevance for many churches and Christians today.

— 3:14 —

Christ called Himself "the Amen, the faithful and true Witness." To understand the significance of this title, we need to turn to the Old Testament. Isaiah 65:16 refers to God as the "God of truth" (lit., the "God of *Amen*," a Hebrew word acknowledging the veracity of something). So we might actually translate verse 14 like this: "The Amen, that is, the faithful and true Witness." As "Amen," Christ embodies faithfulness and truth in all He says and does (John 14:6). Unlike the Laodiceans, Christ is no hypocrite. He is the personification of authenticity.

Christ also called Himself, according to the New American Standard Bible, "the Beginning of the creation of God" (3:14). The word translated "beginning" is *archē*, a word with numerous meanings and nuances in Greek. It can mean "beginning," "elementary principle," "first," "summary," "origin," "first cause," "ruler," "authority," "domain," and even "corner."[55] With so many possibilities, how do we know the meaning of 3:14, where Christ calls Himself "the *archē* of God's creation"? Given the immediate context and the content of the letter to the Laodiceans, Christ as *archē* seems to identify Him as the Source and Ruler of all creation (John 1:1–3; Col. 1:16–18; Rev. 1:5).

When Christ identified Himself as the Amen, the faithful and true Witness, and the supreme Source and Ruler of all creation, the church at Laodicea must have bristled. They may even have squirmed. He was preparing to speak the truth, to bear true witness against that church dealing in falsehood. And as He outlined the real situation in Laodicea, He did so not as a casual observer giving a few pieces of constructive criticism. He was their Sovereign Lord, who could make or break that church in an instant.

— 3:15–17 —

At this point in the message, the sophisticated congregation in Laodicea probably got a little nervous. The Embodiment of Truth, who calls it as He sees it, who is the Creator and King of all, looked the church in the eye and said, "I know your

Condition of the Church in Ephesus

Because of its pathetic condition of self-reliance, the church in Laodicea had nothing good to offer.

deeds." The church was in a wretched state. In fact, you'll recall, He exposed them as "lukewarm," neither hot nor cold.

When Christ wished that the Laodiceans were either cold or hot rather than lukewarm, He could have been referring to their hypocritical nature—they claimed to be a certain way, but their words and their deeds didn't match. Or Christ could have been saying that the Laodiceans were simply useless in their works. A little geography and history help us better understand the analogy. Ten miles to the east was Colossae, known for its refreshing cold springs. Six miles to the north was Hierapolis, which had hot springs. Laodicea, located on a high plateau far from any springs, had to pipe in its water through stone aqueducts. By the time it reached the city, the water was always tepid, lukewarm, and sometimes even bitter or chalky to the taste after traveling for miles through all that stone.

Like their municipal water, Laodicea's works were lukewarm, neither hot nor cold. Cold water has therapeutic and culinary uses, as does hot water, but lukewarm water is unpleasant, insipid, and useless. Similarly, the book of James addresses the issue of those who profess to have faith but fail to demonstrate it in their works. Such fruitless faith is said to be "useless" (James 2:20). Christ expressed disdain for the same type of sin in Laodicea: the works of the Christians living there were done solely in the flesh and therefore were halfhearted, insincere, and self-indulgent. They reflected nothing of the love that comes from Christ through the power of the Holy Spirit. Christ's reaction to the complacent, listless spiritual condition of the Laodiceans could not have been more vivid: "I will spit you out of My mouth" (3:16). It's hard to think of a less flattering reaction, especially from the only Man in the universe whose opinion really matters. Put bluntly, He said, *You make me sick!*

The next comment highlights the specific nature of their self-indulgent lifestyle (3:17). That city and church were so wealthy they considered God unnecessary. In reality, they were spiritually bankrupt. They had clothed themselves in fine apparel, but inwardly, where it really counted, they were naked of virtue. Though their city boasted of near-miraculous eye salve, only Christ had the power to remove their pervasive spiritual blindness. Though worldly rich, well-dressed, and healthy, spiritually they were poor, naked, and blind.

Commendations and Condemnations in the Letters to the Seven Churches

Church	Commendation	Condemnation
Ephesus	Good works, endurance, discernment	Departed from first love
Smyrna	Faithfulness in persecution	None
Pergamum	Some faithfulness in persecution	Idolatry, false teaching, immorality
Thyatira	Some love, faith, service, endurance	Idolatry, false teaching, immorality
Sardis	Worthy remnant kept clean	Hypocrisy, incomplete works
Philadelphia	Good works, endurance, faithfulness	None
Laodicea	None	Pride, materialism, laziness

—— 3:18–19 ——

I can't speak for you, but if somebody told me that everything about me made him want to vomit, I wouldn't expect to hear from him again. Yet while Christ's nature as the "faithful and true Witness" meant He held nothing back in his honest indictment of the Laodiceans' spiritual condition, He never set aside His love and grace. As the Source and Ruler of all God's creation, He offered the Laodiceans the possibility of turning things around. It wasn't too late!

First, Jesus gave them serious advice that can be summed up in a straightforward command: "Stop trusting in yourselves—turn to Me!" In place of dependence on worldly wealth that brought spiritual poverty, Christ offered true spiritual riches. In place of relying on their outer appearance that left them spiritually naked, Christ offered to clothe them in His own righteousness. Instead of a physical salve to heal blurred sight, Jesus offered them spiritual eye salve to cure the cataracts on their character.

Second, Christ reassured them of His love. Though He had rebuked the Laodiceans with severity, He added words of tough love: "Those whom I love, I reprove and discipline" (3:19). This echoes the language of Proverbs 3:12, which says, "For whom the Lord loves He reproves, even as a father corrects the son in whom he delights." In even more detail, Hebrews 12:7 – 11 explains that God's discipline is not out of spite, hatred, or even anger; rather, it is out of love and genuine concern for His children:

> It is for discipline that you endure; God deals with you as with sons; for what son is there whom his father does not discipline? But if you are without discipline, of which all have become partakers, then you are illegitimate children and not sons. Furthermore, we had earthly fathers to discipline us, and we respected them; shall we not much rather be subject to the Father of spirits, and live? For they disciplined us for a short time as seemed best to them, but He disciplines us for our good, so that we may share His holiness. All discipline for the moment seems not to be joyful, but sorrowful; yet to those who have been trained by it, afterwards it yields the peaceful fruit of righteousness.

The Laodiceans were steeped in self-reliance. They shamelessly trusted in themselves, their riches, and their own strength. Yet out of a fatherly love for His children, Christ presented a clear solution: "Be zealous and repent" (3:19).

— 3:20 – 22 —

The image of Christ knocking at the door brings to mind a call for intimate fellowship (3:20). In this case, Christ desired fellowship with the lukewarm believers at Laodicea whose pride, self-sufficiency, and hypocrisy had kept Him at arm's length. Though this passage has some application for evangelism, the Lord was primarily concerned here with moving Christians from halfhearted commitment to full-blown repentance.

It seems fitting that in a letter emphasizing Christ's sovereign rule over God's creation (3:14), Christ should extend a promise of reigning with Him when He returns (3:21). Just as Christ overcame sin and death to sit at the right hand of the Father, so believers in Christ will one day rise from the dead and sit with Christ on His throne in the future earthly kingdom (2:26 – 27; 20:6).

With the letter to Laodicea, Christ's messages to the seven churches conclude and the second part of the Lord's inspired outline of the book of Revelation comes to its conclusion (cf. 1:19). John first wrote *the things which he saw* — the spectacular vision of Christ (1:10 – 20). Then he wrote *the things which are*, pertaining to the local churches from Ephesus to Laodicea. That would also include any who have ears to hear and apply the messages to those seven churches (chs. 2 – 3). We now move into the third part of this inspired outline, *the things which will take place after these things* (1:19).

Application

Hot, Cold ... or Lukewarm ?

The Laodiceans had several serious problems. In the midst of their affluence and pride, self-sufficiency had taken hold. Because they had it all, the Laodiceans rested their faith, hope, and love on their health and wealth rather than on Christ. Their good works were halfhearted and ineffective. Their security rested on fleeting riches. Their deepest spiritual needs were filled by physical means. But the real problem with the church in Laodicea was that they didn't even realize they had a problem.

Sound familiar?

As I consider our culture of worldly excess, extreme individualism, and self-reliance, it's difficult to avoid the realization that Christ's message to Laodicea has special application to us today. Too many Christians live in luxury, but they have little interest in the lost. We employ the latest church growth gimmicks, but we add few new believers to our numbers. In so many ways we have exchanged influence for affluence, concern for comfort, and passion for passivity. Our physical prosperity and resulting self-sufficiency can mask the fact that we're spiritually "wretched and miserable and poor and blind and naked" (3:17).

Let's take some time to examine our true spiritual condition, letting Christ's message to Laodicea penetrate our own hearts. Set your watch aside and offer Christ your undivided attention. The following chart summarizes the ailments

---

The Laodicean Condition

You think you are prosperous because of God's blessing, but you are spiritually poor.

Diagnostic Questions

- Do I spend more time thinking about finances than about ministry?
- Do I give regularly and generously, or do I withhold gifts?
- Do I spend far more time and money on myself rather than on others?

Answering Christ's Knock

"Do not store up for yourselves treasures on earth, where moth and rust destroy, and where thieves break in and steal. But store up for yourselves treasures in heaven, where neither moth nor rust destroys, and where thieves do not break in or steal; for where your treasure is, there your heart will be also." (Matt. 6:19–21)

According to Matthew 6:31–33 and Philippians 4:19, how should believers receive the things they really need?

The Laodicean Condition

You think you are self-sufficient and in need of nothing, but you are spiritually wretched and miserable.

Diagnostic Questions

- Do you hide your needs from friends, family, and church members out of embarrassment?
- When you struggle with temptation, sin, or addiction, do you try to conquer it alone, or do you seek help?
- When making life decisions, do you think through it yourself or seek the counsel of others?

Answering Christ's Knock

"Two are better than one because they have a good return for their labor. For if either of them falls, the one will lift up his companion. But woe to the one who falls when there is not another to lift him up. Furthermore, if two lie down together they keep warm, but how can one be warm alone? And if one can overpower him who is alone, two can resist him. A cord of three strands is not quickly torn apart." (Ecc. 4:9–12)

According to Hebrews 10:24–25, James 5:16, and 1 Peter 4:8–10, how can you take practical steps to counter an attitude of self-sufficiency?

The Laodicean Condition

You think you are aware of your own spiritual condition, but you are blinded by your own sin.

Diagnostic Questions

- Do you compare your spiritual life and growth to that of others rather than to the perfect standard of Christ?
- Do you allow "small" sins to linger because they aren't really harming anybody?
- When nobody is looking, do you say or do things that you wouldn't want others to see?

Answering Christ's Knock

"For the word of God is living and active and sharper than any two-edged sword, and piercing as far as the division of soul and spirit, of both joints and marrow, and able to judge the thoughts and intentions of the heart. And there is no creature hidden from His sight, but all things are open and laid bare to the eyes of Him with whom we have to do." (Heb. 4:12–13)

According to 2 Peter 1:5–9 and 1 John 2:11, what is necessary to avoid being spiritually "blind or short-sighted"?

The Laodicean Condition
You think your life is clothed in good works, but you are spiritually naked.
Diagnostic Questions
• Are you satisfied with simply having faith without a changed lifestyle to go with it?
• Do you often point out personal good works for others to see, or do you keep your deeds anonymous?
• Do you have a "persona" you wear around church people that's significantly different from close family and friends?
Answering Christ's Knock
"For all of us have become like one who is unclean, And all our righteous deeds are like a filthy garment." (Isa. 64:6)
"For I say to you that unless your righteousness surpasses that of the scribes and Pharisees, you will not enter the kingdom of heaven." (Matt. 5:20)
"You believe that God is one. You do well; the demons also believe, and shudder. But are you willing to recognize, you foolish fellow, that faith without works is useless?" (James 2:19–20)
"You believe that God is one. You do well; the demons also believe, and shudder. But are you willing to recognize, you foolish fellow, that faith without works is useless?" (James 2:19–20)
According to Isaiah 61:10, 1 Corinthians 1:30–31, and Philippians 2:12–13, where does true righteousness and resulting good works come from?

that brought about Laodicea's "lukewarm" condition. Prayerfully consider each of the following four "Laodicean Conditions," using their related diagnostic questions to examine your own life in light of Christ's admonitions. Then study the texts and question under "Answering Christ's Knock" to begin addressing these very serious problems.

Christ is knocking at the door of your life. Won't you let Him in? He wants to bless you with *eternal* riches, provide your *true* spiritual needs, open your eyes to your *real* condition, and clothe you with *His* righteousness and works empowered by the Holy Spirit. Stop! Don't go any further in this book until you have opened the door of your heart to Him.

NOTES: Messages of the Majestic Savior (Revelation 1:1–3:22)

1. Palmer, *1, 2, 3 John, Revelation*, 114.
2. After the title and blessing in verses 1–3, John addressed his original audience in a sort of "cover

letter" for the book. John received his unexpected series of visions while in prayer on the Lord's Day—Sunday (1:10). As he experienced these visions, he obviously had access to paper and pen, for he was able to take notes along the way (10:3). Most likely, after receiving these visions, John composed his notes into a complete, unified record, including some interpretive statements along the way (5:6, 8). He prefaced this complete account of his visions with an introductory greeting to the seven churches in Asia Minor (1:4–8), followed by a few words that provide the setting of the first vision (1:9–11).

3. Alan Johnson, "Revelation," in *The Expositor's Bible Commentary*, vol. 12, *Hebrews–Revelation* (ed. Frank E. Gaebelein; Grand Rapids: Zondervan, 1981), 420.

4. See G. K. Beale, *The Book of Revelation: A Commentary on the Greek Text* (The New International Greek Testament Commentary; ed. I Howard Marshall and Donald A. Hagner; Grand Rapids: Eerdmans, 1999), 187–89.

5. In the Greek translation of the Hebrew Bible, the seven qualities differ slightly—"the spirit of wisdom and understanding, the spirit of counsel and strength, the spirit of knowledge and godliness shall fill him; the spirit of the fear of God." See Lancelot C. L. Brenton, *The Septuagint with Apocrypha: Greek and English* (London: Samuel Bagster & Sons, 1851; reprint, Peabody, MA: Hendrickson, 1998), 846–47.

6. David E. Aune, *Revelation 1–5* (Word Biblical Commentary 52; ed. David A. Hubbard et al.; Dallas: Word, 1997), lvii–lx. See also Lorman M. Petersen, "Patmos," in *The New International Dictionary of the Bible* (ed. J. D. Douglas and Merrill C. Tenney; Grand Rapids: Zondervan, 1987), 756.

7. See an early account in Eusebius of Caesarea, *Ecclesiastical History* 3.17–20.

8. The phrase "in the Spirit" has a number of meanings in the New Testament. When referring to the human spirit, it denotes sincerity or deep commitment (Rom. 1:9). When referring to the Spirit of God, it describes the spiritual unity believers have with God and with each other by the indwelling Holy Spirit (John 4:23–24; Acts 1:5; Rom. 14:17; Eph. 6:18; Col. 1:8). Sometimes the phrase refers to special abilities given by the power of the Spirit, such as the ability to perform miracles (Matt. 12:28) or to speak or write as a prophet under the inspiration of the Spirit (Matt. 22:43–44; Eph. 3:5). In 2 Corinthians 12:1–4, Paul implied that the Holy Spirit miraculously transported him into the spiritual realm ("the third heaven"; "paradise"). Each of John's four uses of "in the Spirit" refers to a dramatic change in the focus of the revelatory visions he received (Rev. 1:10; 4:2; 17:3; 21:10).

9. *Shepherd of Hermas, Revelation* 5. See Michael W. Holmes, *The Apostolic Fathers: Greek Texts and English Translations* (Grand Rapids: Baker, 1999), 345.

10. John F. Walvoord, "Revelation," in *The Bible Knowledge Commentary: New Testament Edition* (ed. John F. Walvoord and Roy B. Zuck; Wheaton, IL: Victor, 1983), 933.

11. G. L. Borchert, "Ephesus," in *The International Standard Bible Encyclopedia* (rev. ed.; ed. Geoffrey W. Bromiley et al.; Grand Rapids: Eerdmans, 1982), 2:115.

12. Edward M. Blaiklock, "Ephesus," in *The New International Dictionary of Biblical Archaeology* (ed. R. K. Harrison and David R. Douglass; Grand Rapids: Zondervan, 1983), 181.

13. Borchert, "Ephesus," 2:115.

14. E. M. B. Green and C. J. Hemer, "Ephesus," in *New Bible Dictionary* (2nd ed.; ed. J. D. Douglas et al.; Wheaton, IL: Tyndale, 1982), 337.

15. Borchert, "Ephesus," 2:117.

16. Ignatius, *To the Ephesians* 1.3. In Holmes, *The Apostolic Fathers*, 137.

17. See "Nicolaitans," in *The New International Dictionary of the Bible*, 708.

18. Edward M. Blaiklock, "Smyrna," in *The New International Dictionary of the Bible*, 950.

19. Robert North, "Smyrna," in *The International Standard Bible Encyclopedia*, 4:555–56.

20. John H. Leith, ed., *Creeds of the Churches: A Reader in Christian Doctrine from the Bible to the Present* (3rd ed.; Louisville: John Knox, 1982), 35.

21. Gerhard Kittel and Gerhard Friedrich, *Theological Dictionary of the New Testament: Abridged in One Volume* (trans. Geoffrey W. Bromiley; Grand Rapids: Eerdmans, 1985), 334–35.

22. John Keith, "How Firm a Foundation," in *The Hymnal for Worship and Celebration* (Waco, TX: Word Music, 1986), no. 275.

23. *Merriam-Webster's Collegiate Dictionary* (10th ed.; Springfield, MA: Merriam-Webster, 2000), s.v. "compromise."

24. Ibid.

25. See Beale, *The Book of Revelation*, 211–12.

26. Robert H. Mounce, *The Book of Revelation* (rev. ed.; Grand Rapids: Eerdmans, 1977), 79; Grant R. Osborne, *Revelation* (Baker Exegetical Commentary on the New Testament; ed. Moisés Silva; Grand Rapids: Baker, 2002), 140–41.

27. C. J. Hemer and M. J. S. Rudwick, "Pergamum," in *New Bible Dictionary*, 912.

28. Robert North, "Pergamum," in *The International Standard Bible Encyclopedia*, 3:768.

29. Ibid., 3:768–69.

30. Walvoord, "Revelation," *The Bible Knowledge Commentary*, 936.

31. See Osborne, *Revelation*, 148–49.

32. Daniel Taylor, "Are You Tolerant? (Should You Be?): Deconstructing the Gospel of Tolerance," *Christianity Today* 43:1 (January 11, 1999): 42–52.

33. Robert North, "Thyatria," in *The International Standard Bible Encyclopedia*, 4:846.

34. Edward M. Blaiklock, "Thyatira," in *The New International Dictionary of Biblical Archaeology*, 450.

35. North, "Thyatira," 846.

36. Because of the similar descriptions in Dan. 10:5–6 and Rev. 1:13–16, it is probably best to see these descriptions as general marks of heavenly beings, not as marks that equate the two. It should be noted that the being in Daniel 10 has limited power, unable to overcome the angelic rulers of Persia. Also, it should be noted that the description of Christ in Revelation 1 also draws on imagery that is clearly associated with the divine "Ancient of Days" in Daniel 7:9 — specifically His hair, which was white as pure wool. So, the symbolic elements that John witnessed were not meant to identify Christ with an angel of the Old Testament, or with God the Father Himself, but as a divine figure of heavenly origin.

37. See Beale, *The Book of Revelation*, 268–69; Mounce, *The Book of Revelation*, 90–91; Palmer, *1, 2, 3 John, Revelation*, 142–43.

38. Many of these tongue-in-cheek descriptions of a literal "dead church" are adapted from Steven J. Lawson, *Final Call* (Wheaton, IL: Crossway, 1994), 151–52.

39. See "Sardis," in *The New International Dictionary of the Bible*, 897; Robert North, "Sardis," in *The International Standard Bible Encyclopedia*, 4:336–37.

40. E. M. B. Green and C. J. Hemer, "Sardis," in *New Bible Dictionary*, 1073.

41. See comments on 1:4 above, pages 28-29.

42. Walter Bauer and Frederick W. Danker, *A Greek-English Lexicon of the New Testament and Other Early Christian Literature* (3rd ed.; Chicago: University of Chicago Press, 2000), 667–68; Kittel and Friedrich, *Theological Dictionary of the New Testament: Abridged in One Volume*, 627–28.

43. Raf Casert, "Rom Houben, Man in Coma for 23 Years, Was Fully Conscious, Mom Says," *Huffington Post* (November 23, 2009), available at www.huffingtonpost.com/2009/11/23/rom-houben-man-in-coma-fo_n_367798.html (accessed 5/17/2010). For counterarguments on this case, see Manfred Dworschak, "Communicating with Those Trapped Within Their Brains," *Der Spiegel Online International* (February 13, 2010), available at www.spiegel.de/international/world/0,1518,677537,00.html (accessed March 17, 2010).

44. Green and Hemer, "Sardis," 1073.

45. Johnson, "Revelation," 452.

46. G. B. Caird, *The Revelation of Saint John* (Black's New Testament Commentary; ed. Henry Chadwick; London: A & C Black, 1966; reprint, Peabody, MA: Hendrickson, 1999), 51–53.

47. M. J. S. Rudwick and C. J. Hemer, "Philadelphia," in *New Bible Dictionary*, 925.

48. Robert North, "Philadelphia," in *The International Standard Bible Encyclopedia*, 3:830; Edward M. Blaiklock, "Philadelphia," in *The New International Dictionary of Biblical Archaeology*, 360.

49. North, "Philadelphia," 830.

50. See Ignatius of Antioch's *Letter to the Philadelphians*, dated around AD 110.

51. On the phrase "synagogue of Satan," see comments on 2:9, page 46 above.

52. Mark Hassall, "Romans and Non-Romans," in John Wacher, ed., *The Roman World* (London: Routledge, 2002), 2:685–700.

53. Edward M. Blaiklock, "Laodicea," in *The New International Dictionary of the Bible,* 582.

54. M. J. S. Rudwick and C. J. Hemer, "Laodicea," in *New Bible Dictionary*, 681.

55. Bauer and Danker, *A Greek-English Lexicon of the New Testament*, 137–38.

WORSHIP OF THE WORTHY LAMB (REVELATION 4:1–7:17)

I grew up in what many have called the "Golden Age of Cinema." Films from that era included *Gone with the Wind*, *The Wizard of Oz*, *The Ten Commandments*, and *Lawrence of Arabia*. One thing I remember about those movies is that they were long—so long, in fact, that we used to have intermissions in the middle of the movies, a break of about fifteen minutes to let you stretch, socialize, or buy more popcorn! Originally the intermissions were used in live stage productions to give actors much-needed breaks, musicians a chance to rest, and stage hands an opportunity to change the set before the next act.

If the book of Revelation were a staged production, there probably would be several of these brief intermissions. In a number of places the audience's perspective suddenly changes, the drama abruptly shifts its emphasis, and the stage is rearranged to present a new series of visionary scenes to point us to Christ. After the curtains close on the first episode of this apocalyptic drama, which we titled "Messages of the Majestic Savior" (1:1–3:22), we experience the first of several such transitions as the scene instantly cuts from the earthly, present reality of the church to the heavenly, future reality of the coming judgments. Having followed the Lord's original command in 1:19 to write "the things which you have seen" (ch. 1) and then "the things which are" (chs. 2–3), John now prepares to write "the things which will take place after these things."

I have titled this second major section of Revelation "Worship of the Worthy Lamb." It extends from Revelation 4:1 through 7:17. As the curtains open on the first scene of this episode, the apostle John is suddenly caught up into the spiritual realm—to the very throne room of heaven (4:1–2). There he witnesses the worship of God the Father and Jesus Christ—the "Lamb of God" who alone is worthy to reveal events of the future through the ceremonial breaking of a seven-sealed scroll (4:3–5:14). Through symbolic visions, the "scroll judgments" begin to reveal the first stages of divine wrath upon the earth (6:1–17). In the midst of these judgments, however, John sees a vision of the redeemed from the nation of Israel and the Gentile nations, reminding us that even in the midst of judgment God's grace and mercy prevail (7:1–17).

The brief intermission is over. The theatre lights dim. The next act in the Bible's portrayal of coming events is about to begin. In a few moments you'll be caught up with John to the heavenly stage, witnessing a powerful drama of Christ's person and work nearly too awesome for words.

Standing before God's Awesome Throne (Revelation 4:1–11)

[1]After these things I looked, and behold, a door *standing* open in heaven, and the first voice which I had heard, like *the sound* of a trumpet speaking with me, said, "Come up here, and I will show you what must take place after these things." [2]Immediately I was in the Spirit; and behold, a throne was standing in heaven, and One sitting on the throne. [3]And He who was sitting *was* like a jasper stone and a sardius in appearance; and *there was* a rainbow around the throne, like an emerald in appearance. [4]Around the throne *were* twenty-four thrones; and upon the thrones *I saw* twenty-four elders sitting, clothed in white garments, and golden crowns on their heads.

[5]Out from the throne come flashes of lightning and sounds and peals of thunder. And *there were* seven lamps of fire burning before the throne, which are the seven Spirits of God; [6]and before the throne *there was something* like a sea of glass, like crystal; and in the center and around the throne, four living creatures full of eyes in front and behind. [7]The first creature *was* like a lion, and the second creature like a calf, and the third creature had a face like that of a man, and the fourth creature *was* like a flying eagle. [8]And the four living creatures, each one of them having six wings, are full of eyes around and within; and day and night they do not cease to say,

> "Holy, holy, holy *is* the Lord God, the Almighty, who was and who is and who is to come."

[9]And when the living creatures give glory and honor and thanks to Him who sits on the throne, to Him who lives forever and ever, [10]the twenty-four elders will fall down before Him who sits on the throne, and will worship Him who lives forever and ever, and will cast their crowns before the throne, saying,

> [11]"Worthy are You, our Lord and our God, to receive glory and honor and power; for You created all things, and because of Your will they existed, and were created."

Angels recline on puffy clouds, strumming harps and singing blissful choruses of praise. Doves and butterflies flitter about, shimmering in radiant light. A fine, white mist blankets the ground, and except for the streets of gold, everything glimmers a bright, iridescent white.

That's heaven, right?

Or is it?

KEY TERMS

ἄξιος [axios] (514) "worthy, deserving, fit"

Worthiness stands out as a major theme in Revelation 4 and 5. The word *axios* means "deserving." God the Father is "worthy" or fit "to receive glory and honor and power" because He is the Creator of all things (4:11). Jesus Christ is also deemed to be worthy by the heavenly worshipers "to receive power and riches and wisdom and might and honor and glory and blessing" (5:12) because He is the Redeemer and heir of all things (5:9).

σφραγίς [sphragis] (4973) "seal, signet"

Though the term *sphragis* only appears three times in the rest of the New Testament, the book of Revelation uses it thirteen times. It most often refers to a literal seal, such as a wax seal with an identifying impression as from a signet ring (5:1; 6:1). The word also refers to a great regal seal used to place a distinguishing mark on the remnant of Israel in 7:2. Because seals in the ancient world indicated ownership, the use of this term reveals that God holds the events of the future — and His chosen people — firmly in His hands.

δόξα καὶ τιμή [doxa kai timē] (1391 + 5092) "glory and honor"

In the New Testament, the pairing of these two terms is regarded as the future reward for believers in Christ (Rom. 2:7, 10; Heb. 2:7). This reward will not be based on any merit of their own but wholly on the merits of Christ, who was "crowned with glory and honor" because He willingly suffered on behalf of all people (Heb. 2:9). In the book of Revelation, the twenty-four elders, likely representing the rewarded saints, are seen casting their glorious crowns of honor before the throne, acknowledging that God alone is worthy to receive ultimate "glory and honor" from His creatures (4:9, 11).

One author summarizes it this way: "The popular head picture of heaven is one of changeless perfection, sometimes in imagery of harps, halos, and clouds, sometimes in imageless concepts of abstract spirituality. That may be heaven for angels, but it's more like hell for humans."[1] Maybe "hell" is too strong, but many would consider such a state as eternally *boring*—like an ethereal retirement home. Is heaven really like this? Is this surreal notion of a dreamy, uneventful bliss what we have to look forward to, forever and ever?

Hardly! Read on...

— 4:1–3 —

Revelation 4 begins with two important Greek words—*meta tauta*, "after these things." These words suggest that John was pointing out a transition into the next part of his apocalyptic journey—the things that would happen immediately after what he described in Revelation 2–3. Recall that the inspired outline in Revelation 1:19 included three aspects of John's visions: (1) the things you have seen, (2) the things that are, and (3) the things that will take place after these things. (See the chart on page 33.)

Even though Christ warned John in advance that he would see things to come, nothing could have prepared the apostle for what he experienced that day. This would be much more than a few mild prophetic truths whispered in a morning doze or mid-afternoon slumber. John was about to be spiritually snatched from the tiny island of Patmos and ushered straight into the indescribable presence of God. No boredom here!

After recording the final words of Jesus to the church in Laodicea, John slowly lifted his pen from the scroll. Those last words are significant, especially in light of what John would see next. Christ said, "Behold, I stand at the door and knock; if anyone hears My voice and opens the door, I will come in to him and will dine with him, and he with Me. He who overcomes, I will grant to him to sit down with Me on My throne, as I also overcame and sat down with My Father on His throne" (3:20–21). Having just described Christ knocking at a closed door, calling out in a gentle voice, and promising a throne to the one who overcomes, a contrasting vision suddenly seized the aging apostle's attention. He saw an open door, he heard a booming voice, and he witnessed an eternal throne (4:1–2). With a door standing open in heaven, Christ called to John, "Come up here, and I will show you what must take place after these things" (4:1).

Immediately John found himself "in the Spirit"—caught up through the open door to the throne of God. It's worth noting that in the following description John didn't attempt to depict God precisely. Instead, we are given merely a glimpse of His glory, which is already enough to overwhelm us. John used the term *homoios* ("like, similar to") in verse 3 to put an indescribable vision into accurate yet inadequate words. John saw God's matchless worth represented by precious stones and His brightness and beauty shining like a rainbow (4:3). His power burst forth like thunder and lightning (4:5). Even in John's vivid description, however, the Father Himself remained hidden from sight, veiled (as Paul put it) "in unapproachable light" (1 Tim. 6:16).

On the one hand, the Bible clearly says that God is invisible and unseen (1 Tim. 1:17). For example, people can "see" His power and character through His works of creation (Rom. 1:20). As a spirit being, however, God is invisible to human perception.[3] On the other hand, the Old Testament says that some have seen God and lived, contrary to their clear expectations that they would die (Gen. 32:30; Judg. 13:22; Isa. 6:1–7). These Old Testament *theophanies* (from *theos*, "God," and *phainō*, "to appear") were temporary and limited representations of God's presence.[4] Consider that God allowed some to "see" Him in a limited sense (Ex. 33:20), and that Jesus said, "Not that anyone has seen the Father, except the One who is from God; He has seen the Father" (John 6:46; cf. 1 John 4:12).

The same apostle who witnessed the glorious vision of the Father on the throne in Revelation 4 also helped solve this problem of the visible yet invisible God when he wrote in his gospel, "No one has seen God at any time; the only begotten God

THE THREE HEAVENS

The various ways people perceive the universe in the twenty-first century differ from the ways people understood the cosmos in the first century. Today many scientists believe all existence is simply matter and energy. For them, "the heavens" simply refer to outer space, while "the earth" describes our globe. In contrast, people who believe in a spiritual dimension of the universe often view the supernatural dimension as existing alongside of or within the present material universe, or perhaps existing in a completely separate plane of reality.

In the ancient world in which John experienced his apocalyptic visions, a number of cosmologies competed for adherents. The Gnostics viewed the universe as comprised of dozens or even hundreds of levels of being, each inhabited by distinct ranks of creatures. Others viewed the world as having two basic realms, the spiritual and the physical, which were constantly in conflict as good versus evil or light versus dark. The biblical Jewish and Christian view of the cosmos reflects a moderate hierarchical and mild dualistic worldview. Unlike most other religious and philosophical literature of the time, the Bible doesn't precisely spell out details of cosmology. It rather utilizes categories and concepts of the day, leaving much to mystery, science, and speculation.

What is this biblical view of the cosmos? The Bible understands three basic "levels" of the universe — the heavens, the earth, and below the earth.[2] The term "heavens" may be further divided into three levels. The "first heaven" includes the sphere surrounding the earth. Today we call this the "atmosphere" or "sky," in which birds fly and clouds drift. The "second heaven" includes everything in the cosmos above the earth's atmosphere — the moon, sun, planets, stars, and galaxies. From a modern worldview perspective, both the first and second "heavens" are technically still part of the physical universe. Not so with the "third heaven." In the biblical sense, the "third heaven" was the term used to describe the dwelling place of God, the angels, and any other spirit beings. Paul says that he was "caught up to the third heaven ... into Paradise" (2 Cor. 12:2, 4). We might call this today the "spiritual realm," a plane of reality accessible only by heavenly invitation, like the one John received in Revelation 4:1.

The realm of existence "below the earth" also has both a physical and spiritual dimension. Physically, it may refer simply to the grave or to underground spaces from which water may flow or lava may spew. Or it may refer to the place of spirits who have departed from the earthly plane but have not been admitted into the presence of God. In both cases the same terms are often used — *sheol* in the Old Testament or *hadēs* in the New. Context helps determine whether the text is referring to the physical or the spiritual realm.

So, when John was taken up into heaven, he was not transported to another planet or even another galaxy. Rather, he was caught up to the "third heaven," to the presence of the living God.

FIVE VIEWS OF THE TWENTY-FOUR ELDERS

Different views from varying theological backgrounds have been proposed for the identification of the twenty-four elders. Here are just five examples.

1. Twelve Old Testament patriarchs and twelve New Testament apostles representing the entire redeemed people of God (21:12–14).
2. The great saints of the Old Testament, to be distinguished from New Testament saints (5:9–17; 15:2–4).
3. Representatives of the New Testament church wearing victory crowns and fulfilling the promise of 3:21.
4. God's angelic "council of holy ones" leading worship before the throne of God, as implied in Psalm 89:7.
5. A special human priesthood chosen from among the redeemed to worship before the throne in rotation, as in the Old Testament priestly orders (1 Chron. 24:4–5; 1 Peter 2.9, Rev. 1:6).

who is in the bosom of the Father, He has explained Him" (John 1:18). In other words, the Son of God—who is the divine "image of the invisible God" (Col. 1:15)—reveals the invisible God to us (Heb. 1:2–3). Jesus said, "He who has seen Me has seen the Father" (John 14:9). Interestingly, early theologians of the church argued that when God appeared to people in the Old Testament, it was actually the Son appearing from heaven before He became the incarnate God-man, Jesus. In this way, God the Father always remained immortal, invisible, and unseen—but fully revealed to us through God the Son.[5]

Although John didn't see the fullness of God the Father in a physical, corporeal sense, his vision nevertheless communicated some profound truths about Him. The Father is the center and source of all creation. Everything points to and revolves around Him. He occupies the sovereign place of rule and has unshakable authority over all things (Ps. 115:3; Dan. 4:35). His sovereign rule is fixed, permanent, and unshakable. Once we personally come to grips with John's vision of God, our response can be nothing less than utter awe, unwavering commitment, and deep reverence for the eternal King.

— **4:4–8** —

After wrestling with words to describe the indescribable, John's gaze moved from God the Father as the center of attention to others in the throne room. First, John described twenty-four elders in white with golden crowns of victory on their heads (4:4).[6] Who are these elders? Bible scholars have produced at least thirteen views regarding their identification.[7] We can't be sure whether these elders are symbols, actual beings, representatives of a larger group, or a future order of beings not yet dwelling in heaven.

Though John never clearly identifies the heavenly elders, I understand them to be a select number of the redeemed chosen to worship and serve before the throne of God. Are they a permanent number or a rotating office? Are there ever more or less than twenty-four? Are they Old Testament saints or New Testament saints — or both? These questions are left unanswered, so we'd be wise to not speculate.

After the elders, John's attention returned to God the Father as thunder boomed and lightning flashed from the throne (4:5). Next he noticed something he had overlooked in the midst of the glorious vision — seven burning lamps, representing the seven Spirits of God.[8] John then observed something that looked like a "sea of glass" before the throne (4:6). Once again, we are at a loss to explain what this is, though John described it as crystal clear, perhaps representing purity. In any case, John's description of the throne room of God finally landed on four "living creatures" surrounding the throne, constantly praising and exalting God (4:6–8).

To help us understand the astonishing imagery in Revelation 4, we need to look back to similar visions in the Old Testament, particularly in the prophetic writings of Isaiah and Ezekiel. I find it easiest to see these connections in the form of a chart.

Angelic Beings in Revelation, Isaiah, and Ezekiel

Revelation 4	Isaiah 6 and Ezekiel 1; 10
Heavenly throne (4:2–6)	I saw the Lord sitting on a throne, lofty and exalted, with the train of His robe filling the temple. (Isa. 6:1)
Rainbow (4:3)	As the appearance of the rainbow in the clouds on a rainy day, so was the appearance of the surrounding radiance. (Ezek. 1:28)
Thunder/lightning (4:5)	As I looked, behold, a storm wind was coming from the north, a great cloud with fire flashing forth continually and a bright light around it, and in its midst something like glowing metal in the midst of the fire. (Ezek. 1:4)
	In the midst of the living beings there was something that looked like burning coals of fire, like torches darting back and forth among the living beings. The fire was bright, and lightning was flashing from the fire. And the living beings ran to and fro like bolts of lightning. (Ezek. 1:13–14)

Spirit of God (4:5)	Wherever the spirit was about to go, they [the living beings] would go (Ezek. 1:12)
Glassy crystal sea (4:6)	Now over the heads of the living beings there was something like an expanse, like the awesome gleam of crystal, spread out over their heads. (Ezek. 1:22)
Four living creatures (4:6–8)	Within it [the storm] there were figures resembling four living beings. (Ezek. 1:5)
Full of eyes (4:6)	As for their rims they were lofty and awesome, and the rims of all four of them were full of eyes round about. (Ezek. 1:18) Their whole body, their backs, their hands, their wings and the wheels were full of eyes all around, the wheels belonging to all four of them. (Ezek. 10:12)
Lion, calf, man, eagle (4:7)	As for the form of their faces, each had the face of a man; all four had the face of a lion on the right and the face of a bull on the left, and all four had the face of an eagle. (Ezek. 1:10) And each one had four faces. The first face was the face of a cherub, the second face was the face of a man, the third the face of a lion, and the fourth the face of an eagle. Then the cherubim rose up. They are the living beings that I saw by the river Chebar. (Ezek. 10:14–15)
Six wings (4:8)	Seraphim stood above Him, each having six wings: with two he covered his face, and with two he covered his feet, and with two he flew. (Isa. 6:2)
Singing "Holy, holy, holy" (4:8)	And one [of the Seraphim] called out to another and said, "Holy, Holy, Holy, is the Lord of hosts, the whole earth is full of His glory." (Isa. 6:3)

The similarities between these three accounts lead me to conclude that the four living creatures are angelic beings called "seraphim" in Isaiah 6:2 and "cherubim" in Ezekiel 10:15. The Hebrew term *seraphim* literally mean "burning ones," indicating their nature as heavenly beings. The term *cherubim*, however, emphasizes their function as protectors or "guardians" of the throne of God. Of course, God doesn't need protection from anything in heaven or on earth. Rather, it may be that these intermediate beings serve to protect other creatures from being consumed by the blazing glory of God! These four living creatures — the highest-ranking angelic beings — lead all creation in worship of their Almighty Creator.

— 4:9–11 —

Following the lead of the four living creatures (4:9), the twenty-four elders joined in the worship, falling down before God and casting their golden crowns of reward at His feet (4:10). Though the elders apparently earned their rewards, they acknowledged that everything they had came from God. Everything they achieved was by His strength. Everything they had done was for His glory. Therefore He alone deserves the glory, honor, power, and thanks (4:9, 11). Thus, in this chapter we hear what might be called a glorious "Hymn of Creation." The twenty-four elders praise God as the eternal and Almighty Creator: "You created all things, and because of Your will they existed, and were created" (4:11). In the next chapter we'll hear the second movement of this great symphony of praise, in which all creation worships God with a "Hymn of Redemption."

In the midst of the flashes of lightning, flaming torches, crashing thunder, beating wings, clanging crowns, and loud antiphonal praises reverberating throughout the heavenly throne room, the apostle John stood in absolute awe. We who dwell in the earthly sphere can scarcely imagine what that must be like. Yet we look forward to that day when we join that heavenly throng standing before God's awesome throne, gathering with other saints and singing praises to that same awesome God who created all things.

> Holy, holy, holy! All the saints adore Thee,
> Casting down their golden crowns around the glassy sea;
> Cherubim and seraphim falling down before Thee,
> Who was, and is, and evermore shall be.[9]

Application

Restoring the Missing Jewel of the Church

Back in the 1960s, the late A. W. Tozer described worship as "the missing jewel in modern evangelicalism." He was a prophet ahead of his time. If truth be told, many of us in the twenty-first century don't have a clue what real worship is. We wonder:

- Does worship mean I have to hold my hands up when I sing and pray, as some Christians do?
- Does worship mean I need to close my eyes and envision something heavenly, lest I become distracted by something earthly?
- Does worship mean I have feelings that are a little bit ecstatic, maybe bordering on the supernatural?

My great concern is that we tend to play the game of "church." We learn how to dress, how to sit, and how to look. We even learn the words of the songs. But what about our focus as we sing them? While we sing, "A mighty fortress is our God," we're thinking, *Why did she wear a dress like that?* We belt out, "A bulwark never failing," and wonder, *Did I turn my headlights off?* We can do that and not even change our expressions. That's not worship—that's playing the church game.

What, then, is worship? Simply put, worship is ascribing "worth" to something or someone. We attribute value, honor, and devotion to our object of worship. When we truly worship God, we turn all of our attention, affection, and adoration toward Him. That's the missing jewel—worshiping God by ascribing to Him supreme worth, for He alone is worthy. God alone is the subject of our praise and the object of our worship. We miss it when our focus becomes horizontal—riveted on people and things—rather than vertical—centered on God and God alone. It has become too common for Christians to surrender everything for their work, but at the same time to sacrifice nothing in worshiping the One who gave His life to save ours. Stop and think. Is that you?

Our great need is to restore the missing jewel of worship in our churches . . . and in our lives. Ask yourself some probing questions. Answer honestly: Are you more preoccupied with the pastor's preaching style than with the One he preaches? Are you more concerned about the lyrics than the One listening? Do your thoughts wander or do they take in the wonder? Look again at Revelation 4. Notice the focus of the twenty-four elders and four living creatures. God alone is at the center of their attention. They praise Him for Who He is and for what He has done. They aren't distracted by each other, by the furniture of the throne room, or by their own wandering thoughts. Instead, they keep their eyes and ears on the One who is worthy of all praise.

Do I? Do you?

Think about how you can refocus your worship from yourself and your surroundings to God and His glory. Many find it helpful to wake up a little earlier on Sunday morning to prepare their hearts and minds for worship. Maybe during worship you need to close your eyes to shut out the world around you and keep your attention on God. Perhaps you need to move closer to the front during worship to keep from being distracted by the things and people around you. Whatever it takes, keep God at the center of your attention.

Worthy Is the Lamb (Revelation 5:1–14)

[1]I saw in the right hand of Him who sat on the throne a book written inside and on the back, sealed up with seven seals. [2]And I saw a strong angel proclaiming with a loud voice, "Who is worthy to open the book and to break its seals?" [3]And no one in heaven or on the earth or under the earth was able to open the book or to look into it. [4]Then I *began* to weep greatly because no one was found worthy to open the book or to look into it; [5]and one of the elders said to me, "Stop weeping; behold, the Lion that is from the tribe of Judah, the Root of David, has overcome so as to open the book and its seven seals."

[6]And I saw between the throne (with the four living creatures) and the elders a Lamb standing, as if slain, having seven horns and seven eyes, which are the seven Spirits of God, sent out into all the earth. [7]And He came and took the book out of the right hand of Him who sat on the throne. [8]When He had taken the book, the four living creatures and the twenty-four elders fell down before the Lamb, each one holding a harp and golden bowls full of incense, which are the prayers of the saints. [9]And they sang a new song, saying,

"Worthy are You to take the book and to break its seals; for You were slain, and purchased for God with Your blood *men* from every tribe and tongue and people and nation. [10]You have made them *to be* a kingdom and priests to our God; and they will reign upon the earth."

[11]Then I looked, and I heard the voice of many angels around the throne and the living creatures and the elders; and the number of them was myriads of myriads, and thousands of thousands, [12]saying with a loud voice,

"Worthy is the Lamb that was slain to receive power and riches and wisdom and might and honor and glory and blessing."

[13]And every created thing which is in heaven and on the earth and under the earth and on the sea, and all things in them, I heard saying,

"To Him who sits on the throne, and to the Lamb, *be* blessing and honor and glory and dominion forever and ever."

[14]And the four living creatures kept saying, "Amen." And the elders fell down and worshiped.

I never cease to marvel at the advances of the modern world. The field of medicine has given us a life expectancy higher than ever. In many countries even those living in "poverty" live longer and have more comforts than kings of the past. Technology has sped up communication and transportation, essentially shrinking the globe. Within seconds a person in Canada can chat with a friend in Thailand. Within a day they can shake hands. At least in the Western world, humans have overcome many social and political problems, learning to face new challenges in the twenty-first century. We human beings have certainly come a long way!

Or have we?

Over a century ago many liberal theologians thought we were on the verge of ridding ourselves of the barbarism, imperialism, and superstition that had led the world astray for so long. This included what they saw as the "mythical" trappings of Christianity—things like the virgin birth, the deity of Christ, and the bodily resurrection of Jesus. Armed with modern science and philosophy, those enlightened intelligentsia were convinced that people could finally mold the world into what it was meant to be—an enduring kingdom of peace and prosperity on earth. In short, they believed that humanity, equipped with the latest ideologies and technologies, was *worthy* to forge a glorious destiny, trusting in human ability rather than trusting in God.

As you probably know, this overconfidence in humanity evaporated like a morning fog. In 1914 Germany ignited the fire that exploded into World War I. The Kaiser's army was armed to the hilt with the most advanced weapons produced at the time. And they had the unwavering support of Germany's leading philosophers and even theologians! That great conflict, dubbed "The War to End All Wars," was quickly followed by the terror and atrocities of World War II, in which mass killing was reduced to a science at Auschwitz and science was used for mass killing through the atomic bomb. More recently has come the horrors of terrorism, which military authorities say is here to stay. The reality of human depravity has dashed the misplaced hopes of humanistic philosophy and liberal theology. Today the world is left wandering in unbelief, doubt, uncertainty, and fear. People wonder whether anyone or anything is able to truly remove the evil around us.

Is anyone worthy to vanquish wickedness and usher in a world of true peace and prosperity? As the world continues its desperate and disappointing search for worldly answers to life's problems, the Bible reveals the solution in clear words and vivid images. In Revelation 5 we witness the inexpressible joy that John felt when the attention of all creation finally centers on the only One who can take the reigns of history and tame a world spinning out of control—Jesus, the worthy Lamb.

—5:1–7—

Like many chapter breaks in the Bible, the division between chapters 4 and 5 is somewhat arbitrary. Revelation 5:1 doesn't begin a new vision or even a new scene in the heavenly drama witnessed by the apostle John. Rather, the wide-angle shot that panned the throne room of God slowly zooms in on a few vital details. The twenty-four elders and the four living creatures lay with their faces on the floor in worship of the Lord God, the eternal Creator of all things, the only One worthy to receive glory, honor, and power (4:11). Suddenly something caught John's eye—a seven-sealed scroll with writing inside and out, held in the right hand of the divine Majesty on the throne.

John would easily have identified this type of document from the ancient world as a title deed or last will and testament—an instrument of ownership that could be opened only by a legal redeemer or rightful heir. In the ancient world, sealed scrolls with writing on both sides were often "private contracts kept from the public."[10] Globs of wax pressed onto the end of the scroll sealed the rolled document. On the outside of these legal documents one could read a brief summary of its content, like a modern book cover with the author and title on the front and a description of the contents on the back.

Clearly, the scroll in Revelation 5 revealed the events of the future tribulation. In the Old Testament the prophet Ezekiel had a similar scroll presented to him, "written on the front and back," in which were recorded "lamentations, mourning and woe" (Ezek. 2:9–10). So, in light of the allusion to the legal documents of the ancient world, we may conclude that the events of coming judgment were a means to a glorious end. As the scroll is opened, Jesus Christ receives His inheritance as the Son of God (Rom. 8:17; James 2:5). Furthermore, the scroll seems to suggest the image of a title deed, demonstrating Christ's ownership of the world created by the Father through the Son (John 1:1–3). Taken together, Revelation 4 and 5 reveal both themes—the

© Robert Gaither

A seven-sealed scroll, likely a legal document of inheritance.

world's ownership by the Father and Son as well as the saints' inheritance and rule with Christ (4:11; 5:9–14).

In our day-to-day affairs, the rule of God often gets obscured by the rebellion of humanity and the disorder that has characterized the world since the fall (Gen. 3). Instead of fulfilling their responsibility as creatures created according to the image of God in order to exercise rule over the earth on their Creator's behalf (Gen. 1:26–28), humans have surrendered their God-appointed role as mediators of God's reign on earth and have submitted to the power of Satan and his demons (Acts 26:18; 2 Cor. 4:4; Eph. 6:12). Even the most righteous saints of the Old Testament were unworthy to reclaim this calling as the *perfect* "image of God" to exercise God's reign over the earth. So all creatures eagerly wait for the day when the title deed will be opened, the will read, and the inheritance bestowed on a descendant of Adam who is worthy to fulfill his "image of God" calling. Only then will the universe be set free from the curse of sin and death (Rom. 8:19–23).

John then describes what might be called a cosmic recruitment effort. An angel cries out, "Who is worthy to open the book and to break its seals" (5:2)? Yet after scouring every level of the universe, no one could be found who qualified (5:3). In response to the failed attempt at locating even one worthy candidate, John began to weep uncontrollably (5:4). John knew that if no one had been found worthy, the hopeless condition of the present world would continue indefinitely. The suffering, pain, sickness, and death that characterize everyday life would never come to an end. Yet John's weeping may have another dimension. For more than sixty years he had placed all his hope in Jesus Christ to ultimately turn the world right-side-up. This means that if heaven's search for a worthy heir failed, so would his confidence in Jesus Christ.

Yet John's tears proved too hasty. God's mercy and grace would never allow the world to drown in a sea of hopelessness! Nor would His plans for Jesus Christ fail to come to fruition. One of the twenty-four elders comforted John by saying, "Stop weeping; behold, the Lion that is from the tribe of Judah, the Root of David, has overcome so as to open the book and its seven seals" (5:5).

Through tear-filled eyes now sparkling with renewed hope, John looked for the Lion, but instead he saw a Lamb (5:6)! The symbols and images John used to describe this spectacle are rich with meaning. The Lamb appeared to have been slain, just as Christ suffered—the Lamb of God who takes away the sins of the world (Isa. 53:6–7; John 1:29). The vision's seven horns represent perfect strength (1 Sam. 2:10). The seven eyes represent the Spirit of God whom Christ sent into all the earth (Zech. 3:8–9; 4:10; John 15:26). As John observed this symbolic image, it dissolved into the glorious Person it represented—the God-man, Jesus Christ, the worthy Lamb who stepped forward and took the scroll from His Father's right hand (5:7).

From My Journal

From Earthly Choir to Heavenly Chorus

As a teenager, I remember my mother wanting our whole family to sing in the annual presentation of Handel's *Messiah* at a church in Houston led by a superb conductor. She took my older brother, sister, and me, and she had us audition. Amazingly, we all made it! We proudly took our various parts home and began to practice in our rooms. Not quite the venue for a profound worship experience, but we all worked hard to get our parts right.

Eventually we began rehearsals with the conductor accompanied by a piano, and for a while I simply didn't get it. If you've ever prepared for a performance like this, you know it's a lot of tedious work singing the same words over and over again—starting, stopping, repeating, concentrating on breathing in all the right places. It doesn't feel at all like worship. It feels like work!

Then I remember the day we all filed into the sanctuary for a dress rehearsal. The conductor swapped the piano for the majestic pipe organ. The level of magnificence suddenly increased and I began to glimpse the weightiness of what we were doing. The gravity only intensified when the full orchestra joined in to rehearse their parts with us.

Then came the first performance. I remember standing up, surrounded by trained voices exercised to perfection, flanked by a full orchestra, many of whom were professionals. There I was, adding my thin teenaged voice to about 250 others. Just a few minutes into the *Messiah* the strangest thing happened. *I couldn't sing!* Instead, I was moved to tears with the sound of the organ, all those instruments, the resonance and harmony of all the voices, and the conductor leading us all in praise to the glory of God. Finally I got it! This was my first encounter with corporate worship. It was glorious!

But you know what? The earthly elation I experienced as I joined my untrained voice to that volunteer choir doesn't hold a candle to the glorious worship that awaits us in the heavenly chorus. Brothers and sisters, one day we'll join together, face the throne of God, and cry out, "Hallelujah! For the Lord God omnipotent reigneth! And He shall reign forever and ever!"

— 5:8–14 —

When the incarnate Son of God took the scroll from the Father, everything changed. The rule of humanity over all creation had been derailed by the fall and wrecked by the curse (Gen. 1:28; 3:17–19). This rule will be restored, however, through the God-man, Jesus Christ. As a truly human descendant of Adam, Jesus Christ is qualified to fulfill the original calling of humanity to exercise dominion over the earth and to subdue it, restoring the conditions of Paradise throughout the whole world. As the truly divine Son of God, Jesus Christ has the power and authority to fulfill this calling where Adam failed. Don't miss this! In 5:8 we see the beginning of the process of God putting everything in its right place by placing everything in the right hands.

What a reason to rejoice! In fact, as soon as Jesus took hold of the seven-sealed scroll, everything changed from weeping to worshiping. All creatures in heaven and earth burst forth in praise. Uncontainable jubilation exploded from the epicenter of God's throne. In one wave after another, creation poured forth praise to the Lamb of God. Why? Because not only is He the Suffering Servant who took away the sins of the world by His sacrificial death (Isa. 53), but He is also the risen, glorified Judge who will execute judgment on the wicked and bestow blessings on the righteous. All authority to judge has been given to Him alone (John 5:21, 22, 27).

Don't miss the order of worship around the throne (5:8). It began with the heavenly worship directors — the cherubim, the highest of God's creatures. They fell flat on their faces before Jesus Christ as if responding to the biblical exhortation, "Let all the angels of God worship Him" (Heb. 1:6). Then the twenty-four elders, the highest of God's redeemed, joined in with accompaniment and offered the prayers of the saints, symbolized by bowls of incense. By the way, don't ever think your prayers are insignificant! Even if God doesn't answer your pleas for help now, one day when Christ reverses the curse and rights all wrongs, your desperate cries for His intervention will be counted. God never tosses your prayers into a trash bin. He's storing them up in bowls, and one day He will answer them in ways beyond your imagination. Be patient!

Notice that the cherubim and elders sang a "new song" — a chorus never

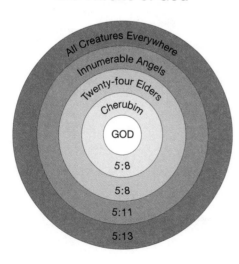

Waves of Worship from the Throne of God

All Creatures Everywhere
Innumerable Angels
Twenty-four Elders
Cherubim
GOD
5:8
5:8
5:11
5:13

heard before (5:9). Fresh lyrics . . . a fresh melody . . . and a fresh experience of worship. Now look at the purposes for their praise in 5:9–10. In chapter 4 the four living creatures and twenty-four elders praised God for His work of creation (4:11). In chapter 5 they praised Christ for His work of redemption:

- Christ is worthy to take the book and break its seals because of His work of redemption.
- His blood covers every tribe, tongue, people, and nation.
- He purchased people from the hopeless slave market of sin and death and made them kings and priests of God.

The waves of praise don't end with the elders. As if caught up in rapturous joy, two more groups joined in. First, innumerable angels encircling the throne offered their own response to the new song: "Worthy is the Lamb that was slain to receive power and riches and wisdom and might and honor and glory and blessing" (5:11–12). Then all creatures in every corner of creation worshiped the Father and the Son together for their work of creation and redemption (5:13), while the four living creatures and elders continued their unceasing worship (5:14).

John's gaze first followed the waves of worship from the center of the throne of the triune Godhead to the extremes of creation. Then John's eyes returned to Jesus Christ, the worthy Lamb, who raised the scroll and readied Himself to break the seven seals.

Application

Finding Your Way through the Worthy Lamb

Do you ever wonder if you're on the right path, headed for the right future and focused on the right priorities? I'm sure all of us have felt confused, disoriented, and in desperate need of a divine GPS navigation system to guide us in our next step through life. Revelation 5 offers at least three important principles that will help us triangulate our position in this life and point us in the right direction.

First, *if you are a believer in Jesus Christ, your ultimate destination is clear.* We are not literally reigning with Christ yet, but our destiny is secure—one day we will rule with Him over all the earth (5:9–10). Knowing our future as kings and priests for God should affect our earthly perspective and plans. We should invest our time, finances, and giftedness in the coming kingdom and focus on Christ as the center, source, and goal of our lives. Consider your regular contributions to the promotion of God's kingdom through proclaiming the gospel to the world. What are you investing? What more could you be doing?

Second, *it's reassuring to know that the Lamb of God qualifies to carry out God's plan.* When you set out to help in the process of kingdom building, you can trust that Christ is in control, even when you can't understand how He's working. The only One who is worthy to exercise judgment and rule over the earth will accomplish His will through your life. Though human history is littered with the wreckage of failed attempts to fix humanity's problems, we can turn to Christ, who has paid the price to bring about a glorious future. When we trust in Christ instead of ourselves, the evil and opposition of the world seem much less daunting. It's all subject to Him! When we see His brilliant splendor looming on the horizon, we can endure this present darkness with ever-increasing hope.

Third, *it's thrilling to engage in worship and praise while we wait and pray.* Anyone and everyone can worship. Revelation 5 shows us that every kind of creature from every level of creation has something to offer the triune God. Through new songs or old hymns, with beautiful instruments or bold voices, by heartfelt prayers or hearty "Amens," all people can reorient their hearts and minds toward God. The powerful preview of worship in the throne room of God gives us a rare insight into the spontaneity and variety of genuine praise.

Let me suggest that you participate in a short exercise. Study Psalm 148, 149, and 150. Circle the attributes and actions for which God is praised. Underline the various places and ways in which He is worshiped. Then consider the "mighty deeds" God has done in your life. Finally, consider ways you can respond *today* to His work with your worship. When you anticipate your destiny, accept Christ's sovereignty, and refocus your adoration, you'll not only be reminded where you are in this world, but you will realize where you need to be.

The Judgments Begin (Revelation 6:1–17)

¹Then I saw when the Lamb broke one of the seven seals, and I heard one of the four living creatures saying as with a voice of thunder, "Come." ²I looked, and behold, a white horse, and he who sat on it had a bow; and a crown was given to him, and he went out conquering and to conquer.

³When He broke the second seal, I heard the second living creature saying, "Come." ⁴And another, a red horse, went out; and to him who sat on it, it was granted to take peace from the earth, and that *men* would slay one another; and a great sword was given to him.

⁵When He broke the third seal, I heard the third living creature saying, "Come." I looked, and behold, a black horse; and he who sat on it had a pair of scales in his hand. ⁶And I heard *something* like a voice in the center of the four living creatures saying, "A quart of wheat for a denarius, and

three quarts of barley for a denarius; and do not damage the oil and the wine."

[7]When the Lamb broke the fourth seal, I heard the voice of the fourth living creature saying, "Come." [8]I looked, and behold, an ashen horse; and he who sat on it had the name Death; and Hades was following with him. Authority was given to them over a fourth of the earth, to kill with sword and with famine and with pestilence and by the wild beasts of the earth.

[9]When the Lamb broke the fifth seal, I saw underneath the altar the souls of those who had been slain because of the word of God, and because of the testimony which they had maintained; [10]and they cried out with a loud voice, saying, "How long, O Lord, holy and true, will You refrain from judging and avenging our blood on those who dwell on the earth?" [11]And there was given to each of them a white robe; and they were told that they should rest for a little while longer, until *the number of* their fellow servants and their brethren who were to be killed even as they had been, would be completed also.

[12]I looked when He broke the sixth seal, and there was a great earthquake; and the sun became black as sackcloth *made* of hair, and the whole moon became like blood; [13]and the stars of the sky fell to the earth, as a fig tree casts its unripe figs when shaken by a great wind. [14]The sky was split apart like a scroll when it is rolled up, and every mountain and island were moved out of their places. [15]Then the kings of the earth and the great men and the commanders and the rich and the strong and every slave and free man hid themselves in the caves and among the rocks of the mountains; [16]and they said to the mountains and to the rocks, "Fall on us and hide us from the presence of Him who sits on the throne, and from the wrath of the Lamb; [17]for the great day of their wrath has come, and who is able to stand?"

Our daily rituals are often the same, day-in and day-out. Wake up. Get up. Wash and dress. Eat breakfast (if there's time). Dash off to school or work or other activities. Like a religious rite, we expect our routines to repeat themselves every day. Each one of us, however, has experienced an unexpected disruption along the way. A flat tire … a sick child … a fender-bender … a phone call out of the blue relaying tragic news. Situations like these interrupt our routines with unwelcome stress—even severe trials. Occasionally these unexpected events can overturn a person's entire life.

For most, God's judgment during the end times will be unexpected and unwelcome, disrupting life's routine with more than just minor irritation. The great tribulation of Matthew 24:21 will affect more than just one family, city, or nation. The period of God's final judgment will affect the whole world (Luke 17:26–30; 1 Thess. 5:1–3; Rev. 3:10).

From My Journal

"Sinner, Oh, Sinner, Where Will You Stand?"

I still remember the first time I faced the reality of God's coming judgment. My older sister, Luci, came home from college with an album called *God's Trombones*. That was long before albums were square pictures on your computer screen you clicked to download. An album was a thick folder of cardboard sleeves packed with a large vinyl disk. (About three of you reading this know what I'm talking about!) My sister said to me, "Babe" — (Yes, she called me "Babe." Still does.) — "I want you to listen to this. You'll love it." The seventh poem has struck me all my life because it deals with the terrors of the final judgment.

I was sixteen years old at the time. Listening to that performer paint such a vivid picture of judgment that it nearly scared my shorts off! Even though the author took a lot of creative license, he drew on imagery from the book of Revelation, Daniel, and Zechariah. It makes you look at yourself and ask the question repeated over and over in those terrifying verses:

Sinner, oh, sinner,
Where will you stand
In that great day when God's a-going to rain down fire?[11]

Some people deny that God will judge anybody for anything. After all, they reason, isn't God a loving God? Doesn't He abound in mercy? Whatever happened to divine compassion and forgiveness? Clearly, God's coming judgment strikes at the very heart of our theology — our view of the nature and character of God Himself. It's no wonder that people find much that disturbs them in the book of Revelation. Yet when we discover that God's mercy and wrath work hand in hand and that through judgment God will bring about redemption, then we will have a much clearer and more balanced understanding of the God we love and serve.

— 6:1–8 —

In the first leg of John's heavenly journey, he visited the glorious throne room of God (chs. 4–5). There he witnessed the Almighty holding a seven-sealed scroll — a title deed of absolute ownership of the universe. Only one Person in heaven and earth was found worthy to take that scroll, to open its seals, and to begin the step-by-step process of snatching control of the world from evil and forever vanquishing sin and death: Jesus Christ. The steps necessary for preparing the world for His kingdom on earth, however, involve a period of unparalleled judgment.

In the book of Revelation three symbols represent three distinct series of future judgments: seven seals, seven trumpets, and seven bowls. Each series of seven describes unique events that will take place in the coming tribulation period. John witnessed the visions of these judgments in an interesting order. The seventh of each series brings the judgment to a close as well as opens up a new vision in which the next series begins (see chart). We will see later, however, that when these various judgments are fulfilled in the coming tribulation period, the seals generally refer to conditions during the early part of the tribulation. The trumpets portray

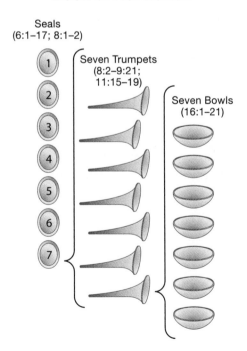

The Seals, Trumpets, and Bowls in the Book of Revelation

Seals
(6:1–17; 8:1–2)

Seven Trumpets
(8:2–9:21;
11:15–19)

Seven Bowls
(16:1–21)

judgments near the middle of the tribulation, and the bowls clearly refer to the most severe judgments at the conclusion of the tribulation. We'll see proof of this later.

The first thing you'll notice is that the first four seals in Revelation 6:1–8 follow a similar pattern: (1) Christ breaks the seal; (2) one of the four living creatures cries out, "Come"; and (3) a colored horse and rider leap onto the scene. Although these "four horsemen of the Apocalypse" have long puzzled commentators, the big picture is apparent: *severe judgment is coming, but God has everything under control.* Beyond this truth, some familiarity with the possible meanings of these symbols will help us understand how God will work out His plan for the future.

The rider on the white horse (6:1–2) most likely represents bloodless conquest—false peace and security. Notice that he carries a bow without arrows. The type of crown on his head is the *stephanos*—not a crown of regal authority but a victor's crown.[12] The tribulation period will begin with a deceptive peace accompanied by a counterfeit spirituality and false religion. We see this same general condition described in 1 Thessalonians 5:3, where Paul wrote, "While they are saying, 'Peace and safety!' then destruction will come upon them suddenly like labor pains upon a woman with child, and they will not escape." Also, we see the coming of false religion in Christ's own description of the end times in Matthew 24:4–5.

Immediately after the rider on the white horse brings in false religion and false peace, the rider on the red horse breaks the promise (6:3–4). The red color symbolizes the fire and blood of war. Rather than an arrowless bow, this dreaded rider wields a sword. This sword is not the *rhomphaia* of order and justice that comes from the mouth of Christ (1:16). It's the dagger-like *machaira* of assassination, uprising, and warfare.[13] This corresponds to Jesus' reference to "wars and rumors of wars" in the end times (Matt. 24:6–7).

When Christ broke the third seal, John saw a black horse gallop onto the scene. As this symbol of the famine and poverty that result from warfare comes in view, desolation and despair flood the world like a global tsunami. The measuring scales and the voice shouting prices indicate that this period of time will be characterized by economic inflation and starvation. One commentator writes:

> The prices listed here are about eight to sixteen times the average prices in the Roman Empire at the time.... Therefore, those suffering from the famine will only be able to buy limited food quantities for their family, and there will be nothing left over to provide for any of the other necessities of life such as "wine and oil."[14]

With the opening of the fourth seal, the fourth horse with its rider charged into John's view. The Greek word describing its color is *chlōros*, indicating a "yellowish green," the sickly color of illness and death.[15] In this terrifying scene, John saw the grim reaper and the grave digger moving together across the face of the earth. Death slays the body while Hades swallows up the soul. These two symbols represent the massive number of deaths that will follow in the wake of the first three horsemen. One-quarter of the world's population will be lost in their rampage! This symbolic vision corresponds to Jesus' literal description of the death and destruction that will characterize the end times (Matt. 24:7, 9).

I must admit, it's hard to come to terms with the severity of these judgments. This stampede of deception, wars, pestilence, death, and destruction makes every tragedy we've learned from world history pale by comparison. Only the emotionally numb will fail to wonder, "How could God allow such things to happen ... much less decree them?" Where in the world is our loving heavenly Father?

In the midst of our concern about these judgments, we must never forget that God is absolutely just and fair in punishing evil. Wickedness deserves to be judged. Yet in His abundant grace, God continually tempers His wrath and demonstrates mercy. For example, in Mark 13:20, Jesus taught that God will put a limit on the days of the tribulation. This may not seem significant until we realize that if He doesn't, everyone in the world will perish!

We should also recognize that most of the judgments in Revelation come through the work of evil agents. God *allows* evil in the world, but He is not the author of evil. One theologian writes, "Specifically, it will not do to accuse God of evil intentions or malevolent acts. He is sovereign, but not blameworthy, for He is righteous in all His deeds (Ps. 11:7; Dan. 9:14). He oversees all things in accord with His will, but He is not the source, the cause, or the author of sin."[16]

As we continue to study the judgments in this book, it may appear that the world is spinning out of control because of the terrible judgments unleashed across the globe. Remember, though, that God remains in control. He is uncompromisingly just, and He never lets go of His goodness. In fact, look at it from another angle. The fact that God *allows* the future judgments to take place indicates that in the present time, He is actively holding back the wickedness of humanity. When the dam of His gracious restraint is broken, disaster pours forth like a flood.

— **6:9–17** —

After watching the four horsemen gallop across the darkening landscape, the apostle John witnessed the Lamb breaking the fifth seal (vv. 9–11). This marks the next event of the tribulation, providing us with some information regarding believers during the tribulation. The church, having been rescued before the tribulation by being caught up to heaven at the rapture, will already have been rewarded in their glorified bodies (3:10).[17] Those who were left behind and who come to faith in Christ *during* the seven-year tribulation period, however, will face the greatest persecution the world has ever known (Matt. 24:21). These martyrs who suffer at the hands of the Antichrist described in Revelation 13 will ultimately be vindicated when God pours out His wrath on His enemies.

The fact that these souls are "underneath the altar" (6:9) indicates that their untimely deaths will be valiant martyrdoms—lives given for the sake of the gospel and in the service of their Savior (6:9). During this time those who violently depart this life will be in a bodiless state awaiting resurrection. As such, they will cry out to God for vengeance: "How long, O Lord, holy and true, will You refrain from judging and avenging our blood on those who dwell on the earth"? (6:10). This plea to God for justice and vengeance finds its roots in the Old Testament imprecatory psalms—prayers calling God to take His stand against the enemies of righteousness. Psalm 94:1–5 provides a perfect example of this sentiment.

> O Lord, God of vengeance,
> God of vengeance, shine forth!
> Rise up, O Judge of the earth,
> Render recompense to the proud.
> How long shall the wicked, O Lord,
> How long shall the wicked exult?
> They pour forth words, they speak arrogantly;
> All who do wickedness vaunt themselves.
> They crush Your people, O Lord,
> And afflict Your heritage.

This prayer for judgment and vindication acknowledges several important theological truths. God is a God of justice, holiness, and truth, who will keep His promises of salvation for His people and retribution against His enemies. But the psalmist—like the saints under the altar in Revelation 6—acknowledges that such vengeance is a strictly divine prerogative. Romans 12:19 says, "Never take your own revenge, beloved, but leave room for the wrath of God, for it is written, 'Vengeance is Mine, I will repay.'" Though the martyred saints will have to wait a little longer while their fellow tribulation martyrs join them (6:11), the Lord will keep His promise to avenge the murder of His saints (2 Thess. 1:6–8). In fact, the fulfillment of this promise of vengeance against the enemies of God's people is portrayed in the sixth seal.

Although many believers in Christ will suffer persecution and martyrdom, the perpetrators of these horrors will not go unpunished. Answering the tribulation martyrs' cries for vindication, the sixth seal reveals the horror of unbelievers who must face the full wrath of God and His appointed Judge, Jesus Christ. The absolute panic experienced by these wicked people doesn't grip them because God is unjust, but because they know He will give them exactly what they deserve!

My guess is that if you asked the average person on the street to describe the end of the world, they would unknowingly allude to language and images from the sixth seal of Revelation 6. With this seal we begin to witness what we might call the "classic" images of the end times—

- the earth quakes
- the sun turns black like sackcloth
- the moon appears red as blood
- stars rain down upon the earth
- the sky splits like a scroll
- the mountains and islands shift from their places

Such images highlighted in *God's Trombones* struck me with fear as a teenager. John used the most descriptive terms he could to represent the severity of these upheavals of both heaven and earth. Today we can imagine the types of geological

WHITE ROBES

In Revelation 6:11, the martyred saints are given "white robes." The Greek term for these robes is *stolē*, which refers to a "long, flowing robe."[18] In the ancient world, the *stolē* marked a person's high social or religious status (Mark 12:38; Luke 15:22). Angelic beings also are seen in these white robes, pointing out their high-ranking authority as ambassadors of God (Mark 16:5). The saints martyred during the great tribulation also wear a *stolē* (Rev. 7:9, 13, 14). Elsewhere in Revelation the image of wearing white signifies a future reward for worthiness (3:3–4; 4:4).

In the first-century Jewish mind-set, white robes symbolized the glorious state of the rewarded saints in the future kingdom. In a passage from the Dead Sea Scrolls we read this description of the coming kingdom of God: "It shall be healing, great peace in a long life, and fruitfulness, together with every everlasting blessing and eternal joy in life without end, a crown of glory and a garment of majesty in unending light."[19] So, the color white represented God's glory, majesty, and brilliance, reflected in the lives of His redeemed saints.

When the Lord God uses this symbol in John's visions, we see an important Christian distinction to the common symbolism. The saints "have washed their robes and made them white in the blood of the Lamb" (7:14). These robes were not made white by their own good works, but by the finished work of Christ's death in their place. "For this reason," Scriptures says, "they are before the throne of God" (7:15).

events that might cause such phenomena. A great earthquake shakes the entire globe and volcanic eruptions spew ash and gases into the atmosphere, veiling the sun like a dark, rough, burlap cloth. Putrid air distorts the color of the moon, and the heavens rain down meteors. When people head for the mountains, they discover that their hiding places have collapsed. When they head for the islands to escape the mass hysteria, they quickly realize the islands have been submerged. Whatever the ultimate fulfillment of these images may be, we can agree with one commentator who writes, "The scene ... is one of catastrophe and distress for the inhabitants of the earth."[20]

Many of these images have appeared earlier in the Bible. The prophet Joel warned regarding the future day of the Lord: "Let all the inhabitants of the land tremble, for the day of the LORD is coming; surely it is near.... The heavens tremble, the sun and the moon grow dark and the stars lose their brightness" (Joel 2:1, 10). Yet this stark warning is accompanied by a call to repentance: " 'Yet even now,' declares the LORD, 'return to Me with all your heart, and with fasting, weeping and mourning; and rend your heart and not your garments' " (2:12–13a). To this statement Joel himself adds some vital theological truths: "Now return to the LORD your God, for He is gracious and compassionate, slow to anger, abounding in lovingkindness and relenting of evil" (2:13).

It is interesting that Peter himself quoted Joel 2 in his sermon at Pentecost (Acts 2:20), suggesting that the same kind of judgments would come upon the nation of Israel in his own day if the people didn't repent of their rejection of Jesus as the Messiah. Though a form of this judgment came upon Jerusalem in AD 70 with the destruction of the temple and dispersion of the Jewish people, the book of Revelation—written some twenty-five years later—warns that a far more severe global day of the Lord is yet to come.

Following the horrific events described in 6:12–14, John recorded a frightful scene: the complete and utter panic of the entire population of the world. Every kind of person—rich and poor, elite and common—will cry out in dread, hiding themselves like hunted animals in the cracks and crevices of the earth. Rather than rushing into God's merciful and loving presence by grace through faith, they will flee from Him (6:15–17). Instead of bowing before Him in worship, they will bury themselves in caves, overcome with frenzied fear. The late Bible teacher John Walvoord noted that the scene of judgment in Revelation 6 "raises the important question contained in the closing words of verse 17: **Who can stand?** Only those who have availed themselves of the grace of God before the time of judgment will be able to stand when God deals with the earth in this final period of great distress."[21]

Again, that haunting refrain from *God's Trombones* emerges, asking a sobering question that should awaken all of us from our spiritual slumber.

Sinner, oh, sinner,
Where will you stand
In that great day when God's a-going to rain down fire?

Application

Knowing God through His Judgments

How can we personally respond to the details of judgment seen in the first six seals? Let me highlight three important truths about the Lord our God revealed in this dramatic text of Scripture.

First, *the warning itself demonstrates God's love and grace.* I'm not a perfect parent. No one is. But in parenting my children when they were young, I resisted the urge to suddenly lash out in anger or arbitrarily punish them for wrongdoing without giving them opportunities to correct their misbehavior. Good parenting sets clear boundaries as well as clear consequences if those boundaries are crossed. In many cases it also involves warnings when children start veering off the right path. In the same way, far in advance God reveals the seriousness and severity of His future judgments against unbelief and sin. His judgments never occur prematurely. This demonstrates His grace in allowing people ample opportunity to heed the warning and turn, in faith, to His Son (see 2 Peter 3:3–9).

Second, *each series of judgments grows in severity.* Although God would certainly be justified in choosing to end the world in one quick flash, by His mercy He has determined to allow numerous opportunities for repentance even after the judgments begin. Again, this demonstrates something important about the character of God. He is longsuffering, patient, and merciful. As such, not only does He act out of His holiness and righteousness in judging the wicked, but He also acts in love and grace to allow persistently wicked people to repent.

Third, *God's judgments are completely under His control.* Whether they are expressed through natural disasters or through depraved, disobedient human beings, God never compromises His sovereignty. In the book of Revelation we find that the initial action bringing judgment originates in heaven. Then and only then are the actors on earth commanded or allowed to act. This order guarantees that God's judgments are tempered by His grace and remain in complete harmony with His dual purpose of establishing His kingdom and ushering in righteousness. Unlike the acts of unrighteous humans, God's actions never spiral out of control or do more damage than He intends. As always, His ultimate purpose demonstrates His matchless power and glory, even through justice and wrath (Rom. 9:22).

An Interlude: Earthly Restraint and Heavenly Worship (Revelation 7:1–17)

[1]After this I saw four angels standing at the four corners of the earth, holding back the four winds of the earth, so that no wind would blow on the earth or on the sea or on any tree. [2]And I saw another angel ascending from the rising of the sun, having the seal of the living God; and he cried out with a loud voice to the four angels to whom it was granted to harm the earth and the sea, [3]saying, "Do not harm the earth or the sea or the trees until we have sealed the bond-servants of our God on their foreheads."

[4]And I heard the number of those who were sealed, one hundred and forty-four thousand sealed from every tribe of the sons of Israel: [5]from the tribe of Judah, twelve thousand *were* sealed, from the tribe of Reuben twelve thousand, from the tribe of Gad twelve thousand, [6]from the tribe of Asher twelve thousand, from the tribe of Naphtali twelve thousand, from the tribe of Manasseh twelve thousand, [7]from the tribe of Simeon twelve thousand, from the tribe of Levi twelve thousand, from the tribe of Issachar twelve thousand, [8]from the tribe of Zebulun twelve thousand, from the tribe of Joseph twelve thousand, from the tribe of Benjamin, twelve thousand *were* sealed.

[9]After these things I looked, and behold, a great multitude which no one could count, from every nation and *all* tribes and peoples and tongues, standing before the throne and before the Lamb, clothed in white robes, and palm branches *were* in their hands; [10]and they cry out with a loud voice, saying,

"Salvation to our God who sits on the throne, and to the Lamb."

[11]And all the angels were standing around the throne and *around* the elders and the four living creatures; and they fell on their faces before the throne and worshiped God, [12]saying,

"Amen, blessing and glory and wisdom and thanksgiving and honor and power and might, *be* to our God forever and ever. Amen."

[13]Then one of the elders answered, saying to me, "These who are clothed in the white robes, who are they, and where have they come from?" [14]I said to him, "My lord, you know." And he said to me, "These are the ones who come out of the great tribulation, and they have washed their robes and made them white in the blood of the Lamb. [15]For this reason, they are before the throne of God; and they serve Him day and night in

His temple; and He who sits on the throne will spread His tabernacle over them. [16]They will hunger no longer, nor thirst anymore; nor will the sun beat down on them, nor any heat; [17]for the Lamb in the center of the throne will be their shepherd, and will guide them to springs of the water of life; and God will wipe every tear from their eyes."

The staggering scene at the end of the sixth seal ended with people all over the earth rushing to caves and screaming, "Who is able to stand" (6:17)? Those panicked screams echoed into the distance as Christ's thumb lingered at the seventh and final seal of the scroll. Based strictly on the rapid-fire judgments he had witnessed to that point, John might have reasonably concluded that the answer to that question was, "Nobody! Not one soul will be able to stand!"

Chapter 7 reveals, however, that two distinct groups of redeemed will, in fact, stand. One will stand strong on earth throughout the tribulation period, having received God's personal seal of protection. The other group, after suffering martyrdom at the hands of God's enemies, will stand in heaven before God's awesome throne in worship and praise. What a sharp contrast to the screaming panic of the pagan world! While the earthbound heathen will cower from God in fear and scramble in vain to find relief across the earth, the heaven-bound saints will stand before their glorious God in faith, ascended into the heights of paradise.

—7:1-8—

As the hoofbeats of the four horsemen echoed into the distance and the cacophony of geological and cosmic upheavals stilled, John's attention turned to the center of the earthly end-time drama: the land of Israel. Throughout history the people of Israel have been conquered, delivered, devastated, exiled, and restored, over and over again, as military threats bombarded them from every side. Yet at the beginning of the tribulation, just as the land of Israel is about to endure the most devastating war in all of history, God's intervention reminds us that He will keep His promises to Israel.

At the opening of the vision in Revelation 7, God sent four angels to restrain "the four winds of the earth"—an idiom for the four cardinal directions. The reference to "winds" symbolizes the coming judgments that will affect both land and sea (7:1–2). An angel then rushed onto the scene, holding "the seal of the living God" to mark the "bond-servants" of God on their foreheads (7:3).

What follows is a detailed roster of Hebrew people from twelve tribes of Israel— 144,000 total (7:4–8). If we compare this list of the twelve tribes with other lists in the Old Testament, we notice several differences.[22] Even the lists in the Old Testament are seldom in the same order and often omit certain tribes (see the chart below). In fact, how the twelve tribes are listed depends on the purpose of the author.[23]

Comparison of Four Biblical Lists of the Twelve Tribes of Israel

Genesis 35 (Summaries of Births)	1 Chronicles 4–7 (Genealogical Records)	Ezekiel 48 (Future Land Allotments)	Revelation 7 (Sealing for Tribulation)
Reuben	Judah	Dan	Judah
Simeon	Simeon	Asher	Reuben
Levi	Reuben	Naphtali	Gad
Judah	Gad	Manasseh	Asher
Issachar	Half Tribe of Manasseh	Ephraim	Naphtali
Zebulun	Levi	Reuben	Manasseh
Joseph	Issachar	Judah	Simeon
Benjamin	Benjamin	Benjamin	Levi
Dan	Naphtali	Simeon	Issachar
Naphtali	Manasseh	Issachar	Zebulun
Gad	Ephraim	Zebulun	Joseph
Asher	Asher	Gad	Benjamin

I suspect that if John were composing the book of Revelation from his own imagination, he would have followed one of the lists of the twelve tribes found in the Old Testament, quite likely the end-time list of Ezekiel 48. According to Revelation 7:4, however, John simply wrote down what he heard. No imagination ... no questions asked. Perhaps later, as he reviewed the names of the twelve tribes, he scratched his head, asking the same questions we would ask today. *The list includes Levi? It leaves out Dan? It replaces Ephraim with Joseph?*

Commentators of every category have tried to answer these and other questions. The question regarding Ephraim and Joseph is relatively easy to answer. Throughout the Old Testament, the inheritance of Jacob's son Joseph was divided into two tribes for his two sons, Ephraim and Manasseh. In the list of Revelation

7, God retains the name Manasseh, but apparently refers to the people of Ephraim with the name of the original patriarch, Joseph. No tribes are lost there. In fact, one tribe is gained, and if the list would have included the rest of the eleven sons of Jacob, there would have been thirteen tribes in the list! Commentator John Walvoord makes these remarks:

> If Dan were included, there would have been 13 tribes.... The tribe omitted was usually Levi, from which the priesthood came. Inasmuch as it is normal to have only 12 and not 13 tribes, the omission of Dan is not significant. Perhaps Dan was omitted here because it was one of the first tribes to go into idolatry (Jud. 18:30; cf. 1 Kings 12:28–29). However, Dan is mentioned in Ezekiel 48:2 in the millennial land distribution.[24]

Though we may not be able to fully explain why these particular tribes were selected to make up the 144,000 sealed in Revelation 7, we can be certain that God has His reasons. Let's not get sidetracked over a few minute details we can't quite figure out. Instead, we should zoom out our mental lens to focus once again on the big picture.

These 144,000 Hebrews will serve as faithful, courageous, and diligent witnesses for Christ during the darkest period of the earth's history. Because they will be miraculously preserved from harm during the tribulation, God will use them to fulfill the ancient Old Testament calling of the Hebrew people to be God's witnesses among the nations

A FUTURE FOR ISRAEL?

Many Christians today are convinced that God's plan for ethnic Israel has come to an end. Some believe that the promises of a glorious nation and blessing in the Holy Land have been abolished because of Israel's unfaithfulness. Others have determined that these promises were fulfilled in a spiritual sense through Christ in the church. Some theologians propose that Israel has been replaced by the church and that ethnic Jews have been divorced by God, without a future in God's plan.

The New Testament, however, assures us that God plans to bring about the fulfillment of those promises through Jesus Christ. Although most ethnic Jews have been in a state of unbelief since the time of Jesus, God will one day bring a remnant to faith in Christ and restore them in the land promised to their forefathers (Gen. 13:15). Jesus Himself promised the apostles, "In the regeneration when the Son of Man will sit on His glorious throne, you also shall sit upon twelve thrones, judging the twelve tribes of Israel" (Matt. 19:28). Before Christ's ascension, the disciples eagerly inquired about the timing of that earthly kingdom when they asked, "Lord, is it at this time You are restoring the kingdom to Israel?" (Acts 1:6). It is significant that Jesus didn't reject their literal interpretation and expectation of a future fulfillment of these earthly promises. Instead, He told them that they would not know the timing of this restoration (Acts 1:7–8).

Years later, the apostle Paul addressed the problem of the present unbelief of most Hebrews by declaring that this rebellion would one day be reversed: "A partial hardening has happened to Israel until the fullness of the Gentiles has come in; and so all Israel will be saved" (Rom. 11:25–26). In other words, when God has accomplished His purposes through the church, He will again turn His attention to the nation of Israel and bring them to faith in Christ. We can see the beginnings of this future for Israel with the sealing of the 144,000 in Revelation 7:1–8.

Why is the restoration of Israel so important? Because God's very reputation as a promise keeper is at stake! With explicit reference to the calling of Israel, Paul said, "For the gifts and the calling of God are irrevocable" (Rom. 11:29). It's as simple as this: If we cannot trust God to keep His promises to Israel (Jer. 31:35–37), how can we trust Him to keep His promises to us (Rom. 8:35–39)? Never doubt it: God will do what He says He will do!

(Isa. 43:1–12). God's plan for Israel was always for the people to serve as the light of truth for the Gentiles. In the tribulation they will serve as Christ's servants who finally fulfill this mission. This believing remnant from ethnic Israel will not only be sealed for power and protection, but they will also survive the tribulation period and become the firstfruits of the nation of Israel when it is restored to the land during the coming millennial kingdom.

— **7:9–17** —

One of the most frequently asked questions in regard to the tribulation is whether anyone will come to saving faith in Jesus Christ during that horrific time. We already have observed that 144,000 people from various tribes of Israel will be set apart for special service to the Lord, but they won't stand alone! Perhaps through the stellar testimonies of the 144,000, God will call to Himself numerous believers in Jesus "from every nation and all tribes and peoples and tongues" (7:9). In contrast to the protected number of Hebrew believers in 7:1–8, however, these Gentile believers will be subject to persecution and martyrdom. In fact, John's vision of the great multitude opened with these believers already pictured in heaven, having suffered physical death at the hands of God's enemies during the tribulation.

Note the differences between the redeemed in 7:1–8 and those in 7:9–17.

This countless multitude waved palm branches before God's throne, represent-

Contrasts between the 144,000 and the Great Multitude	
The Redeemed in 7:1–8	The Redeemed in 7:9–17
144,000	Innumerable
From twelve tribes of Israel	From every nation, tribe, people, and language
Standing on earth	Standing before God's throne
Sealed for protection	Ascended after persecution

ing celebration, deliverance, and jubilation (7:9). They didn't cry out in screams of pain but with praises to "God who sits on the throne, and to the Lamb" (7:10). At this point one of the twenty-four elders interpreted the vision for John, so we aren't left wondering about the identity of this great multitude. He said, "These are the ones who come out of the great tribulation, and they have washed their robes and made them white in the blood of the Lamb" (7:14). Clearly these are tribulation believers who, because of their conversion to Christ, will suffer earthly affliction, disaster, tears, pain, anguish, grief, sorrow, and tragedy. This great multitude will fully understand the meaning of Paul's words, "For I consider that the sufferings of this present time are not worthy to be compared with the glory that is to be revealed to us" (Rom. 8:18). Notice their eternal glory described in 7:15–17:

- They are before God's throne.
- They serve in God's temple day and night.
- God grants them His favor and protection.
- They no longer hunger or thirst.
- The elements can no longer harm them.
- Christ will shepherd and nourish them.
- God will relieve all their sorrows.

The interlude in Revelation 7 teaches us that even in the midst of wrath, God does not forget His mercy. Those who come to believe during the tribulation will be in one of two groups. The first group of believers will be the remnant of physical Israel sealed for protection and called to testify concerning Christ (7:1–8). Their presence reminds us that God is always faithful to His promises. He won't break a single one! The second group of believers will be composed of the masses of Gentiles who believe in Christ and suffer persecution and martyrdom for their faith. These martyrs will come out of the tribulation through death, but their suffering will instantly give way to victorious worship (7:9–17). Their presence in this vision teaches us that even when we suffer to the uttermost, God never fails to reward those who remain faithful to the end.

NOTES: Worship of the Worthy Lamb (Revelation 4:1–7:17)

1. Peter J. Kreeft, *Heaven: The Heart's Deepest Longing* (San Francisco: Harper & Row, 1980), 50.
2. All three are reflected in Psalm 139:7–10, indicating that God is everywhere present and active. We are told that Christ's sovereignty also extends to all spheres of existence, as one day every knee will bow to Him "in heaven and on earth and under the earth" (Phil. 2:10). These same three levels are reflected in Revelation 5:3, 13.
3. Millard J. Erickson, *Christian Theology* (2nd ed.; Grand Rapids: Baker, 1998), 294.

4. Robert L. Saucy, "Scripture: Its Power, Authority, and Relevance," in *Understanding Christian Theology* (ed. Charles R. Swindoll and Roy B. Zuck; Nashville: Nelson, 2003), 29–30.

5. John A. Witmer, "Jesus Christ: Knowing Jesus as Man and God," in *Understanding Christian Theology* (ed. Charles R. Swindoll and Roy B. Zuck; Nashville: Nelson, 2003), 304–5.

6. The normal word for a monarch's crown is *diadēma*, whereas the victor's crown is the *stephanos*. The twenty-four elders are each crowned with the *stephanos*, suggesting that they may represent saints who have been rewarded at the judgment seat of Christ (2 Cor. 5:10).

7. Johnson, "Revelation," 12:462.

8. For an explanation of the "seven Spirits of God," see comments on 1:4.

9. Reginald Heber, "Holy, Holy, Holy," in *The Hymnal for Worship and Celebration*, no. 262.

10. Osborne, *Revelation*, 248.

11. James Weldon Johnson, *God's Trombones*. You can listen to the full poem at www.youtube.com/watch?v=NZrm-RymP7k.

12. Bauer and Danker, eds., *A Greek-English Lexicon of the New Testament*, 943–44.

13. Osborne, *Revelation*, 278.

14. Beale, *The Book of Revelation*, 381.

15. Bauer and Danker, eds., *A Greek-English Lexicon of the New Testament*, 1085–86.

16. Robert A. Pyne, "Humanity and Sin," in *Understanding Christian Theology* (ed. Charles R. Swindoll and Roy B. Zuck; Nashville: Nelson, 2003), 758.

17. For a brief discussion of the timing of the church's rapture to heaven, see comments on Revelation 3:10, page 74.

18. Bauer and Danker, eds., *A Greek-English Lexicon of the New Testament*, 946.

19. Geza Vermes, ed., *The Complete Dead Sea Scrolls in English* (New York: Penguin, 1997), 102.

20. Johnson, "Revelation," 12:476.

21. Walvoord, "Revelation," *The Bible Knowledge Commentary*, 949.

22. Johnson, "Revelation," 12:482.

23. For example, the list found in Genesis 35 intends to record the actual physical sons of Israel. The list in 1 Chronicles 4–7 gives a genealogical record of several sons of Israel but leaves out Zebulun even after listing him as one of the sons of Israel in 2:1. Instead, the author splits the tribe of Joseph into two—Manasseh and Ephraim—and replaces Zebulun with an additional half tribe of Manasseh with no explanation. The list of the twelve tribes in Ezekiel 48 points to an end-time allotment of the Promised Land in the future kingdom, describing the boundaries geographically. As such, it also splits Manasseh and Simeon in two and relegates Levi to a special portion of the land.

24. Walvoord, "Revelation," *The Bible Knowledge Commentary*, 949.

JUDGMENTS OF THE RIGHTEOUS REDEEMER (REVELATION 8:1–10:11)

I grew up in Houston, Texas—a part of the country that has seen more than its fair share of disastrous weather. It's the kind of weather that can change your life ... or ruin it. When hurricane season arrives, all the communities along the Gulf Coast make sure they have fresh batteries in their flashlights and fill the generators with fuel and their bathtubs with water, as they brace themselves for whatever comes. Sometimes several years go by with only heavy rains or a few fallen trees that probably were on the city's list to cut down, anyway. But then other years the Big One hits ... or the Big Two ... or Three.

The routine is always the same. A few panic. Most calmly react. They load their families and pets into their cars and drive north on Highway 45 or hop onto Highway 90 and head west. Others nail plywood on the windows, lock the doors, and stare at their TVs until the power goes out. They pray that the hurricane will suddenly turn to the north or east, even though they're praying for it to hit somebody else! With any "luck," the storm will blow itself out as it makes landfall. Then they'll have to repair only a roof rather than rebuild half a house.

Insurance companies call storms like these "acts of God." Technically, they're right. Nothing happens in this world without our Sovereign's permission. Yet there's nothing divinely *special* about the natural disasters we all experience. The storms that intrude on so many peoples' lives are a part of the natural deterioration of the fallen world, a result of the curse on creation first mentioned in Genesis 3:17–19. Romans 8:21 calls it creation's "slavery to corruption." So everybody in the world—the righteous and the wicked—are subject to the brutal effects of the fall. The rain falls on the just and the unjust (Matt. 5:45).

We need to distinguish this condition of judgment on creation in general from the specific judgments that God pours out on particular people at particular times. Though we may all experience hurricanes, earthquakes, floods, and fires, when judgment comes directly from God, the result is always severe. Throughout history God has unleashed his righteous wrath on sinful, rebellious people: the world of Noah, Sodom and Gomorrah, the Egyptians, the Babylonians—the list could go on. Yet these biblical examples of God's judgment all foreshadow the ultimate judgment that will engulf the entire globe in the future tribulation.

In the unfolding drama of Revelation, I've titled this episode "Judgments of the Righteous Redeemer" (8:1–10:11). In this section we will observe a sudden

KEY TERMS

ἀστήρ [astēr] (792) "star"

Besides its literal reference to the countless celestial lights in the heavens, the Greek word astēr ("star") has numerous figurative meanings in the Bible. In Genesis 37:9 stars symbolize the twelve tribes of Israel (see Rev. 12:1). In Revelation stars symbolize both the messengers of the seven churches (1:20) and Jesus Christ Himself (22:16). In the midst of the visions of future events, however, falling stars represent wicked demons responsible for destruction (8:10–12; 9:1; 12:4).

οὐαί [ouai] (3759) "alas, woe"

Loud wailing during times of deep sorrow was common in the ancient world. In fact, funerals of the rich were sometimes accompanied by professional "wailers" to increase the perception of grief at the loss of a person who may have had more enemies than allies. The exclamation ouai intends to mimic this cry of anguish. Doubling the word in ancient writing indicated severe anguish. Revelation 8:13 repeats the term three times, pointing to the extremely sorrowful nature of the judgments and the acute sadness associated with the wickedness of the world that calls for such judgments.

σάλπιγξ [salpinx] (4536) "trumpet, horn"

The ancient instrument known as the salpinx was not a musical instrument used for entertainment. Rather, it was a horn employed on solemn occasions. For example, it was used to call soldiers to battle (1 Cor. 14:8), to proclaim a sacred assembly (Matt. 24:31), or to call attention to the presence of an important — often royal — person (Heb. 12:19). The seven trumpet judgments in Revelation 8 and 9 use the salpinx to pronounce divine judgment against the earth — a solemn and somber occasion.

increase in the severity of end-time judgments. Along the way, though, God intersperses needed reminders of His mercy and grace. Following a half-hour respite at the breaking of the seventh seal, the second series of seven judgments commences—the seven trumpets (8:1–5). These trumpet blasts announce the next stage in divine wrath: a more intense display of God's righteous judgments against stubborn, unrepentant sinners (8:6–21). Just as the trumpet blasts approach a deafening crescendo, the soundings cease and John experiences another hiatus in which God's mercy is affirmed. During that brief interlude John is recommissioned to prophesy concerning "peoples and nations and tongues and kings" (10:1–11).

We all experience "acts of God" that refocus our minds on the important things in life. Yet as we will see in the vivid descriptions of the trumpet plagues, God will one day act decisively to snare the attention of a wayward humanity hardened by sin.

The all-important question is, will they listen?

First Blasts of the Trumpet Plagues (Revelation 8:1–13)

---

¹When the Lamb broke the seventh seal, there was silence in heaven for about half an hour. ²And I saw the seven angels who stand before God, and seven trumpets were given to them.

³Another angel came and stood at the altar, holding a golden censer; and much incense was given to him, so that he might add it to the prayers of all the saints on the golden altar which was before the throne. ⁴And the smoke of the incense, with the prayers of the saints, went up before God out of the angel's hand. ⁵Then the angel took the censer and filled it with the fire of the altar, and threw it to the earth; and there followed peals of thunder and sounds and flashes of lightning and an earthquake.

⁶And the seven angels who had the seven trumpets prepared themselves to sound them. ⁷The first sounded, and there came hail and fire, mixed with blood, and they were thrown to the earth; and a third of the earth was burned up, and a third of the trees were burned up, and all the green grass was burned up

⁸The second angel sounded, and *something* like a great mountain burning with fire was thrown into the sea; and a third of the sea became blood, ⁹and a third of the creatures which were in the sea and had life, died; and a third of the ships were destroyed.

¹⁰The third angel sounded, and a great star fell from heaven, burning like a torch, and it fell on a third of the rivers and on the springs of waters. ¹¹The name of the star is called Wormwood; and a third of the waters became wormwood, and many men died from the waters, because they were made bitter.

¹²The fourth angel sounded, and a third of the sun and a third of the moon and a third of the stars were struck, so that a third of them would be darkened and the day would not shine for a third of it, and the night in the same way.

¹³Then I looked, and I heard an eagle flying in midheaven, saying with a loud voice, "Woe, woe, woe to those who dwell on the earth, because of the remaining blasts of the trumpet of the three angels who are about to sound!"

We humans are a stubborn lot. Spiritual blindness, self-will, and an inborn habit of disobedience all work against the humility and submission God desires. Believers who should know better have a hard time with the simple directive to "trust and obey." For people who grope in the darkness and stumble in ignorance, the situation is worse! How can a righteous Redeemer snare the attention of a wicked world?

Christian apologist C. S. Lewis approached that question this way:

> Anyone who has watched gluttons shoveling down the most exquisite foods as if they did not know what they were eating, will admit that we can ignore even pleasure. But pain insists upon being attended to. God whispers to us in our pleasures, speaks in our conscience, but shouts in our pains: it is His megaphone to rouse a deaf world.[1]

In the process of calling people to repentance, God uses a variety of means. For example, Saul of Tarsus was literally heading down the wrong path in his persecution of the early church (Acts 9:1–2). Though God already had been working at goading Saul's conscience (26:14), it ultimately took a powerful encounter with the risen Savior, accompanied by a brief stint of blindness, to get his attention (9:3–8). In a similar way, God will one day get the attention of the entire world. Over the centuries He has called sinners to repentance through the gospel. He has offered the witness of fulfilled prophecy and changed lives. He has even revealed coming judgments, warning the world of things to come. However effective these methods may have been, a day is coming when the hardness of the unbelieving hearts of the unregenerate will intensify. When that happens, God will turn to other means to get through to a deaf and stubborn world.

In the book of Revelation we foresee God using an intensifying series of judgments to capture the world's attention for the purpose of redemption. In fact, a major purpose of God's judgments in Revelation is to seize the world's attention when it refuses to listen. The redeemed martyrs in Revelation 7 tell us that many will respond to God's end-time call. The rest of Revelation, however, tells us that most will harden their hearts even more.

— **8:1–6** —

After John witnessed Christ opening the first six seals of the seven-sealed scroll (Rev. 5–6), he caught a backstage glimpse of the multitude of Hebrews and Gentiles who would be saved during the tribulation (ch. 7). Following this brief intermission, the next act of God's judgments is ready to begin at the opening of the seventh seal (8:1). To draw the eyes, ears, minds, and hearts of the world to Himself, heavenly angels will sound a series of trumpets—unmistakable signs of His power over the earth. For some, the sounds serve as calls to redemption, but for most, they will become terrifying reminders of wrath.

The Greek term used for "trumpet" (*salpinx*) refers to an instrument of pronouncement, alarm, or call to arms. The New Testament never uses this term to

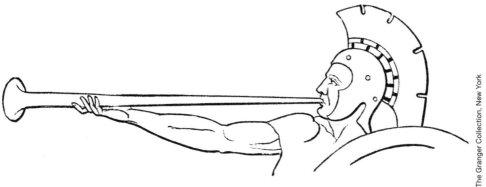

A *salpinx*, or herald's trumpet

identify a musical instrument. Instead, it refers to its military use, similar to a bugle used on a battlefield. In Revelation, as in several Old Testament passages (Isa. 27:13; Joel 2:1), the *salpinx* announces the coming of the day of the Lord.[2]

Until this moment in John's visions, there have been sounds of enormous volume—all creatures in antiphonal worship, angelic hosts belting out hallelujahs, a cacophony of earthly calamities, and a reverberating celebration of praise among the redeemed. Yet when Christ broke the seventh and final seal and a distinct group of seven unidentified angels were handed seven trumpets, all that explosion of noise turned to silence.

How appropriate! When God prepares to intensify His wrath, every creature is reduced to open-mouthed silence. In fact, silence is the only proper response to looming judgment. This theme runs throughout the Old Testament. Psalm 76:8 declares, "You caused judgment to be heard from heaven; the earth feared and was still." God proclaimed through Isaiah, "Coastlands, listen to Me in silence, and let the peoples gain new strength; let them come forward, then let them speak; let us come together for judgment" (Isa. 41:1). Zephaniah 1:7 warns, "Be silent before the Lord God! For the day of the Lord is near."

During this interlude of reverent silence, an angel approached the altar holding a golden censer of incense (8:3). This saucer-shaped bowl was used in temple worship to hold burning incense, "an aromatic substance made of gums and spices."[3] In both the Old and New Testaments, the use of incense is sometimes associated with prayer (Ps. 141:2; Luke 1:10). In Revelation 8, this association is explicit. The offering of incense symbolizes the earlier impatient prayers of the martyred saints in Revelation 6:10: "How long, O Lord, holy and true, will You refrain from judging and avenging our blood on those who dwell on the earth?" We are commonly taught that God's answer to any prayer will be "yes," "no," or "wait." In this case, we observe that unanswered prayers are sometimes stored up until God chooses to answer them in His perfect timing.

Beginning in 8:5, the time has finally come to answer those desperate pleas for God's intervention. As Deuteronomy 32:35–36 says,

Censer

> Vengeance is Mine, and retribution,
> In due time their foot will slip;
> For the day of their calamity is near,
> And the impending things are hastening
>   upon them."
> For the LORD will vindicate His people,
> And will have compassion on His servants,
> When He sees that their strength is gone,
> And there is none remaining, bond or free.

John Phillips writes, "What a potent force is prayer! The saints go into their bedrooms, close the doors, kneel down, and pray. They spread out before God their petitions, and God hears. The prayers are placed in the scales of judgment."[4] How true! In fact, 8:5 reveals God's initial response to the saints' prayer of 6:10. Phillips continues:

> Preliminary rumblings are heard, presaging the great upheavals soon to take place. Voices! Thunderings! Lightnings! Earthquakes! In its essence, this formula, sometimes called a formula for catastrophe, is repeated four times in the Apocalypse (4:5; 8:5; 11:19; 16:18). Prayer that can precipitate such things truly must be potent indeed! So the silence ends.[5]

— 8:7–13 —

With the conclusion of silence, the deafening blasts of the trumpets began. In 7:3 God had allowed a pause in His judgments long enough for the 144,000 Israelites to be marked for divine protection. In that vision the earth, the sea, and the trees could not be affected by judgment until God's servants were sealed. As we arrive at the seven trumpet judgments beginning in chapter 8, however, that temporary restraint of God's wrath will be removed. The first four trumpets will sound in short, rapid, staccato blasts, taking up only six verses. In contrast, the events surrounding the fifth through the seventh trumpet judgments will extend from chapter 9 to 11. The first four trumpet blasts will partly impact both the ecosystem and atmosphere of the earth, drastically altering living conditions on the planet. The latter judgments will describe spiritual warfare affecting people directly.

Note that all of the trumpet judgments will be limited in scope. For the most part, only one third of the planet will be affected by the first four plagues. The demonic torment of the fifth trumpet is limited to only five months. The deadly spiritual attack of the sixth trumpet affects only one third of the world population. The limits placed on these judgments remind us that God will still be exercising restraint in the early stages of the tribulation, allowing room for repentance and salvation even in the midst of wrath.

The first trumpet blast. The first trumpet will unleash a judgment targeting one third of the earth's vegetation and all of its green grass (8:7). This no doubt will decimate crops and forests, filling the air with smoke and ash. Though this first judgment is not directly aimed at human beings, it will indirectly affect food supplies, the global economy, and health on a massive scale.[6]

The second trumpet blast. The first trumpet targeted the earth. The second blast will affect one third of the sea. This enormous devastation strikes both life in its depths and ships on its surface (8:8–9). In John's symbolic vision, he witnessed "something like a great mountain" engulfed in flames cast into the sea. The image of water turning to "blood" recalls the divine judgment of God through Moses described in Exodus 7:17–19. Whether this is literal blood or a description of massive pollution as a result of the catastrophe, we cannot be sure. It may be that the "mountain" envisioned by John describes an asteroid that will strike the ocean. The tsunami alone caused by this kind of impact would inflict the extent of death and destruction described in verse 9. The impact on human life would be inestimable. Those who depend on ocean life for food would suffer hunger and hardship on an unprecedented scale. The destruction of seafaring vessels would cause disruption in global trade as well as a crisis of security when the navies of world powers are significantly reduced.

The third trumpet blast. As if the judgments on land and sea weren't enough to bring the world to its knees, the third trumpet will bring another dreadful blow (8:10–11). John saw an object like a star falling from heaven, which impacted one third of the fresh water springs, rivers, and bodies of water. These waters will be contaminated, rendered fatal to those who drink. John said the name of the star that caused this plague was "Wormwood" (8:11). Similar to the sagebrush, wormwood is a "bitter, aromatic herb ... with clusters of small, greenish yellow flowers" that grows in desert regions and often symbolizes the bitterness of life.[7] This name indicates that the waters that had once provided fresh nourishment to one third of the world's population will become polluted and poisonous. As a result, many will perish (8:11).

The fourth trumpet blast. As the first three catastrophes strike the vegetation, the oceans, and the fresh rivers and bodies of water, people might turn their hopeful attentions to the skies. The fourth trumpet blast will strike one third of the sun, moon, and stars, dimming their light by one third (8:12). Those places in the area hit hardest by these plagues will have already lost power and deteriorated into desperation and despair. Add natural darkness to this situation and the result will be anarchy and chaos. Rioting, looting, and crime will exacerbate the horrors experienced around the globe.

The judgments announced by the first four trumpets are so shocking and severe that our natural tendency is to doubt their literal meaning. Of course, Revelation uses numerous symbols to communicate the future, but these symbols always point to real events. When we feel tempted to water down this language, soften its severity, or overspiritualize the interpretations, we must remember Christ's ominous words: "For then there will be a great tribulation, such as has not occurred since the beginning of the world until now, nor ever will" (Matt. 24:21). So, whether we take these visions as literal or more symbolic, one thing is clear. *The judgments described in Revelation 8 will be so dreadful that no amount of government aid, relief efforts, or advanced preparation will be able to bring recovery.*

The first four trumpet judgments, like the first four seals of Revelation 6, form a distinct cluster. They are loud, rapid-fire blasts that seize the attention of the world. Following these, however, three additional judgments will transpire. These will be slower, longer, and even more excruciating than the previous four. Before God unleashes

© Anna Yu/www.istockphoto.com

Wormwood

these, He will make a bold pronouncement while He has the world's attention.
John described the vision as follows:
"Then I looked, and I heard an eagle flying in midheaven say with a loud voice,
"Woe, woe, woe to those who dwell on
the earth, because of the remaining blasts
of the trumpet of the three angels who are
about to sound!" (8:13).

THE SEVEN TRUMPETS AT A GLANCE

One third of the earth, trees, and grass burned (8:7)
One third of sea creatures and ships destroyed (8:8–9)
One third of the rivers and springs poisoned (8:10–11)
One third of celestial bodies darkened (8:12)
Five-month torment by demons (9:1–12)
One third of people killed by warfare (9:13–21)
Goal of the Judgments: Christ reigns! (11:15–19)

In other words, the worst is yet to come.

Application

Responding to Tomorrow's Judgment Today

As we step away from these judgments for a moment, we can't help but follow the
example of heaven and respond with silence. No natural disaster or act of war can
compare with what John has already seen. Any tragedy we suffer in this life is only
a foreshadowing of what's to come upon the earth during the tribulation. We dare
not let these troubling truths leave us unaffected. God communicated them for a
purpose. So, as I reflect on the events described in Revelation 8, I walk away with
three practical principles.

First, *God uses physical disasters to communicate spiritual messages.* Have you
noticed that following disasters like fires, hurricanes, or earthquakes, people seem
much more likely to talk about God? Many hearts become open to spiritual things.
I've also noticed that people's hopes and prayers get suddenly transformed by tragedy. Before the event they may have been praying for material things. After the
disaster they express thankfulness for what they have. The reality is that even
today—just as in the future—God often uses suffering to draw our attention from
the world to Him.

This truth is difficult to accept, especially for many who in recent years have
endured the ravages of terrible disasters. Think about your own life. How has God
used trials, suffering, or disasters to get your attention, correct your way, or lead
you to a new path? Would you have heard that message without that experience?
Consider your own path of spiritual growth. Have you grown more spiritually
while sailing smoothly along in clear waters, or when rough waters threatened to
overturn your life and you desperately needed help?

Second, *God's harsh judgments have a holy purpose.* Nobody denies that the first four trumpet judgments result in devastation, hardship, and death. Yet we are wise never to question God's motives. Even in the face of God's most severe discipline, we must submit, surrender, and release our wills to Him as we accept His perfect plan. I know it feels tempting to shake our fists toward heaven and doubt the goodness of God in the midst of suffering. Yet the spiritually mature will humble their hearts during harsh times. May I challenge you to read Hebrews 12:5–11, slowly and aloud? Think through the proper response of God's children to His painful discipline. It's best to work through a biblical perspective on suffering before the storm hits rather than scrambling to think through this issue in the midst of chaos and confusion.

Finally, we need to remember that *God won't stop until His plan is accomplished.* This is a hard lesson to accept—and even harder to live through. The sad reality of the first four trumpet judgments is that they are only the beginning. In our own lives, we can choose to heed the warnings of God's Word, or we can harden our hearts. Either way, God eventually will work out His plan, which is our sanctification (1 Thess. 4:3). Has God impressed on you a plan that you've been resisting? Stop! Instead, ask the Lord to soften the stubbornness of your heart toward His purposes and to conform you to His will. Only when God's purpose is accomplished will you receive His peace and a reprieve.

Releasing Demons from the Abyss (Revelation 9:1-12)

---

¹Then the fifth angel sounded, and I saw a star from heaven which had fallen to the earth; and the key of the bottomless pit was given to him. ²He opened the bottomless pit, and smoke went up out of the pit, like the smoke of a great furnace; and the sun and the air were darkened by the smoke of the pit. ³Then out of the smoke came locusts upon the earth, and power was given them, as the scorpions of the earth have power. ⁴They were told not to hurt the grass of the earth, nor any green thing, nor any tree, but only the men who do not have the seal of God on their foreheads. ⁵And they were not permitted to kill anyone, but to torment for five months; and their torment was like the torment of a scorpion when it stings a man. ⁶And in those days men will seek death and will not find it; they will long to die, and death flees from them.

⁷The appearance of the locusts was like horses prepared for battle; and on their heads appeared to be crowns like gold, and their faces were like the faces of men. ⁸They had hair like the hair of women, and their teeth were like *the teeth* of lions. ⁹They had breastplates like breastplates of iron; and the sound of their wings was like the sound of chariots, of many horses rushing to battle. ¹⁰They have tails like scorpions, and stings; and in their

tails is their power to hurt men for five months. ¹¹They have as king over
them, the angel of the abyss; his name in Hebrew is Abaddon, and in the
Greek he has the name Apollyon.

¹²The first woe is past; behold, two woes are still coming after these things.

An invisible war rages. The warriors strike unsuspecting victims without warning, afflicting them at their weakest moments. Their insidious attacks leave individuals and families reeling in pain and heartache. This war has been rumbling
for centuries—even millennia. I'm not referring to political battles over borders
fought between nations and kingdoms. This isn't a social or cultural war against
terrorism, poverty, drugs, or pornography. No, this is spiritual warfare between the
kingdom of darkness and the kingdom of light—and every human is in danger
of imminent attack.

Satan and his demons have been at work tempting and attacking humans since
the infamous sneak attack in the garden of Eden eons ago (Gen. 3). They have never
ceased pursuing their ultimate goals of destroying the dignity of humanity and driving a wedge between humans and their Creator. Revelation 9, however, shows us
that a time will come when the invisible warfare of today will become insignificant
compared to the frontal assault of the enemy's army during the tribulation. As we
study John's vision and observe the armies of darkness battling in the future, we can
better understand how similar spirits of wickedness try to torment us today.

— 9:1–6 —

The dreadful seal judgments unfolded in 6:1–8:6, then the more intense trumpet judgments began to resound through 8:7–11:19. We've examined the first
four already (8:7–13). Now we begin the last three, identified by the three uses
of "woe" in 8:13. The first of these great end-time woes begins to play across the
screen of heaven in chapter 9.

As soon as the fifth angel sounded his trumpet, John watched another star fall
from heaven. The star is often used symbolically in Scripture to refer to a prominent person (Num. 24:17), to Satan (Isa. 14:12–17), to angelic beings (Job 38:7),
to human leaders of churches (Rev. 1:20), or even to Christ, the "bright morning
star" (22:16). Some understand the star in this passage to be Satan falling from
heaven.[8] But it could simply be a high-ranking angel given authority over the abyss.

The terms "abyss" and "bottomless" in 9:1–2, 11 come from the same Greek
word, *abyssos*. In biblical writings, *abyssos* means "depth" or "underworld."[9] It can
refer to the physical depths of the earth (Gen. 7:11) or to the dwelling place of

Mori Chen/AP Images

Swarming locusts

departed spirits awaiting release or judgment (Rom. 10:7; cf. Eph. 4:8–10; 1 Pet. 3:19). Apparently, the abyss is also the place where certain demons have been kept in prison until judgment (Luke 8:30–31; cf. 2 Peter 2:4). Given the context of the end-time judgments, it appears that the opening of the abyss in Revelation 9 forecasts a short-term release of demons prior to their final condemnation in the lake of fire (20:14–15; cf. Matt. 25:41).

When the door of the abyss swung open, smoke spewed forth, darkening the sun and blackening the sky (9:2), and a swarm of insect-like creatures emerged from the smoke. John calls them simply "locusts" (9:3), though when he describes them in more detail in verses 7–10, we realize these are like no locusts any human has ever seen. Remember, John was using words and images of his world as he attempted to describe spiritual realities that have no direct parallels. So when John says he saw a swarm of locusts, *don't think Jiminy Cricket!*

Because of their shocking capacity for devastation, locust swarms were greatly feared in biblical times. Entire regions—including essential crops—could be stripped by a locust plague: "Areas up to 1000 sq. km. (400 sq. mi.) can be covered by locust swarms, which leave a barren, denuded landscape in their wake. It is easy to see why the locust is identified as one of biblical man's greatest calamities."[10] The locusts from the abyss in 9:3, however, were far worse than normal locusts. These creatures were able to sting their victims like scorpions.

We can marvel at the overwhelming number and startling appearance of these supernatural locusts, but we shouldn't miss the limitations placed on them. First, note that their power will be "given" to them (9:3). The word "power" (*exousia*) means "authority" or "permission." It may appear at first that this swarm is completely out of control, but we must remember that they can do nothing apart from God's permission.

Second, they will not be permitted to harm the things locusts usually devour — vegetation, crops, or grass (9:4). These aren't your average hungry locusts! Their target will not be plants but people.

Third, though they will be told to harm humans, they can inflict their torment only on certain people — "men who do not have the seal of God on their foreheads" (9:4). This recalls the remnant of Israel, sealed for protection in 7:2–3. Those saints will be spared from the suffering inflicted by the locusts.

Fourth, they will be given authority to torment, not to kill (9:5). This torment will be similar to the torment of a scorpion sting — excruciating, burning, even debilitating, but in this case, not deadly.

Finally, God will place a limit of five months on their mission of torment (9:5). Yet in that five months the physical, mental, emotional, and spiritual agony these people will suffer will drive them mad. Some of the most haunting words in all of Scripture describe the desperate situation: "And in those days men will seek death and will not find it; they will long to die, and death flees from them" (9:6).

— 9:7–12 —

John describes the locusts in greater detail in verses 7–10. Ponder the analogies he uses:

Like horses prepared for battle (9:7)
Crowns like gold on their heads (9:7)
Humanlike faces (9:7)
Hair like women (9:8)
Teeth like lions (9:8)
Breastplates like iron (9:9)
Sound of wings like horses and chariots (9:9)
Tails like scorpions (9:10)

What a monstrous sight! Note the repeated word "like," warning us not to take this description completely literally. John was using the vocabulary available to him in order to describe something virtually indescribable. Based on the symbolic picture of these locusts, however, we can draw a general description of their character. They will be warlike, brutal, and fierce. Unstoppable, they will pursue without flinching their purpose of torment. They are intelligent creatures, perhaps even alluring, utilizing deception and persuasion to attract people. In the end, however, their goal will be to torture, to tear apart, and to destroy.

Clearly, the "locusts" are spiritual, demonic creatures, not literal earthly animals. They aren't members of the insect kingdom, but supernatural soldiers in the kingdom of darkness. The symbolic descriptions John saw were meant to communicate ferocity, aggression, power, and intelligence. In fact, John also mentioned that this army of wicked spirits will be led by a "king" (9:11). Known as "the angel of the abyss," his name in Hebrew is *Abaddon,* and in the Greek he has the name *Apollyon.* Both of these words mean "Destroyer."

Though some scholars identify this demonic ruler of the abyss as Satan himself, this doesn't seem likely. Satan's abode is not in the abyss—at least not until he is cast into that bottomless pit at the end of the tribulation (Rev. 20:1–3). By contrast, this king's authority seems limited to the demonic hoard from the abyss itself. So who is this "angel of the abyss"? We cannot be dogmatic, but he's probably a high-ranking lieutenant of Satan who will do his dark lord's bidding.[11]

In any case, at the close of this frightening vision, John gives this ominous warning: "The first woe is past; behold, two woes are still coming after these things" (9:12). Though the release of the demons is unspeakably dreadful, something even worse is coming.

Application

Treading on Serpents and Scorpions

During His earthly ministry, Jesus gave authority to seventy of His followers to preach, to heal, and to cast out demons (Luke 10:1–16). Upon returning from their "short-term mission," they exclaimed, "Lord, even the demons are subject to us in Your name" (10:17). After acknowledging that their ministry of spiritual warfare had caused Satan to fall from his stronghold in the heavenly realm (10:18), Jesus said to them: "Behold, I have given you authority to tread on serpents and scorpions, and over all the power of the enemy, and nothing will injure you. Nevertheless do not rejoice in this, that the spirits are subject to you, but rejoice that your names are recorded in heaven" (10:19–20).

Obviously, none of those "seventy" are around today. We don't have that same bestowal of Christ's authority as they did during His earthly ministry. This doesn't mean, however, that we are helpless victims in the face of demonic attack. In fact, Paul clearly states that we are armored and armed for spiritual battle against forces of wickedness in heavenly places (Eph. 6:11–17). So, in light of the reality of our own spiritual warfare, how does the five-month demonic attack of the future tribulation relate to us? I can think of four important ways that these verses inform our own situation.

First, *we must remember that although they are invisible, demons are real and aggressive.* Not all demons are confined to the abyss (see Luke 8:31). Countless spirits of wickedness roam freely, and so long as they do, they are in search-and-destroy mode. They'll pounce at any opportunity to strike both believers and unbelievers. Sometimes we'd rather pretend that these beings don't exist or that they are so limited in power that we don't need to worry about them. Not true! Ignorance of our enemies gives them an advantage over us. Don't be naïve!

Second, *we are reminded that demons are organized and committed to our destruction.* Like a battle-hardened army, Satan's forces know how to wage an efficient war to conquer the hearts and minds of all people. From subtle tricks to a full-blown spiritual Blitzkrieg, they are ready to use whatever means necessary to win. Take a close look at 1 Peter 5:8. How can you be more "sober" and "alert" in light of this warning? Peter gives us some hints in 1:13–16. In light of this passage, are you prepared for inevitable spiritual attacks?

Third, *we should be encouraged that although these demons are powerful, they have limitations.* We see that even during the tribulation these wicked angels can do only what they are allowed to do. Today—in the age of the Spirit's restraining power through the church—their abilities are even more limited (2 Thess. 2:6–8). But don't underestimate the deceptive and destructive powers of the enemy (Jude 8–10). As soon as we drop our guards, we're doomed. We can't neglect our spiritual lives, forsake our assembling with other believers, or trust in our own strength.

Finally, *we must never forget that these aggressive and insidious creatures flee at the name of the Lord Jesus Christ.* At His matchless name they cower in fear, run for cover, and scramble for survival. With a single syllable of rebuke, Jesus Christ can flatten Satan's entire army. They are no match for Him (Luke 8:26–31). Let Christ handle your spiritual battles for you. Submit to Him. Release all your anxieties to Him through prayer (1 Peter 5:6–7). Resting in Christ, resist the devil in faith and trust that He alone can shut the mouth of the roaring lion and quench the flaming arrows of the evil one.

Be encouraged! Through Christ we can be victors over the forces of darkness, not victims of their evil schemes.

Demons, Death, and Defiance
(Revelation 9:13–21)

> [13]Then the sixth angel sounded, and I heard a voice from the four horns of the golden altar which is before God, [14]one saying to the sixth angel who had the trumpet, "Release the four angels who are bound at the great river Euphrates." [15]And the four angels, who had been prepared for the hour and day and month and year, were released, so that they would kill a third of mankind. [16]The number of the armies of the horsemen was two hundred million; I heard the number of them. [17]And this is how I saw in the vision the horses and those who sat on them: *the riders* had breastplates *the color* of fire and of hyacinth and of brimstone; and the heads of the horses are like the heads of lions; and out of their mouths proceed fire and smoke and brimstone. [18]A third of mankind was killed by these three plagues, by the fire and the smoke and the brimstone which proceeded out of their mouths. [19]For the power of the horses is in their mouths and in their tails; for their tails are like serpents and have heads, and with them they do harm.
>
> [20]The rest of mankind, who were not killed by these plagues, did not repent of the works of their hands, so as not to worship demons, and the idols of gold and of silver and of brass and of stone and of wood, which can neither see nor hear nor walk; [21]and they did not repent of their murders nor of their sorceries nor of their immorality nor of their thefts.

When did you last worship an idol?

I'm not talking about the glimmering gold, silver, or bronze statues made to look like beautiful gods or goddesses. I don't mean grotesque wooden or stone gargoyle-like figures often unearthed by archaeologists. I'm pretty sure most of us don't make a habit of offering incense at the graves of dead ancestors or bow down before their bones or ashes. Though some cultures and religions around the world engage in these more explicit practices, if you're reading this, chances are you're not from one of those traditions — but that doesn't mean you're off the hook!

Even though most of us may never kiss relics or exalt effigies, we're all sometimes guilty of idolatry. Consider the following description of idolatry in our culture:

> Idolatry in our society is not so obvious but is just as real as it was in John's day. By definition idolatry is turning an earthly thing into a god and worshiping it rather than the God of creation. Whatever we place ahead of God in our lives is our idol. Therefore, the modern world is replete with idols: money, possessions, power, pleasure, sex, success, fame, drugs. These are all tools of Satan, and there are countless stories in which these very things have tortured and killed those who pursue them. We must warn people of the cosmic powers in control of this secular world and call them to God.[12]

If we understand idolatry as an issue of the heart, we can honestly confess that all of us constantly struggle with temptations toward idolatry. Unbridled ambition, pride, and arrogance turn our full devotion from God toward something else, and that something else is usually the unholy trinity of Me, Myself, and I. Most people who become wrapped up in the things of this world—material possessions, people, fame, and fortune—never realize that they follow a path that leads to a hardened heart and a rejection of God. This slippery slope of idolatry can end only in discipline or judgment. A rejection of God leads to a godless lifestyle, which results in either discipline from a loving heavenly Father (if you're one of His children) or the deserved wrath from a righteous divine Judge.

The book of Revelation describes God's wrath coming on the inhabitants of the world because of their rejection of God and their idolatrous self-indulgence. We might expect that the increasingly severe judgments and constant opportunities for repentance throughout the tribulation would result in a massive revival. As the intensity of judgment grows, however, we get a clearer picture of the hardness and depravity of the human heart. In Jeremiah 17:9 we read, "The heart is more deceitful than all else and is desperately sick; who can understand it?" The answer to this enigma comes in the next verse: "I, the LORD, search the heart, I test the mind, even to give to each man according to his ways, according to the results of his deeds."

—9:13–15—

At the sounding of the fifth trumpet, we witnessed the opening of the abyss and the release of tormenting demons swarming the earth like locusts, driving people mad. Then, at the blast of the sixth trumpet, John described four angels of death who had been held captive near the Euphrates River in modern day Iraq. When they were released, all of the forces of hell broke loose across the face of the earth. Step by grueling step, the restraining grace of God was removed from the world, allowing Satan, his demons, and sinful humans to destroy the earth—and each other.

Note that this scene of judgment centers on a particular part of the world—what we today call the Middle East. For somebody reading the book of Revelation in, say, colonial America in the seventeenth century, that might be a little surprising. They might have felt tempted to interpret such a statement allegorically. But we who live in the twenty-first century shouldn't be surprised that much of the book of Revelation seems to center on Israel and its surrounding nations. In fact, for nearly the last one hundred years, many Bible students have viewed the Middle

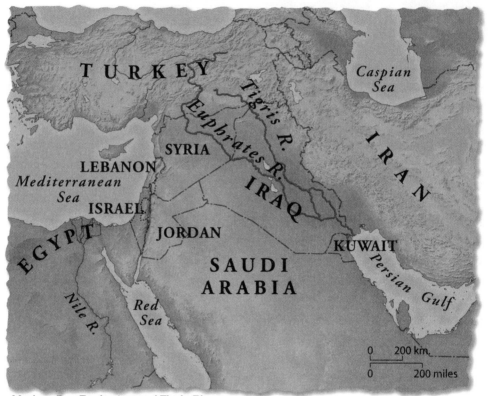

Modern Day Euphrates and Tigris Rivers

East as a ticking time bomb, ready to explode and move the whole world into the end times at any moment.

I'm not trying to sound like a sensationalist, because the "times and seasons" of the end are in God's hands alone. He can bring them tomorrow or centuries from now. Still, I want to take the Bible at face value. Let it say what it says. If it says "the great river Euphrates," we should have in mind no river but the one that flows right through the heart of the Middle East. Both the Tigris and the Euphrates River originate in modern-day Turkey. The Euphrates snakes through Syria, flows straight through the center of Iraq, and then joins the Tigris before emptying into the Persian Gulf.

The four angels released at the Euphrates River are never identified either as angels of heaven or wicked demons (9:14). Most likely, these are four high-ranking fallen angels that figure prominently among the demonic hoard of Satan's emissaries. They may well be the invisible influences behind four ungodly nations in power during the future tribulation period. Demonic "principalities" and "powers" have stood behind world leaders throughout history.

Daniel 10 gives us a glimpse of the kind of spiritual warfare that occurs in the invisible realm. Daniel learned that an angelic messenger had fought against the "prince of Persia" in order to deliver his message to Daniel. He then stated that the archangel Michael had come to his aid (10:13). He also mentioned the "Prince of Greece" (10:20) as another spiritual power. Similarly, Ezekiel 28 may refer to both the human ruler of Tyre (28:1) and the invisible spiritual "king of Tyre" (28:12)—perhaps even Satan himself—who gave the human leader his power and authority.

So, in Revelation 9, the four angels bound at the Euphrates may be the spiritual powers of wickedness that stand behind four nations who will oppose God and His people during the coming tribulation.[13] Though their power to influence the world may be limited today, during the tribulation the divine restraints will be lifted.

Let's not forget that their release will follow God's timetable. They cannot move their human puppet rulers to action until the exact moment God allows. Though they serve their master, Satan, they cannot act apart from the sovereign permission of God. In fact, God has planned their release for a specific "hour and day and month and year" (9:15). Never think that life is merely a series of haphazard events tossed into the air by blind fate for us mortals to catch or dodge! On the contrary, we can rest in the confidence that whatever comes our way is known not only by our all-knowing, omnipotent God, but it is directed by Him according to His good purposes. As we read in Romans 8:28, "We know that God causes all things to work together for good to those who love God, to those who are called according to His purpose." As we'll soon see, those things that work together for the good of God's elect do not always mean the good of everybody.

When the angels of death are released, they go out to kill a third of humanity (9:15). Verse 18 reveals that they will succeed. Don't run past this figure too quickly! A third of humanity today is over two billion people! Don't forget that by this time many people on earth have already suffered destruction in which a quarter of the earth's population had been decimated (6:8). No wonder God has actively restrained these wicked angels for so many centuries! Second Peter 3:9 declares, "The Lord is not slow about His promise, as some count slowness, but is patient toward you, not wishing for any to perish but for all to come to repentance." God's gracious disposition toward the world staves off the relentless wrath of the forces of evil, but when this present window of opportunity for repentance closes, a dark cloud of wrath will quickly close in. The several verses fill in the details of how this holocaust will be accomplished.

— **9:16–19** —

John first mentioned the number of an army commissioned to carry out the deadly intentions of the four angels of death. Here we have the largest number in the Bible—200 million! The number of these soldiers sounds barely believable today. Just imagine hearing a number that large in a world with a population drastically less than our own. Yet John clearly heard the number (9:16).[14] Before we start adding up the population of China or India and pondering the logistics of transporting 200 million of anything from Asia to the Middle East, however, let's take a closer look at the context. These are the armies of the four angelic beings who had just been released from the Euphrates (9:15). The 200 million strong army is responsible for carrying out the four angels' bloody mission (9:18).

John described the "armies of the horsemen" in some detail, using the best analogies he could muster from his own day. They are unlike any cavalry the world has ever seen (9:17). Though the horses' heads looked more like the heads of lions, John mentioned nothing remarkable about the riders themselves except for the color of their armor. The three colors on the riders' breastplates matched the

Breastplate Colors	Three Plagues
Fiery red or orange	Fire
Deep hyacinth blue	Smoke
Sulfuric yellow	Brimstone

color of the "plagues" that proceeded from the mouths of their horses (9:17). These plagues will be responsible for the death of a third of humankind (9:18). Not only did the horses' lion heads have power to inflict this carnage, but John said, "Their tails are like serpents and have heads, and with them they do harm" (9:19).

Some commentators have tried desperately to identify this grotesque image with modern or futuristic weapons like helicopters, tanks, or fighter jets. But because these creatures are identified as the armies of the four wicked angels of the Euphrates, it seems most reasonable to conclude that they are symbols for an army of demons unleashed to bring death and destruction upon the inhabitants of the world.

This is now the second demon-inspired attack on the human race. The first was by means of a swarm of locusts, but they were not permitted to kill anyone during the five months of their torment (9:5). In contrast, this next wave of demonic

From My Journal

Finding God's Way in the Storm

Blow that layer of dust off the prophetic book of Nahum in your Bible and catch a glimpse of the last part of 1:3: "In whirlwind and storm is His way."

That's good to remember when you're caught in a rip-snortin' Texas frog-strangler as I was some years back. I nudged myself to remember God's presence as the rain-heavy, charcoal clouds hemorrhaged in eerie, aerial explosions of saw-toothed lightning and ear-shattering thunder. Witnessing that atmospheric drama, I reminded myself of its Director, who was, once again, having "His way … in the whirlwind and the storm." I took the Texas highway through Weatherford, Cisco, Abilene, and Sweetwater. There was no doubt that the Lord, the God of the heavens, was "in the storm" across west Texas. Nature never lets you ignore her Master.

But life has its own storms—hurricanes that descend from blue sun-filled skies or clear starry nights. What about the whirlwinds of disease, disaster, and death? Or the storms of interruptions, irritations, and inconveniences? If Nahum's words apply to the heavenly sphere, do they also apply to the earthly? Surely if God's way is in the murky, threatening sky, He's also in the difficult, heart-straining contingencies of daily life. The Director of the heavenly and earthly theaters is One and the same. The cast may be different, the plot may be altered, the props may be rearranged, but just offstage stands the Head, the Chief—overseeing every act, every scene, every line.

It would take several volumes much bulkier that this one to list the God-appointed whirlwinds and storms I've personally endured in my Christian walk. They affected not only me, but also my wife, my now-grown children, and my grandkids, as well as siblings, lifelong friends, church members, and colleagues. I can't help but sigh as these episodes roll through my memories. But two things comfort me as I ponder the storms. First, these squalls surge across *everyone's* horizon. God is not picking on me. There's no dark raincloud following me around while others have nothing but sunny days. It may occasionally appear that way, but take a closer look and you'll see that everybody goes through dizzying cyclones from time to time.

Second, I remind myself that as much as we dislike the storms, we all *need* them. God has no other method more effective at getting the attention of these hard hearts of ours. The massive blows and shattering blasts (not to mention the little, constant irritations) smooth us, humble us, and compel us to submit to *His* script and bow before *His* chosen role for our lives.

attack will be granted the ability to kill. It may be that these demons will inflict their plagues directly or they may use earthly means to do so. They may inspire armies of various Middle Eastern nations or a certain nation's military divisions. We can't be certain about the meaning of these visions. Yet the big picture remains clear: as the tribulation proceeds, the judgments will increase in severity.

Tragic images fill our minds as we try to imagine the chaos, confusion, grief, and shock that will sweep the globe at that time. Humans will completely forget previous natural disasters, military strikes, and terrorist attacks in light of these unparalleled events. Considering that a fourth of humankind will be killed during the fourth seal judgment (6:7–8) and another third will be lost in the massive army in the sixth trumpet judgment (9:13–19), we can estimate that over half the world's population will be sent to meet their Creator and Judge by that time. Many people, however, will survive this onslaught. What will happen to those who live through it? How will they respond? Surely they will turn to their righteous Redeemer in repentance for their wickedness … *right*?

— 9:20–21 —

Perhaps more disturbing than the death and destruction just depicted is the reaction of the survivors of these plagues in the next two verses. I can hardly bear to read them.

We would love to imagine that the unbelieving world will see the supernatural events, hear the cataclysmic disasters, and finally heed the preaching of the 144,000 missionaries who passionately call for repentance and faith in Christ. In fact, I wish I could tell you that 9:20–21 declares that the rest of humanity, upon seeing these things, will turn from their wicked ways and acknowledge their righteous Redeemer as Lord and God. Out of love and compassion for the lost, we desperately hope that hardship, calamity, and the fear of death will soften the hearts of men and women devoted to idolatrous false religions. Sadly, John's vision reveals the opposite will occur. One author evaluates this shocking turn of events:

> Those content to give their good days to the devil's service, seldom come to reformation in their evil days. While the pressure of judgment is on them, they may cry, God have mercy! And think to lead a different life; but their vows and prayers vanish with their sorrows, and they are presently where they were before, only the more hardened in their iniquities.[15]

As difficult as it is to believe, most people living during this awful time of judgment will become even more hardened than ever against God. They will stubbornly hold onto their demon worship and idolatry (9:20). They will refuse to repent from murder, sorcery, immorality, and theft (9:21). In short, the survivors of the first several judgments will close their ears to God's message of mercy and grace, choosing instead to accept the wrath that will continue to increase in severity. Hard to believe, isn't it? The great preacher Donald Barnhouse puts 9:13–21 into painful perspective:

> There is no evidence in the Bible; there is no evidence in history; and there is no evidence in prophecy which would indicate that men have ever been brought to God in great numbers through tribulation. One-third of the race may die, but the other two-thirds do not for that reason move toward God. Reluctantly we are forced to accept the verdict, "There is none that understandeth, there is none that seeketh after God" (Rom. 3:11).[16]

Clearly, idolatrous addictions to the world's treasures and pleasures can harden people's hearts to such a degree that the most extreme judgments will be unable to capture the world's attention. But idolatry is not a sin that will enslave only the unsaved during the tribulation. It's a strong temptation for believers of every age, including our own. This truth convinces me that material things in our present generation are slowly calcifying our hearts to the spiritual things of God. Where that is happening, we too need to heed God's warning and repent.

Application

Turning from Dead Idols to the Living God

When we stand beside the apostle John and witness the devastating impact of future judgments through his visions, we discover something utterly astounding about the depths of human depravity. *No matter how extensive human suffering may be, the curse of spiritual depravity remains overwhelming.* Eugene Peterson's loose but vivid translation of 9:20–21 highlights the hardness of the human heart:

> The remaining men and women who weren't killed ... went on their merry way—didn't change their way of life, didn't quit worshiping demons, didn't quit centering their lives around lumps of gold and silver and brass, hunks of stone and wood that couldn't see or hear or move. There wasn't a sign of a change of heart. They plunged right on in their murderous, occult, promiscuous, and thieving ways. (Rev. 9:20–21 The Message)

Idolatry of various forms stands at the heart of humanity's rebellion against God. It leads to greater sin and stronger defiance even in the midst of His obvious judgments and merciful calls to repentance and salvation. Idolatry blinds fallen humanity to the Word of God. We must keep in mind, however, that modern forms of idolatry can negatively affect the lives of believers as well. Dead "idols" can distract us from the living God. Because of the rampant materialism and self-centered egoism in the world today, let's take some time to work through practical questions regarding our own struggles with the powerful temptations in our world.

Read Ephesians 5:5 – 6 and Colossians 3:5 – 6. What types of behavior are associated with idolatry in these passages? What are the ultimate effects of idolatry?

What idols are enshrined in your own life? Complete the following chart to identify some potential or present "idols" that may be wooing you away from single-minded devotion to the one true God. Remember that these things may not be sinful in themselves. As they drive a wedge between us and our Savior, however, they can become destructive to our spiritual growth. Think prayerfully and honestly about these five areas.

Material possessions	
Important people	
Worldly positions	
Uncontrolled passions	
Selfish pursuits	

Consider what specific steps you can take to loosen the stranglehold that these idols have on your life. What relationships do you need to reconsider? What cherished things do you need to remove from your life? What positions do you need to release? What passions need to be restrained? What pursuits need to be stopped? Finally, write a prayer of repentance. Ask your Heavenly Father to forgive you and to free you from any idols that threaten to distract your attention from Him.

A Strong Angel, a Strange Assignment (Revelation 10:1 – 11)

---

¹I saw another strong angel coming down out of heaven, clothed with a cloud; and the rainbow was upon his head, and his face was like the sun, and his feet like pillars of fire; ²and he had in his hand a little book which was open. He placed his right foot on the sea and his left on the land;

³and he cried out with a loud voice, as when a lion roars; and when he had cried out, the seven peals of thunder uttered their voices. ⁴When the seven peals of thunder had spoken, I was about to write; and I heard a voice from heaven saying, "Seal up the things which the seven peals of thunder have spoken and do not write them." ⁵Then the angel whom I saw standing on the sea and on the land lifted up his right hand to heaven, ⁶and swore by Him who lives forever and ever, who created heaven and the things in it, and the earth and the things in it, and the sea and the things in it, that there will be delay no longer, ⁷but in the days of the voice of the seventh angel, when he is about to sound, then the mystery of God is finished, as He preached to His servants the prophets.

⁸Then the voice which I heard from heaven, *I heard* again speaking with me, and saying, "Go, take the book which is open in the hand of the angel who stands on the sea and on the land." ⁹So I went to the angel, telling him to give me the little book. And he said to me, "Take it and eat it; it will make your stomach bitter, but in your mouth it will be sweet as honey." ¹⁰I took the little book out of the angel's hand and ate it, and in my mouth it was sweet as honey; and when I had eaten it, my stomach was made bitter. ¹¹And they said to me, "You must prophesy again concerning many peoples and nations and tongues and kings."

Epic stories affect us at an emotional level, where the impact and meaning go beyond what mere words can describe. They draw us in to a dramatic narrative. We are swept up by the action, become a victim of the conflict, or share the conquest with the hero. Some of the greatest novels and movies of our day—though fictional—illustrate powerful truths about humanity, redemption, grace, and justice. They portray heroism, illuminate struggle, and resonate with real emotions.

Christian author John Eldredge notes three truths that surface in every good story, including God's true story of creation and redemption:

- Things are not what they seem.
- This is a world at war.
- We have a crucial role to play.[17]

Undoubtedly, the book of Revelation tells a compelling drama in which we can recognize each of the three elements of a great story. First, *things are not what they seem.* Although we dwell in a physical reality, an unseen realm also exists, which influences our everyday lives. This spiritual realm will become increasingly more "visible" in the future.

Second, *this is a world at war.* Since the devil's successful temptation of Adam and Eve in the garden of Eden (Gen. 3), the battle has continued. It has affected not only human history; it will one day engulf the whole world in deception and destruction.

This leads to the third element of the book of Revelation: *we have a crucial role to play*. This battleground is no place for embedded reporters or remote observers. Like it or not, our very presence on earth as members of God's redeemed people demands our full-throttle participation.

Though Revelation tells the true story of how God vanquishes wickedness and brings ultimate victory for the righteous, its intensifying images of judgment can feel overwhelming even for the "victors." God does, however, provide a few necessary interludes along the way. Each brief intermission allows the reader to pause,

Revelation's Series of Sevens with Interludes

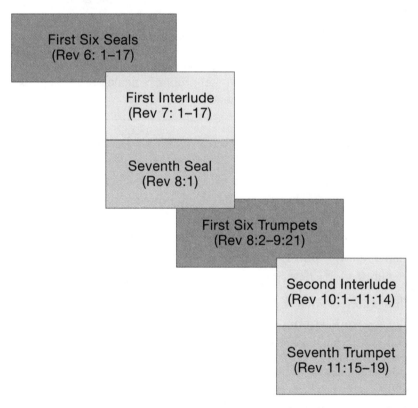

First Six Seals
(Rev 6: 1–17)

First Interlude
(Rev 7: 1–17)

Seventh Seal
(Rev 8:1)

First Six Trumpets
(Rev 8:2–9:21)

Second Interlude
(Rev 10:1–11:14)

Seventh Trumpet
(Rev 11:15–19)

take stock of what has happened, and prepare for what is to come. The first interlude between the sixth and seventh seals revealed two groups of redeemed believers who will be saved during the tribulation (ch. 7). Beginning in Revelation 10, a second interlude interrupts the sequence between the sixth and seventh trumpets. In this interlude, we see a change of emphasis from the outpouring of wrath on unbelievers to the consolation and encouragement of believers. At the same time, the apostle John is recommissioned for the second half of his prophetic role.

—10:1–4—

At the sounding of the fifth and sixth trumpets, John witnessed several powerful wicked angels leading armies that inflicted unparalleled torment and destruction—the "angel of the abyss" heading up an army of demons permitted to torment the unrepentant (9:11) and four angels of death bent on destroying a third of humanity (9:15). While the horrific sights and sounds of these wicked angels and their demonic throngs still impress themselves upon our minds, a strong angel from heaven suddenly injected himself into the scene (10:1).

The appearance of this great angel was so magnificent that he made the previous wicked angels look plain by comparison. Clothed with a cloud, a face shining like the sun, feet like pillars of fire—all these things reaffirm his heavenly origin. A rainbow crowns his head, perhaps indicating God's covenant of mercy with humanity in Genesis 9:13–16, in which the Creator promised never to destroy all flesh with a flood. The character of God hasn't changed from the days of Noah. His grace and mercy endure even in the midst of judgment.

This strong angel stood on both land and sea and held a "little book" open in his hand (10:2). When the angel cried out with a voice like a roaring lion, seven thunders spoke (10:3). Perhaps these thunderous voices originated from the cloud that engulfed the angel. Clearly they were audible voices with a clear message. But a voice from heaven explicitly instructed John to "seal up" the words of the seven thunders, keeping them shrouded in mystery (10:4). One day in heaven we may learn what they said, but until then, we can only assume it must have been a frightful message of judgment.

—10:5–7—

Similar to our own custom of swearing an oath in court by placing our right hand on the Bible and raising our left, the strong angel lifted up his right hand and "swore by Him who lives forever and ever" (10:5–6). God the Creator, who made heaven, earth, and sea, received an oath that there would no longer be any delay (10:6). The angel swore that the sounding of the seventh trumpet would rapidly bring an end to the mystery of God (10:7).

What is the "mystery of God . . . as He preached to His servants the prophets"? John Walvoord explains this cryptic phrase:

> This mystery had been previously announced to God's prophets. The reference, therefore, is not to hidden truth but to the fulfillment of many Old Testament passages which refer to the glorious return of the Son of God and the establishment of His kingdom of righteousness and peace on the earth. While God's purposes are not necessarily revealed in current events where Satan is allowed power and manifestation, the time will come when Satan no longer will be in power and the predictions of the Old Testament prophets will be fulfilled.[18]

At this point it would be wise to recall 6:10, when the tribulation martyrs cried out, "How long, O Lord, holy and true, will You refrain from judging and avenging our blood on those who dwell on the earth?" The mighty angel of Revelation 10 announces that God's response to those prayers will soon come to an end. The final number of the redeemed will be fulfilled and the judgment of the wicked will be complete.

—10:8–11—

As the great angel fell silent, the booming voice from heaven spoke again. This time the voice gave John a strange but significant assignment: take the book from the hand of the strong angel and eat it (10:8–9). The angel warned John that the book would taste sweet in his mouth but make his stomach sour—a heavenly recipe for "sweet and sour scroll"! By this time in his life John had learned to obey instantly even the strangest commands of the Lord, so he did exactly as he was told (10:10).

This isn't the first time one of God's prophets was told to eat a scroll. In Ezekiel 2:8–3:4, we read the following interesting exchange between God and the prophet Ezekiel:

> "Now you, son of man, listen to what I am speaking to you; do not be rebellious like that rebellious house. Open your mouth and eat what I am giving you." Then I looked, and behold, a hand was extended to me; and lo, a scroll was in it. When He spread it out before me, it was written on the front and back, and written on it were lamentations, mourning and woe.
>
> Then He said to me, "Son of man, eat what you find; eat this scroll, and go, speak to the house of Israel." So I opened my mouth, and He fed me this scroll. He said to me, "Son of man, feed your stomach and fill your body with this scroll which I am giving you." Then I ate it, and it was sweet as honey in my mouth.

Then He said to me, "Son of man, go to the house of Israel and speak with My words to them."

The consumption of the scroll was a symbol of complete appropriation of the prophetic message. When Ezekiel opened his mouth, he would utter the very words of God against the people of Israel — words of "lamentations, mourning and woe." In the same way, John was told to fully consume the message of judgment in Revelation 10, a message that made his stomach churn (10:10).

In contrast with Ezekiel's mission to the people of Israel, however, John's mission had a much broader scope. He was to "prophesy again concerning many peoples and nations and tongues and kings" (10:11). This recommissioning of John marks a watershed in the book of Revelation. From this point on the judgments would become decidedly more severe.

The brief interlude in Revelation 10 reinforces the fact that things in this world are not what they seem. Believers know there's a war going on and that at any moment the sporadic attacks and brief skirmishes in the battle between good and evil will erupt into the worst spiritual and physical conflict in history. Yet God emphasizes another truth in Revelation 10. The apostle John had a crucial role to play — proclaiming the mystery of God to "many peoples and nations and tongues and kings" (10:11).

Just like John, we have roles to play in God's ultimate plan. We can't call ourselves "apostles," and we don't receive literal visions and revelations from God. We're not required to swallow prophetic books to utter inspired words. But each of us has been given a crucial mission to share the good news of salvation with the world (Matt. 28:19–20). Yet just like John, we must first internalize the message, allowing it to become a part of our own lives.

It's true that the gospel of Jesus Christ involves both bad news and good news — bad news about lost humans subject to divine judgment, but good news about the righteous Redeemer, Jesus Christ, who paid the complete penalty for us and saves us when we simply trust in Him. As ambassadors for Christ in this age, we must not only understand and accept the gospel ourselves, but we must also be able to communicate that message to others.

Have you accepted God's commission on your life?

Or, like John, are you ready for a recommissioning from God?

NOTES: Judgments of the Righteous Redeemer (Revelation 8:1–10:11

1. C. S. Lewis, *The Problem of Pain* (New York: Macmillan, 1962), 93.

2. For the various uses of the trumpet in the Old and New Testaments, see Osborne, *Revelation*, 342–43.

3. Douglas and Tenney, eds., *The New International Dictionary of the Bible*, 465.

4. John Phillips, *Exploring Revelation* (rev. ed.; Chicago: Moody Press, 1987), 118.

5. Ibid.

6. Some have suggested a contradiction between the burning of "all the green grass" in 8:7 and the reappearance of grass in 9:4. Two answers are possible. The word "all" in 8:7 may be limited to all the grass in the areas affected by the judgment. For example, "the prayers of *all* the saints" in 8:3 probably doesn't refer to the prayers of every saint who ever lived, but probably to the prayers of the saints under the altar in 6:10. Nevertheless, we can also take "all" as referring literally to all grass on the earth. If this is the case, we must remember that many types of grass quickly regrow after a fire. Because the fifth trumpet judgment itself lasts five months, we can assume that during this time much of the vegetation—including trees and grass—begins to grow again.

7. Douglas and Tenney, eds., *The New International Dictionary of the Bible*, 806.

8. Walvoord, "Revelation," *The Bible Knowledge Commentary*, 952.

9. Bauer and Danker, eds., *A Greek-English Lexicon of the New Testament*, 2.

10. G. L. Keown, "Locust," in *The International Standard Bible Encyclopedia*, 3:358.

11. See Osborne, *Revelation*, 373.

12. Ibid., 388.

13. Today the nations directly associated with the Euphrates River are Turkey, Syria, and Iraq. We can't be sure what nations will exist in the future, but it may be that political borders before or during the tribulation will change. It is also possible that the four angelic beings mentioned in 9:14 do not directly correspond to four future nations, but to four human rulers of the future who have a direct influence on nations of that region. Another possibility may be that they correspond to the angelic rulers of past nations who had exercised control over that region—Babylon, Medo-Persia, Greece, and Rome.

14. The Greek number here is *dismyriades myriadōn* (lit., "two myriads of myriads," or "twenty thousand of ten thousands"). Greek scholars generally agree that in the ancient world numbers this large focused less on the literal figure and more on the vastness of the multitude. One Greek lexicon defines the phrase as "an indefinitely large number ... countless, incalculable" (Johannes E. Louw and Eugene A. Nida, eds., *Greek-English Lexicon of the New Testament Based on Semantic Domains*, vol. 1, *Introduction and Domains* [2nd ed.; New York: United Bible Societies, 1988], § 60.9). Without allegorizing or taking this passage "spiritually," it should be recognized that John intended to relay the meaning, "a vast, incalculable number." However, scholars also acknowledge that the number may be literal.

15. J. A. Seiss, *The Apocalypse: Lectures on the Book of Revelation* (6th reprint ed.; Grand Rapids: Zondervan, 1966), 221.

16. Donald Grey Barnhouse, *Revelation: An Expositional Commentary* (Grand Rapids: Zondervan, 1971), 177.

17. John Eldredge, *Waking the Dead: The Glory of a Heart Fully Alive* (Nashville: Nelson, 2003), 26–34.

18. Walvoord, "Revelation," *The Bible Knowledge Commentary*, 954.

RIVALS OF THE SOVEREIGN LORD (REVELATION 11:1–13:18)

In theatrical productions, intermissions often give stagehands a chance to rearrange the set in preparation for a change of scenery, a new perspective in the play, or a sudden twist in the storyline. In the apostle John's vivid portrayal of end-time events, interludes function in the same way. After assimilating the prophetic scroll of coming judgments (10:9–10), John continued to record the amazing things he saw and heard. This transitional interlude continues into chapter 11, but this time we shift our point of view.

Let's call the fourth movement in the story of Revelation "Rivals of the Sovereign Lord" (11:1–13:18). Following John's recommissioning in chapter 10, the perspective of the great drama shifts from heavenly wrath to earthly conditions—particularly future events that will concentrate world attention on the Promised Land. The initial scene begins with the embattled ministry of two chosen witnesses prophesying in Jerusalem. It culminates in their tragic execution and triumphant resurrection (11:1–14). After the seventh trumpet announces the arrival of Christ's kingdom (11:15–19), John will witness a series of visions detailing Satan's final world empire. Through this wicked kingdom, Satan will fiercely oppose Christ, His people, and Almighty God Himself.

In this dramatic portrayal, we witness two tyrants as they take center stage—one political, the other spiritual. Directed by Satan himself, these two brutal dictators will be permitted to rule the world virtually unchecked for three and a half years (12:1–13:18). Yet when humanity appears to be teetering at the brink of total self-destruction, we are reminded that God's sovereignty places clear and firm boundaries on even the most wicked and willful sinners.

Two Fearless, Future Witnesses (Revelation 11:1–14)

---

¹Then there was given me a measuring rod like a staff; and someone said, "Get up and measure the temple of God and the altar, and those who worship in it. ²Leave out the court which is outside the temple and do not measure it, for it has been given to the nations; and they will tread under foot the holy city for forty-two months. ³And I will grant *authority* to my two witnesses, and they will prophesy for twelve hundred and sixty days,

clothed in sackcloth." ⁴These are the two olive trees and the two lamp-stands that stand before the Lord of the earth. ⁵And if anyone wants to harm them, fire flows out of their mouth and devours their enemies; so if anyone wants to harm them, he must be killed in this way. ⁶These have the power to shut up the sky, so that rain will not fall during the days of their prophesying; and they have power over the waters to turn them into blood, and to strike the earth with every plague, as often as they desire.

⁷When they have finished their testimony, the beast that comes up out of the abyss will make war with them, and overcome them and kill them. ⁸And their dead bodies *will lie* in the street of the great city which mystically is called Sodom and Egypt, where also their Lord was crucified. ⁹Those from the peoples and tribes and tongues and nations *will* look at their dead bodies for three and a half days, and will not permit their dead bodies to be laid in a tomb. ¹⁰And those who dwell on the earth *will* rejoice over them and celebrate; and they will send gifts to one another, because these two prophets tormented those who dwell on the earth.

¹¹But after the three and a half days, the breath of life from God came into them, and they stood on their feet; and great fear fell upon those who were watching them. ¹²And they heard a loud voice from heaven saying to them, "Come up here." Then they went up into heaven in the cloud, and their enemies watched them. ¹³And in that hour there was a great earth-quake, and a tenth of the city fell; seven thousand people were killed in the earthquake, and the rest were terrified and gave glory to the God of heaven.

¹⁴The second woe is past; behold, the third woe is coming quickly.

When they come to us in the form of bestselling novels, prime time television, epic poems, or blockbuster movies, the heroes in classic stories tend to follow a common formula. They often portray average individuals who endure and conquer overwhelming adversity at tremendous personal sacrifice in order to accomplish seemingly impossible goals. Think about some of the great films of the last generation—*Star Wars, Rocky, Titanic, Braveheart*—you get the picture. Such tales motivate us to overcome our weaknesses and accomplish great objectives. Enemies attack. Obstacles get hurled into their paths. Tragedies strike. But the heroes of great stories find a secret source of strength beyond themselves. Such strength enables them to vanquish even the most potent adversaries.

When the people are real and the events are true, the story inspires us all the more. Consider the brave men and women of the "Greatest Generation" who sac-rificed their own comfort and even their lives to defeat the forces of evil during World War II. We remember individuals like Corrie Ten Boom, who risked her life to help Jews escape the clutches of the Nazis. In fact, history—especially church

KEY TERMS

ἐξουσία [*exousia*] (1849) "power, authority"

A major theme in Revelation 11–13 is the dramatic transfer of "authority" (*exousia*) from the two witnesses (11:3–13) to the two beasts (13:1–18). The two witnesses will first have absolute authority to call down judgments and perform signs and wonders on the earth (11:6). At the midpoint of the tribulation, however, the beast and the false prophet will receive authority not only to kill the two witnesses, but also to draw all of the world's power to themselves (13:2, 4, 5, 7, 12). This transfer of *exousia* indicates that God will gradually release the world to its own devices as an act of intensifying end-time judgment.

μαρτυρία [*martyria*] (3141) "testimony, witness"

The English word "martyrdom" comes from a Greek term meaning "testimony." By the second century the word began to take on a technical sense of giving one's life for the faith (*Martyrdom of Polycarp* 2.1), but it originally referred to any verbal testimony concerning one's faith in Jesus Christ (Rev. 11:7; 12:11, 17). The scene of the two "witnesses," or "martyrs," in Revelation 11 includes not only proclamation, but also a sealing of their testimony with death. This represents a transition from the first-century to second-century uses of the term *martyria*.

σημεῖον [*sēmeion*] (4592) "sign, distinguishing mark"

Ancient peoples often viewed "signs" in the sky, such as lightning or eclipses, as omens of terrible things to come (Matt. 16:3). The term *sēmeion* could also refer to miraculous feats that pointed to a person's supernatural origin or authority (12:38). In Revelation the term is used to indicate amazing symbolic visions that point to epochal events (Rev. 12:1, 3), but it also refers to false wonders and miracles used by Satan to turn people away from God (13:13–14).

history—is filled with moving stories of saints, mere men and women like you and me, who took a stand for Christ and paid the ultimate price for their courageous convictions. Though their flames were extinguished in their own dark generation, the light of their valor continues to burn brightly.

The book of Revelation also presents us with the story of "underdogs" who stand against overpowering and intimidating forces. John himself stood strong under the persecution of the emperor Domitian (1:9). Members of the early church courageously stood against trials and temptations (2:9–11). Now, in 11:3–14, we'll encounter two end-time prophets, simply called the "two witnesses," who take a stand in the midst of the worst generation in human history.

—11:1–2—

Gripping action scenes in movies often begin with what screenwriters call an "establishing shot"—a distant, wide-angle image of a building, a city, or even a planet. The establishing shot helps to orient the audience to the setting within which the scene will take place. If the establishing shot reveals a building marked "Police Headquarters," you know the tough-looking guy at the desk shuffling papers in the next scene isn't a kindergarten teacher. Or if the camera shows a train rolling into a dusty western town in the middle of a vast prairie, you can guess that the next shot of a cowboy walking down the street isn't going to a costume party. The goal of the establishing shot is to establish *context*. Without context, disorientation and misunderstanding can occur. Revelation 11:1–2 is like a cinematic "establishing shot." It sets the context and tone for the following detailed scene, which helps us better understand the events that follow.

In this establishing shot, John himself is involved in the scene. Presumably an angel handed John a measuring rod—not unlike a modern yardstick. A voice instructed him to measure the temple of God, the altar, and the worshipers (11:1). This may sound like a strange thing to do in the midst of the crossfire of earth-shaking judgments, but remember that John was still licking his lips and rubbing his belly after eating a sweet and sour scroll. Strange assignments seem to have been the order of the day!

At this point we need to pause and consider a less obvious oddity about John's task. John had this vision around the year AD 96. Even though he had been living in a cave for months, he knew as well as any Jew that the temple in Jerusalem had been leveled to the ground by the Romans more than twenty-five years earlier. In fact, when the voice told John to measure God's temple, his first thought could have been, *Temple? What temple?*

Nevertheless, John also knew that prophecies from the Old Testament, the Lord Jesus, and the apostle Paul all pointed to a future temple that would stand during the tribulation. Daniel 9:26–27 mentioned both the destruction of the "city and the sanctuary" (9:26) and a future interruption of apparently reestablished temple worship (9:27; 12:11). Jesus quoted Daniel's prophetic words with reference to the "abomination of desolation" being set up in "the holy place" in Judea (Matt. 24:15–26). Paul was a little more detailed in his description of the same future events when he described the coming Antichrist as "the man of lawlessness ... the son of destruction, who opposes and exalts himself above every so-called god or object of worship, so that he takes his seat in the temple of God, displaying himself as being God" (2 Thess. 2:3–4).

Bible scholar Charles Ryrie suggests that the temple mentioned in Revelation 11:1–2 is "the temple that will be built during the tribulation, in which Jewish

Model of the temple and temple mount in the time of Jesus

worship will be carried on during the first part of that seven-year period and in which, at the midpoint, the man of sin will exalt himself to be worshiped."[1] In other words, the temple will be rebuilt during a time of unparalleled global tension centered in the Middle East. This is probably why John was given a measuring rod—an implement used in construction.

Yet John also was told to leave something out of his measurements—the outer court. The outer court was usually called the "Court of the Gentiles," the closest a non-Jew could get to the temple without falling under the sentence of death. This tells us two things. First, those worshipers at the temple will be far fewer in number than those left out. John was able to quickly measure those within ... but those on the outside were too numerous to count. This serves as an important reminder that God can and does work out His plan through a remnant.

Second, we see that God has set in advance a limit on the time when the nations will be permitted to "tread under foot the holy city." The "forty-two months" here likely refers to the second half of the tribulation period during which the future Antichrist and his False Prophet will reign (see 13:5). As we'll soon see, the end-time regime of that diabolical duo won't come to full power until God has first delivered His last prophetic words through his own duo of divine spokesmen—the two witnesses.

—11:3–6—

Having established the context of Jerusalem and noting that it would be delivered into the hands of God's enemies for forty-two months, John's zoom lens focused on the dynamic ministry of God's two witnesses. God will grant them special authority to prophesy for "twelve hundred and sixty days" in sackcloth—the garb of mourning. Commentators disagree on whether these two witnesses prophesy during the first half, the second half, or the middle of the seven-year tribulation period.[2] It seems doubtful that their ministry will take place during the last half of the tribulation. That would mean the Antichrist, False Prophet, and all their wicked followers will be celebrating and sending gifts in the very last hours of the tribulation while God pours out His wrath (cf. 11:10 with 16:10–11).

The "who" question, however, is far more common than the "when" question. The first thing readers ask when they see these strange two witnesses is, "May I please see some identification?" No one can blame them, since the two witnesses play a prominent role in the chapter and stand at the center of the action in the book of Revelation. Some have identified the witnesses as Moses and Elijah. After all, they already made a cameo appearance during Jesus' transfiguration, discussing Christ's mission in Jerusalem (Luke 9:30). Others have identified the two witnesses as Enoch and Elijah—the only two people in the Old Testament who departed this world without dying physically (Gen. 5:24; 2 Kings 2:11–12; cf. Heb. 11:5). Finally, those who believe that this part of Revelation refers not to future events but to events that occurred in the first century have identified the two witnesses as Peter and Paul, or James and John, or even two high priests killed by the Romans in AD 68![3]

We are given few specifics about these two individuals. We know they will be given authority to prophesy for three and a half years, during which time they will be protected from harm and given special power to call down plagues and judgments on their wicked adversaries (11:3–6). Because the symbols of the two olive trees and two lampstands in 11:4 correspond directly to the symbols representing Zerubbabel and Joshua in Zechariah 4:3–14, it may be that the testimony of the two witnesses will somehow relate to the rebuilding of the temple in Jerusalem. Most importantly, the miraculous authority given to the two witnesses by God is similar to that of Moses, Elijah, and other Old Testament prophets, demonstrating the crucial nature of their ministry during the future tribulation.

In the end, we must exercise prudence and admit that we simply don't know the identity of these two witnesses. To name them goes beyond what is written. We can at least say with confidence that these two figures appear to sum up the kind of miraculous and prophetic ministry that has marked other periods of biblical history. During those periods, God was making epochal changes in His plan or delivering great amounts of new revelation. We can identify five such periods of signs, wonders, and miracles in the Bible.

Periods of Concentrated Signs and Wonders in the Bible

Period	People	Progress
Years of exodus and conquest of the Promised Land	Moses and Joshua	Change from the age of the patriarchs to the age of the law
Days of the wayward kings of Israel and Judah	Elijah and Elisha	The eve of judgment and exile because of unfaithfulness to the Law
Period of exile and captivity in foreign lands	Daniel and friends	Preservation of God's people in exile and preparation for their return
Years of Christ's earthly ministry and the early Church	Jesus and apostles	Change from the Old Testament to the New, birth of the Christian church
Period of the future tribulation	The two witnesses	Judgments leading to the second coming of Christ and His kingdom

— 11:7–12 —

Like all the prophets before them, these two end-time prophets will frustrate their enemies. Invulnerable and unstoppable for the duration of their God-empowered ministries, they will be impervious to assault. Yet when God says, "Mission accomplished," He will lift His hand of protection from them, and their enemies will be permitted to kill them (11:7).

What a startling turn of events! Remember the scroll John ate in the previous scene? It was first sweet like honey in his mouth — like the days of victory experienced by the two witnesses during their ministry. Then the scroll turned sour in John's stomach — like the bitterness of their ultimate defeat at the end of their time of testimony. I find it interesting that the Greek word translated "testimony," *martyria*, is the same root from which we get our English words "martyr" and "martyrdom." Originally, to be a martyr meant to give public testimony about the truth. But that public witness could lead to sealing that testimony with death.

Thus, these two "martyrs" of the future will follow their Savior and countless saints before them in the path of martyrdom for the sake of the gospel of Jesus Christ.

In verse 7 we see the first reference to "the beast" in the book of Revelation. More detailed descriptions of this end-time figure, also called the "Antichrist," will appear in chapters 13 and 17. This coming beast, who will rise to full power at the midpoint of the seven-year tribulation, will be responsible for conquering and killing the two witnesses after their three-and-a-half-year, short-term mission (11:7). Following their deaths, the world's utter contempt for these men will display itself. The populace will leave their bodies in the street of Jerusalem for three and a half days—an utter affront to the Jewish culture, which demands a quick and dignified burial (11:8). On top of that, the whole world will rejoice at the news of their deaths, so tormented were they because of those two prophets (11:10).

Yet the gift-giving merriment and mockery will be suddenly cut short. While the witnesses' enemies will leave their bodies lying in public for all to see, God will step in and raise them to life again after three and a half days (11:11). As their mockers look on in fear, the dead prophets will leap to their feet and ascend to heaven in the sight of all (11:12).

The ministry of the two witnesses will certainly leave a profound mark on the lives of those who witness their exploits. Yet as we examine the lives of those prophets, we see that they will have no basis for personal boasting. Everything that sets them apart—their incredible preservation, their miraculous powers, and their convicting preaching—comes from the sovereign hand of God. When their mission ends, their enabling power ends, too. But God doesn't abandon His vessels like disposable shells. Instead, he will turn tragedy into triumph, whisking His two fearless witnesses into His heavenly presence.

— **11:13–14** —

With the world still gawking at the shocking events of the resurrection and ascension of the two witnesses, the city of Jerusalem will shake violently with an earthquake. This disaster will cause a tenth of the city to collapse, leaving seven thousand people dead (11:13). The survivors of that quake will immediately break into what looks like a "forced confession." We can't be sure how many of those terrified people who suddenly give "glory to the God of heaven" will be exercising genuine, saving faith. Throughout history, untold numbers of people have acknowledged the power and wrath of God without actually confessing Him as their personal Lord and Savior.

Yet one thing is certain. The great Jerusalem earthquake following the ascension of the two witnesses will mark the end of an era. Revelation 11:14 tells us that the second woe (announced earlier in 8:13) has come to pass. The window of repentance for all humanity is closing quickly; the time for the final judgments is swiftly approaching.

Application

From Tragedy to Triumph

God's unchanging plan remains in motion and on target. When His hand empowers a person's life and ministry, that ministry continues until He brings it to completion. Even death cannot stop the legacy of a faithful minister of God! While it may be possible to silence the voice of one who bears witness to the truth, the truth that has been proclaimed remains indestructible.

One major truth emerges from the account of the two witnesses: *God transforms tragic situations into triumphant events.*

Underdogs become overcomers.

Weakness is changed to strength.

Overwhelming obstacles lead to magnificent opportunities.

Today, positive thinkers and motivational speakers try to inspire us to accomplish great things, embrace our potential, and achieve our personal goals—all in our own strength. Many Christian leaders advocate a life of success, health, wealth, and personal happiness. Yet when we contrast this me-centered philosophy with the heroes of the Bible and the saints of history who accomplished great things *for God by His power*, both the motivation and the outcome stand in sharp contrast: all the glory is God's, *not ours.*

The Bible is filled with examples in which God used outcasts and underdogs to accomplish His will: David versus Goliath, Elijah versus the prophets of Baal, Gideon's three hundred versus thousands of Midianites, Esther versus Haman. Our God delights in turning the tables on the world's mind-set of "bigger is better" and "only the strong survive." In a world that sets success and accomplishments as the ultimate standard for determining a person's worth, it's easy to forget that God often chooses the small over the large and a remnant over the masses.

I challenge you to dig deeply into one or two of these great stories over the next few days. Focus on the weakness or tragedy of that person's life, how God enabled him or her to overcome this handicap, and what great things He accomplished through that individual. Then look at your own weaknesses and look back over your own life, noting the kinds of obstacles, tragedies, or disappointments you've endured. Ask God—the only source of true spiritual power—to turn your weaknesses into strengths. Count on Him to transform your tragedies into triumphs.

Person and passage	Weaknesses or tragedies	What God accomplished	Your weaknesses and tragedies
Moses (Ex. 1–12)			
Gideon (Judg. 6–8)			
Samson (Judg. 13–16)			
Ruth (Ruth 1–4)			
David (1 Sam. 16–31)			
Esther (Esth. 1–10)			
Daniel (Dan. 1–6)			

The Sounding of the Seventh Trumpet (Revelation 11:15–19)

[15]Then the seventh angel sounded; and there were loud voices in heaven, saying, "The kingdom of the world has become *the kingdom* of our Lord and of His Christ; and He will reign forever and ever." [16]And the twenty-four elders, who sit on their thrones before God, fell on their faces and worshiped God, [17]saying,

"We give You thanks, O Lord God, the Almighty, who are and who were, because You have taken Your great power and have begun to reign. [18]And the nations were enraged, and Your wrath came, and the time *came* for the dead to be judged, and *the time* to reward Your bond-servants the prophets and the saints and those who fear Your name, the small and the great, and to destroy those who destroy the earth."

[19]And the temple of God which is in heaven was opened; and the ark of

His covenant appeared in His temple, and there were flashes of lightning and sounds and peals of thunder and an earthquake and a great hailstorm.

Every hour of every day, in hundreds of languages throughout the world, Christians recite one of the most familiar prayers in Scripture. The prayer begins with two familiar words: *Patēr hēmōn … Pater noster … Vater unser … Notre Père … Padre nostro … Our Father*. Many churches frequently incorporate the Lord's Prayer of Matthew 6:9–13 into their worship services. Believers the world over recite it as an act of personal devotion. In fact, this tradition goes all the way back to the first century, when Christians would recite the Lord's Prayer three times every day.[4] By the time John wrote Revelation, reciting the Lord's Prayer together had likely become a widespread practice.

Interestingly, though the faithful have offered that prayer to God daily since the founding of the church, some elements of that ancient prayer have never been answered literally. In Matthew 6:10, Christ prayed, "Your kingdom come." I'm no expert on global affairs, but I know the world would look a lot different if this part of the Lord's Prayer had already been answered! Nothing in the world today gives us any sense that Christ's earthly kingdom has already come down from heaven. In fact, when we flip on the news, it sometimes feels like hell is working its way up.

Though believers help to advance the spiritual kingdom of God through preaching the gospel (Acts 28:31; Col. 1:13), the day is coming when all aspects of the Lord's Prayer will be fulfilled literally (Rev. 11:15–19). Christ will one day reign over all the earth, the world will be transformed, sin and death will be eradicated, and ultimately God's purposes will be accomplished "on earth as it is in heaven" (Matt. 6:10).

What a glorious day that will be! Yet we must never forget that the arrival of Christ's kingdom will be prefaced by a period of judgment. A trumpet blast, a booming voice, and a celestial chorus resound before a heavenly temple. Flashes of lightning, claps of thunder, shuddering earthquakes, and devastating hail will rock the earth. With the sounding of the seventh and final trumpet, God prepares John for the seven dreadful bowls of wrath that will usher in Christ's glorious reign.

— 11:15 —

Perspective is everything. Though the events described in 11:15–19 await fulfillment at God's final judgment and the second coming of Christ, the loud voices of praise from heaven refer to future events in the past tense because John sees them as they happen. None of us today see things from that same prophetic perspective, but

IS THE SEVENTH TRUMPET THE "LAST TRUMPET"?

At this point I need to clarify a common misunderstanding about this seventh trumpet. In 1 Corinthians 15:51 – 52, Paul writes, "Behold, I tell you a mystery; we will not all sleep, but we will all be changed, in a moment, in the twinkling of an eye, at the last trumpet; for the trumpet will sound, and the dead will be raised imperishable, and we will be changed." Referring to the same event, Paul writes in 1 Thessalonians 4:16 – 17, "For the Lord Himself will descend from heaven with a shout, with the voice of the archangel and with the trumpet of God, and the dead in Christ will rise first. Then we who are alive and remain will be caught up together with them in the clouds to meet the Lord in the air, and so we shall always be with the Lord."

Some scholars equate the "last trumpet" announcing the rapture of the church in 1 Corinthians 15:52 and 1 Thessalonians 4:16 with the "seventh trumpet" of Revelation 11:15. On the surface this may seem like a reasonable assumption, given that the "seventh trumpet" in Revelation appears to be the "last trumpet" of the series. But a close examination reveals that these two trumpets refer to separate prophetic events.

The seventh trumpet of 11:15 clearly announces the final phase of the wrath of God, the beginning of Christ's reign, and the praises of the heavenly chorus in response to this epochal exchange of power. In contrast, Paul's end-time trumpet refers to the bodily resurrection and the "catching up" of believing saints from the earth. When we set all these accounts side-by-side, we observe that the only thing these passages have in common is the mention of a trumpet. So, is it still possible that Paul's "last trumpet" and John's "seventh trumpet" are the same?

we can be just as certain of the ultimate reign of Christ "forever and ever."

Chronologically, the seventh trumpet both introduces and includes the final period of God's wrath symbolized by the seven bowls in Revelation 16. John Walvoord writes, "The fact that this will be fulfilled as the Second Coming makes it clear that the period of the seventh trumpet chronologically reaches to Christ's return. Therefore the seventh trumpet introduces and includes the seven bowl judgments of the wrath of God revealed in chapter 16."[5] In Revelation 12 – 16 we will observe more details of the final three-and-a-half years of the tribulation as the effects of the seventh trumpet are played out on the earthly stage. For now, though, the prophetic song of heaven summarizes in short form what will be described in more detail later.

Let's not miss the big picture of what the trumpet is announcing. The voices in heaven summarized the detailed worship chorus in verses 15, 17 – 18. They declared, "The kingdom of the world has become the kingdom of our Lord and of His Christ; and He will reign forever and ever." In his musical masterpiece *Messiah*, Handel incorporated this refrain into his famous "Hallelujah Chorus." The words emphasize the great change of power from wicked humanity under the spiritual bondage of Satan (the kingdom of the world) to Christ and the saints under the sovereign headship of God the Father (the kingdom of our Lord and of His Christ). To affect this change, however, the kingdom of darkness must be judged and the kingdom of light must cast its brilliance on the face of the earth.

—11:16–18—

When the seventh angel sounded his trumpet, heaven broke forth in praise. The age-old prayer of the church, "Your kingdom come," will be fulfilled. Finally, the kingdom prophecies that span both the Old and New Testaments will be realized.

In John's vision, these events are viewed as already accomplished, but we should not let this fact confuse us. From our perspective, all of these events described in verses 16 through 18 are yet future. But because the purposes of God cannot change and the prophesied events are certain, we can join in the heavenly throng and praise God for what He *will* do.

- There *will be* a victory in which the kingdom of this world will become the kingdom [of our Lord and of his Christ] (11:15–16).
- There *will be* a time of intense wrath in which the nations under the control of Satan will be vanquished, which will make way for the establishment of Christ's throne on this earth (11:17–18).
- There *will be* a time at the end of that thousand-year reign when the nations will once again rebel, and

THE "LAST TRUMPET" AND "SEVENTH TRUMPET" CONTRASTED

1 Corinthians 15:51–52	1 Thessalonians 4:14–17	Revelation 11:15–18
Last trumpet sounds	Trumpet of God sounds	Seventh angel sounds
	Voice of archangel shouts	
	Christ descends from heaven	
Dead saints raised	Dead saints raised	
Living saints changed		
	Living saints caught up	
	Resurrected and raptured saints meet Christ in the air	
		World kingdom becomes Christ's kingdom
		God takes His power and begins to reign
		God's wrath came
		Dead judged
		Prophets and saints rewarded

To answer this question, we need to keep in mind that Paul wrote 1 Thessalonians around AD 50 and 1 Corinthians around AD 55. Because John had his visions and wrote Revelation around AD 96, Paul would not have been aware of the series of seven trumpet judgments. So, we can confidently conclude that Paul himself was not referring to the seventh trumpet of Revelation when he mentioned the "last trumpet." But could John have been referring back to Paul's final trumpet when he mentions the angel sounding the seventh trumpet in Revelation 11:15? Had it been John's intention to make this connection, probably he would have used the term "last trumpet" to erase any doubt. Or at least he would have made a specific reference to the saints' resurrection and rapture, or to the descent of Christ.

In light of this, it appears that these two trumpet blasts refer to separate prophetic events. Paul's "last trumpet" announces the resurrection, rapture, and rescue of the Church from the earth prior to the beginning of the seven-year tribulation period. The seventh trumpet blast here brings the series of trumpet judgments to a close, previews both the wrath and reign of Christ, and makes way for the visions leading up to the seven bowls of wrath (chs. 12 – 16).

those hostile powers will ultimately be defeated (11:18).

- There *will be* a final judgment and final reward, when the wicked will be raised and sent to eternal punishment while the righteous will receive the full inheritance promised to the saints (11:18).

No matter what the world looks like today, no matter how out of control things appear, in the end, God wins! Never forget that essential truth. With the twenty-four elders (11:16), we, too, can fall on our faces and worship God in light of this great promise.

— **11:19** —

In the beginning of chapter 11, John was told to measure the temple of God on earth (11:1). At the end of the chapter, John returned to a temple, but this time it's the temple of God in heaven (11:19). The temple in heaven indicates unbroken fellowship with God — its doors remain open to all. Within this temple John saw the ark of the covenant, a symbol of God's holiness as the basis for His just wrath.

The ark of the covenant contained the tablets of the Ten Commandments (Deut. 10:2), a constant reminder of God's righteous standards. The presence of a heavenly ark of the covenant reminds us that God will never forget the provisions of His covenant. Because of His mercy and grace, God grants complete access to His throne to those who believe. Yet on the basis of His unalterable standards of law and justice, He exercises wrath and judgment against unbelievers. This judgment is symbolized by the flashes of lightning, peals of thunder, an earthquake, and the hailstorm mentioned in 11:19. When God reveals His righteousness, He unleashes His wrath against those who have broken His covenant. But to those of us who know Him through His Son, Jesus Christ, and have taken refuge in mercy and grace through Christ's blood, we enjoy unhindered access to the throne of God.

Centuries ago Christ taught His first disciples to pray, "Your kingdom come. Your will be done, on earth as it is in heaven" (Matt. 6:10). When we look heavenward, we see the model of how things should be on earth. One day the ideal will

The ark of the covenant

be real; faith will become sight; the hidden will be revealed. In the meantime, we can live our lives in light of both the justice and mercy of God.

Application

Current Access for Future Kings

As we reflect on the panoramic preview of future events announced by the seventh trumpet, two timeless truths stand out.

First, *we have unlimited access to God by His grace.* The image of the open temple in heaven (11:19) communicates that believers stand in an open relationship with God. Based on the forgiveness purchased for us by the blood of Christ, we can have confidence as we approach Him. Not only this, but as His beloved children, we are free from His coming wrath (1 Thess. 1:9–10; Rev. 3:10). Christians will never experience the seventh trumpet judgment—nor any of the trumpet judgments described in Revelation. Instead, we will have already been transformed and taken to heaven at Paul's "last trumpet" (1 Thess. 4:16). While the wicked endure tribulation on earth, the church will be preparing to return with Christ and reign with Him over the earth (Rev. 17:14; 19:14).

At this point, I urge you to pause and ask yourself, "Have I trusted in Christ? Have I accepted God's free gift of eternal life? Do I know for certain that I have a personal, intimate relationship with God and will be delivered from the coming wrath?" To be eternally saved, a person must simply believe the good news about

Jesus Christ—that He died in our place to pay the complete payment for all of our sins and that He rose again from the dead to be our ever-present Savior.

Again, I ask: "Have you accepted this truth personally?" If so, never forget that you now have direct access to God. Hebrews 4:16 says, "Therefore let us draw near with confidence to the throne of grace, so that we may receive mercy and find grace to help in time of need." What is your greatest need today? Have you boldly approached God with that need through prayer? If the doors of heaven are open to you as a child of God, take hold of your birthright and enjoy unlimited access to your heavenly Father.

A second powerful and reassuring truth that can be drawn from this passage is that *our sovereign King will reign and reward us.* This truth is so clear and so certain that the vision expresses this future fulfillment in the past tense. Our response must be one of trust and confidence in this hope. We should also diligently serve until he returns. Believers are called to proclaim the gospel of salvation until He comes (Matt. 28:18–20). In what ways are you personally working to advance His spiritual kingdom on earth?

Exposing the Ultimate Evil Empire (Revelation 12:1–17)

¹A great sign appeared in heaven: a woman clothed with the sun, and the moon under her feet, and on her head a crown of twelve stars; ²and she was with child; and she cried out, being in labor and in pain to give birth.

³Then another sign appeared in heaven: and behold, a great red dragon having seven heads and ten horns, and on his heads *were* seven diadems. ⁴And his tail swept away a third of the stars of heaven and threw them to the earth. And the dragon stood before the woman who was about to give birth, so that when she gave birth he might devour her child.

⁵And she gave birth to a son, a male *child*, who is to rule all the nations with a rod of iron; and her child was caught up to God and to His throne. ⁶Then the woman fled into the wilderness where she had a place prepared by God, so that there she would be nourished for one thousand two hundred and sixty days.

⁷And there was war in heaven, Michael and his angels waging war with the dragon. The dragon and his angels waged war, ⁸and they were not strong enough, and there was no longer a place found for them in heaven. ⁹And the great dragon was thrown down, the serpent of old who is called the devil and Satan, who deceives the whole world; he was thrown down to the earth, and his angels were thrown down with him. ¹⁰Then I heard a loud voice in heaven, saying,

"Now the salvation, and the power, and the kingdom of our God and the authority of His Christ have come, for the accuser of our brethren has been thrown down, he who accuses them before our God day and night. ¹¹And they overcame him because of the blood of the Lamb and because of the word of their testimony, and they did not love their life even when faced with death. ¹²For this reason, rejoice, O heavens and you who dwell in them. Woe to the earth and the sea, because the devil has come down to you, having great wrath, knowing that he has *only* a short time."

¹³And when the dragon saw that he was thrown down to the earth, he persecuted the woman who gave birth to the male *child*. ¹⁴But the two wings of the great eagle were given to the woman, so that she could fly into the wilderness to her place, where she was nourished for a time and times and half a time, from the presence of the serpent. ¹⁵And the serpent poured water like a river out of his mouth after the woman, so that he might cause her to be swept away with the flood. ¹⁶But the earth helped the woman, and the earth opened its mouth and drank up the river which the dragon poured out of his mouth. ¹⁷So the dragon was enraged with the woman, and went off to make war with the rest of her children, who keep the commandments of God and hold to the testimony of Jesus.

Satan hates us. All who love and follow Christ and His teachings must never forget those three words. He wants nothing more than to sabotage our love for God and for others, to tempt us into a moral catastrophe, and/or to see us choose a lifestyle of sin rather than a walk with the Lord Jesus Christ. When we falter, he stands ready to accuse us before God. When we pass the tests of temptation, he looks beyond that and is already strategizing his next attack. Satan hates us with a relentless passion.

Most often his methods are indirect—establishing and fortifying moral pitfalls in the world in order to lure, snare, and destroy unsuspecting victims. He has only to sit back and laugh as people wander headlong into his sinister traps. Sometimes he employs more direct methods—bringing made-to-order temptations into our lives to deceive us. The truth is, if God were to allow it, Satan would unleash his entire arsenal against humanity, marching both spiritual and physical armies across the face of the earth to destroy all men, women, and children.

Satan's ultimate evil empire has been spreading its influence for millennia. Masquerading as an angel of light (2 Cor. 11:14), Satan rarely exposes his demonic empire to the light of truth. A day is coming, however, when God will remove His restraining power from the earth, and Satan will be allowed to run amok for a brief season. Paul writes about this future removal of His restraining force in 2 Thessalonians 2:6–8: "And you know what restrains him now, so that in his time he will be revealed. For the mystery of lawlessness is already at work; only he who now restrains will do so until he is taken out of the way. Then that lawless one will be revealed." At that time deception, destruction, and despair will ravage the planet. Yet even then, Satan's acts will be those of a desperate villain who knows his time is short.

Throughout the ages people have played into the hands of the Adversary by falling into one of two errors in their thinking about him. In his classic work *The Screwtape Letters*, C. S. Lewis mentions these extremes:

> There are two equal and opposite errors into which our race can fall about the devils. One is to disbelieve in their existence. The other is to believe, and to feel an excessive and unhealthy interest in them. They themselves are equally pleased by both errors, and hail a materialist or a magician with the same delight.[6]

Understanding that Satan is neither all-powerful nor completely powerless will help us come to terms with the real challenges we face as we do battle with his evil empire in its current form. I say "current form" because it's important to understand that Satan's ability to unleash his fury on God's people is limited in the present age. One day, however, Satan's empire will be allowed to strike the world in full force—before it crumbles at the coming of Christ.

—12:1–6—

In Revelation 11 we heard a heavenly chorus sing about the final judgments and the certainty of Christ's reign on earth. This victorious proclamation climaxed with a dazzling display of God's glory when the ark of the covenant appeared in the heavenly temple, followed by thunder and lightning, an earthquake, and a hailstorm. As this vision dissolved, its trembling and rumbling subsided, and John received a new vision.

In this new scene, according to 12:1, "a great sign appeared in heaven." The Greek word *sēmeion* ("sign") indicates a mark or symbol that carries a special meaning or points us to something beyond it.[7] This new vision contains symbolic characters that point to real people or events in history—past as well as future. Let's familiarize ourselves with the five main characters or groups of characters that appear in Revelation 12. The following overview will help us understand the significance of this sweeping drama of judgment and redemption:

This vision begins with a rapid review of the first coming of Christ. The righteous remnant of Israel in the first century eagerly anticipated the coming of the Messiah. We see members of this remnant not only in Mary and Joseph, but in such figures as Simeon and Anna, who had awaited the coming of the Christ and

Cast of Characters in Revelation 12

Symbolic characters	Literal identification	Explanation and interpretation
Woman (12:1–2, 6, 13–17)	The righteous remnant of Israel	The key identification is found in Genesis 37:9–10, where the same symbols are used to represent the twelve tribes of Israel. It's best, however, to see this woman in Revelation as representing the elect, righteous remnant described by Paul in Romans 9:1–8, rather than all ethnic Israel. Elsewhere in Revelation this same group is represented by the 144,000 elect from the twelve tribes of Israel (Rev. 7:1–8; 14:1–5).
Dragon and his armies (12:3–4, 7, 9, 12–17)	Satan and his demons working through the wicked world powers	The dragon is clearly identified as "the devil and Satan" (12:9). The symbol of the seven heads and ten horns corresponds with the same number of heads and horns in Daniel's beastlike representations of the nations that opposed Israel in the Old Testament — Babylon, Medo-Persia, Greece, and Rome (Dan. 7). Satan always has used ungodly nations in his attempts to destroy God's people, and a host of wicked angels have assisted him in his plans.
Male Child (12:5, 13)	Christ the King of kings and Lord of lords	The male Child is identified as the One who will "rule all nations with a rod of iron" (Rev. 12:5). This is a messianic reference similar to Psalm 2:9 and Revelation 19:15. Though Satan sought to destroy Him, Christ ultimately triumphed, leading the way for all those who believe in Him to also reign with Him in the coming kingdom (Rev. 2:26–27). Clearly Christ is the main character in Revelation, appearing under a number of names, including the Lamb that was slain (5:6), the Lion of Judah (5:5), and finally the King of kings and Lord of lords (19:16).
Michael and his armies (12:7–8)	The archangel Michael and elect angels	Michael is described as "one of the chief princes" who stands guard over Israel and battles demonic forces for God's people (Dan. 10:13, 21; 12:1). As the commander of the heavenly army of good angels, Michael is, in fact, Satan's angelic counterpart, who stands toe-to-toe with the devil (Jude 9).
Offspring (12:17)	The tribulation saints	While the woman (the remnant of Israel) will be protected, the "rest of her children" — all believers in Christ during the future tribulation — will be subject to persecution and martyrdom.

rejoiced at His arrival (Luke 2:25–32, 36–38). Yet the birth of Christ was met with great opposition, especially from Herod the Great, who tried to destroy the Child (Matt. 2:7–18). In fact, throughout Christ's life Satan utilized numerous means to oppose His mission in order to destroy the Messiah. In the end, however, the Son of God emerged from this world victorious, having inherited all authority in heaven and on earth (28:18). Thus, the whole story of the four Gospels is represented by the birth of the male Child and His being caught up to God's throne (Rev. 12:5).

Between verses 5 and 6 of Revelation 12, however, the perspective rushes forward in time. If this were a movie, we might imagine a few words on the bottom of the screen that read something like, "Thousands of years later." The entire history of the church is simply passed over. Why is this? For one thing, the emphasis in Revelation is not on what happens to the church during the present age, but what will happen to Israel and Gentile believers during the future tribulation. Second, because the church since Pentecost has been spiritually united with Christ through the baptism of the Holy Spirit (1 Cor. 12:12–13), we share with Christ in His destiny. Just as the male Child was caught up to God and rescued from Satan's earthly wrath, the church also will be caught up to God to be rescued from the coming wrath of the tribulation (1 Thess. 4:17; 5:9–10).

So, verse 6 begins to describe what happens to the restored, elect remnant of Israel during the tribulation period. In 7:1–8, we've already seen that this future remnant will be composed of the 144,000 from the twelve tribes of Israel, sealed for protection with a special calling by God. Under the symbol of the woman, we see that God will take special care of His people, Israel, during the final three and a half years of the tribulation, providing a place for her in the wilderness to protect her during the most intense period of judgment and wrath (12:6).

— **12:7–12** —

Revelation 12 portrays two great conflicts—one in heaven and the other on earth. Though distinct, these battles are closely related. In the first conflict, we observe a clash between Satan and the archangel Michael (12:7–8). Michael, who has been defending God's people for millennia (Dan. 10:13, 21), will defeat the armies of Satan in heaven and cast them down to the earth. This future event probably will occur at the beginning of the seven-year tribulation, at the same time as the rapture of the church.

Although popular ideas of Satan imagine him as the "king of hell" ruling over demonic servants and damned sinners, this is not true according to the Bible. Walvoord notes, "While the concept of Satan in heaven is difficult to comprehend, it is clear that he is now the accuser of the saints (cf. Job 1:6; Rev. 12:10). Though Satan was defeated at the first coming of Christ (John 16:11), his execution was delayed and is in stages."[8]

In our own day, Satan has limited access to both heaven and earth. He continually brings charges against the saints, pointing out our sins and accusing us before God for the wrongs we commit. But when the rapture occurs and the redeemed suddenly receive sinless, immortal bodies, all bases for accusations against the saints will vanish and Satan will have nobody to slander. So, when Satan is cast down from heaven (which will then be filled with the victorious bride of Christ), a voice will cry out with words of victory for those in heaven, but with words of woe to those left behind.

Think about the words of 12:10–12 in light of the catching up of the saints to heaven and the casting down of Satan to earth at the beginning of the tribulation. Members of the church, destined to reign with Christ in His kingdom, will have received the fullness of their salvation and power and will be preparing to join Christ at His return to earth to establish the earthly kingdom (12:10). At the same time, Satan—the accuser of the brethren—will be cast down to earth. Though he had accused the mortal and sinning saints while they struggled with temptation on earth, Satan will no longer be able to make a case against believers. Their sinful inclinations and mortal flesh will have been replaced by a new nature and a new, glorified flesh (1 Cor. 15:53–54). Finally, the church will be described as overcoming Satan—not by personal strength but by the blood of the Lamb and through His Word (12:11). Because of this, the resurrected and raptured saints who will dwell in heaven can rejoice (12:12).

The beginning of the tribulation and Satan's final fall from heaven, however, will not be good news for anyone left on earth. The voice in heaven also pronounced woe on those left behind, because the devil, knowing he has a short time before his final doom, will be inspired and energized by great wrath (12:12). This wrath of Satan on earth is portrayed in verses 13–17.

— **12:13–17** —

When Satan and his demons are cast out of heaven, several significant changes result. First, he will no longer be able to gain an audience with God to accuse the Lord's people. Second, he will no longer have access to the presence of God and be granted permission to test and tempt the saints. Third, the horrors of earthly evil will increase. Even as cries of victory resound from heaven, earthly woes ring out as

From My Journal

Check ... Check ... *Check-Mate*

The devil has come down to you, having great wrath, knowing that he has only a short time. (Rev. 12:12)

Every time I read about Satan's final desperate days on earth, I recall teaching my boys to play chess. It was a bad decision on my part, I might add. They perfected their game as time passed. Both of them got to where they couldn't wait to play me because over the years they had studied me, learned my patterns, and anticipated my moves. Eventually the eager teacher became the easy target.

I remember sitting at a campground one summer vacation. We were relaxing under the glow of our Coleman lantern. Everything was going well until one of them pulled out the chessboard and asked me to play. You know you're in trouble when one of the kids invites you to play a game of chess and he has this wily grin on his face, as if he's impersonating the Cheshire cat. When that happened, deep down inside I knew I had "only a short time." Escaping that fate wasn't an option. This was vacation. We had nothing better to do. So there I sat, my son ogling my every move, squirming impatiently on his campstool, and laughing smugly every time I moved. It's the kind of laugh I might imagine a spider would make when it sees a fly caught in its sticky web: "Gotcha! Heh heh heh hehhhhh!"

Soon the dynamics of the board start to change—fewer of my black pieces and more of his whites. Those ivory soldiers start marching in on me; then the dreaded word breaks the silence: "Check!" I pull back the knight, keep my hand on its little pointed head, and anticipate the next several moves. And I try to look like the wise father I'm not. Again that ominous word, "Check!" All the while I'm sweating, he's chuckling. He knows my time is short. Ultimately, it's "check-*mate*!" As the lantern slowly fades, I have to admit, I have met my match.

I know we've been taught never to laugh at Satan. But I have to admit, occasionally it's hard to hold back a subtle grin when I realize the devil's a loser. His time is short and he knows it. That slithering serpent can make all the crafty moves he wants, but in the end, *God wins*. Check ... check ... check—every move he makes on the chessboard of world events brings him closer to the end, when heaven will finally cry out those glorious words: "*Check-mate!*"

Satan desperately attempts to inflict as much damage as possible during the final countdown to his own ultimate defeat.

Immediately after Satan is thrown down, he will attempt to erase Israel from the face of the earth (12:13). Throughout history the Jews have been the special object of hatred, ridicule, and persecution. During the Middle Ages, they were looked on with suspicion and treated as outcasts in a world dominated by a form of political Christianity that viewed all Jews as Christ-killers. During World War II, the Nazis attempted to obliterate the Jewish people in a holocaust driven by absolute evil. Even after the birth of the modern nation of Israel in 1948, neighboring nations in the Middle East have often talked of driving the Jews into the sea and retaking the land. Anti-Semitism has a long and sordid history. Satan has inspired countless attempts at destroying God's special covenant people. Yet God has continued to fulfill His promise to preserve Israel even in her spiritually blind condition of rejecting Jesus as her Messiah (Rom. 11:28–29).

During the tribulation, God will continue to preserve the righteous remnant of Israel from harm (7:1–8). Represented by the symbol of the woman in Revelation 12, Israel will receive supernatural protection from Satan's military attack, which is signified here by a flood flowing from the dragon's mouth (12:14–16). This image of a flood overtaking Israel is also seen in Daniel 9:26, a prophetic reference to the invasion of Israel by the Roman army in which the city of Jerusalem was destroyed, along with the temple: "And its end will come with a flood; even to the end there will be war; desolations are determined."

Those events in the first century represent eloquent types of the future tribulation, when Satan will inspire the Gentile nations to once again invade the nation of Israel with hopes of destroying God's covenant people. This invasion of the Promised Land evidently will take place during the first three and a half years of the seven-year tribulation. Perhaps in league with the two witnesses who prophesy during this same period (11:3–6), the remnant of Israel will be miraculously protected from Satan's attempts at physical annihilation. Following these attempts, the remnant will flee from the land of Israel into the "wilderness" to be protected by God during the second half of the tribulation (12:14).

By the middle of the seven-year tribulation, Satan will have grown increasingly frustrated with his foiled attempts at destroying Israel through conventional means. With wicked cunning, he will intensify his plan of attack: "So the dragon was enraged with the woman [the remnant of Israel], and went off to make war with the rest of her children [the tribulation saints], who keep the commandments of God and hold to the testimony of Jesus" (12:17).

What new madness will Satan use to make war with the saints during the second half of the tribulation? We will see these startling tactics in Revelation 13.

Application

Standing on the Promises of God

Through the vivid vision of Revelation 12, we witness an incredible series of dramatic events that span heaven and earth and span thousands of years from the birth of Christ through the future seven-year tribulation. Yet the great epic begun in chapter 12 introduces a few practical points that will help us in our everyday lives.

First, Revelation 12 teaches us that *Israel may be blind and disobedient as a nation, but God has never forgotten her.* He never will. His reputation as a promise keeper is at stake. God will remember His people and preserve them. He will protect them when persecution arises, and He will ultimately fulfill His promise to return them to their own land under the Messiah. Although most ethnic Jews have not accepted Jesus as their Messiah, God has still preserved them as a distinct people over the last two thousand years. In Romans 11:1 Paul wrote, "God has not rejected His people, has He? May it never be!" The fact of God's faithfulness, even to faithless Israel, should give us hope as well. The same God who stands by His promises to Israel stands by His promise to each of us: "I will never desert you, nor will I ever forsake you" (Heb. 13:5).

Second, Revelation 12 teaches us that *although Satan is a powerful and aggressive foe, he will not triumph.* Satan accuses us before God every day and night (12:10), while at the same time Jesus Christ, our advocate, ceaselessly intercedes for us (Heb. 7:25). One day God will resurrect the saints and transform their corruptible bodies into new, immortal ones (1 Cor. 15:51–53). On that day Satan's mouth will be shut, for he will no longer have any basis to accuse us. When that happens, he will be cast out of heaven, and the countdown to his doom will begin. As you examine your own life, what sins could Satan accuse you of today? Read Romans 8:1–3, 31–39 and 1 John 2:1. Why aren't believers condemned for their sins? The answer drips with grace! All of our sins—past, present, and future—have been paid in full by the blood of Christ! No accusation from Satan can stick to us or soil our reputation, because God's grace and mercy have washed us clean from our transgressions.

Third, Revelation 12 shows us that *we may be open and assaulted targets today, but we need not fear.* The events of Revelation 12 have yet to occur, so Satan still operates under the restraining hand of God. When we draw near to God, He will protect us from any attack Satan can unleash against us. Remember the promise in James 4:7, "Resist the devil and he will flee from you." We need not fear! In the face of spiritual attack, the following passages of Scripture can help you stand firmly and fearlessly. I would encourage you to write them down. Refer to them regularly. Memorize them. In fact, take a few moments and read through them now, slowly and aloud, to remind you of the victory you enjoy as a member of the Body of Christ.

- Luke 22:31–32
- Ephesians 6:12–13
- 2 Timothy 1:7
- 1 Peter 5:8–10
- James 4:7–8
- 1 John 4:4

A Tale of Two Beasts: Antichrist and His Lieutenant (Revelation 13:1–18)

[1]And the dragon stood on the sand of the seashore.

Then I saw a beast coming up out of the sea, having ten horns and seven heads, and on his horns *were* ten diadems, and on his heads *were* blasphemous names. [2]And the beast which I saw was like a leopard, and his feet were like *those* of a bear, and his mouth like the mouth of a lion. And the dragon gave him his power and his throne and great authority. [3]*I saw* one of his heads as if it had been slain, and his fatal wound was healed. And the whole earth was amazed *and followed* after the beast; [4]they worshiped the dragon because he gave his authority to the beast; and they worshiped the beast, saying, "Who is like the beast, and who is able to wage war with him?" [5]There was given to him a mouth speaking arrogant words and blasphemies, and authority to act for forty-two months was given to him. [6]And he opened his mouth in blasphemies against God, to blaspheme His name and His tabernacle, *that is*, those who dwell in heaven.

[7]It was also given to him to make war with the saints and to overcome them, and authority over every tribe and people and tongue and nation was given to him. [8]All who dwell on the earth will worship him, *everyone* whose name has not been written from the foundation of the world in the book of life of the Lamb who has been slain. [9]If anyone has an ear, let him hear. [10]If anyone *is destined* for captivity, to captivity he goes; if anyone kills with the sword, with the sword he must be killed. Here is the perseverance and the faith of the saints.

[11]Then I saw another beast coming up out of the earth; and he had two horns like a lamb and he spoke as a dragon. [12]He exercises all the authority of the first beast in his presence. And he makes the earth and those who dwell in it to worship the first beast, whose fatal wound was healed.

¹³He performs great signs, so that he even makes fire come down out of heaven to the earth in the presence of men. ¹⁴And he deceives those who dwell on the earth because of the signs which it was given him to perform in the presence of the beast, telling those who dwell on the earth to make an image to the beast who had the wound of the sword and has come to life. ¹⁵And it was given to him to give breath to the image of the beast, so that the image of the beast would even speak and cause as many as do not worship the image of the beast to be killed. ¹⁶And he causes all, the small and the great, and the rich and the poor, and the free men and the slaves, to be given a mark on their right hand or on their forehead, ¹⁷and *he provides* that no one will be able to buy or to sell, except the one who has the mark, *either* the name of the beast or the number of his name. ¹⁸Here is wisdom. Let him who has understanding calculate the number of the beast, for the number is that of a man; and his number is six hundred and sixty-six.

Every great drama has a villain—sometimes, several. Storytellers call them "antagonists." Their role in the plot is to antagonize the hero. That may involve engaging the hero in hand-to-hand combat or pulling strings behind the scenes. It could include intimidating and stalking, or throwing obstacles in the hero's path, or deceiving him by pretending to be an ally. If you think of any successful novel or film, you'll be able to identify the villains. They embody the wickedness of classic conflicts between good and evil. Yet the most insidious and potentially destructive nemesis in any kind of plot is *the villain who appears to be the hero.*

The Bible describes an antagonist who relentlessly assaults and attacks. We first saw him tempting Adam and Eve in the garden of Eden, causing the fall of humanity and ushering sin and death into the world (Gen. 3). Throughout history he has worked through depraved individuals, wicked rulers, and godless empires to deceive the world and destroy the righteous (Rev. 12). Ultimately he will empower the worst deceiver and destroyer the world will ever see—an adversary of God's people who makes Nero, Hitler, Stalin, Mao, and Osama bin Laden pale by comparison.

Since the birth of Christianity, faithful believers have expected a coming evil dictator and his deceptive right-hand man, who will have an enormous, evil influence over the world. This diabolical duo will derive their power from none other than Satan himself. Revealed in Scripture under various titles, the clearest and most definitive description of the Antichrist and False Prophet is set forth in Revelation 13. These powerful end-time antagonists will emerge on the world stage like beasts rising up out of the sea (13:1) and bursting out of the land (13:11). Together these two monstrous emissaries of evil will become the most persuasive and dynamic political and religious leaders of all time.

Though believers today need not fear these embodiments of evil and deception, Scripture warns us that we are to be on the alert. The "mystery of lawlessness" and "the spirit of the antichrist" are already at work in the world through the activities of Satan (2 Thess. 2:7; 1 John 4:3). So, knowing the schemes and devices of the end-time Antichrist and False Prophet will help us stand strong in our present battle against the antichrists and false prophets of our own day.

—13:1–4—

As soon as Israel flees into the wilderness for her three-and-a-half year protection, the dragon (Satan) will stand on the seashore and summon his greatest personification of deception in history (13:1). From the churning waters of the sea, John saw a beast rise up—a horrific mongrel of monsters bent on destroying everything in its path.[9] We've already established that Revelation is filled with symbolic visions, but these symbols point to literal realities that will come to pass in the future. What do the seven heads and ten horns represent about the future Antichrist?

The exotic—even bizarre—symbols used to describe the Beast are not merely frightening features conjured up to illustrate the monstrous character of the Antichrist (13:2). The vision of the Beast is drawn from specific images in the book of Daniel in order to communicate the reality of this end-time dictator. In Daniel 7 the great prophet had a vision of four beasts rising up from the sea—the first like a lion, the second like a bear, the third like a four-headed leopard, and the fourth "dreadful and terrifying and extremely strong" with ten horns (Dan. 7:3–8). These four symbols corresponded to Nebuchadnezzar's earlier dream of the four metals of the statue (Dan. 2). Bible scholar J. Dwight Pentecost rightly interprets these four beasts of Daniel for us as the successive empires that opposed Israel in the ancient world: Babylon, Medo-Persia, Greece, and Rome.[10] If we add up the number of heads and horns on the four beasts in Daniel 7, they equal the seven heads and ten horns of the Beast in Revelation 13. All this deserves a closer examination. Perhaps a chart will help.

John Walvoord explains the symbolism of the Beast this way: "In Revelation 13:2 the beast was seen to gather in the symbolism of the three preceding empires—Greece (a leopard, cf. Dan. 7:6), Medo-Persia (a bear, cf. Dan. 7:5), and Babylon (a lion, cf. Dan. 7:4)."[11] This symbolism suggests that the Antichrist of the future tribulation will embody the sum total of all the world empires that opposed God and His people throughout history (see the above chart). He will be directly empowered by Satan himself, acting as the ultimate dictator and leading the mother of all evil empires.

Revelation 13 Compared with Daniel 2 and 7

Statue of Daniel 2	Beasts of Daniel 7	Meaning in Daniel	Beast of Revelation 13	Possible meaning in Revelation
Head of fine gold	Like a lion with wings of an eagle	Babylon under Nebuchad–nezzar	Mouth like a lion	Like Babylon in its one pagan religion and single language as a "return to Babel"
Breast and arms of silver	Like a bear with three ribs in its mouth	The Medo-Persian Empire	Feet like a bear	Like Medo-Persia, devours its opponents
Belly and thighs of bronze	Like a leopard with four heads and four wings	The Greek Empire under Alexander, then his four generals	Like a leopard	Like Greeks, rapidly conquers and unifies the world
Legs of iron and feet (with ten toes) of iron mixed with clay	Monstrous beast with iron teeth and ten horns, and a boastful little horn speaking blasphemies	The Roman Empire, fragmented into pieces, but restored under a future dictator	Seven heads and ten horns; one head having a mortal wound that was healed	Like Rome, unites remote and diverse nations under one dictator, promising peace but bringing war

The meaning of the healed "fatal wound" on one of the seven heads (13:3) has been greatly debated for centuries.[12] Some have said the wound refers metaphorically to the kingdom of the Beast—that he will suffer a "deadly" political blow and survive. The Greek phrase translated "as if it had been slain," however, is the same expression used to describe the Lamb of God (i.e., Jesus) in 5:6, whose death was clearly real and resulted in a literal, bodily resurrection. This suggests that the Antichrist of the future will attempt to mimic Christ's death and miraculous resurrection through his own deceptive injury and resuscitation.

How like Satan! The one who "disguises himself as an angel of light" (2 Cor. 11:14) will provide the world with a copycat "christ" to match all their man-centered ideals of personality, politics, and power. No wonder the whole world will be swept off its feet by this attractive, persuasive figure (13:3)! In fact, we are told the world will worship the dragon through their worship of the Beast. In this rabid fit of hypernationalism that will make Hitler's Third Reich look like a high school sporting event, the world will cry out, "Who is like the beast, and who is able to wage war with him?" (13:4).

—13:5–10—

The Antichrist will snare the attention of the unbelieving world through deceptive satanic miracles. His resulting totalitarian regime could accurately be described as "hell on earth." Consider this. If James 3:6 describes the believer's unbridled tongue as metaphorically "set on fire by hell," we probably can't imagine the hellish words that will spew from the mouth of Satan's personal pawn. Revelation 13:5 calls them "arrogant words and blasphemies." The prophet Daniel said he "will speak monstrous things against the God of gods" (Dan. 11:36). Paul said that Antichrist "opposes and exalts himself above every so-called god or object of worship" (2 Thess. 2:4). Clearly his tongue will be "set on fire by hell." In fact, his motives and manipulative manner of deception will be fueled by the unrestrained power of none other than the consummate antagonist, Satan.

For forty-two months the Antichrist will blaspheme God, heaven, and everything in it (13:6). Yet his attention will not be focused on those saints who dwell safely in the heavens. He will direct his devil-inspired wrath toward the unprotected saints on earth. Unlike the first half of the seven-year tribulation, during which God's special servants enjoyed miraculous protection from the dragon's direct assault (11:3–6), the last forty-two months of the tribulation will be characterized by victory of the Beast over the saints (13:7). In fact, we should recall that the two witnesses, who will be protected during their ministry, will be killed shortly after the rise of the Antichrist from the sea (11:7). Their murder will mark only the beginning of a bloodbath of martyrs at the brutal hands of the Beast. No words can adequately portray the awful scenes.

The Two-Part Tribulation: From Dimming to Darkness

Daniel 7:25; 9:27; 12:7
Revelation 11–13

3½ years	3½ years
2 Witesses	2 Beasts
Temple Restored	Temple Desecrated
Israel Flees	Israel in Wilderness
Saints Protected	Saints Martyred
Trumpets	Bowls

7 years

No wonder this military giant will be able to exercise authority "over every tribe and people and tongue and nation," coaxing the entire unbelieving world to worship him like a god (13:7–8). Paul's second letter to the Thessalonians also gives us a glimpse of this same figure, including an insight into his ability to draw the adoration of the whole world: "the one whose coming is in accord with the activity of Satan, with all power and signs and false wonders, and with all the deception of wickedness for those who perish, because they did not receive the love of the truth so as to be saved" (2 Thess. 2:9–10).

Of course, not everybody will play Satan's end-time game of "follow the leader." Those whose names are written in the Lamb's book of life will have the spiritually enlightened eyes to see through the polished politics and not be intimidated by the military might of the Antichrist. They will see him for the monster he really is. Yet resistance to his military might will have its dreadful consequences. Those who refuse to worship the Beast will suffer severely. Revelation 13:9–10 admonishes the reader to snap to attention and heed a solemn warning: "If anyone has an ear let him hear. If anyone is destined for captivity, to captivity he goes; if anyone kills with the sword, with the sword he must be killed. Here is the perseverance and the faith of the saints."

Pause for a moment. Try hard to imagine yourself as one of those faithful saints enduring those fateful days. They will sometimes huddle together for mutual defense and sometimes stand alone before their persecutors. Think about that. Enter into their existence as you allow your imagination to run free. How might they feel during their time of trial? How will they endure? Revelation 13:10 tells us that they may be taken captive or killed. Revelation 6:11 and 7:9–17 informs us that a great number of tribulation believers will suffer martyrdom during this period. Clearly, this persecution will require a level of spiritual stamina unparalleled in history.

—13:11–15—

Revelation 13:1–10 describes the rapid rise of a political and military dictator, the Antichrist. Satan's most sinister and destructive weapon against humanity, however, will carry twice the punch as many realize. Just as the two comings of Christ were not clearly understood from the Old Testament prophecies, early Christians didn't clearly understand that the end-time villain would be twofold until John penned Revelation 13. Along with the Antichrist (the Beast from the sea), John witnessed the rise of a second figure who will serve as the Antichrist's right-hand man. Revelation 13:11–18 opens the curtain to unveil the personification of deception—the Beast from the earth, also called the "False Prophet" (16:13; 19:20).

If we compare the first and second beasts, we immediately recognize that these are not merely two symbols for the same person.

Comparison of the Two Beasts of Revelation 13

First Beast	Second Beast
Rises from the sea (13:1)	Rises from the land (13:11)
Seven heads with blasphemous names (13:1, 3)	One head (13:11)
Ten horns with crowns (13:1)	Two horns like a lamb (13:11)
Authority given to him by the dragon (13:2)	Exercises authority of the first beast (13:12)
The whole world worships the dragon because of the beast (13:3–4)	Causes people to worship the first beast (13:12)
Speaks blasphemies against God for forty-two months (13:5–6)	Performs amazing signs to deceive the whole world into worshiping the first beast's image (13:13–15)
Makes war with the saints and overcomes them (13:7)	Forces the world to receive the mark of the beast or suffer severe persecution (13:16–17)

You may have noticed that the dragon, the Beast from the sea, and the Beast from the land will work together in their plan to deceive, convince, and conquer. In fact, many have noticed what they have called an "unholy trinity." It appears that Satan's end-time deception will sell the world a cheap imitation of the Holy Trinity of biblical Christianity. One commentator describes the "unholy trinity" this way:

> The dragon, Satan, appears in Rev. 12:3ff. as the antagonist to the woman and the child. The beast from the sea/Antichrist appears in chapter 13 and receives his throne and authority from the dragon. The beast from the earth is called "the false prophet" to indicate the counterfeit miracles and prophecies that characterize him.... These three evil beings form a parody or imitation of the divine Trinity.[13]

This unholy distortion represents Satan's final attempt at blaspheming God and deceiving the world by twisting the truth into a grotesque caricature of the one true God—Father, Son, and Holy Spirit. Today Satan seeks the same goal of deception. He disguises himself as an angel of light to disarm the unsuspecting, and then tricks those people into worshiping and following him (2 Cor. 11:13–15). During the coming tribulation, however, the potential for spiritual deception will be far greater. In the midst of the worldwide chaos caused by natural disasters, political upheavals, and widespread death, the False Prophet will present a compelling creed. His false religion will offer false hope for a starving world.

The Greek verb translated "deceives" in 13:14 comes from *planaō*, which means "cause to wander" or "lead astray."[14] Our English word *planet* comes from the same root. The ancient world looked into the night sky and saw a few wandering "stars" amidst an unchanging field of sparkling constellations. (Nowadays if you see a wandering "star" it's more likely an airplane than a planet!) One might wish that Satan's deceptions would affect only a handful of people, but the reality should boggle the mind. The False Prophet of the end times will deceive the majority of the world through his hellish antics.

Blinded by unbelief and sin, the world will easily fall prey to the second Beast's deceptive message and methods. Intellectually attracted to him, emotionally drawn by his appealing style, and convinced by his amazing signs, they will voluntarily submit and obey. One commentator notes:

> His arguments will be subtle, convincing, and appealing. His oratory will be hypnotic, for he will be able to move the masses to tears or whip them into a frenzy. He will control the communication and media of the world and will skillfully organize mass publicity to promote his ends. He will be the master of every pro- motional device and public relations gimmick. He will manage the truth with guile beyond words, bending it, twisting it, and distorting it. Public opinion will be his

to command. He will mold world thought and shape human opinion like so much potter's clay. His deadly appeal will lie in the fact that what he says will sound so right, so sensible, so exactly what unregenerate men have always wanted to hear.[15]

In the midst of his persuasive message, which will likely reach the whole world through cutting-edge technology, the false prophet will lead people on the earth to make an image of the Antichrist. People have come up with any number of wild theories about the "image of the beast." Over more than forty-five years of ministry, I think I've heard most of them! When the television set first came on the scene, some people thought that might be the image of the Beast. Or maybe the computer connected to the Internet! Some folks, bewitched by sci-fi movies, tossed around the idea that the image might be a supercomputer that gains consciousness ... or a 3-D hologram ... or a subhuman clone of the Antichrist! All of these get "A"s for creativity, but I would give them "F"s for faithfulness to Scripture. It's best to let the text speak for itself: what do we know for sure about the "image of the Beast"?

- Those who dwell on the earth will be motivated to make an image of the Antichrist (13:14).
- The False Prophet will be able to give breath to the image so it can speak (13:15).
- The image will be an object of mandatory worship (13:15).

That isn't a lot to go on, is it? We don't know if this will be one giant statue or a mass-produced "image." Just as the singular "mark" of the Beast refers to many marks, the "image" of the beast could refer to many similar images around the world. We simply do not know. My own tendency is to take this literally. The image will be some kind of idol that visually represents the Antichrist—not a robot, or a clone, or a supercomputer.

It may be that Satan and his demons will infest and possess the idol (or idols) in order to be the direct objects of the world's worship. It wouldn't be the first time. Throughout history demons have connected themselves with idols in order to receive the worship and adoration they so desperately crave. In 1 Corinthians 10:19–20, Paul writes, "What do I mean then? That a thing sacrificed to idols is anything, or that an idol is anything? No, but I say that the things which the Gentiles sacrifice, they sacrifice to demons and not to God; and I do not want you to become sharers in demons." That statement should send a chill down our spine regarding idols! Though idols themselves are lifeless things, they become a means for worshiping demons.

You might also remember that earlier in the book of Revelation, during the trumpet judgments, John saw people of the earth refusing to repent of "the works of their hands, so as not to worship demons, and the idols of gold and of silver and of brass and of stone and of wood, which can neither see nor hear nor walk" (9:20). During the second half of the tribulation, the attention of those who worship lifeless idols will be drawn to something new — an idol that appears miraculously to live and breathe! This may very well be the judgment on wicked humanity mentioned by Paul in 2 Thessalonians 2:11–12, "For this reason God will send upon them a deluding influence so that they will believe what is false, in order that they all may be judged who did not believe the truth, but took pleasure in wickedness." Having rejected God's offer of repentance, the unbelievers will be lured by a deception so grand that only true believers will be able to see through the illusion and, as a result, stand firm in the face of persecution.

— 13:16–18 —

Imagine that you live in an oppressive regime in which confessing to be a Christian is outlawed by those in authority and punishable by death. You cower in a small apartment at night as the heavy boots of soldiers can be heard on sidewalks and streets as people in the neighborhood are arrested, suspected of being Christians. Suddenly you hear a knock. As you pray that the troopers will pass you by, they force themselves through the door. Lights flash around the room, boots stomp across the floor, and suddenly you find yourself looking into the barrels of automatic weapons.

"Tell me," barks the man pointing his rifle at you, "are you a Christian?"

You have a choice to make. Either deny Christ and live, or confess him and die on the spot.

Chances are, most believers reading this would think, "I'd confess Christ. Of course I would. That soldier can't threaten my faith in Jesus as my Lord!"

Now let's intensify that scene.

Imagine that you aren't alone. Instead, when the soldiers barge through the door, they point their weapons not at you, but at your spouse and your three small children. "Reject Christ or *they* die!"

Dying for your faith is one thing; letting others die for your faith is quite another. Yet this is just the kind of sickening scenario Satan will inspire in the dreadful future John is describing. Because of the impact of earthly disaster, food will be scarce. Yet people will still need to buy and sell food to provide for their families. The alternative to participation in the Antichrist's economy is a long, slow death by starvation. The book of Revelation tells us that the Antichrist's regime will force believing parents to choose between feeding their families and defending their faith. As a father and grandfather, I can't imagine a crueler test of faith than this.

The last few verses of Revelation 13 describe the False Prophet's devilish economy, governed by the infamous "mark of the beast" (13:16). This mark—displayed on either the right hand or the forehead—will permit all worshipers of the Beast to buy and sell the necessities of life. What happens to those who refuse to worship the Beast, to those who do not bear the mark? Let's make this clear.

No worship—no mark.

No mark—no buying or selling.

No buying or selling—no groceries, no clothing, no medicine, no shelter . . . no life.

The commerce of the tribulation will revolve around that identifying mark, mysteriously calculated as 666—"the name of the beast or the number of his name" (13:17). John informs us that this number is "that of a man" (13:18), somehow related to the Antichrist's name. Of course, this kind of thing has drawn the attention of countless calculations throughout history as Bible believers have tried to identify the man behind the mark. One commentator aptly notes, "The number of the beast down through the centuries has been linked with literally hundreds of different possibilities."[16] In Latin, Greek, and Hebrew, letters stand for numbers, so anyone with a calculator and a good dose of creativity can slap the "666" label on a number of prominent personalities.

The following men have been seriously proposed by some overzealous Bible students as being the villain of the end times.

Antichrist Identifications throughout History

Nero Caesar	Adolf Hitler
Emperor Constantine	Benito Mussolini
Mohammed	Franklin Delano Roosevelt
The Popes	John F. Kennedy
Martin Luther	Mikhail Gorbachev
Napoleon Bonaparte	Saddam Hussein
Abraham Lincoln	Osama bin Laden

As it turns out, none of these men fulfilled the job description of Revelation 13, did they? In fact, we can glean some tried-and-true wisdom from one of the ancient prophecy teachers of the church. After discussing various false identifications of the Antichrist prevalent even in his own day (around AD 180), Irenaeus of Lyons wrote, "It is therefore more certain, and less hazardous, to await the fulfillment of the prophecy, than to be making surmises, and casting about for any names that may present themselves."[17] What excellent advice the church through the centuries should have listened to! If history has taught us nothing else about the coming Antichrist and his mysterious number, it's that we cannot identify the Antichrist until he has already taken control. Then *and only then* will the "man of lawlessness" be revealed (2 Thess. 2:3).

We do know this for certain: the commerce of the future will revolve around the identifying mark, whatever that mark may be. Possessing the mark will prove one's allegiance to the Antichrist. Refusing the mark will demonstrate faith in Jesus Christ. No other time in history will make the identity of true Christians so clear. In that day the questions and riddles revolving around the identity of the Beast, the nature of the mark, and the calculation of the number 666 will be answered for those who possess divine wisdom and discernment (13:18). Until then, we must continue to contend with the various means of spiritual deception aggressively at work in our present age. Each of us must, therefore, equip ourselves for spiritual battle with reliable knowledge, keen discernment, and God-given wisdom.

So much for then; what about now? In light of Satan's strategies for deception and destruction, are you equipped with those three essentials to face the challenges of his relentless and ruthless attacks? It's one thing to be aware of the Adversary's plan for the future; our first responsibility is to be alert and engaged in resisting him today.

NOTES: Rivals of the Sovereign Lord (Revelation 11:1 — 13:18)

1. Charles C. Ryrie, *The Ryrie Study Bible: New International Version* (expanded ed.; Chicago: Moody Press, 1994), 1961.

2. Charles Ryrie suggests that this refers to the first three and a half years of the tribulation (Charles C. Ryrie, *The Ryrie Study Bible*, 1961). Another scholar, John Walvoord, suggests it refers to the second half (John F. Walvoord, *The Prophecy Knowledge Handbook* [Wheaton, IL: Victor Books, 1990], 573–75).

3. See Beale, *The Book of Revelation*, 572–73; Osborne, *Revelation*, 417–18.

4. The *Didache*, one of the earliest Christian writings outside the New Testament, instructs believers to pray a prayer like the Lord's Prayer three times every day (*Didache* 8.2–3).

5. Walvoord, "Revelation," *The Bible Knowledge Commentary*, 959.

6. C. S. Lewis, *The Screwtape Letters* (New York: Macmillan, 1961), 3.

7. Louw and Nida, eds., *Greek-English Lexicon of the New Testament*, vol. 1, § 33.477.

8. Walvoord, "Revelation," *The Bible Knowledge Commentary*, 959.

9. Later in Revelation the "waters" from which the Beast rises is interpreted as "peoples and multitudes and nations and tongues" (17:15). His will be a truly global empire.

10. J. Dwight Pentecost, "Daniel," in *The Bible Knowledge Commentary: Old Testament Edition* (ed. John F. Walvoord and Roy B. Zuck; Wheaton, IL: Victor , 1985), 1350–55.

11. Walvoord, "Revelation," *The Bible Knowledge Commentary*, 960.

12. See a discussion of the variety of interpretations of the "fatal wound" in Osborne, *Revelation*, 495–97; Walvoord, *Prophecy Knowledge Handbook*, 582–83.

13. Osborne, *Revelation*, 591.

14. Bauer and Danker, eds., *A Greek-English Lexicon of the New Testament*, 821–22.

15. Phillips, *Exploring Revelation*, 171.

16. Osborne, *Revelation*, 519.

17. Irenaeus, *Against Heresies* 5.30.3.

VENGEANCE OF THE GLORIOUS DELIVERER (REVELATION 14:1–19:10)

When the curtain closed on the previous act of the end-time drama, the situation looked bleak. The evil Antichrist and his fiendish False Prophet had taken center stage, trampling Jerusalem underfoot and sending countless saints to the sword (chs. 11–13). The only way for people to save their lives and the lives of their families was to fall prostrate before a satanic false messiah. To reject the Antichrist's visible mark of allegiance to his wicked regime meant persecution and execution. If the story were to end here, we would think that evil had won the day and that God had forgotten His promises and forsaken His people.

Yet as the house lights dim and the curtain parts for the next act in this apocalyptic saga, the tide decisively turns. Instead of darkness and gloom, the stage blazes with divine brilliance. The brutal Beast and his deceptive lieutenant have been cleared from the scene. In their stead we see the glorious Lamb of God standing on Mount Zion with His elect saints. The long-expected Hero has stepped foot on the earth, and with His presence the wicked kingdoms of the world begin to scramble. In fact, from this point on we will witness the ultimate defeat of the real evil empire and the establishment of a perfect kingdom of righteousness and peace.

I have titled this fourth episode of the book of Revelation "Vengeance of the Glorious Deliverer" (14:1–19:10). It begins with a preview of coming events as the blasphemous exploits of the two beasts give way to a series of visions that predict the final gathering of the earth for deliverance and harvesting of the earth for judgment (14:1–20). This forecast then dissolves into a new vision of the most severe plagues of the end times—the seven bowls of wrath (15:1–16:21). Then, just as the armies of the earth gather at Armageddon, the frame freezes (16:16). During this suspended action, an angel takes John aside to interpret some of the symbols, including a detailed description of the evil empire's judgments and the victorious celebration of God's people (17:1–19:10).

Amidst these profound visions of Babylon, Armageddon, and the bowls of wrath, we also find practical truths for us today. As history rushes toward its final destiny, all of us are called to live in anticipation of our final destination.

KEY TERMS

ἀλληλουϊά [hallēlouia] (239) "Praise the Lord, Hallelujah" (Rev 19:1, 3, 4, 6)

Though the word "Hallelujah" appears frequently in the Old Testament book of Psalms and is common in Christian parlance — including prayers, preaching, and praise — the word itself only appears four times in the New Testament, all of them in Revelation 19:1–6. The word is the exact equivalent to the Hebrew phrase *hallelujah*, meaning "Praise the LORD." Its presence in Revelation indicates that *praise* is the proper response to Christ's coming as Judge and King.

θυμός [thymos] (2372) "wrath, passion, anger"

Two Greek words are often translated "wrath" in the New Testament. The most common term, *orgē*, refers to anger expressed through some kind of judgment (Heb. 3:11). The term *thymos*, by contrast, emphasizes the emotion behind one's actions (Rev. 12:12). These terms are coupled closely in Revelation 16:19 and 19:15, indicating both God's anger toward sin and His decisive actions against the ungodly. Unlike human anger and rage, divine wrath is always a function of God's perfect holiness and righteousness.

πληγή [plēgē] (4127) "blow, wound, plague"

Our English word "plague" is derived from the Greek word *plēgē*. Though we often think of plagues today as communicable diseases run rampant, a biblical "plague" was a supernatural manifestation of judgment. "Plagues" in Revelation appear mostly in the second half of the book, when God directs the fullness of his fury against rebellious humanity (11:6; 15:1).

φιάλη [phialē] (5357) "dish, censer, vial, bowl"

Revelation 15–16 describe a series of seven "golden bowls full of the wrath of God" poured upon the earth. The *phialē*, from which we derive our English word "vial," refers to a basin often used in ceremonial acts. Such bowls were used in the tabernacle and temple (Ex. 27:3; 1 Kings 7:26). Similar sacred vessels appear in the heavenly temple, symbolically containing "the prayers of the saints" (Rev. 5:8). It may be that the final bowls of wrath represent God's response to pleas for vindication — a holy and sacred offering of justice on behalf of God's people, who had suffered so greatly.

A Surprising Preview of Coming Attractions (Revelation 14:1–13)

¹Then I looked, and behold, the Lamb *was* standing on Mount Zion, and with Him one hundred and forty-four thousand, having His name and the name of His Father written on their foreheads. ²And I heard a voice from

heaven, like the sound of many waters and like the sound of loud thunder, and the voice which I heard *was* like *the sound* of harpists playing on their harps. ³And they sang a new song before the throne and before the four living creatures and the elders; and no one could learn the song except the one hundred and forty-four thousand who had been purchased from the earth. ⁴These are the ones who have not been defiled with women, for they have kept themselves chaste. These *are* the ones who follow the Lamb wherever He goes. These have been purchased from among men as first fruits to God and to the Lamb. ⁵And no lie was found in their mouth; they are blameless.

⁶And I saw another angel flying in midheaven, having an eternal gospel to preach to those who live on the earth, and to every nation and tribe and tongue and people; ⁷and he said with a loud voice, "Fear God, and give Him glory, because the hour of His judgment has come; worship Him who made the heaven and the earth and sea and springs of waters."

⁸And another angel, a second one, followed, saying, "Fallen, fallen is Babylon the great, she who has made all the nations drink of the wine of the passion of her immorality."

⁹Then another angel, a third one, followed them, saying with a loud voice, "If anyone worships the beast and his image, and receives a mark on his forehead or on his hand, ¹⁰he also will drink of the wine of the wrath of God, which is mixed in full strength in the cup of His anger; and he will be tormented with fire and brimstone in the presence of the holy angels and in the presence of the Lamb. ¹¹And the smoke of their torment goes up forever and ever; they have no rest day and night, those who worship the beast and his image, and whoever receives the mark of his name." ¹²Here is the perseverance of the saints who keep the commandments of God and their faith in Jesus.

¹³And I heard a voice from heaven, saying, "Write, 'Blessed are the dead who die in the Lord from now on!'" "Yes," says the Spirit, "so that they may rest from their labors, for their deeds follow with them."

"Coming soon . . ."

Those words grab our attention and pique our interest. The entertainment moguls strategically use previews of coming attractions in their attempt to generate buzz about an upcoming book, movie, or television show. "Teaser trailers" snare audiences with exciting scenes from movies long before they're finished. A few rapid-fire snippets can generate eager anticipation among a community of fans who have never even seen the film! But we all know the disappointment that can come when the reality fails to live up to the hype. How many times have you paid hard-earned cash for a movie, only to realize the best scenes were all portrayed in the preview? Sometimes the preview of coming attractions leads us to expect one thing when the filmmaker delivers something completely different.

We can be certain that God's preview of future events in the book of Revelation will never disappoint. Not only does He know the future, He also controls it. He's not simply the leading actor in the coming end-time drama; He's the writer, producer, and director! So when He gives us previews of things to come, we should pay close attention. These scenes aren't meant to satisfy our curiosity, but to warn the rebellious and to encourage the righteous. Now, before we return to the details of this final message to humanity, I need to make a few comments about how Revelation 14 fits in the chronology of the book.

In the historical books of the Bible like Exodus, Judges, 1 Kings, or the book of Acts, the story usually unfolds in chronological order. In prophetic writings such as Jeremiah, Daniel, or Zechariah, however, the narrative often takes the reader on a prophetic journey that moves in and out of chronological order. The book of Revelation is no exception. Sometimes a vision will describe the nature of the future tribulation as a whole. Other times it may portray judgments that will be fulfilled in strict sequence. Occasionally the vision will back up and fill in details. Other times it will leap forward to summarize events that will be described in greater detail later.

The visions recorded in Revelation 14 fall into this last category. We might call it an overture of the final judgments—brief vignettes, like a teaser trailer for an upcoming movie. In this thematic preview of coming attractions, we step closer to the end of the great tribulation, but the judgments aren't over. We'll see God's full wrath revealed in chapters 15 and 16; but before that, the Lord interjects several snapshots of hope. In this way Revelation 14 ties the whole book together, reminding us of its major message and pointing us forward to the ultimate vengeance of the glorious Redeemer.

—**14:1–5**—

At the end of chapter 13, we were told that the followers of the Antichrist will be identified by a mark on the right hand or forehead (13:16)—a visible proof of their loyalty to Satan's earthly empire. When we move immediately into chapter 14, we meet 144,000 faithful followers of the Lamb. They have a different mark "written on their foreheads" (14:1)—the names of the Father and the Son, symbolizing God's mark of ownership. This group of Hebrew believers was originally seen at the beginning of the tribulation, with 12,000 sealed from each tribe of Israel, for protection during the coming judgments (7:1–8). Revelation 14 then pictures these same Jewish saints as they stand triumphantly at the end of the tribulation "on Mount Zion" (14:1). This vision foreshadows the gathering of the remnant of Israel after the tribulation when the Son of God returns to earth.

This group of 144,000 from the tribes of Israel will be converted to their Messiah after the rapture of the church at the beginning of the seven-year tribulation. During that time they will confront unbelievers, call them to Christ through repentance and faith, and proclaim the catastrophes of the coming judgments. Though they will endure hardship and flee persecution, they will be divinely protected through those terrible times and eventually enter into the thousand-year earthly reign of Christ. In fact, they will fulfill numerous Old Testament prophecies that the nation of Israel would one day be restored in the Promised Land under their Messiah-King. Isaiah 37:31–32 states, "The surviving remnant of the house of Judah will again take root downward and bear fruit upward. For out of Jerusalem will go forth a remnant and out of Mount Zion survivors. The zeal of the LORD of hosts will perform this." Similarly, Micah 4:6–7 says, " 'In that day,' declares the LORD, 'I will assemble the lame and gather the outcasts, even those whom I have afflicted. I will make the lame a remnant and the outcasts a strong nation, and the LORD will reign over them in Mount Zion from now on and forever."

While John observed this glorious gathering of saints on Mount Zion, music began to pour forth from heaven around the throne of God (14:2–3). Only the 144,000 will understand the celestial chorus, for they will be the firstfruits of the messianic kingdom (14:4). As God's select and chosen few, these saints are described as undefiled, chaste, and blameless—having followed the Lamb of God wherever He led them throughout the tribulation period (14:4–5). These are saved, sealed, sanctified, and spotless saints. As such, these tried and true survivors become the means by which God will fulfill His promise that Israel will bless all nations during Christ's reign over the earth (Gen. 26:4).

—14:6–13—

After giving us a glimpse of the remnant of Israel standing with Christ on Mount Zion, the stage clears and the backdrop changes as we read of another series of climactic announcements. Keep in mind that these proclamations do not appear in chronological order. Instead, they deal with themes and events that stretch across the tribulation period and find their ultimate climax in its final days. The first three proclamations here come through angels, the last through a booming voice from heaven.

First announcement: the gospel (14:6–7). The first angel proclaims "an eternal gospel [good news]," calling all people to worship God the Creator rather than Satan, who will soon be judged. Note a few important points about the gospel from these two verses. First, it is eternal in nature (14:6). Though the means of communicating may change throughout the centuries, the message itself never changes.

Second, the gospel is universal in scope (14:6). It isn't just for one people group, one race, or one nation, but for "every nation and tribe and tongue and people." The free gift of salvation through Jesus Christ is for anyone who believes (John 3:16). Third, the gospel is focused on the living God (14:7). Remember that during the tribulation the Antichrist will require all people on earth to fear, glorify, and worship him as a god. The gospel, by contrast, calls all people to turn "to God from idols to serve a living and true God" (1 Thess. 1:9).

Second announcement: judgment (14:8). The second angel proclaims in advance the ultimate destruction of the Antichrist's massive evil empire, "Babylon the great" (14:8). The repeated phrase "fallen, fallen" emphasizes the certainty of the coming collapse. A detailed description of that future judgment awaits us in chapters 15–18, but before that God wants everybody to know that the Beast's doom is sure. With the fall of the evil religious, political, and economic systems called "Babylon," all those intoxicated by her immorality also will fall.[1]

Third announcement: doom (14:9–11). The third angel pronounces judgment on all those who fail to believe the eternal gospel and enter into a right relationship with God through faith alone in Christ alone. Those who reject Christ will succumb to the deceptions of the Beast, receiving his mark of ownership rather than God's seal of the Spirit (14:9). Once a person makes that decision, his or her fate will be sealed. In the final judgment of the wicked, those who reject the one true God will be subject to the fullness of God's wrath (14:10). In fact, the strongest language of damnation in all of Scripture is reserved for those future worshipers of Satan in the great tribulation: "And the smoke of their torment goes up forever and ever; they have no rest day and night, those who worship the beast and his image, and whoever receives the mark of his name" (14:11). The stakes could not be higher, nor could the consequences be more severe.

Fourth announcement: blessing (14:12–13). With these warnings as a dark backdrop, God's Word brings a brief but vivid ray of hope. John Walvoord reminds us, "The stern warning addressed to all worshipers of the beast is also an encouragement to those who put their trust in Christ in the time of great tribulation. Though some of them will face martyrdom and others will need to go into hiding, they are assured that their lot is far preferable to those who accept the easy way out and worship the beast."[2] This truth is confirmed by the fourth pronouncement from a voice in heaven, calling for the saints to persevere in their faith in Christ (14:12). Though they may be put to death for their faithfulness to Christ, the Holy Spirit proclaims that those who die after having placed their trust in Christ can look forward to irrevocable rewards for their deeds (14:13). In short, they will be eternally blessed, wonderfully relieved, and abundantly rewarded.

Application

Saved, Sealed, Sanctified . . . and Sent

The description of the 144,000 in 14:1–5 should convict all of us who claim to be followers of Christ. Look again at that stunning description of those faithful saints:

- They are sexually chaste.
- They follow the Lamb without hesitation.
- They have no lies on their lips.
- They are blameless.

We might generalize that description in another way. In their relationship with others, they are pure. In their relationship with God, they are obedient. Surrounded by deception and lies, they exhibit remarkable integrity. They have an unimpeachable character that results in an impeccable record. They are a living reproof to their peers, displaying proof of the gospel by their very lives.

This same kind of people has a compelling testimony today. If you and I are corrupt like those around us, we have no credible message for those who are confused and lost in the corruption. If our mouths are filled with lies, the world won't believe us when we claim the gospel to be true. If we are known for moral failures, nobody will listen when we claim to be followers of the one true God.

As believers in Christ, we know we are sent into the world to preach the gospel. Many of us can quote the Great Commission by heart: "Go therefore and make disciples of all the nations, baptizing them in the name of the Father and the Son and the Holy Spirit, teaching them to observe all that I commanded you" (Matt. 28:19–20). Yet too often we forget that having a right *manner* of life is just as important as having the right *message* in our lives. Jesus Himself said, "Let your light shine before men in such a way that they may see your good works, and glorify your Father who is in heaven" (Matt. 5:16). The disciple Peter remembered his Master's words when he wrote, "Keep your behavior excellent among the Gentiles, so that in the thing in which they slander you as evildoers, they may because of your good deeds, as they observe them, glorify God in the day of visitation" (1 Peter 2:12).

Take some time to do a little self-examination. Ponder these penetrating and personal questions quietly before the Lord and answer honestly:

- Is your lifestyle an unspoken testimony of God's grace?
- Do you keep yourself pure and above reproach in your relationships with others — especially those of the opposite sex? Or do you compromise, blurring the line between appropriate and inappropriate behavior and questionable speech?

- Do you practice immediate obedience to the statements of Scripture? Or do you delay, rationalize, and pick and choose what to obey?
- Do you measure your speech against the standard of absolute truth? Or do you serve up "white lies," half-truths, and deceptions?
- Do you cultivate a blameless lifestyle that remains the same in private and in public? Or would the people who know you best testify to double standards and hypocrisy? Are you hiding secret sins?

God's most effective witnesses are those who are not only saved and sealed, but also walking in the light—set apart for God and willingly available to be sent as lights into a dark and corrupt world.

God's Terrible, Swift Sword (Revelation 14:14 – 20)

---

¹⁴Then I looked, and behold, a white cloud, and sitting on the cloud *was* one like a son of man, having a golden crown on His head and a sharp sickle in His hand. ¹⁵And another angel came out of the temple, crying out with a loud voice to Him who sat on the cloud, "Put in your sickle and reap, for the hour to reap has come, because the harvest of the earth is ripe." ¹⁶Then He who sat on the cloud swung His sickle over the earth, and the earth was reaped.

¹⁷And another angel came out of the temple which is in heaven, and he also had a sharp sickle. ¹⁸Then another angel, the one who has power over fire, came out from the altar; and he called with a loud voice to him who had the sharp sickle, saying, "Put in your sharp sickle and gather the clusters from the vine of the earth, because her grapes are ripe." ¹⁹So the angel swung his sickle to the earth and gathered *the clusters from* the vine of the earth, and threw them into the great wine press of the wrath of God. ²⁰And the wine press was trodden outside the city, and blood came out from the wine press, up to the horses' bridles, for a distance of two hundred miles.

The rousing words of "The Battle Hymn of the Republic" have stirred men and women to faithful action since Julia Ward Howe penned them in 1861. Most who sing them do not know that she took the word pictures she used directly from the book of Revelation.

Mine eyes have seen the glory of the coming of the Lord;
He is trampling out the vintage where the grapes of wrath are stored;
He hath loosed the fateful lightning of His terrible, swift sword;
His truth is marching on.

He has sounded forth the trumpet that shall never sound retreat;
He is sifting out the hearts of men before the judgment seat;
O, be swift, my soul, to answer Him! Be jubilant, my feet!
Our God is marching on.[3]

These words, based partly on 14:14–20, cut like a double-edged sword. They call God's people to a spiritual battle to advance the gospel throughout the world. At the same time they warn unbelievers of coming judgment, when God's wrath will be unleashed upon the wickedness of the earth.

The Jesus who will carry out the judgments described in 14:14–20 is the same One whose birth we celebrate each Christmas. How different will be His second advent from His first!

The Two Advents of Christ Contrasted

At His first coming …	At His second coming …
He came in meekness as a servant (Matt. 20:28)	He will come in power as judge (Matt. 24:30–31; 25:31–46; John 5:26–29)
He came in humility and gentleness (Matt. 11:29; John 5:41)	He will come in majesty and splendor (1 Thess. 4:16; Rev. 1:7)
He came to seek and save the lost (Matt. 18:11; Luke 19:10; John 3:17)	He will come to judge and reign (Acts 10:40–42; 2 Cor. 5:10; Rev. 11:15)
He came as a Servant to suffer wrath for sinners (Matt. 16:21; 17:12; Mark 9:12)	He will come as a Conqueror to rescue the righteous from wrath (1 Cor. 15:51–52; 1 Thess. 4:15–17)
He came to sow the seed of the gospel (Matt. 13:3–9; Luke 8:11)	He will come to reap the harvest (Matt. 13:37–42)

The hour is fast approaching when Jesus Christ will return from heaven with power and glory. All the misconceptions about who Jesus was and is will be dispelled at that time, and the whole world will stand face-to-face with the one true Christ. The one-sided meek and mild Jesus of Sunday school songs will give way to the fuller picture of Christ as Judge and conquering King. In that day the true but incomplete picture presented in "Jesus Loves Me" will be fulfilled by the Christ of "The Battle Hymn of the Republic."

In 14:1–13, John gave us a preview of coming events—the gathering of the remnant of Israel on Mount Zion at the coming of Christ (14:1–5). This image of redemption gave way to four proclamations: the eternal gospel (14:6), the fall of Babylon (14:8), the warning of doom (14:9), and promises to tribulation saints (14:12–13). The rest of chapter 14 vividly summarizes the final judgments about to be described in the next few chapters. The grain harvest (14:14–16) previews the seven bowl judgments described more fully in chapters 15–16. The grape harvest (14:17–20) pictures the Battle of Armageddon detailed in 16:13–21 and 19:19–21.

—14:14–16—

After three angels passed by with heavenly messages and a booming voice thundered a final warning from heaven, John's eyes caught a glimpse of something new and startling. A white cloud formed in the heavens, and as it approached, he recognized the image of a man with a crown on His head and a sickle in His hand.

Throughout Scripture, the cloud represents the *shekinah* glory of God—that physical form of divine power that reminded God's people that He was with them. It appears in Exodus 13:21 as the pillar of fire by night and pillar of cloud by day. Its purpose? To lead the Israelites out of Egypt to the Promised Land. The glory of God appeared in this cloud, from which the Lord often spoke to His people (Ex. 16:10; 19:9; 20:21). The cloud also rested on the tabernacle and in the temple, reminding Israel that God graciously dwelled with His people (Ex. 33:9; Lev. 16:2).

In the New Testament the cloud also represents the presence of God's power and glory. On the mount of Christ's glorious transfiguration, a "bright cloud" overshadowed the disciples and God spoke from its midst: "This is My beloved Son, with whom I am well-pleased; listen to Him!" (Matt. 17:5). At Christ's ascension, "a cloud received Him," marking the translation from the earthly to heavenly realm (Acts 1:9). It is therefore fitting that the second coming of Christ in judgment would be portrayed as the Son of Man riding on a white cloud. In fact, centuries ago the prophet Daniel wrote:

> I kept looking in the night visions,
> And behold, with the clouds of heaven
> One like a Son of Man was coming,
> And He came up to the Ancient of Days
> And was presented before Him. (Dan. 7:13)

Jesus quoted that prophetic statement and applied it to Himself when He predicted His second coming in Mark 13:26—"Then they will see the Son of Man coming in clouds with great power and glory."

The expression "Son of Man" in Revelation 14:14 clearly refers to Christ as the fulfillment of the Old Testament prophecies concerning the coming of God's kingdom mediated through a chosen human who also was somehow divine. This Hebrew idiom was often used to emphasize the *humanity* of a person. For instance, Daniel found himself trembling in the presence of angels, who referred to him as a "son of man" (Dan. 8:17). Similarly, Jesus often used the title "Son of Man" to highlight His human qualities (Matt. 8:20; 12:40; 17:12; John 3:14; 8:28). At the same time, "Son of Man" calls attention to the incarnation—God becoming Man to die for sin and to rise victoriously from the dead. The image of the cloud-riding "Son of Man" in Daniel 7:13 places this figure in the realm of heaven—a divine, glorious, exalted Man who alone receives the right to rule.

John's vision of the Son of Man drawing back His sickle to harvest the earth would have been familiar in the agrarian culture of his day. As a field of wheat ripened, the crop a farmer had carefully planted and cultivated would need to be taken in. The day of harvest could not be put off. Similarly, God's plan of redemption began as a simple promise to one day redeem humans through the woman's seed, at the same time defeating the serpent and his wicked offspring (Gen. 3:15). In the passing of thousands of years, God's plan continued to unfold. The covenant promises passed down from Abraham, Isaac, and Jacob to Judah, then to the house of David, and finally to the Person of Jesus Christ. Christ is the ultimate "seed ... to whom the promise had been

Erich Lessing/Art Resource, NY

An ancient sickle (around 1st cent. BC) used for harvesting grain made" (Gal. 3:19). So, by the end of the tribulation, the world will be ripe for harvest.

Wearing the victor's crown and wielding a sickle — the tool for harvesting grain — the Son of Man will respond to the word of the Father through the angel: "Put in your sickle and reap ... because the harvest of the earth is ripe" (14:15). The Greek word translated "ripe" means "dried" or "withered,"[4] suggesting that the condition of wicked humanity had become "overripe." This tells us that the Lord, in His mercy, has delayed judgment as long as possible. Peter affirmed, "The Lord is not slow about His promise, as some count slowness, but is patient toward you, not wishing for any to perish but for all to come to repentance" (2 Peter 3:9). Though God is merciful and restrains His hand of judgment for the sake of those who will repent, there will come a time when He will say, "Enough is enough!" At that epochal moment, the day of harvest will arrive.

Instantly the Son of Man in John's vision swept His sickle over the earth and executed judgment. Robert Thomas notes, "The brevity of the statement dramatizes the suddenness of the judgment."[5] Like an overripe wheat field that demands immediate attention by the harvester, the evil of humanity will call for swift and decisive justice. The apostle Peter, after reminding his readers of the patience of God in delaying judgment, informed his readers, "But the day of the Lord will come like a thief" (2 Peter 3:10). God is patient and merciful, but one day the earth will feel the sharp edge of His "terrible, swift sword."

— 14:17–20 —

While the wheat harvest pictures the sudden, swift intrusion of God's judgment in human history, the grape harvest depicts the severity of that judgment. John saw another angel emerge from the heavenly temple. This one, wielding a sharp sickle, was instructed by another angel to gather the clusters of ripened grapes from the earth (14:18). The word used in verse 18 for "ripe" differs from the word that described the wheat harvest. This term means "to be at the prime."[6] The wickedness of the world had reached a crescendo. A few verses earlier the third angel announced that those who worship the Beast and receive his mark will "drink of the wine of the wrath of God" (14:9–10). For many, their destinies had been sealed. They had aligned themselves against their Creator and Redeemer with the ultimate sign of rebellion — the mark of the Beast — accompanied by a wicked lifestyle to match.

In response to the command to harvest the grapes of wrath, the angel obeyed without delay. He swung the sickle across the earth and hurled the gathered grapes into "the great wine press of the wrath of God" (14:19). This vision draws on another common image in the ancient world. Grapes were harvested at the peak of ripeness. They were then thrown into a large bathtub-shaped vat, usually carved into rock and connected to a lower receptacle by a narrow channel. As the clusters of grapes were crushed underfoot in the upper chamber, the juice flowed into the second vat so it could be collected in jars or wineskins for fermentation.

In the vision of the wine press of God's wrath, John witnessed a dramatic outcome: "And the wine press was trodden outside the city, and blood came out from the wine press, up to the horses' bridles, for a distance of two hundred miles" (14:20). The symbols reveal an unmistakable reality: the battle pictured in this vision will be massive and bloody beyond imagination. Nothing in earth's history has come close. Revelation 14:17–20 describes in breathtaking images the result of the final battle of the Antichrist and the kings of the earth. The grape harvest represents the people who will gather for war in the valley of Har-Megiddo—better known as "Armageddon." That epic battle is described more fully in 16:16 and 19:15–21. We'll examine that location and that "war to end all wars" in more detail there, but for the time being it's important to realize that we are seeing a brief, symbolic preview of that event.

The visions of the grain and grape harvest use common Old Testament images to describe Armageddon. Isaiah 63 pictures the divine Judge's garments stained red from the wine press of His wrath (63:1–3). He cried out, "I trod down the peoples in My anger and made them drunk in My wrath, and I poured out their lifeblood on the earth" (63:6). Joel 3 captures the same end-time judgment in similar terms, helping us better understand the nature of the symbols in Revelation 14:

An ancient wine press with a large upper vat and lower receptacle to gather the fresh grape juice

Put in the sickle, for the harvest is ripe.
Come, tread, for the wine press is full;
The vats overflow, for their wickedness is great.
Multitudes, multitudes in the valley of decision!
For the day of the LORD is near in the valley of decision.
The sun and moon grow dark
And the stars lose their brightness.
The LORD roars from Zion
And utters His voice from Jerusalem,
And the heavens and the earth tremble.
But the LORD is a refuge for His people
And a stronghold to the sons of Israel. (Joel 3:13–16)

The "valley of decision" refers to the Jezreel Valley near the biblical city of Megiddo. There the armies of the world will be gathered for judgment, far outside the city of Jerusalem. Though Armageddon will spell certain doom for the enemies of God, it will also mean salvation for His people. Christ and the armies of heaven will return to destroy the Antichrist and his armies. Then the King of kings will establish His everlasting kingdom (Rev. 19:11–16).

Application

Christ's Double-Edged Sword

As we peer into the future through the apostle John's prophetic words and see Jesus as the sickle-wielding Judge of the earth who treads the wine press of God's wrath, two principles present themselves. One relates to God's grace, the other to His justice. Ponder both carefully.

First, *God's grace gives us the freedom to choose righteousness.* In Genesis 2:15–17, God taught humanity its first lesson: with the gift of free choice comes accountability. Adam and Eve were created with the capacity to obey *or disobey.* They could submit to God *or rebel against Him.* When they sinned, they became slaves to sin, sending humanity headlong into a state of sin and death (Rom. 5:14; 1 Cor. 15:22). Christ's death, however, has set us free from slavery to sin (Rom. 6:5–7). Furthermore, the Holy Spirit gives us the ability to choose righteousness instead of wickedness (Phil. 2:12–13). As believers in Christ, Paul's exhortation calls us to use this freedom in the service of God, not self. Read the following words carefully and underline the specific commands.

> Therefore do not let sin reign in your mortal body so that you obey its lusts, and do not go on presenting the members of your body to sin as instruments of

unrighteousness; but present yourselves to God as those alive from the dead, and your members as instruments of righteousness to God. (Rom. 6:12–13)

Second, *God's justice holds every person accountable.* Many Christians believe that because they're eternally saved by grace, they are no longer subject to the scrutiny of God. This represents a distortion of the biblical teaching regarding Christians and judgment. It is true that there will be no condemnation for those who are "in Christ Jesus" (Rom. 8:1), and believers will be spared from suffering the *wrath* of God (1 Thess. 5:9). Scripture is also clear, however, that "we will all stand before the judgment seat of God" (Rom. 14:10). Paul expounds on this fact in more detail. Again, don't rush through these verses. Take their warnings seriously . . . *and personally.* Your current joy and future reward are at stake:

> For no man can lay a foundation other than the one which is laid, which is Jesus Christ. Now if any man builds on the foundation with gold, silver, precious stones, wood, hay, straw, each man's work will become evident; for the day will show it because it is to be revealed with fire, and the fire itself will test the quality of each man's work. If any man's work which he has built on it remains, he will receive a reward. If any man's work is burned up, he will suffer loss; but he himself will be saved, yet so as through fire. (1 Cor. 3:11–15)
>
> For we must all appear before the judgment seat of Christ, so that each one may be recompensed for his deeds in the body, according to what he has done, whether good or bad. (2 Cor. 5:10).

A day of divine examination is coming. Are you using your freedom in Christ to live a life free from sin's domination? Or have you forgotten that there will be an accounting of your works at the judgment seat of Christ? What can you expect from the One who said, "I am He who searches the minds and hearts; and I will give to each one of you according to your deeds" (Rev 2:23)?

The Original Temple of Doom (Revelation 15:1–8)

¹Then I saw another sign in heaven, great and marvelous, seven angels who had seven plagues, *which are* the last, because in them the wrath of God is finished.

²And I saw something like a sea of glass mixed with fire, and those who had been victorious over the beast and his image and the number of his name, standing on the sea of glass, holding harps of God. ³And they sang the song of Moses, the bond-servant of God, and the song of the Lamb, saying,

> "Great and marvelous are Your works,
> O Lord God, the Almighty;

> Righteous and true are Your ways,
> King of the nations!
> ⁴ Who will not fear, O Lord, and glorify Your name?
> For You alone are holy;
> For all the nations will come and worship before You,
> for Your righteous acts have been revealed."

⁵After these things I looked, and the temple of the tabernacle of testimony in heaven was opened, ⁶and the seven angels who had the seven plagues came out of the temple, clothed in linen, clean *and* bright, and girded around their chests with golden sashes. ⁷Then one of the four living creatures gave to the seven angels seven golden bowls full of the wrath of God, who lives forever and ever. ⁸And the temple was filled with smoke from the glory of God and from His power; and no one was able to enter the temple until the seven plagues of the seven angels were finished.

You sit outside the office, fidgeting nervously as the secretary frequently glances up at you over her wire-framed glasses. The plush chair beneath you was meant to be comfortable, but you might as well be strapped in an electric chair. The clock on the wall ticks away. Your heartbeat quickens. At any moment the door will open and you'll learn your fate. You see, behind that door people in authority are discussing numerous accusations against you:

- falling behind on deadlines
- dereliction of duties
- insubordination
- incompetence

The reason you're at the brink of panic is that *everything they're saying about you is true*! You're guilty of every charge. Your months of irresponsibility have finally caught up with you, and now it's time to face the consequences.

All of us have, at one point or another, been through a similar situation. Maybe it was facing the principal after cheating on a test, or your parents after breaking their rules, or an employer after wasting company time and resources. Nobody likes that feeling of genuine guilt that leads to breathless fear. It's not just the fear of being found out. Deeper than that, it's the fear of being held accountable.

Truth be told, the whole world stands guilty before a righteous and holy God who knows our every thought, word, and deed. Romans 3:23 says, "All have sinned and fall short of the glory of God." Though we don't like to admit it, every human has a sense of moral accountability to the divine Lawgiver. He has inscribed His moral law on the hearts of every man, woman, and child (Rom. 2:14–15). The result? *Guilt. Fear.* While secular psychologists suggest all sorts of rationalizations to purge this overwhelming sense of guilt, the Bible repeatedly reminds us that "people are appointed to die once, and then to face judgment" (Heb. 9:27 NET).

As kooky as they appear on the street corners wearing sandwich board signs proclaiming doom, the message of the big-city prophets is essentially correct:

REPENT!
THE END IS NEAR!
JUDGMENT IS COMING!

This same message sums up the eight verses of Revelation 15 — a message of doom from the temple of God. Before recording the appalling visions of the seven bowls of wrath in chapter 16, John describes a snapshot scene of coming judgment (15:1), a glorious scene of triumphant joy (15:2–4), and a dreadful scene of wrathful doom (15:5–8).

— **15:1** —

The opening line — "Then I saw another sign in heaven" — marks the beginning of a new vision, a prelude to the bowl judgments detailed in Revelation 16. You may recall that a significant portion of John's revelation describes the coming judgments of God against an increasingly wicked and rebellious humanity. I need to remind you, though, that if you have come to know Jesus Christ as Savior, you need not fear these cataclysmic judgments. Those who accept Christ will be rescued from those dreadful days of doom. Those who reject the gospel, however, will remain and suffer the wrath to come.

From this verse we discover two important facts. First, the bowls represent seven plagues concentrated near the end of the future seven-year tribulation period. The word translated "plague" in this verse literally means a "blow" or "wound."[7] These judgments are not long, drawn-out epidemics like influenza or HIV. Rather, these plagues come with sudden impact — swift, severe, destructive, and fierce. Second, the seven bowl judgments will be the last expression of God's wrath toward the inhabitants of the earth. They will climax at the Battle of Armageddon and the return of Christ.

This snapshot preview of coming judgment should give hope to all people of faith in Christ. God's judgment will accomplish its purpose and come to an end. Its purpose is to avenge the holocaust inflicted on the saints at the hands of the Antichrist and his henchmen during the great tribulation. Its end will be the reward of the resurrected saints when they come to life and reign with Christ for a thousand years.

From My Journal

Facing Reality

I arrived at my office unusually early. The sky was heavy and overcast, a typical fall morning. My mind was on my schedule as I fumbled with the keys. In standard Swindoll fashion I pushed the door wide open in a hurry—only to be stopped dead in my tracks. A chill crept up my back as I peered into the dark, eerie study. The light switch was across the room, so I stood there at the door staring at the most startling reminder of reality imaginable!

In the middle floor of my church study was a *casket* with a wilted spray of flowers. On top of the closed casket was a picture of *me*! Now, my friend, if you want to know how to awaken someone from early morning drowsiness, this routine will surely do it. I suppose I stood there three full minutes without moving a muscle as I blinked and gathered my senses, half expecting the Ghost of Christmas Future to show up. I checked my watch and felt pleased to see the second hand still moving. I wasn't in some Charles Dickens nightmare after all. All my reflexes responded correctly, and my heartbeat reassured me that I was still alive.

But the fact is, I won't always be. That's *reality*. The practical joker who rolled that coffin into my office taught me a jolting and unforgettable lesson. Some future day, some quiet, heavily overcast morning, the sun will rise again on this old earth, but I will be gone—absent from this body. Dust will settle on my books and somebody else will carry my keys, answer my phone, pick up the mail, and fill that room with his own laughter and tears. Painful and difficult as it may be to tolerate such thoughts, *that's reality.*

I would much prefer to live my life on the sharp, cutting edge of reality than dreaming on the soft, phony mattress of fantasy. Reality is the tempered poker that keeps the fires alive; it's the spark that prompts the engine to keep running—the hard set of facts that refuses to let feeling overrule logic. It's reality that forces every Alice out of her Wonderland. Its undaunted determination has pulled many a wanderer, lost in the maze of meanderings, back to the real world of right and wrong, true and false. Reality, I remind you, is the world from which most every emotionally and mentally disturbed patient has escaped, and the point to which they must return before health is restored. Hard as it may be to bear, reality brings a practical security second to none. It is, unquestionably, the healthiest place on earth.

Some quiet morning, whether we like it or not, you and I will be *forced* to face reality. The secondhand on our inner watch will suddenly stop. Time will be no more. At that moment—even before the casket gets ordered—my spiritual passport will be clutched in my hand. How about you? What will it read? For many it will bear the stamp

"CONDEMNED," but because of the grace of God through Jesus Christ, mine will read "REDEEMED." Again I ask: What will yours say?

While our world is sinking in the mire of human opinion, theories, philosophies, and dreams, our Lord invites us to stand firmly on the rock of reality. And what does that realistic mind-set look like? It includes such things as:

- Man is a depraved sinner in need of a Savior.
- Our hope is in Jesus Christ's death and resurrection.
- Receiving Him brings instant and eternal forgiveness.
- Death is certain, but not the end.
- Heaven is real ... and so is hell.
- We cannot escape standing before Him.
- The time to prepare is *now.*

Face it. That's reality.

—15:2–4—

Along with wrath, God reveals His grace. This is an unyielding principle of God's character. With vengeance, He couples victory. With judgment, he sends joy. So, 15:2–4 presents the mirror opposite of the somber doom of the seven angels of wrath in verse 1. While those angels bearing the bowls of wrath were filing in, John saw an untold number of the redeemed bearing harps and standing on the sea of glass spread out before the throne of God. Who are these people? John describes them as those who were victorious over three horrendous pressures to reject Christ during the tribulation:

- *political pressure* through the first Beast's compelling, charismatic military prowess
- *religious pressure* through the second Beast's deceptively miraculous image
- *economic pressure* through the number of the Beast, necessary to buy and sell

These pressures, described earlier in chapter 13, pushed all people to the edge of a life-and-death decision. Either they could worship the Beast and save their lives, or they could resist His regime and lose them.

The redeemed standing on the sea of glass chose faithfulness to Christ—a foolish decision in the midst of unparalleled persecution. But to quote the famous line of missionary and martyr Jim Elliot, "He is no fool who gives what he cannot keep, to gain what he cannot lose."[8]

This vast throng of the redeemed will sing a song of victory before the throne of God. Each will play a lyre—a stringed instrument held in the hands, not the large harp we see in a modern orchestra. Unlike teaching and preaching, musical ministry will endure throughout eternity! Singing and praising will never cease, because the more that finite beings like us get to know our infinite God, the more reason we'll have to praise Him. That's why we love to sing that last verse of "Amazing Grace":

Ancient lyre

Z. Radovan/www.BibleLandPictures.com

When we've been there ten thousand years
Bright shining as the sun.
We've no less days to sing God's praise
Than when we've first begun.[9]

In verses 3–4, John notes that this heavenly choir will sing two songs: "the song of Moses" and "the song of the Lamb." Commentators offer several theories for the identity of these songs. Most agree that the song of Moses probably incorporated lyrics from one or both of two Old Testament passages: Exodus 15:1–18 and Deuteronomy 32:1–43. In essence, these songs refer to deliverance from Egypt through the ten plagues, God's defeat of the Egyptian army, and Israel's preparation for entrance into the Promised Land. How appropriate for victorious saints who were delivered from the judgments of the tribulation to witness the defeat of the Antichrist and the establishment of Christ's earthly kingdom! "The song of the Lamb" appears to be a new song, so John went on to describe the lyrics.

Both songs praise God for who He is and what He has done. He is God the Almighty, the Righteous and true King, who alone is holy. His works are great and marvelous, His ways just, and He is worthy of worship by all nations. This passage points to a profound truth about worship. Whether the songs are old or new, the purpose of worship is to glorify God for His awesome Person and awe-inspiring works.

Regarding the relationship of the two songs sung before the throne, one commentator observes:

> The song of Moses was sung at the Red Sea, the song of the Lamb is sung at the crystal sea; the song of Moses was a song of triumph over Egypt, the song of the Lamb is a song of triumph over Babylon; the song of Moses told how God brought His people out, the song of the Lamb tells how God brings His people in; the song of Moses was the first song in Scripture, the song of the Lamb is the last. The song of Moses commemorated the execution of a foe, the expectation of the saints, and the exaltation of the Lord; the song of the Lamb deals with the same three themes.[10]

—15:5–8—

As John listened to the vast choir of tribulation saints belting out their song of victory, his attention was again turned to the preparations for the final outpouring of God's wrath on the earth. While believers rejoiced in heaven, those who rejected the Lord's free offer of eternal life were about to endure long-delayed judgment.

John saw a temple in heaven, similar to the physical building that once stood in Jerusalem. By the time of John's writing, the earthly temple had lain in ruins for more than twenty-five years. Yet even that earthly temple was a "model" of the heavenly temple fashioned by God Himself (Heb. 8:2–5). Unlike the earthly temple, however, the "most holy place" or "holy of holies" in the heavenly temple was open. In its earthly counterpart, that place where the presence of the Lord dwelled had always been concealed (Lev. 16:2–3; Heb. 9:2–7). Only the high priest could enter the holy of holies once a year to make sacrifices on behalf of sinful people. In heaven, where no sinful people dwell, Christ Himself serves as our eternal High Priest. For the saints in heaven nothing obscures God's glory. For believers the heavenly tabernacle is a temple of unhindered access to God, but for unbelievers that same tabernacle becomes *a temple of doom*.

As the vision proceeded, seven angels emerged from the heavenly temple, each clothed in pure white and adorned in priestly garments (15:6). With solemnity, these angels approached the throne of God. One of the four living creatures mentioned in chapters 4–6 handed each of them a bowl "full of the wrath of God" (15:7). The word translated "bowl" refers to a shallow, saucer-like dish used for boiling liquids as well as for "drinking or pouring libations."[11] One dictionary adds that the use of this term in Revelation is "suggestive of rapidity in the emptying of the contents."[12]

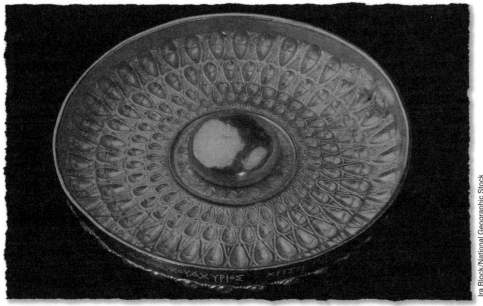

Ancient libation bowl

These bowls may be connected with the bowls filled with the prayers for vindication offered by the martyred believers in 5:8. They are the direct response to that plea for God to avenge their suffering and death. These bowls of wrath also begin to answer the age-old question of why the wicked seem to go unpunished while the righteous suffer injustice. The truth is that God's mercy during the tribulation delayed the full measure of judgment to give people an opportunity to repent (2 Peter 3:9). But we must never presume on God's mercy. Judgment postponed is not the same as judgment denied.

As John continued to stare into the open temple, he saw it "filled with smoke from the glory of God" (15:8). As in the days of Moses, after the earthly tabernacle was completed (Ex. 40:33–35), the heavenly tabernacle was consumed by the glorious holy presence of God. Similarly, when Isaiah witnessed the Lord sitting on His throne, "lofty and exalted" (Isa. 6:1), he saw the heavenly temple "filling with smoke" (6:4).

John's vision of the heavenly temple of doom underscores three important contrasts.

As the temple fills with God's glory ...	... the earth is filled with His wrath.
In the past the wrath of God poured was poured out on Christ to save sinners ...	... in the future the wrath of God will be poured out on sinners to judge them.
While the righteous in heaven rejoice over the triumph of good ...	... the rebellious on earth will suffer with the destruction of evil.

Application

Victory in Heaven ... Vengeance on Earth

A. W. Tozer wrote, "We talk of [God] much and loudly, but we secretly think of Him as being absent, and we think of ourselves as inhabiting a parenthetic interval between the God who was and the God who will be."[13] The song of Moses draws on God's past deliverance; the song of the Lamb looks forward to His future vengeance. Yet John's vision of joy in heaven and sorrow on earth in Revelation 15 should turn our attention to our own situation today.

First, we should *express gratitude for God's promise of protection*. Prior to the tribulation events described in Revelation 15, those people on earth who have placed their faith in Jesus Christ will be "caught up ... in the clouds to meet the Lord in the air" (1 Thess. 4:17). While the final triumph of good over evil is yet future, believers in Christ can offer thanks for victory over the enemy. Regarding this hope of future salvation, Paul wrote:

> Having the first fruits of the Spirit, even we ourselves groan within ourselves, waiting eagerly for our adoption as sons, the redemption of our body. For in hope we have been saved, but hope that is seen is not hope; for who hopes for what he already sees? But if we hope for what we do not see, with perseverance we wait eagerly for it. (Rom. 8:23–25)

Do you nurture this hope of redemption and deliverance? Is it real enough to affect your everyday attitudes? I urge you to go there! If you need a little prompting, you might want to take a closer look at the singing saints before the throne of God who triumphantly sing songs of praise and thanksgiving. If you don't know any by heart, I encourage you to learn them. Besides a Bible, every believer should get to know some of the songs of faith. Treasure the old songs—those great hymns. Learn the new choruses of praise as well. Spend time alone or with family "speaking to one another in psalms and hymns and spiritual songs, singing and making melody with your heart to the Lord; always giving thanks for all things in the name of our Lord Jesus Christ to God, even the Father" (Eph. 5:19–20). A closeness is cultivated when families sing together.

Our second response should be *concern for those who choose to reject Christ*. After the church is raptured and the Antichrist rises to power, many will realize that their choice to reject Christ was a regrettable, tragic error. Others will continue to reject Jesus as their sovereign Lord and undergo horrible suffering as a result. The most important decision in life is the choice to accept God's promise of protection in His Son, Jesus Christ. Therefore, the greatest concern for believers today must be for the lost. How do you express your concern for them in a world increasingly hostile to the claims of Christ?

The apostle Peter answers this question in 1 Peter 3:15. First, "sanctify Christ as Lord in your hearts." Set Christ apart, and let Him set you apart as a holy vessel. Offer yourself for His service—anytime ... anywhere ... for *anyone*. Prepare yourself to be a ready and willing soldier to obey His prompting at any moment.

Second, always be "ready to make a defense to everyone who asks you to give an account for the hope that is in you." Rehearse your own testimony about how Christ saved you. Keep it fresh on your lips. Tell it freely and sincerely. Few things pique the curiosity of unbelievers more than the testimony of a joyous, transformed life.

Finally, treat unbelievers with "gentleness and reverence." Steer clear of anything resembling a self-righteous, modern-day Pharisee. Let God do the judging in His own time. Let's pursue people not with sour derision, but with the sweet fruit of the Spirit: "love, joy, peace, patience, kindness, goodness, faithfulness, gentleness, self-control" (Gal. 5:22–23). Sharing Christ with a fallen world is easier than you realize.

Be a willing witness of the gospel message. Share your testimony of a transformed life. Don't forget to provide a persuasive, winsome picture of God's saving grace.

The Final Seven Super Bowls (Revelation 16:1–21)

¹Then I heard a loud voice from the temple, saying to the seven angels, "Go and pour out on the earth the seven bowls of the wrath of God."

²So the first *angel* went and poured out his bowl on the earth; and it became a loathsome and malignant sore on the people who had the mark of the beast and who worshiped his image.

³The second *angel* poured out his bowl into the sea, and it became blood like *that* of a dead man; and every living thing in the sea died.

⁴Then the third *angel* poured out his bowl into the rivers and the springs of waters; and they became blood. ⁵And I heard the angel of the waters saying, "Righteous are You, who are and who were, O Holy One, because You judged these things; ⁶for they poured out the blood of saints and prophets, and You have given them blood to drink. They deserve it." ⁷And I heard the altar saying, "Yes, O Lord God, the Almighty, true and righteous are Your judgments."

⁸The fourth *angel* poured out his bowl upon the sun, and it was given to it to scorch men with fire. ⁹Men were scorched with fierce heat; and they blasphemed the name of God who has the power over these plagues, and they did not repent so as to give Him glory.

¹⁰Then the fifth *angel* poured out his bowl on the throne of the beast, and his kingdom became darkened; and they gnawed their tongues because of pain, ¹¹and they blasphemed the God of heaven because of their pains and their sores; and they did not repent of their deeds.

¹²The sixth *angel* poured out his bowl on the great river, the Euphrates; and its water was dried up, so that the way would be prepared for the kings from the east. ¹³And I saw *coming* out of the mouth of the dragon and out of the mouth of the beast and out of the mouth of the false prophet, three

unclean spirits like frogs; [14]for they are spirits of demons, performing signs, which go out to the kings of the whole world, to gather them together for the war of the great day of God, the Almighty. [15]("Behold, I am coming like a thief. Blessed is the one who stays awake and keeps his clothes, so that he will not walk about naked and men will not see his shame.") [16]And they gathered them together to the place which in Hebrew is called Har-Magedon.

[17]Then the seventh angel poured out his bowl upon the air, and a loud voice came out of the temple from the throne, saying, "It is done." [18]And there were flashes of lightning and sounds and peals of thunder; and there was a great earthquake, such as there had not been since man came to be upon the earth, so great an earthquake was it, and so mighty. [19]The great city was split into three parts, and the cities of the nations fell. Babylon the great was remembered before God, to give her the cup of the wine of His fierce wrath. [20]And every island fled away, and the mountains were not found. [21]And huge hailstones, about one hundred pounds each, came down from heaven upon men; and men blasphemed God because of the plague of the hail, because its plague was extremely severe.

It seemed like the perfect, quiet Saturday morning. That unusually warm February 1 was a great time to wash our vehicles and run through the next morning's sermon. While in the middle of washing my truck, I heard a loud *BOOM!* I assumed there must have been a major traffic collision a few blocks away. After several minutes, however, I heard no sirens, no more sounds … nothing. The day returned to its stillness. My life went on as if nothing had happened. But on that February morning, far above my head, the space shuttle *Columbia* had disintegrated. As it reentered the atmosphere, breaking up in the blue sky above, it spilled debris across a vast section of north Texas and left permanent open spaces at the dinner tables of seven grieving families.

It may have been a similarly calm day in Corinth when a man named Paul picked up his stylus and wrote to his friend in Thessalonica. In fact, the talk in the public square may have been all about "peace and security," prompting Paul to write these sobering words: "For you yourselves know full well that the day of the Lord will come just like a thief in the night. While they are saying, 'Peace and safety!' then destruction will come upon them suddenly like labor pains upon a woman with child, and they will not escape" (1 Thess. 5:2–3). Some fifteen years later, the apostle Peter used the same word picture of a thief in the night when he warned his readers, "But the day of the Lord will come like a thief, in which the heavens will pass away with a roar and the elements will be destroyed with intense heat, and the earth and its works will be burned up" (2 Peter 3:10). Their message was clear: the period of future judgment on the earth would come without announcement, without a news flash, without warning. Just like the sonic boom above my head on the day of the *Columbia* disaster, it would catch the world in its mode of "business as usual."

Paul and Peter may have warned of the coming judgment, but John witnessed it in a stunning revelation. Revelation 16 describes the final round of ever-increasing judgments on the people who will stubbornly take the side of evil against the Lord in spite of countless warnings throughout the seven-year tribulation period. You may notice some similarities between the final seven bowls of wrath and the earlier seven trumpet judgments. On close examination, however, we make two important observations.

First, God's future judgment will not come as one sudden, catastrophic event at the end of time to annihilate all of life. Rather, it will consist of many judgments throughout the tribulation, each one allowing yet another opportunity for repentance. Second, the judgments will grow progressively more severe, providing greater impetus to submit to the Lord while demonstrating that an ultimate end to all evil will come soon. Although many will trust in Christ during this time, the sad truth is that most will continue in their disbelief and rebellion.

Tribulation Judgments in the Book of Revelation

"Seal" Series (Revelation 6:1–8:5)	"Trumpet" Series (Revelation 8:6–9:21)	"Bowl" Series (Revelation 16:1–21)
1. Conquest 2. Warfare 3. Famine and Poverty 4. Death (¼ population) 5. Mistreatment/ Martyrdom 6. Earthquake 7. Introduction of "Trumpet" Judgments	1. Hail and Fire (⅓ vegetation ruined) 2. Meteor Shower (⅓ sea life killed) 3. Water Pollution (⅓ water supply poisoned) 4. Darkness 5. Demonic Locust Attack 6. Demonic Hordes (⅓ humanity killed) 7. Introduction of "Bowl" Judgments	1. Malignant Sores 2. Poisoned Seas (death of all sea life) 3. Poisoned Fresh Water 4. Humanity Scorched 5. Widespread Darkness/Misery 6. Vast Military Invasion 7. Most Destructive Earthquake/Hail

Increasing Intensity. . . Culminating at Armageddon

When we examine the seven bowls of wrath, we notice that the first four judgments relate to the natural world—the earth, the sea, the rivers, and the sun (16:1–9). The next two bowls affect the political world—the Beast's throne and the armies of the world (16:10–16). Finally, the seventh bowl judgment sums everything up, bringing all judgments to an end (16:17–21). We will look at each of these three sets of judgments in sequence.

— 16:1–9 —

After hearing a loud voice commanding the seven angels to pour their seven bowls of God's wrath upon the earth (16:1), John saw the angels instantly obey. Yet they didn't simply crowd at the edge of heaven and empty their saucers like a mob of kindergartners slinging mud. John's vision portrayed a serious and sobering period in earth's future. John watched as the angels proceeded in a somber manner, one at a time, in a preset order.

The first angel stepped out of the line of seven and splashed his bowl upon the earth (16:2). I don't mean to sound calloused, but the description of the target and results of this first judgment remind me of a heat-seeking missile or smart bomb. The only people affected by the first plague were "the people who had the mark of the beast and who worshiped his image." Clearly, these final bowls of wrath will commence in the very last days of the seven-year tribulation. You might recall that the Beast and False Prophet don't even rise to power until the second half of the tribulation (13:5), during which time they will begin a worldwide program of branding those who worship them or banning those who don't (13:11–18). Although those who received the mark of the beast and worshiped his image will think they have spared their lives and saved their families, the reality is that they only buy themselves about three years ... in exchange for eternity! Worse than that, these Beast-followers will ally themselves with and participate in the war machine that will hunt down, persecute, and kill nonconforming believers in Christ.

Now, as a result of their revolt against God and attack on His people, John saw the people of the earth instantly break out in "a loathsome and malignant sore." John Phillips suggests this sore may be directly related to the mark of the beast they received. He writes, "There, on the right hand, a horrible, putrifying, incurable cancer! There on the face, a loathsome, ugly, disfiguring, and agonizing blotch! Men become horrible to look upon and their pains never end."[14] But those who rejected the mark out of their devotion to Christ are immune! With the first bowl of wrath, everybody will begin to realize that though the Antichrist had been briefly allowed to wreak havoc on the saints, the tide was about to turn.

As the sores continued to bring misery and pain to the afflicted, the second angel arrived with his bowl and poured it upon the saltwater seas. In John's symbolic vision, the water immediately became "blood like that of a dead man." Now, I wouldn't call myself squeamish, but thick, putrid, rotten, coagulated, slimy blood makes my stomach churn. If you've ever been to an ocean beach when jellyfish have washed ashore and died, you have an idea of the kind of stench involved. Yet this vision in Revelation is millions of times worse. Earlier, in the second trumpet judgment, only one third of the sea life was killed by the fiery mountain cast into the ocean (8:8–9). When John saw the sea polluted by this toxic death, however, the waters were so contaminated that nothing could survive. With the devastation of sea life, those who had received the mark of the Beast in order to buy and sell food will be dealt a crushing blow to their economy . . . and their lives.

As the wicked inhabitants of the earth reeled at the realization that their lives were being torn apart, they turned inland toward the rivers and lakes. Yet just as they were about to console themselves, the third angel poured his bowl on "the rivers and the springs of waters," turning them to blood. In the first half of the tribulation, a star called "Wormwood" contaminated only one third of the rivers and springs, causing many to die from the bitterness of the water (8:10–11). This time, at the end, *all* of the fresh water will be turned to blood, resulting in nothing safe to drink. Then the people of earth can turn their attention only to the skies and pray for fresh, pure rain to water their parched lips. Sadly, they had long refused to turn their hearts toward heaven to quench their dry, barren souls!

At this point you may be thinking, *How awful! What kind of God would do this? Do these people really deserve these extreme judgments?* So it's fitting that the angel associated with the waters should break into a brief doxology to set the record straight. John heard him reaffirm that through these judgments God will demonstrate His perfect righteousness and holiness (16:5). This reminds everyone that the direct recipients of this wrath will be personally responsible for a global holocaust against God's people. They will martyr the saints and murder the prophets (16:6), spilling their holy blood upon the earth. Because "justice" means getting what a person deserves, then true justice will be served on the wicked of the world. In fact, the angel's praise concludes, "You have given them blood to drink. They deserve it." Like a responsive refrain, a voice from the altar reiterated this truth: "Yes, O Lord God, the Almighty, true and righteous are Your judgments" (16:8). Neither the angel nor those around the altar left room for anybody to question the righteousness and goodness of God.

After this brief doxology, the fourth angel looked down upon the earth, where the marked men and women waited expectantly for rain to quench their thirst. The angel reached up and poured his bowl upon the sun, causing it to shine with intense heat to "scorch men with fire." Instead of catching soothing drops of rain, the people of earth were burned with searing rays from the sun. Scientists have long been concerned about the possibility of massive, unexpected solar flares that could increase the number of harmful rays that penetrate our atmosphere. It seems that by the end of the tribulation the atmosphere will have been so damaged that the rays of the sun will no longer be filtered or deflected, causing all sorts of climate changes, with catastrophic results. This end-time global warming will make today's hot-earth hysteria resemble nothing more than a warm spring day.

You would think that after a series of four consecutive judgments, which bring wicked humanity to its knees, human hearts would melt. One might expect that the next verse would describe how all those sore-inflicted, starving, thirsting, burning men and women of earth will raise their hands and cry out to God for mercy. Surely a loving God would hear the cries of their hearts, relent of His just wrath, and bring times of refreshing and renewal even at this late stage! In fact, the prophet Joel specifically pointed out this aspect of the Lord's character, even at the brink of total judgment:

> "Yet even now," declares the Lord,
> "Return to Me with all your heart,
> And with fasting, weeping and mourning;
> And rend your heart and not your garments."
> Now return to the Lord your God,
> For He is gracious and compassionate,
> Slow to anger, abounding in lovingkindness
> And relenting of evil.
> Who knows whether He will not turn and relent
> And leave a blessing behind Him? (Joel 2:12–14)

Yet instead of humble repentance, we see nothing but increased hardness. In response to judgment, the worshipers of Satan will blaspheme God (16:9). They will fail to repent. They will refuse to give Him glory. Think about this. Everyone who will be afflicted by the plagues will have had access to the same predictions you're reading about now. They will have had seven years of successive warnings building on the prophecies fulfilled just a short time before. Though they have no excuse for continued rebellion, they will still curse their Creator and rage at their Redeemer.

— 16:10–16 —

Like the earlier trumpet judgments, the first four bowls are directed against the natural realm (earth, sea, waters, and sun). We may call them "natural" disasters, though they have a supernatural cause. The fifth and sixth bowl judgments, however, like their trumpet counterparts, are more obviously supernatural, target-ing the political realm (the Beast's kingdom and the kingdoms of the world).

When John witnessed the fifth angel pour his bowl on the "throne" of the Beast, two results followed: a shroud of darkness descended on the Beast's entire kingdom, and the people were consumed by excruciating pain (16:10). The term "throne" in the Bible isn't concerned with furniture but with the seat of a ruler's authority. In the tribulation, the "throne" specifically refers to the center of the Antichrist's reign, but it will also include his entire kingdom and those over whom he will reign for forty-two months. That kingdom will experience darkness like never before. This affliction recalls the plague of darkness God brought on Egypt millennia ago. Exodus 10:21–23 describes that plague this way:

> Then the LORD said to Moses, "Stretch out your hand toward the sky, that there may be darkness over the land of Egypt, even a darkness which may be felt." So Moses stretched out his hand toward the sky, and there was thick darkness in all the land of Egypt for three days. They did not see one another, nor did anyone rise from his place for three days, but all the sons of Israel had light in their dwellings.

Revelation 16:11 reminds us that the afflictions suffered by the enemies of God are cumulative. The sores brought on by the first bowl will continue to fester as the darkness closes in around them. The water that would have soothed their sun-scorched flesh will stand in stinking, stagnant pools; once-clean water will be pol-luted with decaying blood. Nevertheless, believe it or not, the people will continue to blaspheme God and refuse to repent.

Sadly, this is the final reference to the people's unwillingness to repent. The first five plagues were God's final offer and humanity's final opportunity for repen-tance. There will be no more. The bowls of wrath reveal that the sinful minds, hearts, and wills of those who took the mark have been sealed. They have become like the generation in the days of Noah: "Then the LORD saw that the wickedness of man was great on the earth, and that every intent of the thoughts of his heart was only evil continually" (Gen. 6:5). The apostle Paul describes this state of absolute depravity in Romans 1. Read these words slowly and thoughtfully.

> For the wrath of God is revealed from heaven against all ungodliness and unrighteousness of men who suppress the truth in unrighteousness. (Rom 1:18)

> For even though they knew God, they did not honor Him as God or give thanks, but they became futile in their speculations, and their foolish heart was darkened. (1:21)

> Therefore God gave them over in the lusts of their hearts to impurity. (1:24)

For they exchanged the truth of God for a lie, and worshiped and served the creature rather than the Creator. (1:25)

For this reason God gave them over to degrading passions. (1:26)

This leads to the sixth bowl of wrath, when the stage is set for the infamous battle of Armageddon. At the end of the seven-year tribulation, whatever will be left of the military forces of the world will gather for war at a place called "Har-Magedon" [Megiddo in Hebrew] (16:6). The Bible's depiction of this battle begins in 16:12–16 and is completed, after a pause in the action, in 19:11–21. In this epic clash, the Antichrist and the armies of the earth will be utterly destroyed by Christ and the armies of heaven. John's portrayal of this last battle involves three elements: a river, a coalition of kings, and an unholy trinity.

In John's vision, the wrath from the sixth angel's bowl fell upon the Euphrates River. The Euphrates has been an integral part of world affairs since creation. It was one of four rivers that irrigated the garden of Eden (Gen. 2:14). It was supposed to have provided the northern and eastern boundaries of the land God promised

Route of the Kings of the East

© Michael Svigel

Jezreel Valley today

to Abraham's descendants (15:18; Josh. 1:4). The Hebrew people simply called it "the River," or "the great river." The Greek name, *Euphrates*, meant "sweet water."[15] Near of the end of God's wrath, however, those waters—long embittered by judgment—will dry up, making a way for the "kings from the east."

At first glance, the result of the sixth bowl seems to come to the aid of the kings from the east, who apparently had been itching to move westward and join in the fray. Little do they know, however, that their eagerness to gather in the Holy Land will not be of their own choosing, but rather will be a result of demonic deception. John described what appears to be three "frogs" belching from the mouths of the unholy "trinity"—the dragon, the Beast, and the False Prophet (16:13). These demons, using deceptive signs and wonders, will lead the rulers of the world and their armies to the great plain of Armageddon. One commentator explains this gathering.

> Satan, knowing that the second coming of Christ is near, will gather the military might of the world into the Holy Land to resist the coming of the Son of Man who will return to the Mount of Olives (Zech. 14:4). Though the nations may be deceived in entering into the war in hope of gaining world political power, the satanic purpose is to combat the armies from heaven (introduced in 19) at the second coming of Christ.[16]

While the unholy trinity, the rulers, and the armies of the world will act on their own evil intentions, they will nevertheless behave predictably and will remain under the sovereign control of God. While the Lord is never the author of evil, He will allow wicked people to destroy themselves by their own evil acts (Rom. 1:20–32). So the armies of the world will ultimately gather at Armageddon. The Jezreel Valley will become the battleground for what the kings and armies expect to be the greatest war in the history of the world. But what follows can hardly be considered a battle.

Revelation 16:16 stops the action with the armies of the earth gathered at Armageddon, as if each army awaits its command from their commanders-in-chief. The final outcome of this battle is not described until Revelation 19, when we see the armies of Satan finally meet their match with the armies of Christ. Until then, we reflect on the words of Christ: "Behold, I am coming like a thief. Blessed is the one who stays awake and keeps his clothes, so that he will not walk about naked and men will not see his shame" (16:15).

— **16:17–21** —

As the kingdoms of the world gathered to fight in the expansive Jezreel Valley, the seventh angel tossed the contents of the final bowl into the air. Immediately a loud voice cried out from the temple, "It is done!" The verb translated "done" stresses the present effect of a past event, indicating that "the judgment of God has already occurred, and we are at the end of history. The meaning of [this verb] is related to its meaning 'happen' or 'come to pass.' "[17] In other words, this cataclysmic end of the

HOLY LAND, HOLY WAR

Like any boy growing up in Nazareth, Jesus would have known the local geography and the historical significance of the hills that surrounded His city. The southern ridge of the town, today called the Nazareth Ridge, overlooks the vast Jezreel Valley, the site of countless clashes between the world's greatest armies. If He squinted His eyes, He could have peered across the valley and just made out the town of Megiddo, well-known as the most militarily strategic city in the Middle East.

The international highway that carried troops and commerce from Mesopotamia to Egypt ran the full length of Israel, meandering through the Carmel mountain range. Megiddo guarded the entrance to the most important pass through the ridge. Pharaoh Thutmose III, who fought the Canaanites in 1468 BC, saw the importance of the stronghold and declared, "It is the capture of a thousand cities, this capture of Megiddo."[18] Archaeologists have uncovered no less than twenty distinct levels of civilization built one upon the other, each one recognizing the supreme value of its location for control of Middle Eastern commerce.

For as long as anyone can remember, Megiddo and the surrounding hill country and the Jezreel Valley have been a place for war. As the young Jesus anticipated His earthly ministry, He knew that one day Megiddo would be the rallying point for the armies of the Antichrist. There, those who would gather to defy His sovereign rule will suffer judgment for their rebellion.

world and the evil that corrupted it was ordained long ago, predicted many times throughout history, and with the pouring of the seventh bowl, will be accomplished.

The description that follows in the remainder of Revelation 16 summarizes what John will deal with in detail in Revelation 17:1–22:5. What he described in short order is nothing less than chilling if we read his words using our imaginations.

- Lightning flashes from one end of heaven to the other.
- Thunder roars through the atmosphere.
- The worst earthquake in history shakes the world.
- The Antichrist's capital city splits into three.
- Islands sink into the ocean.
- Mountains collapse into the earth.
- Hundred-pound hailstones pummel the earth.

What's left of human civilization is shaken to its stone-age foundation, clearing the earth for an extreme makeover. Revelation describes nothing less than the end of the world as we know it. Everything about the earth, including its topography, will be prepared for a new regime: the thousand-year reign of Jesus Christ.

Application

Turning the Tables

Rest assured, those who mistreat the innocent and choose evil over good *will* be brought to justice. The Beast-worshipers will commit to his wicked regime to save their lives, and for a few years it will probably look as if they might get away with their persecution and murder of believers. But Revelation 16 reminds us that God's judgment is inescapable.

The same is true for us today. It may appear that the wicked get off scot-free. But one day there will be a reckoning. God has made it clear that the present world system, which rewards evil and punishes good, will come to a tragic end. The images of Revelation 16 can be distilled into two key truths to remember as we navigate the injustices of the present world system.

First, *justice in this world will always appear distorted.* The psalmist lamented:

Behold, these are the wicked;
And always at ease, they have increased in wealth.
Surely in vain I have kept my heart pure
And washed my hands in innocence;
For I have been stricken all day long
And chastened every morning. (Ps. 73:12–14)

In other words, life is often a raw deal. You work hard at school and make a hard-earned B+, but a fellow student cheats or cuts corners and not only gets an "A," he is granted a scholarship. Your wicked coworkers get promoted by flattery and slander, but you follow the rules and lose your job. You maintain insurance on your car, but somebody without insurance hits you and leaves you with the bill. How have you experienced unfairness? How have you expressed your frustrations about the injustices inherent in this fallen world system? Do the words of the psalmist resonate with you?

Second, *escaping the reality of God's judgment is impossible.* The same psalmist, coming to his senses and looking at the world from a divine rather than human perspective, continues:

> When I pondered to understand this,
> It was troublesome in my sight
> Until I came into the sanctuary of God;
> Then I perceived their end.
> Surely You set them in slippery places;
> You cast them down to destruction.
> How they are destroyed in a moment!
> They are utterly swept away by sudden terrors! (Ps. 73:16–19)

Just as the tribulation rebels will be held accountable for their wickedness, so every person will be held accountable for his or her life. It is impossible to escape judgment. Reminding ourselves of this fact will help us come to terms with the brutality of the present world and the injustice that seems to reign. One day the tables will be turned and justice will be served.

Reminding ourselves that the injustices of this world will one day be undone can bring tremendous benefits. The unfairness we endure for righteousness suddenly feels worth the cost. This kind of theology is therapeutic. It can ease our anger, frustration, and even depression. Our striving against sin in this world will not go unnoticed, nor will indulging sin go unpunished.

The Final Exit of Worldwide Religion (Revelation 17:1–18)

---

¹Then one of the seven angels who had the seven bowls came and spoke with me, saying, "Come here, I will show you the judgment of the great harlot who sits on many waters, ²with whom the kings of the earth committed *acts of* immorality, and those who dwell on the earth were made drunk with the wine of her immorality." ³And he carried me away in the Spirit into a wilderness; and I saw a woman sitting on a scarlet beast, full of

blasphemous names, having seven heads and ten horns. ⁴The woman was clothed in purple and scarlet, and adorned with gold and precious stones and pearls, having in her hand a gold cup full of abominations and of the unclean things of her immorality, ⁵and on her forehead a name *was* written, a mystery, "BABYLON THE GREAT, THE MOTHER OF HARLOTS AND OF THE ABOMINATIONS OF THE EARTH." ⁶And I saw the woman drunk with the blood of the saints, and with the blood of the witnesses of Jesus. When I saw her, I wondered greatly. ⁷And the angel said to me, "Why do you wonder? I will tell you the mystery of the woman and of the beast that carries her, which has the seven heads and the ten horns.

⁸"The beast that you saw was, and is not, and is about to come up out of the abyss and go to destruction. And those who dwell on the earth, whose name has not been written in the book of life from the foundation of the world, will wonder when they see the beast, that he was and is not and will come. ⁹Here is the mind which has wisdom. The seven heads are seven mountains on which the woman sits, ¹⁰and they are seven kings; five have fallen, one is, the other has not yet come; and when he comes, he must remain a little while. ¹¹The beast which was and is not, is himself also an eighth and is *one* of the seven, and he goes to destruction. ¹²The ten horns which you saw are ten kings who have not yet received a kingdom, but they receive authority as kings with the beast for one hour. ¹³These have one purpose, and they give their power and authority to the beast. ¹⁴These will wage war against the Lamb, and the Lamb will overcome them, because He is Lord of lords and King of kings, and those who are with Him *are the* called and chosen and faithful."

¹⁵And he said to me, "The waters which you saw where the harlot sits, are peoples and multitudes and nations and tongues. ¹⁶And the ten horns which you saw, and the beast, these will hate the harlot and will make her desolate and naked, and will eat her flesh and will burn her up with fire. ¹⁷For God has put it in their hearts to execute His purpose by having a common purpose, and by giving their kingdom to the beast, until the words of God will be fulfilled. ¹⁸The woman whom you saw is the great city, which reigns over the kings of the earth."

In 1844 Karl Marx famously described religion as "the opiate of the people."[19] That political philosopher viewed all religion as man-made—a crutch that helped people escape the hardships of this world system by resting their hopes, confidence, and comfort on something other than the heartless world around them. The cure for humanity's need for religion, Marx argued, was to overcome the conditions of oppression and inequality that had forced people to seek psychological succor from outside themselves. Marx's solution? Communism—an atheistic system that invoked as much religious zeal in the twentieth century as any of the man-made "religious" systems Marx had criticized.

Marx's critique of religion as the "opiate of the people" often makes Christians cringe. But I think he was right. *Hold on!* Before you label me a Communist (which I'm definitely *not*), let me explain. Marx was right that all "man-made" religion is useless—merely a deceptive psychological crutch to distract people from the real conditions of the world. His unforgivable errors, however, were to lump Christianity into the same category as a "man-made" religion and to propose atheistic communism to replace it. When you stop and think about Marx's words, you realize his criticism of man-made religion was *dead on*, but his own man-made solution was *dead wrong*.

The Bible itself presents a picture of man-made religion that gives us a heavenly perspective on the matter. Travel back with me to the period in human history following the great flood, after Noah's death, to the land of Shinar—the birthplace of worldwide religion. The story of the tower of Babel in Genesis 11:1–9 is familiar to most. Instead of obeying God's command to "be fruitful and multiply, and fill the earth" (9:1, 7), the descendants of Noah moved east to Shinar—the location of ancient Babylon. There they defied God's mandate to spread throughout the world, preferring to band together and build a tower that would symbolize their man-made greatness. Consider their humanistic attitude: "They said, 'Come, let us build for ourselves a city, and a tower whose top will reach into heaven, and let us make for ourselves a name, otherwise we will be scattered abroad over the face of the whole earth'" (11:4). In order to avoid the very thing God commanded (spreading over the face of the whole earth), the people decided to make a name for themselves.

Interestingly, the ancient Jewish historian Josephus pointed out that these ancient people built the tower out of "burnt brick, cemented together with mortar, made of bitumen, that it might not be liable to admit water."[20] In other words, they apparently disbelieved God's promise that He would never again send a global flood and made their tower waterproof to keep from drowning! Furthermore, the entire project was projected heavenward—an attempt to construct a physical means to earn what only God can freely grant, access to heaven. Another ancient source, quoted by Josephus, noted, "When all men were of one language, some of them built a high tower, as if they would thereby ascend up to heaven."[21]

Here we see the three foundations of man-made false religion:

- rejection of God's promises—*faithlessness*
- rebellion against God's commands—*disobedience*
- refusal of God's grace—*legalism*

God responded decisively to this attempt at uniting humanity under a single, nationalistic religion. He confused their single language, producing several indecipherable dialects and breaking their ability to work together toward their godless ends. The result? They were *forced* to obey God's earlier command to branch out and fill the earth. Instead of creating a multitude of diverse nations and cultures united in worshiping the one true God, however, the nations fabricated countless man-made religions and created numerous gods after their own image.

The plane of Shinar, where "Babel" had been built, eventually became the center of one of the world's earliest empires—Babylon. The religious pride of the Babylonians is well documented: "Written Babylonian accounts of the building of the city of Babylon refer to its construction in heaven by the gods as a celestial city.... The Babylonians took great pride in their building; they boasted of their city as not only impregnable, but also as the heavenly city, *bâb–ili* ('the gate of God')."[22] It's no wonder that "Babylon," even after its collapse as an influential political and religious center of the world, became a metaphor for godless, humanistic religion in general.

This brings us to the book of Revelation, which mentions "Babylon" six times:

"Fallen, fallen is Babylon the great, she who has made all the nations drink of the wine of the passion of her immorality." (14:8)

Babylon the great was remembered before God, to give her the cup of the wine of His fierce wrath. (16:19)

On her forehead a name was written, a mystery, "BABYLON THE GREAT, THE MOTHER OF HARLOTS AND OF THE ABOMINATIONS OF THE EARTH." (17:5)

"Fallen, fallen is Babylon the great! She has become a dwelling place of demons and a prison of every unclean spirit, and a prison of every unclean and hateful bird." (18:2)

"Woe, woe, the great city, Babylon, the strong city! For in one hour your judgment has come." (18:10)

"So will Babylon, the great city, be thrown down with violence, and will not be found any longer." (18:21)

Our knee-jerk response may be to interpret this as the historical city named "Babylon," or as the region of ancient Babylon in the present Middle East—Iraq. The name "Babylon," however, already occurs in the New Testament metaphorically for another city, Rome (1 Peter 5:13). In light of Revelation's penchant for symbolic language, it seems best to identify "Babylon" not specifically as a particular city or country, but as representing a final godless, humanistic, and worldwide religious system. In the same way we might refer to "Wall Street" to describe the entire American financial system, Revelation uses "Babylon" to refer to the Antichrist's end-time religious/political/economic empire.

Cast of Characters in Revelation 17

Phrase/Image	Scripture	Explanation
The great harlot	17:1–8	Works-based, humanistic religion, called "the mother of harlots" because it is the foundation of all false religions, drawing its inspiration from pride, self-sufficiency, and a denial of God's grace.
Many waters	17:1, 15	All people and people groups around the world under the influence of the worldwide religion.
The Beast	17:3, 8, 11–14	The Antichrist, ruler of the end-time global empire and object of worship in the worldwide religion.
"Was, and is not, and is about to come up out of the abyss"	17:8, 11	The Antichrist will imitate Christ's death and resurrection in order to amaze the world and win its political and religious devotion (13:3–4). This description contrasts with the divine Christ, who "who is and who was and who is to come" from heaven to rule forever (1:8).
Seven heads	17:3, 7, 9–10	Seven world empires that stood in opposition to God and His people — five that were in John's past (Egypt, Assyria, Babylon, Medo-Persia, and Greece), one that existed in John's present (Rome), and one that will arise in the future (empire of the Antichrist).
"Seven mountains"	17:9	Though ancient Rome was built on seven hills, the idea of a city built on "seven hills" became a way to equate the grandeur of a city with the grandeur of Rome. So, Constantinople was regarded as a city on seven hills, as were other cities in the ancient world. It is uncertain whether this means the capital city of the Antichrist will have seven literal hills.
The eighth king	17:11	The Antichrist, who is one of the preceding kings, is also an "eighth." This may refer to the two phases of his rule — before his marvelous "death and resurrection" (the "seventh" king) and after this astounding feat when Satan turns his local political career into a global empire (as the "eighth" king).
Ten horns	17:3, 7, 12	Ten political powers that will unite to empower the Antichrist, turning all worldly authority over to him.
"Called and chosen and faithful"	17:14	When Christ returns as King of kings and Lord of lords to overcome the beast and the kings of the earth, He will be accompanied by "the called and chosen and faithful." This same group is called the "armies which are in heaven, clothed in fine linen, white and clean" (19:14). The New Testament commonly uses the terms "called," "chosen," and "faithful" to describe saints, so these are likely the resurrected and raptured believers returning with Christ to the earth at the battle of Armageddon.

— 17:1–6 —

With the armies of the earth gathered for the great battle of Armageddon (16:16) and the shocking preview of the final wrath of God still echoed through the halls of heaven (16:17–21), the drama subsided and John heard a gentle voice calling his attention. An angel—one of the seven who had poured out the bowls symbolizing the final wrath of God—suddenly took on the role of "apocalyptic tour guide," leading John through some visionary symbols in order to explain the meaning of the images. We'll eavesdrop on John's private tour in a moment, but before that, let's preview some of the key phrases and images that require some explanation in Revelation 17. The following chart serves as a sort of "tour brochure," giving a broad overview of symbols and their identifications.

With the likely meaning of these images in mind, we can briefly point out some of the details along John's tour. First, the angel intended to point out the judgment that will come on the system of worldwide false religion, also known as "the great harlot" or "Babylon" (17:1). Her religious influence will have spread far and wide. The spiritual immorality associated with idolatry will have caused the world to fall into something like a spiritual drunken stupor (17:2). Indeed, this will be a satanic spiritual "high" like nothing Karl Marx could have imagined when he called man-made religion "the opiate of the people." For this reason, judgment of demonic false religion will mean judgment of its devoted practitioners. We have already seen this in great detail when we witnessed the dumping of the seven bowls of wrath on the Antichrist and his followers (16:1–21).

As the tour continued, the interpreting angel took John on a journey into the spiritual realm, where he witnessed a lewd and disturbing scene. A woman dressed and adorned in the typical fashion of an ancient prostitute held a cup symbolizing her immorality (17:4). She rode atop a beast with seven heads and ten horns (17:3)—the symbol for the Antichrist (13:1).[23] Her name, "Babylon the Great," is a mystery—something that requires interpretation (17:5). As the "mother of harlots and of the abominations of the earth," she will be responsible for numerous religions that follow her example. Together these will lead the world into untold abominations. In fact, the woman, Babylon, is portrayed as drunk "with the blood of the saints," those who will be martyred for Jesus Christ (17:6). This means that the false religious system she represents will lead to the zealous persecution and slaughter of countless true servants of God. In response to this vision, John notes, "When I saw her, I wondered greatly" (17:6).

— 17:7–18 —

The heavenly tour guide, reading the perplexed expression on John's face, reassured him: "Why do you wonder? I will tell you the mystery of the woman and of the beast that carries her" (17:7). The chart above gives several likely explanations for the details of the angel's identifications. So at this point, let's focus on the big picture.

Just as the Beast and False Prophet are seen working together in Revelation 13, so Revelation 17 describes their two respective realms — the global empire and the worldwide religion — inextricably linked. During the three and a half years of the Antichrist's reign, the world will suffer under the ultimate merger between a totalitarian state and an antichristian "church."

The Beast's empire will be supported by an alliance of nations from around the globe, from "peoples and multitudes and nations and tongues" (17:15). All the world powers will surrender their sovereignty to the Antichrist (17:13), who will reign over all the kings of the earth from his great capital city (17:18). That is, the original tower of Babel dream of a worldwide government with one ruler, one language, one religion, and one economy will finally be realized for a brief season — figuratively, "for one hour" (17:10, 12). We already see this desire for religious, spiritual, and political unity at work through such institutions as the United Nations, the World Bank, and the World Council of Churches. These attempts have always failed to bring about true peace and security, and until the Antichrist's hostile takeover, their optimistic attempts will continue to fail. When Antichrist takes the throne, however, the one-world government and one-world religion will finally emerge.

The end of the angel's prophetic explanation brings out a profound irony. The world system bent on bringing glory to humanity will end with a double tragedy. At first the kings of the earth will turn on each other as their fragile alliance crumbles (17:16–17). This will climax in the battle of Armageddon, when the kings of the earth gather to make war with each other (16:12–16). This battle will actually end, however, when the glorious Deliverer descends with His own army of resurrected and glorified saints from heaven to exercise vengeance against the false christ and his armies (17:14; 19:14).

Application

Don't Be Duped by the Devilish

Marx called man-made religion "the opiate of the people." Revelation 17 tells us that in the last days the devil will concoct a spiritual drug so potent that it will make cocaine look like candy! The fulfillment of this worldwide religion awaits the future tribulation, but that doesn't mean the same devilish religious deception isn't alive and well today. In fact, the apostle John warned us, "Just as you heard that antichrist is coming, even now many antichrists have appeared" (1 John 2:18). He added, "The spirit of antichrist . . . is already in the world" (4:3).

This present spell of false religion exchanges God's grace and mercy for self-sufficiency and human effort. It trades God's commands for private definitions of right and wrong. And it brushes aside God's promises with "sophisticated" unbelief. Christians are not immune from being negatively influenced by these devilish deceptions, so let's keep a couple important truths at the forefront of our minds.

First, *religious activity feels full and alive but is, in truth, empty and dead.* Struggling with the purpose behind religious activity is a normal part of a genuine spiritual life in Christ. While believers become new creatures the moment they are saved, we don't automatically start living by the unearned grace that saved us. As we grow, we often revert to our own, self-sufficient, proud ways. We seek to earn God's continued favor on our own. We forget that the unmerited grace that saves us is the same grace that keeps us.

Second, *satanic strategy appears impressive and effective but is, in truth, impotent and deceptive.* Satan, the father of lies, along with his host of demons, has encouraged human beings in their pursuit of eternal life, purpose, and meaning by means of human effort. He deceives people through the lie of self-reliance, seeking to earn God's favor by one's own effort. Or Satan tries to encourage self-condemnation, the lie that a person's bad works render them unlovable by God. Neither is true. In fact, both stem from the satanic lie that *good works* are the basis of our relationship with God. God's offer of salvation solely by grace through faith immediately cuts down Satan's "reasonable" strategy.

To apply these truths directly to your own life, use the chart on page 233. Read the following "Common False Statements" in the left column. Mark the ones you have caught yourself thinking or saying. Then read the corresponding "True Statement" based on the Word of God. When you have finished comparing the true and the false, make a conscious decision to remove the false thoughts and words from your mind by writing a brief commitment in the space below the chart.

From Earthly Horrors to Celestial Hallelujahs (Revelation 18:1–19:10)

---

¹After these things I saw another angel coming down from heaven, having great authority, and the earth was illumined with his glory. ²And he cried out with a mighty voice, saying, "Fallen, fallen is Babylon the great! She has become a dwelling place of demons and a prison of every unclean spirit, and a prison of every unclean and hateful bird. ³For all the nations have

Common false statements of self-reliance or self-condemnation	True biblical statements of reliance on God's grace and mercy
If I'm a good person, I'll go to heaven when I die.	We go to heaven not because of anything we do, but because of what Jesus did on our behalf (Rom. 5:8; Gal. 2:16; Eph. 2:8–9).
The Lord holds back blessings because of my lack of faith or my disobedience.	The Lord's sole motivation for blessing is His own *grace*. He delights to bless His children with gifts they don't deserve and can't earn (Luke 11:11–13; Eph. 3:14–21).
When I go through tough times or suffer, God must be punishing me for my sin or faithlessness.	Though we might experience hardship as part of God's loving *discipline* to mature us (Heb. 12:5–11), God never condemns us eternally for sin (Rom. 8:1, 28). Because we live in a world corrupted by sin (8:20–23), we will experience difficult circumstances, but because of Christ we will never be punished for our sins (8:1, 28). Instead, He disciplines us as a loving Father.
If I strive to live a holy, blameless life, God will protect me from harm.	The Lord never promised to protect us from harm (James 1:2–4; 1 Peter 4:12–14); nevertheless, He promised that everything that happens will be for our good (Rom. 8:28) and that nothing can ultimately separate us from His love and salvation (8:38–39).
God does His part, and I need to do mine. I need to meet Him halfway. After all, "God helps those who help themselves."	God wants us to rely on Him in all things, rather than on our own strength (Ps.31:1–3; John 15:3–5). He will provide all our needs.
Commitment to change from subtle self-reliance to reliance on God's grace alone	

_____

_____

_____

_____

_____

_____

drunk of the wine of the passion of her immorality, and the kings of the earth have committed *acts of* immorality with her, and the merchants of the earth have become rich by the wealth of her sensuality."

[4]I heard another voice from heaven, saying, "Come out of her, my people, so that you will not participate in her sins and receive of her plagues; [5]for her sins have piled up as high as heaven, and God has remembered her iniquities. [6]Pay her back even as she has paid, and give back *to her* double according to her deeds; in the cup which she has mixed, mix twice as much for her. [7]To the degree that she glorified herself and lived sensuously, to the same degree give her torment and mourning; for she says in her heart, 'I sit *as* a queen and I am not a widow, and will never see mourning.' [8]For this reason in one day her plagues will come, pestilence and mourning and famine, and she will be burned up with fire; for the Lord God who judges her is strong.

[9]"And the kings of the earth, who committed *acts of* immorality and lived sensuously with her, will weep and lament over her when they see the smoke of her burning, [10]standing at a distance because of the fear of her torment, saying, 'Woe, woe, the great city, Babylon, the strong city! For in one hour your judgment has come.'

[11]"And the merchants of the earth weep and mourn over her, because no one buys their cargoes any more — [12]cargoes of gold and silver and precious stones and pearls and fine linen and purple and silk and scarlet, and every *kind of* citron wood and every article of ivory and every article *made* from very costly wood and bronze and iron and marble, [13]and cinnamon and spice and incense and perfume and frankincense and wine and olive oil and fine flour and wheat and cattle and sheep, and *cargoes* of horses and chariots and slaves and human lives. [14]The fruit you long for has gone from you, and all things that were luxurious and splendid have passed away from you and *men* will no longer find them. [15]The merchants of these things, who became rich from her, will stand at a distance because of the fear of her torment, weeping and mourning, [16]saying, 'Woe, woe, the great city, she who was clothed in fine linen and purple and scarlet, and adorned with gold and precious stones and pearls; [17]for in one hour such great wealth has been laid waste!' And every shipmaster and every passenger and sailor, and as many as make their living by the sea, stood at a distance, [18]and were crying out as they saw the smoke of her burning, saying, 'What *city* is like the great city?' [19]And they threw dust on their heads and were crying out, weeping and mourning, saying, 'Woe, woe, the great city, in which all who had ships at sea became rich by her wealth, for in one hour she has been laid waste!' [20]Rejoice over her, O heaven, and you saints and apostles and prophets, because God has pronounced judgment for you against her."

[21]Then a strong angel took up a stone like a great millstone and threw it into the sea, saying, "So will Babylon, the great city, be thrown down with violence, and will not be found any longer. [22]And the sound of harpists and

musicians and flute-players and trumpeters will not be heard in you any longer; and no craftsman of any craft will be found in you any longer; and the sound of a mill will not be heard in you any longer; [23]and the light of a lamp will not shine in you any longer; and the voice of the bridegroom and bride will not be heard in you any longer; for your merchants were the great men of the earth, because all the nations were deceived by your sorcery. [24]And in her was found the blood of prophets and of saints and of all who have been slain on the earth."

[19:1]After these things I heard something like a loud voice of a great multitude in heaven, saying,

"Hallelujah! Salvation and glory and power belong to our God; [2]because His judgments are true and righteous; for He has judged the great harlot who was corrupting the earth with her immorality, and he has avenged the blood of his bond-servants on her." [3]And a second time they said, "Hallelujah! Her smoke rises up forever and ever." [4]And the twenty-four elders and the four living creatures fell down and worshiped God who sits on the throne saying, "Amen. Hallelujah!"

[5]And a voice came from the throne, saying, "Give praise to our God, all you His bond-servants, you who fear Him, the small and the great."

[6]Then I heard *something* like the voice of a great multitude and like the sound of many waters and like the sound of mighty peals of thunder, saying, "Hallelujah! For the Lord our God, the Almighty, reigns. [7]Let us rejoice and be glad and give the glory to Him, for the marriage of the Lamb has come and His bride has made herself ready." [8]It was given to her to clothe herself in fine linen, bright *and* clean; for the fine linen is the righteous acts of the saints.

[9]Then he said to me, "Write, 'Blessed are those who are invited to the marriage supper of the Lamb.'" And he said to me, "These are true words of God." [10]Then I fell at his feet to worship him. But he said to me, "Do not do that; I am a fellow servant of yours and your brethren who hold the testimony of Jesus; worship God. For the testimony of Jesus is the spirit of prophecy."

What if the entire world as you know it—people, things, events, and activities—were suddenly to collapse? What if your sources of comfort, luxury, and entertainment were lost forever? Sounds like a bad sci-fi movie, doesn't it? That kind of thought frightens people. Nobody wants the stock market to crash, the power grid to fail, their employer to go bankrupt, or a hurricane to level their city. Too much of our lives depends on the world continuing on just as it is.

Sadly, the same thing is true for many Christians. They have become so rooted in the world that it would take a God-sized rototiller to pull them loose. All my life I've heard people say—only half joking—that they hope there's "X" in heaven, with "X" being whatever source of passing earthly pleasure they happen to prefer. It could be golf, or chocolate, or movies, or television. I've heard a few even say they hope the Lord will delay His return until they're able to do "Y," with "Y" being some earthly activity or event they haven't enjoyed yet—maybe getting married, or retiring, or traveling to Europe.

Comfort . . . convenience . . . luxury . . . recreation. If we're honest with ourselves, we'll probably discover that we're more attached to the things of this world than we care to admit. It's a sobering realization, though, when we arrive at Revelation 18 and learn that all those things of the world that receive so much of our time and attention—all those "X"s and "Y"s of our lives—are marked for burning in the fires of judgment.

—18:1–3—

At the end of Revelation 17 we learned that "Babylon" is the "great city, which reigns over the kings of the earth"; it is the end-time capital of a godless worldwide empire under the Antichrist. That future Mecca of me-theism and Vegas of vanity will be the mother of evil and all forms of false religion. Like Paris, France, she represents a lifestyle of high culture. Like Jerusalem, she's a crossroad of world religion. Like Washington, she's teeming with political power. In fact, if you were to take all the powerful cities of the world and merge them into one grand megalopolis, you'd have "Babylon." The identification of the actual city in the coming tribulation is less important than the fact that it will be the nerve center of Antichrist's final world system directly opposed to God and His people.

But it won't last! In fact, the moment Satan is cast down from heaven he will know that "he has only a short time" (12:12). Before the Antichrist has time to break all his campaign promises, his pseudo-utopia will begin to crumble. Already in 14:8 we were forewarned about its inevitable demise, like a weather man tracking the storm of the century heading straight for a helpless coastal city: "Fallen, fallen is Babylon the great, she who has made all the nations drink of the wine of the passion of her immorality."

Revelation 18 begins with that same pronouncement, plus some added details (18:1–3). Babylon will be a haunt of demons whose mission will be to inspire extreme human wickedness, from sexual immorality to unbridled luxury. The world will lap it up without limits, like a raucous celebration of sin the likes of which the world has never seen. Revelation 18 makes it clear, however, that within a few short years God will finally announce, "The party's over!"

—18:4–8—

At this late hour God will extend one final invitation: "Come out of her, my people, so that you will not participate in her sins and receive of her plagues" (18:4). This language recalls God's Old Testament call for Israel to flee from Babylon before "the LORD's time of vengeance" (Jer. 51:6–9). Just as historical Babylon was judged for its original wickedness, the end-time "Babylon" will fall and take everybody down with it. That's why God will call His people out from its midst before He pours out His final bowls of wrath (18:4).

Chronologically, this call for an exodus of God's people from Babylon will come before the seven bowls of wrath described in Revelation 15–16. So, the calling out of His people may refer to the gathering of the 144,000 on Mount Zion (14:1–5), which was recorded immediately before the final proclamation of the "eternal gospel" (14:6–7) and the loud proclamation of the fall of Babylon (14:8).

With the call to come out of Babylon, the voice also described that Babylon will receive "double" the judgment because of her intense wickedness (18:6). The reason for such a harsh punishment? She "glorified herself," displaying the ultimate pride and self-exultation (18:7). In its most definitive application, Proverbs 16:18 will be fulfilled: "Pride goes before destruction, and a haughty spirit before a fall" (NKJV).

—18:9–20—

Following this warning from heaven, John heard a new sound—this time coming from the earth. Loud lamentations poured forth from those who placed their faith, hope, and love in that last great Babylonian empire. Three times they cried out in deep anguish over her sudden and absolute destruction:

"Woe, woe, the great city, Babylon, the strong city! For in one hour your judgment has come." (18:10)

"Woe, woe, the great city, she who was clothed in fine linen and purple and scarlet, and adorned with gold and precious stones and pearls; for in one hour such great wealth has been laid waste!" (18:16–17)

"Woe, woe, the great city, in which all who had ships at sea became rich by her wealth, for in one hour she has been laid waste!" (18:19)

Amidst these passionate cries of woe, John described the utter implosion of the ungodly religious, political, economic, and cultural empire that enveloped the earth during the three and a half years of Antichrist's reign. Whereas Revelation

17 emphasized the religious hold this system had on the world, chapter 18 emphasizes the luxury enjoyed by those who have invested everything in the system. Not
surprisingly, when that great world empire begins to crumble, her lovers—those
addicted to her power and pleasures—will begin to wail in anguish. The objects
of their absolute devotion—the Antichrist and his empire—will be crushed before
their eyes. At the same time the objects of their hatred—Jesus Christ and His
people—will be poised to take control.

John relayed the lamentations from three groups: the kings of the earth
(18:9–10), the merchants of the earth (18:11–17), and the traders of the sea
(18:17–20). In that great global economy every necessity and luxury will be
obtained (18:11–19), but only by those who receive the mark of the Beast (13:17).
As they watch the empire of the Beast burn amidst its countless treasures, they will
also know that their own time is short. Thinking they had gotten in on an opportunity of a lifetime, those who rested in the lap of Babylon's luxury will suddenly
realize that the tables have been turned. Like the Nazis in Berlin on the eve of the
Allied victory, the reality of the Antichrist's followers' defeat will be obvious as their
satanic Reich disintegrates before their eyes. The last line of their lamentations
indicates this startling truth, but it comes far too late to reverse: "Rejoice over her
[Babylon], O heaven, and you saints and apostles and prophets, because God has
pronounced judgment for you against her" (18:20).

—18:21–24—

Finally, a mighty angel appeared in John's vision with a millstone in his grip. He
plunged it into the depths of the sea as a picture of the finality of the judgment of
God. A stone of that size makes a huge splash with rippling waves as it sinks forever into oblivion. In the same way, the destruction of the world system under the
Antichrist will shake heaven and earth as it vanishes from the world scene, never
to be recovered (18:21).

With the devastation of that world system, all of its worldly luxuries will fade
away, never to be recovered. The mighty angel, who had thrown the millstone
into the sea, listed the things of the world that would never rise in her again. Note
that not one of these things—in and of itself—is wicked. But in the Babylonian
world system, these things that could be used to the glory of God become tools
for glorifying humanity. The disappearance of these everyday things represents a
total destruction of every facet of society, from fine arts to night life, from fine
craftsmanship to common labor. All at once, everything will be gone, as Jeremiah

From My Journal

The Lure of Luxury

For a long time as I drove to my office each morning, I passed a sight that left me drooling. I mashed my nose against the glass and stared as long as I possibly could before returning to reality. The object of my glare was a sleek, shiny boat resting in a driveway of a nearby neighbor. Its shallow fiberglass hull was a deep sparkling blue, and it, along with its tailored trailer, was spotless. The wrap-around windshield shined like a bejeweled diadem, and its engine shined brightly in the light of the dawn. That classy treasure lacked only one thing—*me*! The boat obviously had the wrong owner. My imagination took me to Catalina and back. I would have waxed it and pampered it, tinkered with its details, and whenever I had the chance, I would have skimmed along the surface of lakes and seas with my family and friends.

Now, maybe your thing isn't something that floats. Well, take your pick. When it comes to luxuries, we have all sorts of options for funneling our envy. Yours might be a pool out back, lovely furnishings in the family room, some powerful V–8 with four on the floor, a priceless antique, a mountain cabin, a trip to Rome, the latest electronic gadget, or an exquisite gem. The list of potential luxuries is endless. When it comes to desiring the luxurious, our imagination can run wild.

Understand, the Bible never outright condemns luxuries. Paul openly declared that he had learned "how to live in prosperity … being filled … having abundance" (Phil. 4:12). In and of themselves, prosperity, fullness, and abundance are not sinful. To put it another way, not every luxury places us in Babylon's embrace. Babylon begins to woo us, however, when luxury starts to possess us. On that axis, everything shifts. When that happens, the green ghost of greed invades our dwelling and haunts our once-contended mind—like the farmer whom Jesus mentioned in Luke 12:16–21, who substituted the material for the spiritual. That man, said Jesus, was an outright fool. To him, luxuries were *essential* to life; they were his sole means of peace and source of security.

Over the years I've reminded myself not to get so distracted by the gift that I fail to recognize the Giver. In our luxury-obsessed world, we all need to do the same. When Babylon blinks her eyes and tosses back her hair, beckoning us to join her extravagant lifestyle, we need to refuse her seductive advances and turn our attention to the true Lover of our souls.

prophesied against Judah for her rebellion: "I will utterly destroy them and make them a horror and a hissing, and an everlasting desolation. Moreover, I will take from them the voice of joy and the voice of gladness, the voice of the bridegroom and the voice of the bride, the sound of the millstones and the light of the lamp" (Jer. 25:9–10).

Finally, as if to remind any who might feel God's complete destruction of the world system is too extreme or unjust or simply uncalled for, the angel reminds us why Babylon had to go. Judgment was needed "because all the nations were deceived by your sorcery. And in her was found the blood of prophets and of saints and of all who have been slain on the earth" (18:23–24).

— **19:1–10** —

The classic science-fiction adventure *Star Wars* ended with the dazzling destruction of the Death Star—a moon-sized space station that had terrorized the galaxy as a symbol of evil and tyranny. The epic trilogy *The Lord of the Rings* climaxed with the cataclysmic destruction of the dark tower of Mordor—the center of the demonic Dark Lord Sauron's evil oppression. In the same way, the annihilation of Babylon represents the destruction of everything evil and demonic in the present world system. In the fictional worlds of *Star Wars* and *The Lord of the Rings*, the triumph over evil was celebrated with intense jubilation among the victors. Thus, it should be no surprise that when something as dangerous and despicable as the Antichrist's kingdom meets its just end, God's people will rejoice with a joyful chorus of hallelujahs.

© Michael Svigel

Replica of an ancient millstone used for crushing olives

That common Old Testament exultation, *hallelujah*, appears four times here in the pronouncement of praise (19:1, 3, 4, and 6). It simply means "praise the Lord," and surprisingly this is the only place "hallelujah" appears in the New Testament. Three groups cry "hallelujah" before God: the saints in heaven (19:1–3), the twenty-four elders before the throne of God (19:4), and the great multitude (19:6). In 19:1–10, we see at least four reasons for celebration. As believers we needn't wait until the events of Revelation come to pass. We can join with that heavenly throng today in anticipation of what God will do in the future.

First, *they celebrate because the power of God has vanquished evil* (19:1–2). When Christians today speak of "the end of the world," they often mean the end of the unrighteous world system driven by Satan and steered by wicked men and women. The end of that world of wickedness will be the cause of great rejoicing. The true and righteous punishment of the "great harlot" means vengeance on behalf of the saints who suffered at her hands.

Second, *they celebrate because the Lord God reigns* (19:3–6). Until the moment Christ sets foot on this earth and abolishes all earthly authority, God will allow people freedom to live their own way. But at any moment God could begin to take back the kingdoms of the world. One day the dominion that Adam surrendered to Satan through sin will be returned to the Perfect Man—Jesus Christ. Then all people everywhere can sing together the words of Handel's "Hallelujah Chorus"—not in anticipation of what God will do one day, but in celebration of its arrival: "Hallelujah, for the Lord God omnipotent reigneth!"

Third, *they celebrate because the marriage of the Lamb has come* (19:7–8). As the funeral dirge of the wicked fades, the wedding bells of the righteous begin to resound. When the King of kings conquers evil and begins to reign, then His bride—the church—will stand at His side and reign with Him. No longer will the church be marred with conflict, tainted with division, or soiled with heresy. Rather, as Paul predicted in Ephesians 5:27, Christ will "present to Himself the church in all her glory, having no spot or wrinkle or any such thing; but ... holy and blameless." What a cause for celebration!

Fourth, *they will celebrate because the marriage supper begins* (19:9). Just imagine the gathering for that grand supper together! Christians often speculate about this feast. Is it a literal banquet or a symbol for indescribable blessings? Will it be a sit-down, multicourse dinner or an extravagant buffet? What kind of food will be served? How silly! Though these questions tantalize the imagination, they completely miss the point. That great banquet will not be about the *menu*, but about the *Master*. It's the end-time answer to Christ's words to His disciples at the Last Supper: "But I say to you, I will not drink of this fruit of the vine from now on until that day when I drink it new with you in My Father's kingdom" (Matt. 26:29). With the whole church glorified and united in the kingdom of God, Christ will take His seat with the saints and enjoy that long-anticipated face-to-face fellowship with those He loves.

Just in case some may find these things difficult to swallow, the angel reassured John, "These are true words of God" (19:9). So overwhelming was that scene and so powerful those words of reassurance, that John spontaneously fell prostrate on his face at the feet of the angel to worship him (19:10). Instantly, the angel rebuked John, reminding him that he, too, was merely a fellow servant of Jesus Christ. *God alone is to be worshiped*—not the most glorious angel or the most exalted saint. Only the Father, Son, and Holy Spirit—one true God in three Persons—deserve our praise.

At the end of these astounding visions of earthly horrors and celestial hallelujahs, the angel turned John's attention back to the One to whom the book of Revelation ultimately points. Indeed, He is the one to whom all prophecy has always pointed—Jesus Christ, the "spirit of prophecy" (19:10).

THE BRIDE AND THE GROOM

When we read about the similarity of Christ's relationship with the church to a groom's relationship with his bride, we need to understand the cultural context in which this analogy was made. The marriage traditions of the ancient Near East differ substantially from those of our twenty-first century Western culture. Rather than a single celebration, we see several distinct stages in the Jewish marriage tradition.

The betrothal. This was much more official and legally binding than a modern "engagement." The parents of both the bride and groom sealed a contract; then they began making arrangements for the ceremony, which often took place a year or more later. During this betrothal period, the man and woman were considered legally married (though they didn't live together), and a betrothal could be broken only by a writ of divorce.

The presentation. After preparations for the couples' future home were finished and the arrangements finalized, the next stage in the marriage could commence. Leading up to the festivities prior to the wedding ceremony, the groom would leave his home and travel to the bride's home, where she would be waiting with her friends, the bridesmaids. The groom would then claim her as his own beloved bride.

The ceremony. The presentation of the bride would initiate a lengthy time of festivities known as the "wedding supper," which could last several days. The new bride and groom would depart the marriage supper with full rights, privileges, and responsibilities as husband and wife.[24]

The analogy of the church's marriage to Christ reflects these ancient Jewish wedding customs. In God the Father's foresight, He chose the church "before the foundation of the world" (Eph. 1:4). Then, when sinners are saved, they are betrothed to Christ – a binding relationship that awaits its complete realization. At the presentation, the church will be raptured to meet the Lord in the air (Matt. 25:1–13; 1 Thess. 4:17). Then, at the wedding feast of the Lamb, the final consummation will begin as Christ and the church take their places to reign over the earth (Rev. 20:4–6).[25]

NOTES: Vengence of the Glorious Deliverer (Revelation 14:1 — 19:10)

1. The meaning of "Babylon" and its ultimate collapse will be discussed in greater detail later in the comments on chapters 17 and 18.

2. John F. Walvoord, *The Revelation of Jesus Christ: A Commentary* (Chicago: Moody Press, 1966), 220.

3. Julia Ward Howe, "The Battle Hymn of the Republic," in *The Hymnal for Worship and Celebration*, no. 569.

4. Louw and Nida, eds., *Greek-English Lexicon of the New Testament*, vol. 1, § 23.198.

5. Robert L. Thomas, *Revelation 8–22: An Exegetical Commentary* (Chicago: Moody Press, 1995), 222.

6. W. E. Vine, Merrill F. Unger, and William White, *Vine's Complete Expository Dictionary of Old and New Testament Words* (Nashville: Nelson, 1996), 536.

7. Bauer and Danker, eds., *A Greek-English Lexicon of the New Testament*, 825.

8. Quoted in Elisabeth Elliot, *Shadow of the Almighty: The Life and Testament of Jim Elliot* (New York: Harper & Brothers, 1958), 247.

9. John Newton, "Amazing Grace," in *The Hymnal for Worship and Celebration*, no. 202.

10. Phillips, *Exploring Revelation*, 187.

11. H. G. Liddell and Robert Scott, *An Intermediate Greek-English Lexicon* (Oxford: Clarendon, 1986), 861.

12. Vine, Unger, and White, eds., *Vine's Complete Expository Dictionary*, 76.

13. A. W. Tozer, *The Divine Conquest* (Harrisburg, PA: Christian Publications, 1950), 23.

14. Phillips, *Exploring Revelation*, 190.

15. M. G. Easton, *Easton's Bible Dictionary* (electronic ed.; Oak Harbor, WA: Logos Research Systems, 1996), see "Euphrates."

16. Walvoord, "Revelation," *The Bible Knowledge Commentary*, 968.

17. Osborne, *Revelation*, 597.

18. James Henry Breasted, *Ancient Records of Egypt: Historical Documents* (Chicago: Russell & Russell, 1906), 185.

19. Karl Marx, "Zur Kritik der Hegelschen Rechts-Philosophie," *Deutsch-Französische Jahrbücher* 1 (1844): 72.

20. Josephus, *Antiquities of the Jews*, 1.116.

21. Ibid., 1.118.

22. Allen P. Ross, "Genesis," in *The Bible Knowledge Commentary: Old Testament Edition* (ed. John F. Walvoord and Roy B. Zuck; Wheaton, IL: Victor, 1985), 44–45.

23. Though the dragon (Satan) is also described as having seven heads and ten horns, 17:3 mentions that the beast is "full of blasphemous names," language matching the description of the Antichrist in 13:1.

24. Walvoord, "Revelation," *The Bible Knowledge Commentary*, 975.

25. Renald E. Showers, *Maranatha: Our Lord, Come! A Definitive Study of the Rapture of the Church* (Bellmawr, NJ: Friends of Israel Gospel Ministry, 1995), 164–69.

REIGN OF THE COMING KING (REVELATION 19:11 – 22:21)

Imagine if George Lucas would have ended his classic *Star Wars* trilogy with the second film, *The Empire Strikes Back*. Remember that one? The credits rolled with Han Solo frozen in a metal coffin en route to Jabba the Hutt. The impetuous Luke Skywalker aborted his Jedi training to rescue his friends as his diminutive teacher, Yoda, shook his head in disappointment. And Darth Vader's shocking claims of paternity nagged filmgoers with feelings of incredulity and disgust. To the relief of millions of fans who lined up for days outside theaters to watch the ultimate defeat of the Galactic Empire, George Lucas capped off his space saga with *Return of the Jedi*. Even those who wouldn't consider themselves *Star Wars* fans paid good money to see that final installment. Why? *Because nobody likes loose ends.*

The previous section of Revelation left a number of loose ends begging to be tied up. As far as the main action goes, chapter 16 completed a cycle of seven bowls of wrath at the brink of Armageddon (16:16). With an abrupt pause in the action, chapter 17 interjected the future demise of "Mystery Babylon" and all her lovers, followed by a series of songs proclaiming her complete destruction in chapter 18. Had God ended the story there, the last image in Bible prophecy would have been a once-habitable world lying formless and void. Though God wrought vengeance against the wicked on behalf of His suffering saints, those faithful believers who lost their lives still have not received their promised rewards.

Take heart, my friend! The time has come for the Master Storyteller to finish the script of His end-time drama. In this climactic conclusion, the last chapter of humanity's wretched history will become the first chapter of God's glorious future. I have chosen as my title for this sixth and final episode of the drama of Revelation: "Reign of the Coming King" (19:11 – 22:21). Following the description of the final fate of the wicked rulers, the action of Revelation will resume with a dazzling portrayal of the second coming of Christ with His armies — resurrected and glorified believers (19:11 – 21).

After His return, Christ and the saints commence their thousand-year reign of peace and justice, during which the primeval curse on the world will be lifted and God's earthly Eden will be unleashed. This period of near-perfection will culminate in the final destruction not only of Satan, but of all evil, pain, and death itself (20:1 – 15). Thus the great drama of human redemption will come to a climax in the eternal state of unparalleled prosperity and undiminished perfection — the new

KEY TERMS

δεύτερος θάνατος [*deuteros thanatos*] (1208 + 2288) "second death"

In its basic biblical meaning, *thanatos* means separation from life. Spiritual death involves a relational separation from God, the true Source of eternal life (Gen. 2:17; Eph. 4:18). Physical death refers to the separation of the spirit from the body (James 2:26). Sometimes the term emphasizes a trajectory away from God's ways and works — a "death-like" lifestyle (Deut. 30:15). Revelation introduces a unique term: the "second death." This refers to the death of an unbeliever after the second bodily resurrection of the wicked (Rev. 20:6, 14; 21:8), suggested already in Matthew 10:28: "Fear Him who is able to destroy both soul and body in hell." The "hell" Jesus refers to here is portrayed in Revelation as the "lake of fire" (Rev. 20:14), where the resurrected wicked will suffer torment forever.

δικαιοσύνη [*dikaiosynē*] (1343) "righteousness, justice, fairness"

The term "righteousness" (*dikaiosynç*) has numerous nuances in the New Testament. Paul often uses the term to describe the righteousness of Christ that is accounted to believers through faith, based solely on the grace of God (Rom. 1:17; 3:22). By contrast, James uses the term to emphasize the visible manifestation of right actions — moral uprightness (James 1:20; 2:23). In Revelation 19:11 the term indicates the rightness of Christ's judgment of the world, a fact too easily forgotten in a culture that believes any judgment or punishment is "wrong" or "unfair."

καινός [*kainos*] (2537) "new, fresh"

The term *kainos* always refers to a qualitative newness — not something merely different, but altogether superior. The "new" thing therefore renders the "old" obsolete. There may be some continuity and similarity between the old and the new, but the "new" should never be equated with the old. The "new heaven" and "new earth" described in 21:1, 2, 5, therefore, represent a radically new order of creation, in which the former wickedness and imperfection have been completely done away.

heavens and new earth (21:1–22:5). Finally, like credits rolling during a closing score, the concluding words of the book of Revelation will affirm that Jesus is coming again ... *soon* (22:6–21).

Here Comes the King of Kings
(Revelation 19:11–21)

---

¹¹And I saw heaven opened, and behold, a white horse, and He who sat on it *is* called Faithful and True, and in righteousness He judges and wages

war. [12]His eyes *are* a flame of fire, and on His head *are* many diadems; and He has a name written *on Him* which no one knows except Himself. [13]*He is* clothed with a robe dipped in blood, and His name is called The Word of God. [14]And the armies which are in heaven, clothed in fine linen, white *and* clean, were following Him on white horses. [15]From His mouth comes a sharp sword, so that with it He may strike down the nations, and He will rule them with a rod of iron; and He treads the wine press of the fierce wrath of God, the Almighty. [16]And on His robe and on His thigh He has a name written, "KING OF KINGS, AND LORD OF LORDS."

[17]Then I saw an angel standing in the sun, and he cried out with a loud voice, saying to all the birds which fly in midheaven, "Come, assemble for the great supper of God, [18]so that you may eat the flesh of kings and the flesh of commanders and the flesh of mighty men and the flesh of horses and of those who sit on them and the flesh of all men, both free men and slaves, and small and great."

[19]And I saw the beast and the kings of the earth and their armies assembled to make war against Him who sat on the horse and against His army. [20]And the beast was seized, and with him the false prophet who performed the signs in his presence, by which he deceived those who had received the mark of the beast and those who worshiped his image; these two were thrown alive into the lake of fire which burns with brimstone. [21]And the rest were killed with the sword which came from the mouth of Him who sat on the horse, and all the birds were filled with their flesh.

A friend of mine visiting England one summer happened to be in a part of London about the same time the Queen was scheduled to pass by in her elegant, horse-drawn parade carriage. The citizens had formed early and the street was abuzz. Long before the Queen was to ride by, eager Londoners and tourists vied for space on either side of the street. As Her Majesty rode by in all her splendor, it wasn't difficult to distinguish between her loyal subjects and mere tourists. British subjects were genuinely excited. They held their breath and clasped their hands on their chests. Americans, however, with arms filled with shopping bags, stood back with a detached amusement, like parents watching their small children enjoy a circus parade. Obviously, the supreme monarch of England holds more clout with some than with others.

That scene reminds me of another royal procession, yet future. Though the coming parade will be met by both submissive subjects and resistant rebels, in the end the response will be the same. No matter what their citizenship, regardless of their culture, language, or even religion, one day "every knee will bow, of those who are in heaven and on earth and under the earth, and … every tongue will confess that Jesus Christ is Lord, to the glory of God the Father" (Phil. 2:10–11).

On that day, everything wrong with this world will be sorted out. According to Revelation 19:11–21, justice finally will roll down in the dramatic return of the Lord Jesus Christ—as King for survivors of the tribulation awaiting relief, but also as Judge against those who persecuted and killed God's people. Here, at the epochal battle of Armageddon, God ultimately triumphs over evil. Persecution of the righteous ends. The schemes of Satan and his demons unravel. The political and religious leaders who deceived the world face their doom. And with the royal procession from heaven to earth, the promise of Christ's triumphant return finally becomes a reality.

— **19:11–16** —

John first saw heaven opened in Revelation 4. There he saw a door open in heaven; a voice called him to come up and see what would happen in the future (4:1). That open-door invitation flung John into the spirit realm, starting a series of visions related to the end times. Finally—at the end of the cycle of seals, trumpets, and bowls—John again wrote, "I saw heaven opened" (19:11). This time, though, it was not so John could be carried up to heaven, but so Jesus could come down to earth.

Curiously, this vision of Christ descending to earth on a white horse never identifies the rider as Jesus. Instead, John painted a picture with his words, making

FOUR REASONS FOR CHRIST'S RETURN TO EARTH

When we look at the Bible as a whole, we see four reasons why Christ must literally, physically return to the earth. Until He does so, these four things will remain on hold.

First, *Christ will return to fulfill numerous promises in the Bible.* Zechariah 14:4 says, "His feet will stand on the Mount of Olives," and after Jesus ascended, two angels told the disciples that He "will come in just the same way as you have watched Him go into heaven" (Acts 1:11). Both the Old and New Testaments speak of His coming back to earth. If He doesn't return, these and many other prophecies will not be fulfilled.

Second, *Christ will return to judge the nations for their unbelief.* Solomon writes in Ecclesiastes 8:11, "Because the sentence against an evil deed is not executed quickly, therefore the hearts of the sons of men among them are given fully to do evil." Some day our present era of grace will end abruptly. At that time there will be an accounting for sin. If He doesn't return, long-standing wickedness will only increase.

Third, *Christ will return to remove Satan from his earthly dominion.* Paul refers to Satan as "the god of this world" (2 Cor. 4:4). During the period between the fall of Adam and the return of Christ, Satan and his demons appear to be on the winning side — but God has a regime change planned. One day Satan and his demonic emissaries will be ousted; Christ and His saints will be enthroned.

Fourth, *Christ will return to establish His kingdom on earth.* Isaiah 9:7 states that the Messiah will be established "on the throne of David and over his kingdom." Furthermore, Christ Himself said that one day He would "sit on His glorious throne" (Matt. 19:28). Christ will not reign as an absentee monarch, but from a literal throne on earth.

it clear that our great King is portrayed in splendor. As we remember that the testimony about Jesus is the spirit of prophecy (19:10), it's appropriate that we take a little extra time to examine this figure more closely.

© Ace Stock Limited/Alamy

Typical victor's garland (*stephanos*)

Diadem, found in the burial mound at Khoklach, Sarmatian, (1st century AD)/ Hermitage, St. Petersburg, Russia/The Bridgeman Art Library

Royal diadem (*diadēma*)

First, Christ is riding a white horse (19:11). This isn't the first white horse we've seen in Revelation. When Jesus opened the first seal of the seven-sealed scroll, a "white horse" leaped forth (6:2). We identified its rider as falsehood personified, the deceptive and wicked theocracy established by the Antichrist. That first rider was given a bow and a crown—the *stephanos*, a "victor's crown"—and he set out to conquer to the world. In his wake follow warfare, famine, and death (6:3–8).

The second Rider on a white horse stands in direct contrast with that first one. His name is "Faithful and True" (19:11), in contrast to the Antichrist's agenda of "deception of wickedness for those who perish"

(2 Thess. 2:10). Though the Antichrist will wage a wicked war inspired by arrogance (Rev. 13:4), Christ will judge and wage war based on righteousness (19:11). In John's vision Christ's eyes are ablaze with fire (19:12), just like the original vision in 1:14. This portrays Christ in all His heavenly glory, his very gaze piercing to the center of our souls and exposing our deepest thoughts and motives.

Unlike the Antichrist, who was crowned with the fragile and temporary "victor's garland," Christ wore not one but many "diadems," the golden bands representing sovereign authority. Though most earthly kings would be crowned with just one diadem, Christ's many crowns proclaim that He is "King of kings and Lord of lords." This expresses His absolute sovereignty. This image of the multi-crowned King Jesus inspired Matthew Bridges in 1852 to pen a majestic hymn that God's people still love to sing:

> Crown Him with many crowns,
> The Lamb upon His throne:
> Hark! how the heav'nly anthem drowns
> All music but its own!
> Awake, my soul, and sing
> Of Him who died for thee,
> And hail Him as thy matchless King
> Thru all eternity.[1]

John mentioned a mysterious name written on Jesus—"which no one knows except Himself" (19:12). Why would John bother to mention that Jesus had a secret name? Perhaps the secret name indicates a unique relationship with God the Father that nobody else shares. Interestingly, Jesus earlier extended a promise to believers that He would give *them* a new name "which no one knows but he who receives it" (2:17). This demonstrates the deep personal and inseparable relationship believers enjoy with Christ—a relationship as unbreakable as Christ's relationship with the Father. What Christ is *by nature* (the unique, eternal, divine Son of God), believers will reflect in a limited way *by grace* (adopted, finite, glorified children of God).

Christ's robe was "dipped in blood" (19:13). Whenever we see blood on another's garment, one question comes to mind: "Whose blood is it—yours or someone else's?" In this case the blood-stained robe could symbolize the fact that Christ "tasted death" for everyone, having become the "Lamb that was slain" (5:12). Or it may allude visually to Isaiah 63:3–4, where the conquering King explains why His garments are sprinkled with blood:

> I have trodden the wine trough alone,
> And from the peoples there was no man with Me.

I also trod them in My anger
And trampled them in My wrath;
And their lifeblood is sprinkled on My garments,
And I stained all My raiment.
For the day of vengeance was in My heart,
And My year of redemption has come.

Because the context of Revelation 19 is clearly judgment, this second option is preferred. Christ's blood-stained garment indicates that He has been exercising judgment against His enemies and that His return to earth represents the final victory.

In his gospel, the apostle John began his account of Christ's first coming by identifying Him as "the Word": "In the beginning was the Word, and the Word was with God, and the Word was God. . . . And the Word became flesh, and dwelt among us" (John 1:1, 14). When John described Christ's second coming, he also assigned Him the title "The Word of God" (Rev. 19:13). The "Word" has a rich meaning throughout the Old and New Testaments. It refers to God's revelation, especially contained in Scripture (1 Sam. 9:27; Matt. 15:6; 1 Thess. 2:13). Already in the Old Testament, however, the "Word" is experienced as a physical, personal presence of Yahweh (Gen. 15:1–5; Jer. 1:4–9). So, when John calls Jesus "the Word of God," he is presenting Him not only as a manifestation of God's *revelation*, but a manifestation of *God Himself*, a title of deity. In His case, it's a deity that is personally present, tangible. The "Word of God" is always "God with us," *Immanuel*.

As Christ descended in the clouds, John quickly realized that He did not come alone. Following behind Him, also riding white horses and dressed in fine white linen, are the armies of heaven (19:14). Before we are tempted to identify these riders as angelic beings, we must allow Scripture to interpret itself. Revelation 17:14 already identified this army in advance: "The Lamb will overcome them [the Beast and his armies], because He is Lord of lords and King of kings, and those who are with Him are the called and chosen and faithful." The phrase "called and chosen and faithful" refers to resurrected, glorified, and rewarded saints, who were raptured at the beginning of the seven-year tribulation. They had been preparing to take their seats in order to rule with Christ; hence they will descend with Christ as He executes the final judgment at Armageddon.

Finally, John described a sharp sword flying from Jesus' mouth (19:15; see 1:16; 2:16). This sword indicates that Christ's judgment on the wicked nations will not be conducted with physical weapons of mass destruction, but with the one sure spiritual weapon—the Word of God (Eph. 6:17; Heb. 4:12). In Isaiah 49:2, the Messianic Servant said, "He has made My mouth like a sharp sword, in the shadow of His hand He has concealed Me." Though concealed for a time, one day God's secret weapon will be unleashed to strike the earth with judgment.

John strung together several Old Testament messianic passages in his description of the coming King. Psalm 2:9 identifies Christ as the Davidic king who will strike the wicked Gentile nations with a rod of iron. Isaiah 11:1, 4 elaborates on this psalm, associating the prophecy explicitly with the Messiah, the "stem of Jesse," and demonstrating that the "rod" of judgment is supernatural, not physical: "He will strike the earth with the rod of His mouth, and with the breath of His lips He will slay the wicked." Finally, the Messiah will fulfill the Old Testament predictions when the wicked are gathered in the "valley of decision"—Armageddon—to be crushed in the winepress of God's wrath (Isa. 63:3; Joel 3:13–14). What a remarkable event that will be!

What qualifies Jesus of Nazareth to exercise this kind of judgment? The question is answered clearly by the final title of Jesus—a title so profound that it's written on His robe and on his thigh: "King of kings and Lord of lords." More than any other name for Christ in this vision, this famous title identifies Jesus as the supreme human ruler over all the earth, along with God Almighty. The following chart shows how the titles "King of kings" and "Lord of lords" are used in the Old Testament, giving us a clearer understanding of this title for Christ.

The title "King of kings" always refers to a supreme earthly king. The title "Lord of lords" refers to God Himself

TWO SECOND COMINGS?

In my understanding of how Scripture lays out future events, I distinguish between the coming of Christ *for* His saints and His coming *with* His saints. This doesn't mean I believe in a second coming *and* a third coming. Not at all. If you think about what we mean by Christ's first coming, you'll realize that it included all the events between His birth by a virgin to His ascension into heaven. This first coming included His childhood, baptism, public ministry, crucifixion, and resurrection — a period of more than thirty years. His Second Coming can likewise be viewed as a process. He is currently seated at the right hand of the Father, serving as our High Priest and Mediator (Acts 2:33; Heb. 8:1).

One day Christ will rise from His seat and step into our world, trading in His high priestly garments for a Judge's mantle and a King's robe. From that point on His ministry will be directed toward earth. His first act in His seven-year process of coming as Judge and King will be to escort His followers off the earth before the tribulation begins. Then He will progressively unleash judgments against the forces of wickedness, finally enabling Him to be enthroned in Jerusalem as King. Though this process will take seven years, it can still be regarded as one second coming with several phases.

During this seven-year period, we see Christ either in the air or on the earth personally involved in a number of end-time events. First Thessalonians 4:17 tells us Christ will descend part way into the sky to resurrect and catch up the saints from the earth. Zechariah 14:4 tells us that "His feet will stand on the Mount of Olives," splitting it in two to allow the remnant of Israel to flee the impending judgments. In Revelation 14:1 we see Christ standing on Mount Zion with the 144,000. In fact, we're told that that remnant of Israelites will follow the Lamb wherever He goes (14:4), which *might* suggest that Jesus will make occasional appearances on the earth throughout the tribulation to direct the 144,000 Jewish believers. Finally, at the end of the tribulation Christ appears in the clouds with the armies of heaven to destroy the Beast and his armies gathered at Armageddon. He will then return to earth and take His seat on David's throne in Jerusalem (19:11–20:4). All of these events constitute a single second coming of Christ.

as the supreme divine Lord. In the New Testament Paul applies this title to God, the "only Sovereign" (1 Tim. 6:15); and in Revelation 17:14 and 19:16, the title is applied to Jesus Christ. The case for the full deity and complete humanity of Christ—with accompanying authority over both heaven and earth—could not be more explicit. Jesus Christ is King over all who call themselves "king," and He is Lord above all who call themselves "lord."

— 19:17–21 —

With the earthly powers of Satan gathered at Armageddon (16:14–16; 19:19) and with Christ and His host assembled in the sky (19:11–16), an angel stood in the sun to command the full attention of the world (19:17). Rather than addressing

Old Testament Uses of "Kings of Kings" and "Lord of Lords"			
"King of kings"		"Lord of lords"	
Ezra 7:12	King Artaxerxes describes himself as "king of kings" because of the great extent of his earthly empire.	Deuteronomy 10:17	Yahweh is described as "God of gods" and "Lord of lords," the great, mighty, and awesome God.
Ezekiel 26:7; Daniel 2:37	Nebuchad-nezzar is described as "king of kings" because of the extent of the earthly empire given to him by God.	Psalm 136:2–3	The psalmist gives thanks to Yahweh, "God of gods" and "Lord of lords," because of His everlasting love.

those who dwell on the earth, the angel cried out with a message to the scavenging birds circling far above the battlefield awaiting the inevitable feast of carrion. He invited them to what he called "the great supper of God," to eat the flesh of all those who will die in the battle of Armageddon (19:17–18). One commentator notes that the angel's pronouncement

> is gruesome and powerful, guaranteeing before the battle has been joined that the end result is certain. The angel commands all the birds ... [using] ironically the same verb used in 16:14, 16 for the false trinity "gathering together" the nations for the final battle. At the same time as the evil forces gather for Armageddon, the carrion birds are called to gather for the aftermath of the inevitable slaughter.[2]

It's no use trying to downplay the reality of this vision. Jesus Himself alluded to this final outcome of His coming in judgment: "For just as the lightning comes from the east and flashes even to the west, so will the coming of the Son of Man be. Wherever the corpse is, there the vultures will gather" (Matt. 24:27–28).

The specific result of this coming is described in Revelation 19:20–21. Notice the fate of each of the "players" in the battle of Armageddon. The Beast (Antichrist) and the False Prophet are thrown "alive into the lake of fire" (19:20). So heinous and extreme was their blasphemy against God that they will be the very first creatures in history to be sent to this final place of eternal suffering! After the thousand-year reign of Christ they will be joined by Satan himself and all the wicked of the world (20:10, 14–15). The rest who remain on the battlefield will be killed by the sword from Christ's mouth—struck down with a single word from Christ's lips. John Phillips describes it well:

> Then suddenly it will all be over. In fact, there will be no war at all, in the sense that we think of war. There will be just a word spoken from Him who sits astride the great white horse. Once He spoke a word to a fig tree, and it withered away. Once He spoke a word to howling winds and heaving waves, and the storm clouds vanished and the waves fell still. Once He spoke to a legion of demons bursting at the seams of a poor man's soul, and instantly they fled. Now He speaks a word, and the war is over. The blasphemous, loud-mouthed Beast is stricken where he stands. The false prophet, the miracle-working windbag from the pit is punctured and still.... Another word, and the panic-stricken armies reel and stagger and fall down dead. Field marshals and generals, admirals and air commanders, soldiers and sailors, rank and file, one and all—they fall. And the vultures descend and cover the scene.[3]

Of course, the mind-set of the earthly armies gathered for battle in the valley will be limited to the physical domain. How foolish it will look when those rulers point their guns and missiles at the all-powerful Creator, who spoke the entire universe into existence! How foolish, but how like fallen humanity! Always overestimating their abilities, forever proud of their technology, yet never coming to terms with their own weakness before the all-powerful, all-knowing Lord of the universe.

Let's cut to the chase: Before anybody on earth can utter the word "Armageddon," the battle will be over. When God determines the end has come, it's curtains!

Application

Applying Armageddon?

As we reflect on the implications of Christ's return in power and judgment, three truths will help us bring the reality of Christ's future coming into our present lives.

First, *His presence will determine who stands and falls.* When Christ arrives, two groups will be spared: the 144,000 sealed from the twelve tribes of Israel and the remnant of Gentile believers who will put their faith in Christ during the tribulation and who survive the persecution of the Antichrist. Everybody else will be killed—that is, all those who will choose to remain His enemies and receive the mark of the Beast. Jesus Himself is the standard by which an individual stands or falls on that day.

The same is true today. Hebrews 9:27 – 28 says, "And inasmuch as it is appointed for men to die once and after this comes judgment, so Christ also, having been offered once to bear the sins of many, will appear a second time for salvation without reference to sin, to those who eagerly await Him." Our response today should be one of faith. *If you have not enlisted in Christ's army by trusting in Him alone for salvation, what are you waiting for?*

Second, *His name is and always will be the final authority.* Ever since the people of Babel erected a tower "whose top will reach into heaven" to try to make a name for themselves (Gen. 11:4), humans have sought to replace the name of God with any other authority they could find. They've tried replacing His name with names like Allah, Buddha, and Sun Myung Moon. They've turned to idols of money, fame, power, and possessions. They've invested their whole lives in this present world, assuming that everything will continue to progress as it has for generations, forgetting that when Christ returns the basis of their own power will be swept away (2 Peter 3:4 – 6). They would do well to realize that one day "at the name of Jesus every knee will bow" (Phil. 2:10). In light of this truth, you need to ask yourself an important question: *What person, possession, position, or priority is challenging His place on the throne of my heart?*

Third, *His Word will win the final victory.* Christ's return in power will end Satan's reign as "the prince of the power of the air" (Eph. 2:2) and "the ruler of this world" (John 12:31). With this final battle, Satan will be cast from the world's throne. It won't be with massive weapons of steel or laser-guided rockets that Satan will be defeated, but as the great reformer Martin Luther put it: "One little word shall fell him."[4]

Believers too quickly forget that the same powerful word that will one day defeat Satan is the same Word given to us to battle the spiritual forces of wickedness in our own lives. Ephesians 6:12 says, "Our struggle is not against flesh and blood, but against the rulers, against the powers, against the world forces of this darkness, against the spiritual forces of wickedness in the heavenly places." As an offensive weapon against these demonic forces, God has given us "the sword of the Spirit, which is the word of God" (Eph. 6:17). Through God's Word—the Holy Scriptures—we have access to divine knowledge, wisdom, and power for destroying speculations, ignorance, stray thoughts, and disobedience—all that Satan uses today to drive a wedge between us and our Master (2 Cor. 10:3–6). In response, *what are you doing to sharpen the spiritual sword of Scripture to better equip you for your battle against Satan and sin?*

Turning the World Right-Side Up (Revelation 20:1–10)

---

¹Then I saw an angel coming down from heaven, holding the key of the abyss and a great chain in his hand. ²And he laid hold of the dragon, the serpent of old, who is the devil and Satan, and bound him for a thousand years; ³and he threw him into the abyss, and shut *it* and sealed *it* over him, so that he would not deceive the nations any longer, until the thousand years were completed; after these things he must be released for a short time.

⁴Then I saw thrones, and they sat on them, and judgment was given to them. And I *saw* the souls of those who had been beheaded because of their testimony of Jesus and because of the word of God, and those who had not worshiped the beast or his image, and had not received the mark on their forehead and on their hand; and they came to life and reigned with Christ for a thousand years. ⁵The rest of the dead did not come to life until the thousand years were completed. This is the first resurrection. ⁶Blessed and holy is the one who has a part in the first resurrection; over these the second death has no power, but they will be priests of God and of Christ and will reign with Him for a thousand years.

⁷When the thousand years are completed, Satan will be released from

his prison, [8]and will come out to deceive the nations which are in the four corners of the earth, Gog and Magog, to gather them together for the war; the number of them is like the sand of the seashore. [9]And they came up on the broad plain of the earth and surrounded the camp of the saints and the beloved city, and fire came down from heaven and devoured them. [10]And the devil who deceived them was thrown into the lake of fire and brimstone, where the beast and the false prophet are also; and they will be tormented day and night forever and ever.

Sin spoils everything.

It pollutes skies, encourages corporate greed, leads to physical and emotional illness, destroys marriages, prompts addictions, and inspires wars. Sin corrupts the legal system, corrodes governments, erodes economics, and promotes false religion. No area of society and culture has escaped its sinister influence. Just as sin destroys an individual's life, so it decimates a community, country, and planet. Theologian Robert Pyne notes, "A community built on self-interest typically demonstrates the same kinds of sin as an individual.... It is difficult for individuals to recognize these collective expressions of sin from within the community, and it is equally difficult to avoid them."[5]

Clearly, things aren't as they should be. Everywhere we look, something's wrong. People of honesty and integrity get mocked as "boy scouts." The economy seems to hum along well until we realize it's oiled with greed and corruption. The quiet voices of harmonious churches get drowned out by the explosions of church splits. The concept of a happy marriage sounds like a myth. The legal system tramples on victims while protecting the rights of perpetrators. Poet James Russell Lowell described the situation this way:

> Truth forever on the scaffold,
> Wrong forever on the throne.[6]

Yes, sin spoils everything ... *but one day Christ will redeem everything.*

— **20:1–6** —

The way things are supposed to be is a far cry from the way they actually are. The idealistic dreams fueling the deep yearning of human hearts sound like unrealistic fantasies:

- peace on earth
- justice for all

- strong marriages
- healthy homes
- harmonious relationships
- safe communities
- moral purity
- equal opportunities
- ethical integrity

Will this world ever know such times? Will the deep groaning for a redeemed creation ever be answered (Rom. 8:18–25)? Or will "happily ever after" be forever banished to the final pages of childhood fairy tales? To answer that question, we need to know exactly why things aren't as they should be. Only when we know *why* the world is turned upside down can we discover what needs to happen to turn it right-side up. At the risk of oversimplification, let me offer three reasons why things are not as they should be.

First, *Satan is currently allowed to have his way.* Satan is not a myth or a symbol for humanity's bad choices or corrupt systems; he is real. He is a supernatural, spiritual being who holds sway over many facets of the world—culture, society, politics, economics, and religion (1 John 5:19). For the world to be turned right-side up, Satan must be dethroned. He may be insidious and invisible, but he's not invincible.

Second, *Jesus is not yet exercising direct authority over the earth.* Christ presently sits at the right hand of the Father (1 Pet. 3:22). He has received all authority over heaven and earth (Matt. 28:18), but in the present age He has not yet fully exercised His authority to reign (Heb. 2:8; 10:12–13). Because Jesus has not yet established His kingdom on earth, governments remain corrupt and sinful. For the world to be turned right-side up, Jesus must take His throne and reign.

Third, *unrighteous people are in the majority and in authority.* For every good, righteous, and incorruptible human leader, there are perhaps dozens of bad, wicked, and compromised ones. They aren't necessarily ignorant, insincere, inexperienced, or lazy people. Quite simply, they are sinners, susceptible to the same temptations as every one of us. Proverbs 29:2 says, "When the righteous increase, the people rejoice, but when a wicked man rules, people groan." To turn the world right-side up, righteous rulers must be in the majority and in authority.

The good news is that the book of Revelation promises a golden age in which all weapons of warfare will be fashioned into implements of peace. Prosperity will be shared. Peace will become the banner of all people. The light of justice will illumine every corner of the world. This condition will not be achieved through educational funding, political change, social programs, cultural awakening, or even religious revival. As promising as some of these things may seem in the short term, fallen humanity ultimately foils all efforts of self-reformation. Praying for world peace sounds noble and pious, but such prayers are futile. True global transformation will occur only when Satan and his minions are ousted, allowing Jesus Christ and His glorified saints to rule over the earth. Theologians call this period of Christ's perfect rule the "millennial kingdom" or the "thousand-year reign." We find the primary passage for the millennium in Revelation 20:1 – 6.

As we continue our study of John's vision of the return of Christ, we need to recall where we left off. When John originally wrote Revelation, he didn't mark chapter and verses. Those were added much later to make it easier for us to refer to the text. So, Revelation 19 and 20 were meant to be read back-to-back, without stopping. No break in the action is implied between these chapters. Revelation 19 ended with Christ and the armies of heaven descending toward the earth, the King of kings and Lord of lords having decimated the wicked armies of the world and having consigned the Beast and False Prophet to the lake of fire. The last end-time figure remaining on the scene is Satan — the great red dragon — who has been pictured in John's visions as the ring leader of an unholy "trinity." The dragon gave the Beast his authority and enabled the False Prophet to perform signs and wonders (ch. 13). The dragon, with the Beast and False Prophet, gathered the armies of the earth at Armageddon (ch. 16).

As Christ and His armies stood suspended in the air, another phase of John's progressive vision took place — the binding of Satan. A strong angel arrived on the scene carrying a key and a chain (20:1). This isn't the first time we see the "key" of the abyss in Revelation. In chapter 9 a fallen angel was given the key to the bottomless pit, later called "the abyss" in 9:11. When the wicked angel was given the key, he opened the abyss and released a horde of demons (9:2 – 11). But when the heavenly angel takes hold of the key to the abyss in 20:1, his purpose will be the opposite. Instead of unleashing spirits of wickedness upon the earth, he will bind Satan with a chain, throw him into the abyss, and seal it up (20:2 – 3).

The "abyss" in the ancient world often referred to the spiritual "underworld,"[7] in this case the place where wicked demons are held in prison until the future judgment of the lake of fire (Luke 8:30 – 31; 2 Peter 2:4). So, when Satan is sealed in the abyss, his influence on the earth will not simply be lessened; it will be nonexistent.

Imagine a world in which Satan can no longer manipulate leaders, tempt sinners, take advantage of the weak, or corrupt the strong! *The first reason things are not as they should be will be solved.* The complete inability of Satan to exert his wickedness on the earth for a thousand uninterrupted years will mean that the first and

THE MILLENNIUM — LITERAL OR FIGURATIVE?

Though a literal reading of Revelation 20:4–6 teaches that a real thousand-year kingdom will be ruled by Christ and the resurrected saints, some theologians throughout church history and today have chosen to interpret this passage figuratively. Some view the resurrection described in 20:4 as the spiritual resurrection of believers when they are saved; then the thousand-year reign would be viewed as symbol for the period of church history, during which Christ is reigning spiritually in heaven at the right hand of the Father.[9] This view is often called "amillennialism" — "a" meaning "no," and "millennialism," meaning "thousand years."

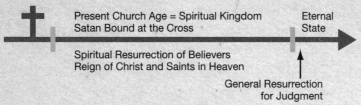

End Times in Amillennialism—The Figurative View

Amillennialists believe that because Christ and the saints are currently reigning over the earth, Satan is figuratively "bound" in the sense that he is unable to exercise *full* deception over the world. Thus, unbelievers are able to believe the gospel and be saved. This view takes the binding of Satan and his banishment to the abyss to refer to a weakening of the devil, not his imprisonment.

But a direct reading of the text argues strongly for a literal kingdom on earth. This view is often called "premillennialism" — "pre" meaning "before," and "millennialism," meaning "thousand years." In this view, Christ returns prior to a literal thousand-year earthly reign. Jesus' own words in other passages of Scripture suggest that He will establish a literal kingdom when He returns (Matt. 19:28–30; Acts 1:6–8). After the apostles, many prominent teachers in the early church — including Papias, Justin, Irenaeus, Tertullian, and Hippolytus — taught that Christ would return before an earthly millennium.[10]

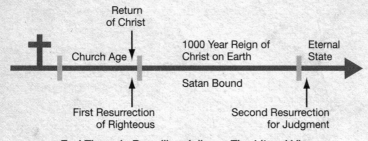

End Times in Premillennialism—The Literal View

This original view of a literal kingdom on earth gradually was replaced by the spiritual amillennial interpretation. Saint Augustine, in the fifth century, changed his view from a literal kingdom to a spiritual one during the course of his Christian life, and his interpretation of Revelation 20 has held sway among Catholic and many Protestant theologians ever since.[11]

worst cause of all sin will be removed from the scene. Revelation 20:3 reminds us, however, that the devil will be cast into *the abyss* when Christ returns, not cast into the lake of fire. Once somebody is thrown into the lake of fire, there is no return. The fact that Satan is cast into the abyss, however, means that he will one day be released, but only "for a short time" (20:3).

I'm surprised at how many commentators read Revelation 20:4 and wonder whom "they" refers to when John wrote, "Then I saw thrones, and *they* sat upon them, and judgment was given to them" (20:4). Grant Osborne writes, "Few verses in the book [of Revelation] are more enigmatic than 20:4."[8] In fact, the simple solution to this "enigma" was actually left standing in mid-air! In the vision begun in Revelation 19 and continuing into chapter 20, "they sat" has to refer to the last ones left in the vision after the Beast, False Prophet, the kings of the earth, and Satan all have be destroyed or removed from the scene—namely, *Christ and His armies*. Once Satan is bound, the King of kings and His army of saints will finish their descent to the earth. John first saw thrones appear, and then Christ and His armies—those last actors remaining in the vision—"sat upon them" (20:4). *At long last the second reason why things are not as they should be will be resolved.* Jesus will take His place of absolute authority over the earth. He will physically reign as King over Israel and His influence and authority will embrace the entire world.

Christ won't reign alone. Already in Matthew 19:28, Jesus promised His disciples, "Truly I say to you, that you who have followed Me, in the regeneration when the Son of Man will sit on His glorious throne, you also shall sit upon twelve thrones, judging the twelve tribes of Israel." Jesus also expanded this promise to all believers: "He who overcomes, and he who keeps My deeds until the end, to him I will give authority over the nations; and he shall rule them with a rod of iron, as the vessels of the potter are broken to pieces" (Rev. 2:26–27), and "He who overcomes, I will grant to him to sit down with Me on My throne, as I also overcame and sat down with My Father on His throne" (3:21). So, the heavenly army clothed in white will include both the original cadre of Jesus' disciples and the church saints, who came to believe because of their preaching (John 17:20).

Yet Revelation 20:4 adds another group to this countless army of ruling saints: those who had been executed during the tribulation, "who had not worshiped the beast or his image, and had not received the mark on their forehead and on their hand." They also will come to life and reign with Christ and the saints for a thousand years. These righteous rulers will not only constitute a moral majority; they will be the only rulers over the earth. Not a single one will be corruptible by money, greed, pride, or power.

No more political conspiracies in the headlines!

No more scandals exposed on the news!

No more bribery, quid pro quo, filibustering, waffling, or broken campaign promises!

The corrupt politics of all earthly governmental systems will be gone forever. Finally, *the third reason that things are not as they should be will be solved.* The righteous, not the wicked, will be in the majority, and a holy leader will be in authority.

God's glorified people will enforce the will of Christ and adjudicate disputes between their subjects. But who are their subjects? Those who survive the tribulation in their mortal, nonglorified bodies (1 Cor. 6:2). This will include the 144,000 preserved remnant of Israel, who will be gathered back to the Promised Land to reestablish the nation of Israel under the Messiah. It will also include Gentile survivors of the tribulation, those who had not received the mark of the Beast but who also had managed to avoid execution at the hand of the Beast and his wicked regime. These mortal survivors — Hebrews and Gentiles alike — will be responsible for repopulating the earth during the thousand-year earthly reign of Christ.

So far we've seen that New Testament saints will have been raptured and resurrected prior to the tribulation and will descend with Christ at the battle of Armageddon (19:11–14; 20:4). We've also seen that the souls of the tribulation martyrs will be rewarded when they come to life and reign with Christ during the thousand-year kingdom (20:4). But what about the Old Testament saints, such as Abraham, Moses, and the prophets? When will they be resurrected?

Though the book of Revelation does not specifically mention them, there are really only two options — either they are resurrected at the same time the New Testament believers are resurrected (1 Thess. 4:17; 1 Cor. 15:52), or they will be raised with the tribulation martyrs at the commencement of the thousand-year reign (20:4). I prefer the second option, based on Daniel 12:13, where an angel says, "As for you, go your way till the end. You will rest, and then at the end of the days you will rise to receive your allotted inheritance" (NIV). In this context, the "end of the days" seems to refer to the end of the tribulation period (12:11–12).

Regardless of exactly when the Old Testament saints join the saints from the church and tribulation periods, we know that when the thousand-year reign begins, all the saved throughout all history will have been resurrected in glorified bodies. Only the unsaved will not be resurrected at that time. In 20:5–6, John describes that all those who partake of this first, multiphase program of resurrection, which began with Christ, will include the church, and it will culminate in the resurrection of all the saints: "This is the first resurrection. Blessed and holy is the one who has a part in the first resurrection; over these the second death has no power, but they will be priests of God and of Christ and will reign with him for a thousand years."

— **20:7–10** —

The Bible clearly declares that Christ's kingdom will last forever. Isaiah 9:7 predicts, "There will be no end to the increase of His government or of peace, on the throne of David and over his kingdom, to establish it and to uphold it with justice and righteousness from then on and forevermore." In answer to this prophecy, an angel told the Virgin Mary, "The Lord God will give Him the throne of His father David; and He will reign over the house of Jacob forever, and His kingdom will have no end" (Luke 1:32 – 33). And loud voices in heaven will one day cry out, "The kingdom of the world has become the kingdom of our Lord and of His Christ; and He will reign forever and ever" (Rev. 11:15). In fact, Daniel 7:18 extends the eternal reign even to the saints who will reign with Him: "But the saints of the Highest One will receive the kingdom and possess the kingdom forever, for all ages to come."

If the kingdom of Christ and His saints will last "forever and ever," why does Revelation 20 refer to the reign of Christ lasting only one thousand years? In truth, the millennial reign is actually the first thousand years of Christ's eternal reign. The condition of peace and righteousness established by Christ *will* last forever. Scripture is clear about that. Satan and his false messiah will never regain power over the earth. Christ and His saints will never be dethroned. The earth will never again be cursed. Yet in another sense, this specific phase of Christ's rule will come to an end after a thousand years and only then will the final phase of His reign begin.

During the thousand-year reign the mortal survivors of the tribulation — Jews and Gentiles — will populate the earth by marrying and having children. By the end of the thousand years the world will be filled with numerous generations of their descendants, who will still have bodies of mortal flesh and, more importantly, *will still struggle with sin and temptation as we now do.* Those subjects of the kingdom will not be like the resurrected rulers, who will be immortal, glorified, and neither marrying nor giving in marriage (Matt. 22:30). And yes, the physical world will be made like Eden during the thousand-year reign — harmonious and peaceful (Isa. 11:6 – 9; 65:20 – 25; Ezek. 36:33 – 36). Yes, the corrupt system of human government underwritten by Satan and his demonic powers will be replaced by Christ and His saints (Dan. 7:21 – 22). But the human population will still have a sinful nature — after the likeness of fallen Adam rather than perfected and glorified after the likeness of Christ.

At the end of the thousand years the descendants of the tribulation survivors will be tested. After his thousand-year imprisonment in the abyss, Satan will be released for a short time (20:7), during which he will rapidly recruit a massive force of rebels willing to march against the King of kings and Lord of lords. How will this be possible? Who in the world would turn against the Messiah enthroned in Jerusalem?

The term "Gog and Magog" may give us a hint. This is a general term in the Bible for the enemies of God spread throughout the remotest parts of the earth (Ezek. 38:2–3; Rev. 20:8). So, those enlisting in Satan's army will likely be *geographically remote*, from among those cities and regions farthest from the center of the Messiah's kingdom in Jerusalem. They also will be *generationally removed* from their original ancestors who had survived the onslaught of the Beast, the memory of which will sound to those distant descendants like mere fables. Finally, the rebels also will be *spiritually distant*, perhaps conforming to the outward expectations of worship and civil duty, but inwardly harboring decades of cynicism, selfishness, and rebellion.

In any case, the dragon will have no problem enlisting an army as numerous as the sands of the seashore. But the "war" masterminded by Satan will never take place. Before a shot is fired, before a blasphemous syllable is uttered, flames from heaven will devour Satan and his vast army of rebels. Then God will finally consign the devil and all of his cohorts not to the temporary abyss, but to the lake of fire (20:10), which originally had been prepared for "the devil and his angels" (Matt. 25:41).

Satan's brief release and humanity's futile rebellion prove two things: *the total incorrigibility of Satan* and *the total depravity of humanity*. As inconceivable as it may seem, not all children born during the millennium will be loving and loyal subjects of Christ. Though Christ's reign will turn the world right-side up, many hearts will remain upside down. Outwardly they may conform, but inwardly they will harbor bitter feelings ripe for harvest when Satan arrives with a message to match their hidden malice. Make no mistake: the human heart remains deceitful and desperately wicked!

Application

Saints Misbehaving

The world, the flesh, and the devil—these three have been engaged in mortal combat with godliness since Genesis 3 plunged all humanity into slavery to sin, susceptibility to Satan, and suffering in the deteriorating world. Today *the world* around us is not our ally: "Do not love the world nor the things in the world.... For all that is in the world, the lust of the flesh and the lust of the eyes and the boastful pride of life, is not from the Father, but is from the world" (1 John 2:15–16). *The devil* is certainly not our friend: "Be of sober spirit, be on the alert. Your adversary, the devil, prowls around like a roaring lion, seeking someone to devour" (1 Peter 5:8). And *the flesh* rouses constant conflict with the Spirit: "For the flesh sets its desire against the Spirit, and the Spirit against the flesh; for these are in opposition to one another, so that you may not do the things that you please" (Gal. 5:17).

When we sin, it's easy to blame the world and the devil, letting our own fallen, depraved nature off the hook. The reality of Revelation 20:7–8, however, makes this "easy out" nothing but a copout. Even with Satan bound for a thousand years and the external world's temptations removed, a host of secret rebels will be ripe for the picking when Satan is released from the abyss. In fact, the devil will find so many hard hearts at the end of the millennium that John said their number was "like the sand of the seashore" (20:8). How could this be? Because those countless men and women born and raised during the thousand-year reign of Christ will still have a sinful nature just like you and me today, and a person's depravity is enough to bring them down.

In light of the example of human depravity in Revelation 20, I want to highlight three vital truths for us today.

First, *when it comes to our sinfulness, we must never play the blame game.* Because Satan is altogether wicked and invisible, there's no better scapegoat than the adversary himself. And because we can't escape the world's uninvited input, it's always easy to point our fingers at this or that worldly trap when we find ourselves caught in its iron jaws. Sometimes, of course, it's true. The devil and the world make it downright difficult to live a holy life. But when this "blame game" becomes a daily habit, we forget that though we are forgiven and declared to be "saints" by God's grace, we are simultaneously sinners by nature. Rather than playing the blame game, we need to take full responsibility for our own disobedience.

This leads to the second truth: *when it comes to our sinfulness, we must never downplay our depravity.* Think through these verses. As much as we hate to admit it, they all apply to us:

> The hearts of the sons of men are full of evil and insanity is in their hearts throughout their lives. (Eccl. 9:3)

> For all of us have become like one who is unclean, and all our righteous deeds are like a filthy garment. (Isa. 64:6)

> There is none righteous, not even one; there is none who understands, there is none who seeks for God; all have turned aside, together they have become useless; there is none who does good, there is not even one. (Rom. 3:10–12)

> For I know that nothing good dwells in me, that is, in my flesh. (Rom. 7:18)

Not until we've come to terms with the depths of our own depravity will we be able to get a grasp of the amazing grace of God.

This brings us to our third important truth: *when it comes to holiness, we must up-play God's work in us.* I'm not saying we sit back and do nothing. I'm not denying free will and personal responsibility. Scripture is clear, however, that believers in Christ—*and only believers*—have been given the empowering grace of the Spirit who works in us, enabling us to live holy lives. Let me encourage you to read a few familiar lines of Scripture. You've probably read them many times before, but read them slowly, as if for the first time.

> For by grace you have been saved through faith; and that not of yourselves, it is the gift of God; not as a result of works, so that no one may boast. For we are His workmanship, created in Christ Jesus for good works, which God prepared beforehand so that we would walk in them. (Eph. 2:8–10)

> Most gladly, therefore, I will rather boast about my weaknesses, so that the power of Christ may dwell in me. (2 Cor. 12:9)

> For this reason I bow my knees before the Father … that He would grant you, according to the riches of His glory, to be strengthened with power through His Spirit in the inner man. (Eph. 3:14, 16)

> For by these He has granted to us His precious and magnificent promises, so that by them you may become partakers of the divine nature, having escaped the corruption that is in the world by lust. (2 Peter 1:4)

> No temptation has overtaken you but such as is common to man; and God is faithful, who will not allow you to be tempted beyond what you are able, but with the temptation will provide the way of escape also, so that you will be able to endure it. (1 Cor. 10:13)

> So then, my beloved, just as you have always obeyed, not as in my presence only, but now much more in my absence, work out your salvation with fear and trembling; for it is God who is at work in you, both to will and to work for His good pleasure. (Phil. 2:12–13)

Did you read every word, or did you skip a line or two? If so, please go back, *carefully and slowly* graze over those six passages. As you just read, Satan and the world cannot always be blamed; our flesh is capable of extreme wickedness, *but* God has provided special strength and unusual ability. So, the choice is ours. The truth is, we *don't* do what's right not because we *can't*, but because we *won't*. The sooner we're willing to stop playing the blame game or throwing personal pity parties, the quicker we'll learn to harness that limitless reservoir of divine power placed in us by the Spirit. Then give *Him* the glory for His miraculous inner work.

Heaven and Hell (Revelation 20:11–21:8)

[11]Then I saw a great white throne and Him who sat upon it, from whose presence earth and heaven fled away, and no place was found for them. [12]And I saw the dead, the great and the small, standing before the throne, and books were opened; and another book was opened, which is *the book* of life; and the dead were judged from the things which were written in the books, according to their deeds. [13]And the sea gave up the dead which were in it, and death and Hades gave up the dead which were in them; and they were judged, every one *of them* according to their deeds. [14]Then death and Hades were thrown into the lake of fire. This is the second death, the lake of fire. [15]And if anyone's name was not found written in the book of life, he was thrown into the lake of fire.

[1]Then I saw a new heaven and a new earth; for the first heaven and the first earth passed away, and there is no longer *any* sea. [2]And I saw the holy city, new Jerusalem, coming down out of heaven from God, made ready as a bride adorned for her husband. [3]And I heard a loud voice from the throne, saying, "Behold, the tabernacle of God is among men, and He will dwell among them, and they shall be His people, and God Himself will be among them, [4]and He will wipe away every tear from their eyes; and there will no longer be *any* death; there will no longer be *any* mourning, or crying, or pain; the first things have passed away."

[5]And He who sits on the throne said, "Behold, I am making all things new." And He said, "Write, for these words are faithful and true." [6]Then He said to me, "It is done. I am the Alpha and the Omega, the beginning and the end. I will give to the one who thirsts from the spring of the water of life without cost. [7]"He who overcomes will inherit these things, and I will be his God and he will be My son. [8]"But for the cowardly and unbelieving and abominable and murderers and immoral persons and sorcerers and idolaters and all liars, their part *will be* in the lake that burns with fire and brimstone, which is the second death."

"Abandon hope, all you who enter here."[12]

Those are the famous words appearing above the gates of Hell in Dante's fanciful epic poem *Inferno*. According to Dante, those who pass beneath that sign will have no hope of ever getting out. Though the details of Dante's fictional picture of heaven, hell, and purgatory range from the fantastic to the heretical, he was right about this: the final destination of the wicked features a one-way entrance. All hope vanishes beyond; there will be no escape from the lake of fire.

Over the last two thousand years, the abrupt paragraph in John's Apocalypse describing the final judgment of the unsaved has instilled fear, sorrow, and disappointment in believer and unbeliever alike. Nobody likes the idea of eternal suffering for sin, but the distinctions between the saved and unsaved are clear, direct, pointed, and unembellished. While the saved will find themselves basking forever in the presence of the Lord, the unsaved will find themselves forever removed from Him. The facts of eternal punishment are set forth without a hint of hope . . . because no hope exists apart from God.

But the glorious truth is that nobody needs to end up in that terrifying place without hope.

— 20:11–15 —

Revelation 20:11–15 describes a terrible scene—an event no one would want to experience. One expositor calls this section "the most serious, sobering and tragic passage in the entire Bible."[13] It will take place after Christ defeats all His enemies at Armageddon, after Satan and his minions are bound for a thousand years while Jesus reigns on the earth, and after evil's last, desperate attempt to attack Christ and regain the world. It will take place after Satan, the Antichrist, and his false prophet have been cast into the lake of fire. In fact, it will be the final reckoning of fallen humanity before God. Even the name is chilling: the great white throne judgment.

Appropriately, Revelation 20:11 begins with God. John saw "a great white throne and Him who sat upon it." The throne is described as "great" because it is God's eternal throne—the seat of His sovereign rule, the place of infinite justice. It is "white" because the verdicts and sentencing that proceed from it will be pure and righteous, reflecting His unimpeachable holiness.

As soon as God the Father appeared in the vision, "earth and heaven fled away" from His presence, like wax melting before a flame or like darkness expelled by the light. In his vision, John saw all existence folding up into nothingness, just as easily as God had called it into existence out of nothing. No words can describe what this image portrays—the eternal, infinite, and magnificent transcendence of God and the absolute temporal, finite, and insignificant contingency of the created universe. The contrast between Creator and creature could not be more dramatic.

With heaven and earth removed, having no purpose in this final judgment (20:11), God will deal with the last group of humans who have not yet been judged—*the unsaved*. They have no place to stand except before their Maker. The first resurrection included all people of God from every age—Old Testament saints, New Testament saints, and tribulation saints. Those raised to life in the second resurrection will include all the rest—all who died apart from the free gift of eternal life in Christ. They're called the spiritually "dead." With heaven and earth dismissed from God's all-consuming presence, the unsaved dead will have no place to hide from God Almighty.

Imagine the different categories of people who will form that group of unsaved from all history:

- those who replaced the Creator with idols and false gods
- those who turned their backs on the free grace of God in favor of a works-based religion
- those who repeatedly heard the gospel of Christ but rejected Him until too late
- those who concluded, based on logic, reason, and experience, that God doesn't exist
- those who lived out their depravity through selfishness, wickedness, and violence

With all the dead gathered before the throne of God, "books were opened" (20:12). Some books contained an accurate record of their deeds, but one of them—the book of life—contained an eternal list of names. The "book of life" image has deep roots in the Old Testament (Ex. 32:32–33; Dan. 12:1–2; Mal. 3:16). Believers during Old Testament times were saved by grace, through faith, as they trusted in God's promises and honored the old covenant. When Jesus initiated the new covenant, He told His disciples, "Rejoice that your names are recorded in heaven" (Luke 10:20). Similarly, Paul encouraged believers with a reminder that their names were written in the book of life alongside other faithful servants of Jesus (Phil. 4:3). Hebrews also declared that the church comprised those "who are enrolled in heaven" (Heb. 12:23).

In order for a person's name to be recorded in the book of life, he or she must reject the notion that a person's own righteousness will suffice. As the apostle Paul wrote, "knowing that a man is not justified by the works of the Law but through faith in Christ Jesus, even we have believed in Christ Jesus, so that we may be justified by faith in Christ and not by the works of the Law; since by the works of the Law no flesh will be justified" (Gal. 2:16). Believers, whose names are written in the book of life, will never receive punishment based on their deeds. Therefore, they will not be summoned to stand before the great white throne.

Revelation 20:12 tells us that another set of books has recorded the good and bad deeds of every person—a symbol indicating that God will never forget a wicked word, thought, or deed. On the basis of this comprehensive knowledge

What Happens to a Person After Death?

"And inasmuch as it is appointed for men to die once and after this comes judgment." (Hebrews 9:27)

	At Death	Bodily Resurrection	Judgment	Eternal Destination
Christian	Christ's Presence — The Grave	Resurrection at the Rapture	Judgment Seat of Christ in Heaven for Rewards	Heaven
Old Testament Believer	Paradise/ Abraham's Bosom — The Grave	Resurrection at Christ's Second Coming	Judgment on Earth for Rewards	Heaven
Tribulation Believer	Christ's Presence — The Grave	Resurrection at Christ's Second Coming	Judgment on Earth for Rewards	Heaven
Unbeliever	Sheol/Hades Torment — The Grave	Resurrection at the End of the Millennium	Judgment at the Great White Throne for Sins	Hell/ Gehenna/ Lake of Fire

Produced by Insight for Living, copyright © Charles R. Swindoll, Inc. Used by permission.

of every unsaved person's wickedness, He will judge justly. We should remember, however, that anyone may have their wicked deeds blotted out, cast away from God as far as the east is from the west (Psalm 103:12). How? Simply by accepting Christ's free offer to write his or her name in His eternal book of life and receive eternal salvation. Each of us has a choice: either enroll in the book of life now and be rewarded at Christ's throne for our good works done in faith … or keep our names out the book of life through unbelief and be judged at God's throne on the basis of our wicked deeds.

Some may think, "I'm not such a bad person, I'll take my chances with the book of deeds." They forget one vital truth: in order to qualify for heaven, his or her entry in the book of deeds needs to be filled with *all* good deeds and *no* bad deeds. God's standard is complete moral perfection (James 2:10). If He finds just one sin recorded there, no matter how small, the sentence will be an eternity of suffering in the lake of fire. No one except the Son of God has ever lived without sinning (2 Cor. 5:21). Because we all have depraved natures and live in a fallen world, no one will ever make it through life without sinning (Rom. 3:23).

In Revelation 20:12–13, the sea, death, and Hades all gave up their dead—from the small to the great. That is, *all people* throughout all time who rejected God's grace will be made to stand before Him and receive their just sentence. As once more you read 20:12–15, note the repetition of the phrase "according to their deeds." The purpose of this appearance before the Creator is to allow the charges to be read to every unbeliever before sentencing. One expositor describes the seriousness of the judgment:

> The accused, all the unsaved who have ever lived, will be resurrected to experience a trial like no other that has ever been. There will be no debate over their guilt or innocence. There will be a prosecutor, but no defender; an accuser but no advocate. There will be an indictment, but no defense mounted by the accused; the convicting evidence will be presented with no rebuttal or cross-examination. There will be an utterly unsympathetic Judge and no jury, and there will be no appeal of the sentence He pronounces. The guilty will be punished eternally with no possibility of parole in a prison from which there is no escape.[14]

The final judgment has three phases—the verdict, the sentencing, and the penalty. The *verdict* is determined simply by confirming that the accused is not, in fact, listed in the book of life. Having determined this, the next step is the *sentencing*, which will be based strictly on the deeds of the accused. The implication is that those who acted more wickedly will receive a greater degree of punishment than others. How this actually works out is up to God. Finally, having determined guilt as well as just sentencing, the Judge assigns the *penalty*—they will be thrown into the "lake of fire," which John calls "the second death."

Although the lake of fire was originally intended for "the devil and his angels" (Matt. 25:41), those who submitted to demonic rule over their lives will find themselves consigned to the same eternal destination where Satan, the Beast, the False Prophet, and the demons were sent (Rev. 19:20; 20:10). No one summoned before the great white throne judgment will be able to escape.

— **21:1–4** —

God created the world to be ideally suited for humankind, whom He created to enjoy an intimate relationship with Him forever. Sin, however, interrupted the Lord's purpose for us. It broke humanity's relationship with God, yes; but it did more than this. It affected creation itself, subjecting it to decay, disharmony, and hostility. When farmers planted vegetables, they harvested weeds. When they tried to grow grain, fruit, and flowers, they got thistles, brambles, and thorns. The evil of humanity resulted in more than just the fall of Adam and Eve. It affected all creation. From the center of Eden to the edge of the cosmos, creation has groaned for redemption since the fall, as Paul wrote:

> For the creation was subjected to futility, not willingly, but because of Him who subjected it, in hope that the creation itself also will be set free from its slavery to corruption into the freedom of the glory of the children of God. For we know that the whole creation groans and suffers the pains of childbirth together until now. (Rom. 8:20–22)

In God's plan, however, sin will absolutely *not* have the last word. After the great white throne judgment, God will replace this present fallen universe with a new one. This "new heaven and ... new earth" (21:1) is the future hope of all who know and love the Lord Jesus Christ. It will be radically different from the sin-twisted, broken, and bruised world we see today. All the things that caused us grief and sorrow will be relegated to the past. Revelation 21:1–8 serves as a short preview for what John will describe in greater detail in 21:9–22:5.

In 21:1, the new heaven and new earth will not be new merely in a chronological sense—as we talk about a "new day," for example. Rather, John describes *qualitative* newness. To use a film metaphor, this isn't a sequel; it's a completely new and different production. It isn't simply a reedited version, enhanced with clearer sound, brighter colors, and a smattering of digitally enhanced special effects. This is no reedit; it's a *remake*! The Greek word *kainos* ("new") means "different from the usual, impressive, better than the old, superior in value or attraction."[15] John had watched as the first heaven and earth "fled away" (20:11), along with all the associated contaminations of sin. In this next vision John saw heaven and earth return — but this time a *new* heaven and a *new* earth, uncontaminated and unaffected by sin (21:1). Created by a perfect God who does perfect work, these will be perfect places existing in a perfect environment. One of today's Christians composers puts it well, *"I can only imagine."*[16]

On the vast stage of the new heaven and new earth, the spotlight suddenly turns toward a descending star: "the holy city, the new Jerusalem" (21:2). This "new city" was promised in chapter 3, when Jesus Himself said, "He who overcomes ... I will write on him ... the name of the city of My God, the new Jerusalem, which comes down out of heaven from My God" (3:12). John described the city in terms of a bride adorned for her husband — pure, radiant, lovely, elegant, and stunning. This beautiful city descends directly from God, erected not by human hands, but

NO MORE SEA?

Most earthlings view the sea as both essential and positive. In elementary school we learned that the oceans are *required* to maintain the weather cycle — the ocean purifies water, which evaporates into the atmosphere, forms clouds, and rains back down onto the earth. Without the oceans, our atmosphere and ecosystem would be drastically different. The oceans also are *relaxing*. The most alluring vacation spots are on or beside the sea — from beaches to islands, from ports to cruise ships. Oceanfront property is expensive — a mark of the elite. Deep-sea recreation, like fishing, sailing, and diving, provide enjoyment for many. Clearly, people view the seas positively.

To people of the ancient world, however, the sea was a mysterious, frightening, and dangerous place, characterized by chaos and possessing the power to kill without warning. No fate could have been worse than to be swallowed up by the sea and have one's remains devoured by fish.[17] Travel by sea was treacherous. Ships had to navigate within sight of land to avoid getting lost or caught in a sudden storm. At the same time, they couldn't sail too close to land, lest they strike a reef or be driven against rocks or jagged cliffs. Trade by sea was both a precarious and lucrative business. If your ship made it back with goods from afar, you were rich. If it didn't, you lost everything — sometimes, your own life.

In the book of Revelation, the sea also served as a symbol, "a principle of disorder, violence, or unrest that marks the old creation (cf. Isa. 57:20; Ps. 107:25–28; Ezek. 28:8)."[18] John's imagery of the sea elsewhere in Revelation designates it as an origin of all kinds of cosmic evil (Rev. 12:12; 13:1). It could also represent the unbelieving nations who persecuted God's people (12:12; 13:1). Clearly, in ancient times, sea stood for chaos and calamity, disorder and destruction.

When John saw the vision of the new heaven and the new earth, he made a point of mentioning that there was "no longer any sea" (21:1). This illustrates that the ordering of the new world will be radically different from the present earth. Though modern readers may be perplexed by this revelation, John's peers would have cheered!

by the word of God Himself. The idea of a dwelling place constructed by God is typical biblical language regarding heaven. Consider these examples:

- "The Most High does not dwell in houses made by human hands" (Acts 7:48).
- "But when Christ appeared as a high priest of the good things to come, He entered through the greater and more perfect tabernacle, not made with hands, that is to say, not of this creation" (Heb. 9:11).
- "For Christ did not enter a holy place made with hands, a mere copy of the true one, but into heaven itself, now to appear in the presence of God for us" (Heb. 9:24).
- "But as it is, they desire a better country, that is, a heavenly one. Therefore God is not ashamed to be called their God; for He has prepared a city for them" (Heb. 11:16).

> **TWELVE THINGS MISSING FROM THE NEW HEAVEN AND EARTH**
>
> *No more sea* — because chaos and calamity will be eradicated (21:1).
> *No more tears* — because hurtful memories will be replaced (21:4).
> *No more death* — because mortality will be swallowed up by life (21:4).
> *No more mourning* — because sorrow will be completely comforted (21:4).
> *No more crying* — because the sounds of weeping will be soothed (21:4).
> *No more pain* — because all human suffering will be cured (21:4).
> *No more thirst* — because God will graciously quench all desires (21:6).
> *No more wickedness* — because all evil will be banished (21:8, 27).
> *No more temple* — because the Father and Son are personally present (21:22).
> *No more night* — because God's glory will give eternal light (21:23–25; 22:5).
> *No more closed gates* — because God's doors will always be open (21:25).
> *No more curse* — because Christ's blood has forever lifted that curse (22:3).

- "But you have come to Mount Zion and to the city of the living God, the heavenly Jerusalem, and to myriads of angels, to the general assembly and church of the firstborn who are enrolled in heaven, and to God, the Judge of all, and to the spirits of the righteous made perfect, and to Jesus, the mediator of a new covenant, and to the sprinkled blood" (Heb. 12:22–24).

Taken together, we get the idea that the dwelling place of God—and the place for which the righteous long—is the new Jerusalem, a city not made by human hands. It currently exists where God is—in the invisible, infinite heavens. Yet one day this city will descend to the new earth. Then and only then can it be truly proclaimed: "Behold, the tabernacle of God is among men, and He will dwell among them, and they shall be His people, and God Himself will be among them"

(21:3, though cf. John 1:14). Don't be misled by the word "tabernacle." Unlike the temporary tabernacle in the Old Testament, the presence of God among humans will be permanent (22:5).

The glorious presence of God on earth brings a number of changes. Because wickedness cannot dwell in His presence, all traces of evil will be eradicated. Anything associated with the old world will have "passed away" (21:4), never to return. In fact, because of the abiding presence of God, it will not even be possible for death, mourning, crying, or pain to make so much as a "cameo appearance." Those former villains in the drama of human history will have been cut from the remake. They will be gone forever. To which we reply: *good riddance*!

— 21:5-8 —

Suddenly, unexpectedly, the glorious Person seated on the throne — God the Father — breaks His typical silence and shouts these marvelous words: "Behold, I am making all things new!" (21:5). That's the sum of the entire vision — in fact, it is the climax of the entire book of Revelation — *out with the old, in with the new.* Think about it. No more terminal diseases, hospitals, wheelchairs, or funerals. No more courts or prisons. No more divorces, breakdowns, or break-ups. No more heart attacks, strokes, Alzheimer's, or debilitating illnesses. No more therapists, medications, or surgery. No famines, plagues, or devastating disasters. *He is making all things new!*

Because God's words are so easily disbelieved (or at least reinterpreted), He pointed at John and commanded him, "Write, for these words are faithful and true" (21:5) — as if to remind him and all who would read his words that God can be trusted to accomplish His promises.

God then added two things in verse 6 that secure the certainty of His decree. First, he said, "It is done." The term carries with it absolute finality. Literally, the Greek word *gegonan* means "they have become." This isn't the same word as Jesus used in his statement on the cross, "It is finished" (*tetelestai*) (John 19:30). That word emphasized something in the past that has come to an end — in Jesus' case, the suffering and payment for the sins of the world. When God declares, "It is done," however, He is pointing forward to a permanent condition that has fully arrived. Moreover, the Holy Spirit led John to use the perfect indicative tense to verify that God's promises are secure, He can express things yet future as completed events with enduring results.

Then He said, "I am the Alpha and the Omega, the beginning and the end." These titles, which also appear in 1:8 and 22:13, remind us that this same God can be trusted to know the future exhaustively and perfectly. He alone dwells outside of our realm of cause and effect. Therefore, He can declare the end from the beginning and utter with confidence: "My purpose will be established, and I will accomplish all My good pleasure" (Isa. 46:10).

Finally, God reiterated both the promise and the warning for all of us (21:7–8). The promise is extended to the one "who overcomes" (21:7). The one who overcomes is not the one who has lived a perfect life, obeyed the Ten Commandments, or observed numerous rites and rituals. Rather, people overcome the world through *faith alone*: "For whatever is born of God overcomes the world; and this is the victory that has overcome the world—our faith. Who is the one who overcomes the world, but he who believes that Jesus is the Son of God?" (1 John 5:4–5). Even in the book of Revelation, John described the saints as those who "overcame [Satan] because of the blood of the Lamb and because of the word of their testimony" (Rev. 12:11). The way a person becomes an "overcomer" is not by his or her own efforts or merits, but solely through faith alone in the Son of God alone. Those believers in Christ, then, will become children of God and heirs of all the good things described in Revelation (cf. 21:7)—hence, "overcomers."

Yet countless people will *not* overcome. That's the flipside of the good news. Not all will abandon their sin and pride as they receive forgiveness and eternal life as a free, unmerited gift. Instead, God declares this sober reminder: the fearful, unbelieving, wicked, murderous, immoral, sacrilegious, idolatrous, and deceptive will be consigned to the lake of fire—the second death (21:8). The fates of these two groups could not be more starkly contrasted. In the future, believers and nonbelievers will live eternally, though in separate and opposite locations. That explains John's primary purpose for writing his gospel: to convince those who had not yet placed their faith in Christ to do so—*immediately* (John 20:31)! In the book of Revelation itself, John repeatedly reminded his readers of God's offer of eternal salvation and of the certain consequences that were sure to follow their failure to respond.

Application

Purifying Promises

In his first letter John wrote, "Beloved, now we are children of God, and it has not appeared as yet what we will be. We know that when He appears, we will be like Him, because we will see Him just as He is" (1 John 3:2). God has revealed enough details about the future to instill hope. While we do not know all the details and

From My Journal

Inheritance

When I read the promise that believers will inherit all "these things" (21:7; cf. 1 Cor. 3:22–23), I can't help but feel greatly excited. The inheritance we'll receive from our heavenly Father is unimaginable. At the same time, though, it reminds me of an earthly inheritance I received when my parents passed away years ago.

After my father died, Cynthia and I were notified that we would inherit a portion of what my mother had received from her father, L. O. Lundy. To our surprise, we had inherited royalties from a natural gas well! Now, being from Texas, we knew all about oil wells and the lucrative industry of natural gas. They were the ones who owned the big houses, dined atop skyscrapers, flew around in private jets, and did pretty much whatever they wanted. Now it appeared that we were about to have a share in all that.

As I read that notice, I shouted, "Cynthia, Look!" She wasn't as impressed as I was. But I persisted: "Wait, look! It's an inheritance. This is going to be *unbelievable*!" Unable to stir much optimism in my superpractical and level-headed wife, I got on the phone and called my sister. "Hey, sis . . . you get the letter?"

"Yeah," she said, "we may be rich!" Finally someone who saw things my way!

"I know it! It's fantastic!"

So week after week went by as we waited eagerly for our ship to come in. How much was a natural gas well worth? I could only imagine off-the-chart amounts of money. I mean, even if it was just worth several thousand a year, that's hundreds of dollars per royalty check . . . and when it's "found money," well, that's nothing to snub your nose at.

Finally, the first royalty check arrived in the mail. With my heart thumping I cracked open that seal and pulled the check from the envelope.

One Dollar and 37/100————————————

To put that in perspective, the paper, processing, and postage cost more than the amount of the check! I finally decided to wade through all the paperwork of the inheritance. It was then that I discovered that we had inherited about one-half of one-eighth of one-tenth of one-thirtieth of one-fiftieth of one-fourth of one-half of one percent! If somebody in Texas was getting rich off that natural gas well, it wasn't anybody named Swindoll. The next check was even less! Exit priceless riches; enter painful reality.

But out of this disappointment, I have great news. The eternal inheritance we'll receive from our heavenly Father won't be like that. Not at all! He said we'll inherit "all things." Each of us will receive 100 percent of God's promise. I can't get my mind around that, but it's true. We're more than "partial heirs" with Christ and our fellow believers. We are "joint heirs"—recipients of eternal life and all the treasures that nobody can imagine this side of heaven.

are unable to grasp the full import of the profound promises, we have enough information to give hope and excite anticipation.

Yet John immediately added another important purpose for knowing the future: "And everyone who has this hope fixed on Him purifies himself, just as He is pure" (1 John 3:3). Knowing about the eternal blessings promised to those who trust in Christ is meant to have a *purifying* effect on our present lives. The process envisioned by John is as follows:

Knowledge of our promises + Hope in our present = Increase in our purity

Just as the coming of the new heaven and new earth will annihilate the impurities of the present corrupt world (Rev. 21:1–4), so too our transforming relationship with Christ and the indwelling presence of the Holy Spirit should progressively purify our own lives. In fact, the apostle Paul used "new creation" language when referring to our conversion to Christ when he wrote, "Therefore if anyone is in Christ, he is a new creature; the old things passed away; behold, new things have come" (2 Cor. 5:17).

We would be wise to take some time to reflect on the "old things" mentioned in Revelation 21:1–8. These are things that will be banished from the new creation. In the following chart, select the few lingering products or practices of sin that affect you the most. Then, study the Scriptures under "How Hope Can Encourage," noting important truths or promises related to the lingering products or practices. Finally, based on the passages describing "How Victory Can Be Won," ponder your own practical application in the right column.

Open House at the Celestial City (Evil not Invited) (Revelation 21:9–22:5)

⁹Then one of the seven angels who had the seven bowls full of the seven last plagues came and spoke with me, saying, "Come here, I will show you the bride, the wife of the Lamb." ¹⁰And he carried me away in the Spirit to a great and high mountain, and showed me the holy city, Jerusalem, coming down out of heaven from God, ¹¹having the glory of God. Her brilliance was like a very costly stone, as a stone of crystal-clear jasper. ¹²It had a great and high wall, with twelve gates, and at the gates twelve angels; and names *were* written on them, which are *the names* of the twelve tribes of the sons of Israel. ¹³*There were* three gates on the east and three gates on the north and three gates on the south and three gates on the west. ¹⁴And the wall of the city had twelve foundation stones, and on them *were* the twelve names of the twelve apostles of the Lamb.

	Lingering Products or Practices of Sin	How Hope Can Encourage	How Victory Can Be Won	Personal Application
Products of Sin	Tears, mourning, and crying (emotional turmoil)	Isaiah 61:1–3	1 Peter 1:6–8	
	Pain and death (physical and mental suffering)	John 11:17–27	1 Thessalonians 4:13–18	
	Thirst (physical desires)	John 4:10–14	Psalm 42:1–11	
	Cowardice (anxiety and worry)	Matthew 6:25–34	1 Peter 5:7	
Practices of Sin	Unbelief (faithlessness and disloyalty)	Mark 9:23–24	Luke 22:31–32	
	Abomination (rebellious and destructive sin)	Hebrews 12:1–11	Revelation 2:5	
	Murder (hatred and violence)		Ephesians 4:26–27	
	Immorality (pornography, extramarital sexual sin)		1 Thessalonians 4:3–5	
	Sorcery (superstition and occultism)		Acts 19:18–19	
	Idolatry (materialism and false religion)		1 Timothy 6:9–11	
	Lying (cheating and dishonesty)		Ephesians 4:25	

¹⁵The one who spoke with me had a gold measuring rod to measure the city, and its gates and its wall. ¹⁶The city is laid out as a square, and its length is as great as the width; and he measured the city with the rod, fifteen hundred miles; its length and width and height are equal. ¹⁷And he measured its wall, seventy-two yards, *according to* human measurements, which are *also* angelic *measurements*. ¹⁸The material of the wall was jasper; and the city was pure gold, like clear glass. ¹⁹The foundation stones of the city wall were adorned with every kind of precious stone. The first foundation stone was jasper; the second, sapphire; the third, chalcedony; the fourth, emerald; ²⁰the fifth, sardonyx; the sixth, sardius; the seventh, chrysolite; the eighth, beryl; the ninth, topaz; the tenth, chrysoprase; the eleventh, jacinth; the twelfth, amethyst. ²¹And the twelve gates were twelve pearls; each one of the gates was a single pearl. And the street of the city was pure gold, like transparent glass.

²²I saw no temple in it, for the Lord God the Almighty and the Lamb are its temple. ²³And the city has no need of the sun or of the moon to shine on it, for the glory of God has illumined it, and its lamp *is* the Lamb. ²⁴The nations will walk by its light, and the kings of the earth will bring their glory into it. ²⁵In the daytime (for there will be no night there) its gates will never be closed; ²⁶and they will bring the glory and the honor of the nations into it; ²⁷and nothing unclean, and no one who practices abomination and lying, shall ever come into it, but only those whose names are written in the Lamb's book of life.

²²:¹Then he showed me a river of the water of life, clear as crystal, coming from the throne of God and of the Lamb, ²in the middle of its street. On either side of the river was the tree of life, bearing twelve *kinds of* fruit, yielding its fruit every month; and the leaves of the tree were for the healing of the nations. ³There will no longer be any curse; and the throne of God and of the Lamb will be in it, and His bond-servants will serve Him; ⁴they will see His face, and His name *will be* on their foreheads. ⁵And there will no longer be *any* night; and they will not have need of the light of a lamp nor the light of the sun, because the Lord God will illumine them; and they will reign forever and ever.

Eleven sets of wide eyes sparkle in the light of the burning lamps. As soon as the door closes behind Judas, the Master begins speaking in His strange ways again. The words make sense, but the eleven men at the table just can't grasp the meaning: "Now is the Son of Man glorified, and God is glorified in Him.... Little children, I am with you a little while longer ... now I also say to you, 'Where I am going, you cannot come.' ... A new commandment I give to you, that you love one another" (John 13:31–34).

They all stare at the Master and hold their tongues ... except for Peter. He ignores the last command to "love" and instead stays focused on the words "you cannot come." Everyone at the table knows you never tell Peter what he *can't* do. Always up for a challenge, Peter expresses loudly what the other ten were thinking: "Lord, where are You going?" (13:36).

Instead of answering, Jesus stares directly at Peter and repeats His statement: "Where I go, you cannot follow Me now; but you will follow later" (13:36).

Peter, with a head like a rock, suddenly takes on a defensive tone: "Lord, why can I not follow You right now? I will lay down my life for You" (13:37).

Jesus shakes his head slowly. "Really, Peter? Will you lay down your life for me?" He sighs. "Actually, this very night you'll deny me three times before a rooster barely has a chance to crow at the dawn" (13:38, paraphrased).

Peter, silenced by the rebuke, stares down at the table and recedes from the flickering beams of lamplight. The uncomfortable silence that follows is suddenly broken with Jesus' words:

> Do not let your heart be troubled; believe in God, believe also in Me. In My Father's house are many dwelling places; if it were not so, I would have told you; for I go to prepare a place for you. If I go and prepare a place for you, I will come again and receive you to Myself, that where I am, there you may be also. And you know the way where I am going. (John 14:1–4)

Those words stir something deep in the hearts of the disciples. Their imaginations begin to soar as they ponder what He might mean. A place? Prepared? *For us?* With Peter reclining in the shadows, stewing over how he could prove His unwavering devotion to Jesus before sunrise, Thomas speaks up: "Lord, we do not know where You are going, how do we know the way?" (14:5).

Jesus' response would stay with them for the rest of their lives: "I am the way, and the truth, and the life; no one comes to the Father but through Me" (14:6).

The apostle John was among the eleven disciples that memorable night, reclining beside Jesus, soaking in every word. Decades later, pondering those events, he recorded Christ's promise that He would come again to receive His church to Himself and provide that special place prepared for them — a place in His Father's house with many chambers. Sixty years later, near the end of the first century, the same John was given a guided tour of the eternal dwelling place of the saints — the new heaven and new earth.

Though it has been the object of much misunderstanding and endless speculation, what Christians commonly call "heaven" is actually the place where we will dwell eternally. Generally speaking, Christians can say that when we die we go to heaven; as Paul said, "to be absent from the body" is to be "at home with the Lord" (2 Cor. 5:8). Though those who depart this world through death will be with the

Lord in the present heavenly realm, our eternal home is actually the new heaven and new earth. And the center of this new order of things will be the new Jerusalem—the permanent dwelling place of the triune God illuminating the city with glorious light. There, in our glorified resurrection bodies, we will forever commune with the Lord God Almighty, the angels, and the redeemed saints of every generation in history, growing together forever in relationship with God and one another.

John's detailed description of the new Jerusalem in 21:9–22:5 answers our most common questions regarding paradise by using unexpected images. As we take in the incredible scenes through the eyes of John, it might help to think of this journey as a guided tour through a gallery of priceless works of art displayed for all to savor. Keep in mind, though, that this is an inspired, prophetic unveiling of our eternal home. While most details remain a mystery to us as we "see in a mirror dimly" (1 Cor. 13:12), this open-house tour of the Celestial City should encourage us to live in joyful anticipation of our ultimate, eternal residence.

— **21:9–10** —

Having just seen what filmmakers call an "establishing shot" of the new Jerusalem, we're about to fly in slowly from our high aerial perspective into the heart of the Celestial City. We'll soar across the glimmering cityscape, examining the details of its structure and basking in its glory. As we join the apostle John in his guided tour of the new Jerusalem, we will have a rare opportunity to explore the *origin, appearance, exterior, dimensions, materials, distinctive characteristic, brilliance,* and *blessing* of God's eternal city.

First, note the *origin of the Celestial City* (21:9–10). As God's final judgment on repentant sinners faded into the distance, one of the seven angels who had poured out the bowls of wrath tugged on John's arm to escort him on his tour of the new Jerusalem. The angel called the city "the bride, the wife of the Lamb" (21:9). The image of the "bride" or "wife" of God has several meanings in Scripture.

- Physical Jerusalem or "Mount Zion" and its inhabitants (Isa. 54:6; 62:5)
- Israel, the Old Testament people of God (Jer. 2:32; Hos. 1:2)
- The church, the New Testament people of God (Rev. 19:7; 22:17)

When we read the description of the new Jerusalem, "the bride, the wife of the Lamb," it seems most likely that the image encompasses these Old and New Testament concepts. So, the new Jerusalem is a real place created by God as the dwelling of *all* the redeemed of *all* ages. Both Old and New Testament believers will dwell in this city from God. This is the place Jesus had in mind when He went to prepare a place for us (John 14:2–3). Hebrews 11:10 and 12:22 describe the heavenly Jerusalem, the eternal Mount Zion, "whose architect and builder is God." After John was carried away in the spiritual realm to a high mountain, he witnessed this Celestial City complete its descent to the earth — coming down out of heaven from God.

— 21:11 —

Second, John focuses on the *appearance of the Celestial City*. In his inspired description of the new Jerusalem, John used two words to convey its stunning appearance: "glory" and "brilliance." The Greek words are *doxa* and *phōstēr*. They are coupled to describe the same thing: the brilliant glory of God. This glory is also mentioned in 15:8 and 21:23. It most likely refers to the fiery, glowing presence of God (called the *shekinah* by Jewish teachers). The Shekinah glory blazed ahead of the Hebrew people as they fled Egypt, shined brilliantly among His people in the tabernacle, and sat enthroned between the cherubim atop the ark of the covenant in the temple (Ex. 40:34–35; Ezek. 43:5).[19]

When John compares this brilliant glory of God to a "jasper" stone (the Greek word *iaspis*), he probably doesn't mean the modern stone called "jasper," but rather an unblemished, perfectly clear diamond. One commentator notes, "Heaven's capital city is thus pictured as a huge, flawless diamond, refracting the brilliant, blazing glory of God throughout the new heaven and the new earth."[20] Nothing on earth begins to compare to what God has prepared for us, since any choice of words fails to capture the breathtaking intensity of His glory.

— 21:12–14 —

Third, the angel's tour led John on a survey of the *exterior of the Celestial City*. John first noticed a great high wall with twelve gates and twelve foundation stones. Regarding the foundations of ancient cities, commentator Alan Johnson notes:

> Foundations of ancient cities usually consisted of extensions of the rows of huge stones that made up the wall, down to the bedrock. Jerusalem's first-century walls and foundation stones have recently been excavated. Huge stones, some of which are about five feet wide, four feet high, and thirty feet long, weighing 80 to 100 tons each and going down some 14 to 19 layers below the present ground level, have been found.[21]

John saw a glorious city, whose walls rested on twelve massive foundations stones, above which stood twelve gates — three on each side of the square city —

guarded by twelve angels (21:12–13). As his eyes adjusted to the blinding light of the city, John noticed words inscribed on the gates and foundations. On the gates were the names of the twelve tribes of Israel, representing the totality of the Old Testament people of God (21:12); on the foundations were the names of the twelve apostles of Christ, representing the New Testament church of God (12:14). Thus, the city will be the dwelling place of the united people of God—Old and New Testament believers—whose salvation rests on the completed work of Jesus Christ.

— 21:15–17 —

Fourth, John discovered the *dimensions of the Celestial City*. The size of the city in John's vision is staggering—nearly 1,500 miles along each wall! At this point the dimensions of the city seem to cross the bounds of credibility. Skeptics have drawn images like the one below, depicting a globe to which is attached a ridiculous cube that would send the earth wobbling in its orbit and perhaps careening into the sun.

This odd configuration has led many interpreters to take John's measurements of the new Jerusalem less literally. But we must remember two things. First, the extraordinary width, length, and height of the city were no less incredible in John's day than they are today. In fact, one might say that in John's day — when 1,500 miles seemed to many like the distance of the entire inhabited world — the number would have sounded even *more* incredible to them than it sounds to us. Second, John himself seems to have understood these measurements to be

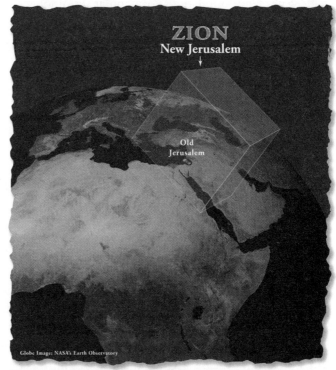

Some interpreters' depiction of the New Jerusalem … on the present earth

human and literal, not spiritual and symbolic. He made a point of noting that the human measurements were the same as angelic measurements (21:17). So, if the measurements are literal, how do we account for the massive size of the city compared to the surface of the earth?

Critics are correct that this massive city could never fit on the *present* earth, but it will be perfectly proportionate to the *new earth*, which God will fashion for the eternal state (21:1). We are never told how large the new earth will be, but we already know that it will be geographically different from the present earth, having no sea (21:1). Furthermore, when we realize that this is the capital city of God's new creation and that its origin is from God Himself, we should not be surprised at its incredible size. It will be the eternal dwelling place of countless saints and innumerable angels.

—21:18–21—

Fifth, John describes the *materials of the Celestial City*. Moving from its structure and size, our lens of Scripture zooms in closer to the actual texture and color of the walls, gates, and foundations. In popular terminology, we could say that the new Jerusalem will be decked out. No wonder John first described the city as "a bride adorned for her husband" (21:2). More specifically, we observe four important characteristics.

(a) The foundations of the city will be adorned with "every kind" of jewel (21:19–20): jasper, sapphire, chalcedony, emerald, sardonyx, sardius, chrysolite, beryl, topaz, chrysoprase, jacinth, and amethyst. Such materials likely symbolize the great diversity of people who will dwell within the city's walls. Elsewhere we read that through His shed blood Christ purchased "men from every tribe and tongue and people and nation" and made them "a kingdom and priests to our God" (5:9–10).

(b) The city itself is "crystal clear," and the massive wall surrounding it is transparent glass (21:11, 18). In the present, fallen world people build walls to maintain privacy and security. These can be physical barriers to keep curious onlookers from watching our every move, but they can also be mental, emotional, or spiritual walls that protect us from harm, hide our shame, or keep people at a distance from us, relationally. This kind of secrecy and security will be unnecessary in the Celestial City. To a certain degree, Christians today can reflect the grace and glory of God, not by hiding in the "inner sanctuary" of private life but by being transparent with others. This means keeping the inside as pure as the outside, and then letting people see the glory of God shine through us.

(c) The gate leading into the city will be created from one giant pearl (21:21). The significance of the "pearly gates" is often missed. John Philips writes:

> All other precious gems are metals or stones, but a pearl is a gem formed within the oyster — the only one formed by living flesh. The humble oyster receives an irritation or wound, and around the offending article that has penetrated and hurt it, the oyster builds a pearl. The pearl, we might say, is the answer of the oyster to that which injured it.[22]

The pearl represents pain resulting in beauty, suffering crowned with glory. When we read of this symbol of the pearl eternally embedded in the doorways of heaven, it should remind us that Christ's suffering had an eternal purpose and opened heaven for us (John 10:9; 14:6). It also assures us that our own suffering for the sake of Christ has a purpose and can be used by Him to reflect His glory in our lives (Rom. 5:3–5; Phil. 3:8–11; James 1:2–4).

(d) The streets of the city will be made of pure gold (21:21). Imagine that! In the new Jerusalem the materials we adore the most in this world will be put to common use. The marble-paved streets of Ephesus, where the apostle John lived out his days, were unusually extravagant, designating it as one of the most opulent cities of the Roman Empire. Yet the opulence of the new Jerusalem will far exceed that of Ephesus or any other city. Gold, for which countless criminals have killed, will be tread upon like asphalt. No vanity. No materialism. No envy or greed. Best of all, no one will be poor in a place that paves its streets with gold.

— **21:22** —

Sixth, let's ponder the *distinctive characteristic of the Celestial City*. The most natural question anyone would ask after taking in the splendor of this vision would be, "What's inside?" We've seen the external measurements and materials of the city and caught a brief glimpse at its streets. But what's inside? If we were to use the biblical and historical Jerusalem as the standard, we might expect to find the temple standing prominently in the center of the city. That would be a good guess — but wrong. Instead, Revelation 21:22 says, "I saw no temple in it, for the Lord God the Almighty and the Lamb are its temple."

Humans tend to associate impressive structures with religious activity, such as the massive, ornate buildings of the Vatican or the Dome of the Rock in Jerusalem, with its enormous golden dome. Even smaller structures such as our own churches represent sacred places to us where we learn about and worship our God. The new Jerusalem, however, will have no need for a special building set aside for worship.

It's true that in the present age of the church, God redirected the location of worship from the physical temple in Jerusalem to the spiritual "temple" of the church itself—the body of believers (1 Cor. 3:16; Eph. 2:19–22). In the future new Jerusalem, in which all the redeemed of every age will dwell, the center of worship will be the Father and the Son. All the inhabitants will worship forever in the presence and by the power of the Holy Spirit.

— **21:23–27** —

Seventh, we observe the *brilliance of the Celestial City.* On the fourth day of the first creation, the Lord created the sun, moon, and stars to illumine the earth and to mark the passing of seasons and years (Gen. 1:14–19). The new creation will not have seasons, nor will it require such sources of light because God will illumine heaven and earth with His own glory.

Throughout the Bible, the images of light and darkness are used to describe two opposing cosmic and spiritual realms:

- truth versus error (John 3:21; 1 John 1:5–8)
- God's perfect order versus sin's corrupt disorder (John 1:1–5)
- pure spirit versus impure flesh (Rom. 13:12–14)
- God's heavenly kingdom versus Satan's worldly kingdom (Col. 1:13–14)

If we look closely at the creation account in Genesis 1, we notice that the presence of light precedes the creation of the sun, moon, and stars (1:3, 14). This may refer to the brilliant effects of God's presence in creation—the Shekinah glory illuminating the universe as He commences His creative work.

After the introduction of sin, the world no longer operated the way God originally designed it. Adam and Eve were the first to experience the withdrawal of God's glorious presence as they were cast into the darkness of the world. Twisted by the fall and obedient to Satan, the world began to function according to a competing system, which poets and other writers have called "darkness."[23] Then, light invaded the darkness in the person of Jesus Christ (John 1:1–5; 8:12; 12:35–36, 46). According to John, the truth that Christ lived, taught, and placed within believers is also the light in which He calls us to walk (1 John 1:5–7).

When John said that night will no longer exist in the new Jerusalem, he was speaking literally, but it has spiritual application. In the new creation, error, sin's corruption, the fallen flesh, and the evil administration of the world will be eradicated (Rev 21:27). As light displaces darkness, so the holy, shining presence of God will drive out all wickedness and falsehood. In this light—the glory of God—all nations will walk (21:24). They will pass through open gates, entering the presence of God without hindrance or hesitation (21:25–26).

— 22:1-5 —

Finally, John describes the *blessing of the Celestial City.* In the beginning God created the earth to be perfectly suited for human life: security without locks, food without famine, work without toil, crops without weeds, relationships without conflict. All of that changed when the first man and woman introduced sin into the world (Gen. 3:14–19). As a direct result, they were expelled from the garden of Eden, unable to access the tree of life and thus live forever (3:22–23). From that moment on, humanity began to decline into disharmony, disease, and eventual death.

In the midst of the new Jerusalem, however, all of the redeemed will have complete access to the tree of life, planted in rows on either side of the river of life flowing from the throne of God and Christ (22:1–2). The complete reversal of the fall and its curse finally will have been accomplished. In fact, the final words of this section are worth repeating. No commentator can improve upon them. Read them slowly, carefully, letting the full truth penetrate your soul:

> There will no longer be any curse; and the throne of God and of the Lamb will be in it, and His bond-servants will serve Him; they will see His face, and His name will be on their foreheads. And there will no longer be any night; and they will not have need of the light of a lamp nor the light of the sun, because the Lord God will illumine them; and they will reign forever and ever. (22:3–5)

Application

Homesick

What a magnificent hope God's people have! When you compare it to the imaginative myths, weird folklore, and false hopes of various religions, you realize why we Christians live our lives homesick for heaven. When I compare the Celestial City to the heavenly hopes of other religions, I cannot help but feel like the most blessed man on earth.

- Buddhists, Hindus, and many New Age religions anticipate repeated reincarnations into other life forms. *That's the spiritual equivalent of spinning your wheels!*

- Taoists view death with indifference. To them it's ultimate oblivion, a state of nondoing. *Talk about boring!*
- Some Muslims believe their religion offers a paradise of seventy virgins satisfying the carnal pleasures of men. *Candidly, that sounds more like Las Vegas than the new Jerusalem!*
- Mormons believe you'll eventually become gods and goddesses of your own world, populating them with your own spirit-babies. *That's just a lot of work!*

Before you jump all over these false views of the afterlife, you can't ignore the fact that some Christians are just as misled with their own ideas of heaven. They imagine floating through the clouds, strumming harps, and having a pair of oversized wings. Instead, we need to think of heaven in more biblical terms. Imagine an eternity with a face-to-face relationship with the One who got you there. No darkness, no disease, no threat of death … everything open and transparent, flooded with light, and filled with the presence of God.

Based on your study of Revelation 21:9–22:5, how does the description of our ultimate destination address your present frustrations, sorrows, or fears? As an experiment over the next week, set aside at least thirty minutes each day to read 21:1–22:5 and then record your thoughts about the new creation in a journal. Take time to mention specific contrasts with current world problems, social ills, and your own current trials. Be specific. Think creatively. Allow your imagination to run free. At the end of this time, reflect on the influence this has had on your attitude, decisions, and relationships with others.

In the Celestial City, evil, sorrow, suffering, sin, and selfishness will not exist. Death will *never* enter our minds. All good things will *never* come to an end as His people give praise and honor to God and enjoy Him forever. *That's* our true home. That's where my mother is. That's where my father is. That's where my believing grandparents and friends and relatives who have passed on have gone. They're home—and they will be there forever.

Feeling homesick yet?

Final Words for a Fallen World (Revelation 22:6–21)

---

⁶And he said to me, "These words are faithful and true"; and the Lord, the God of the spirits of the prophets, sent His angel to show to His bond-servants the things which must soon take place. ⁷And behold, I am coming quickly. Blessed is he who heeds the words of the prophecy of this book."

⁸I, John, am the one who heard and saw these things. And when I heard and saw, I fell down to worship at the feet of the angel who showed me these things. ⁹But he said to me, "Do not do that. I am a fellow servant of yours and of your brethren the prophets and of those who heed the words of this book. Worship God."

¹⁰And he said to me, "Do not seal up the words of the prophecy of this book, for the time is near. ¹¹Let the one who does wrong, still do wrong; and the one who is filthy, still be filthy; and let the one who is righteous, still practice righteousness; and the one who is holy, still keep himself holy."

¹²"Behold, I am coming quickly, and My reward *is* with Me, to render to every man according to what he has done. ¹³I am the Alpha and the Omega, the first and the last, the beginning and the end."

¹⁴Blessed are those who wash their robes, so that they may have the right to the tree of life, and may enter by the gates into the city. ¹⁵Outside are the dogs and the sorcerers and the immoral persons and the murderers and the idolaters, and everyone who loves and practices lying.

¹⁶"I, Jesus, have sent My angel to testify to you these things for the churches. I am the root and the descendant of David, the bright morning star."

¹⁷The Spirit and the bride say, "Come." And let the one who hears say, "Come." And let the one who is thirsty come; let the one who wishes take the water of life without cost.

¹⁸I testify to everyone who hears the words of the prophecy of this book: if anyone adds to them, God will add to him the plagues which are written in this book; ¹⁹and if anyone takes away from the words of the book of this prophecy, God will take away his part from the tree of life and from the holy city, which are written in this book.

²⁰He who testifies to these things says, "Yes, I am coming quickly." Amen. Come, Lord Jesus.

²¹The grace of the Lord Jesus be with all. Amen.

Ravi Zacharias wrote, "Our society is walking through a maze of cultural land mines, and the heaviest price is exacted as we send our children on ahead."[24] Mazes ... landmines ... and exuberant youth who rarely watch where they're going or look before they leap. That about sums up the present world.

The twentieth century saw the rise of a generation who not only rejected much of what their elders held as unassailable truth, but even began to doubt the concept of "truth" itself. The tragic result has been a philosophical system that eggheads call "relativism" or "postmodernism." It's the belief that truth should be defined as merely the commonly held beliefs of a particular culture or society. As such, the belief systems that individuals or groups use to make sense of their world aren't necessarily valid for another person or group. (That wouldn't be "politically correct.")

Through the media, academia, and other opinion formers, this idea continues to shape the thinking of most people in the twenty-first century. Younger generations are left to grope aimlessly through the relativistic maze, feeling insecure, fearful, and overwhelmed. They don't realize that landmines await them around every turn—destructive deceptions and immoral acts that can bring calamity, even an early death.

Paul the apostle warned his young protégé Timothy that a primary characteristic of the latter days would be the widespread rejection of truth (1 Tim. 4:1–2; 2 Tim. 4:3–4). In light of this warning, the book of Revelation provides exactly what the coming end-time generation—and every generation—needs: objective, certified, reliable truth. When armed with this truth, people can face their fallen world with greater security, deeper faith, and stronger courage.

— 22:6–7 —

In verse 6, the pronoun "he" refers to the angel who had been guiding John on his tour of the new Jerusalem (21:9–10, 15–16; 22:1). As John stared breathless at the profound brilliance and incomprehensible magnitude of the vision of our eternal home, the angel knew John needed to hear that "these words are faithful and true" (22:6). The description of the new Jerusalem can be trusted, just as much as the Lord Jesus and God the Father can be believed (3:14; 19:11; 21:5). John, echoing his opening words in 1:1, added this reminder to his readers: "The Lord, the God of the spirits of the prophets, sent His angel to show to His bond-servants the things which must soon take place" (22:6). Then he reiterated the promise of blessing to whoever heeds the words of the book in light of the soon coming of Christ (22:7).

All of this is meant to communicate three important exhortations that are particularly compelling for a confused culture. First, *we are to believe what is faithful and true*. Because the book of Revelation—both its warnings and its promises—comes from God the Father, through Christ, by the power of the prophetic Spirit, it could not be more reliable. This inspired source of truth can be trusted.

Second, *we are to anticipate what has been predicted*. People today doubt whether we can know anything *for certain* about the present and the past—much less about the *future*. As believers in the God of truth, however, we can trust Him when He said, "Truly I have spoken; truly I will bring it to pass. I have planned it, surely I will do it" (Isa. 46:11). We are to live in a constant state of readiness, not neglecting our duties or failing to prepare for the future, but always looking forward to the soon coming of Christ to take us home.

Third, *we are to heed what has been revealed.* Hearing isn't the same as heeding. Heeding implies responding to admonitions and obeying commands. The primary purpose of prophecy is not knowledge but obedience. By seeing the ultimate consequences of sin, we should turn away from wickedness in our own lives. When we consider the blessings of the world to come, a life of gratitude and worship in the present is clearly our best choice.

— **22:8–11** —

Following the verification by the angel, the apostle John stamped his own seal of approval on everything he saw and heard. He placed his reputation on the line when he affirmed that he himself actually saw the things he described (22:8). He was so overwhelmed by the message, however, that he momentarily lost control of his senses and fell down to worship the angel who had just led his heavenly tour.

The exclusive worship of God is a consistent theme throughout Revelation. John's first visions described the worship of God by the heavenly host (chs. 4–5), and as the visions continued to unfold, worship punctuated key events along the way. Then, in chapters 13 and 14, the Beast threatened true worship by presenting himself as a god. I find it surprising, then, that John makes the mistake of worshiping something other than God—not once, but twice (19:10; 22:8–9).

John's impulsive worship of the wrong object should serve as a warning to each of us. How easy it is for finite, fallen creatures to get caught up in the moment and forget the One who deserves our full affection! How prone we are as humans to mistake the gift for the Giver when we receive another of His remarkable blessings. Thankfully, the angel immediately rebuked John, turning his attention back to God—and to God alone (22:9).

The angel completed his message to John by instructing him not to seal up the prophecy of the book (22:10). Though the details of the book will become clearer as the end nears, the big picture of the book is not difficult to discern. It was meant to be read, studied, understood, and applied, not sealed up and stacked on a shelf to collect dust. The warnings of this book must be proclaimed in order to turn as many as possible away from the lake of fire. At the same time, we believers must keep our eternal home in the center of our current hope, letting its truths purify us as we await our coming Lord.

The final words of the angel seem strange. He seems to be encouraging the wicked to continue being wicked instead of repenting: "Let the one who does wrong, still do wrong; and the one who is filthy, still be filthy" (22:11). In light of the many exhortations to repent throughout Revelation, however, this cannot be the intended meaning. Rather, the language may be itself a kind of warning, perhaps paraphrased this way: "You wrong-doers, go ahead and keep doing wrong. Just see what happens. And all unclean sinners, keep rolling in the mud. Just ignore God's offer of cleansing. You've seen what's in store for you. As for you righteous and holy saints, keep practicing righteousness, keep being holy—and you'll get your reward in due time."

— 22:12–16 —

Like a legal document affixed with the signatures of several witnesses, Jesus Himself undersigned the document with His own testimony of its truthfulness. In doing so, He issued four declarations, each of which summarizes a major message of the book of Revelation.

First, Jesus said, "Behold, I am coming quickly" (22:7, 12). After more than two thousand years, Jesus' declaration might appear to be another false claim of a charlatan. It helps to know that the Greek term translated "quickly," however, has less to do with how soon He will come and more to do with the suddenness of the event when it occurs. God alone knows the exact moment of Christ's return, but from our perspective, it could come at any moment. That has been true from the time Jesus uttered those words. Christ's coming is certain and imminent; it could be this very day as you complete your reading of this book.

Second, Jesus said, "My reward is with Me, to render to every man according to what he has done" (22:12). When the Lord Jesus returns to earth, he will bring judgment to those who rejected His free offer of salvation by grace alone through faith alone. The time for repentance will have run its course and each person's eternal destiny will be sealed. The unsaved will receive what he or she deserves for their sins, regardless of fame, wealth, title, or status. In other words, Christ's reward will be just, never prejudiced.

Third, Jesus said, "I am the Alpha and the Omega, the first and the last, the beginning and the end" (22:13). We learned earlier that in the Greek alphabet *alpha* is the first letter and *omega* is the last. Bible expositor John MacArthur makes these interesting observations about Christ's self-designation: "An alphabet is an ingenious way to store and communicate knowledge. The 26 letters in the English alphabet, arranged in almost endless combinations, can hold and convey all knowledge. Christ is the supreme, sovereign alphabet."[25] He is the source of all that is true, from beginning to end.

Fourth, Jesus said, "Blessed are those who wash their robes, so that they may have the right to the tree of life, and may enter by the gates into the city," adding a reminder of those wicked who will never be able to enter the gates of glory (22:14–15). Jesus couples the final beatitude of this book with a severe warning. Note the clear "inside/outside" distinction. There's no ambiguity. Those who favor the relativism of postmodern philosophy reject such rigid categories as "right and wrong," "good and bad," "true and false," "orthodoxy and heresy." When the Light of the world steps into the darkness, those gray matters will be clarified and the darkness will be dispelled once and for all.

Fifth, Jesus said, "I, Jesus, have sent My angel to testify to you these things for the churches. I am the root of the descendant of David, the bright morning star" (22:16). His last statement testifies to the truth of the whole book of Revelation. Like a king affixing a royal seal to an official document, Jesus ties His reputation as Son of David and Son of God to the prophecies of the book. Once the warnings and promises have been uttered, there is no turning back. The words of the book are faithful and true because they were given by the One who is altogether faithful and true.

— **22:17** —

Last words wield influence because they do so much with so little. They have the ability to distill a person's life to its essence. They expose the wit, the angst, the peace, the rage, the pride, and the joy of those who uttered them. The last five verses in Revelation represent the last God-breathed words we have before the return to Christ. In a few lines, the Spirit of God expresses the underlying purpose and message of this entire book.

FAMOUS LAST WORDS

A person's last words often provide a glimpse into his or her character, sometimes revealing what that individual values most. Some parting comments are thoughtful; others are spontaneous and sometimes surprising. Here are the final utterances of well-known people in history.

"I shall hear in heaven. Clap now, my friends, the comedy is done."
— *Ludwig van Beethoven, composer*[26]

"I have been everything, and everything is nothing. A little urn will contain all that remains of one for whom the whole world was too little."
— *Severus, philosopher*[27]

"Ah, is this dying? How I have dreaded as an enemy this smiling friend."
— *Thomas Goodwin, Puritan and president of Magdalen College, London*[28]

"I've never felt better!"
— *Douglas Fairbanks, actor*[29]

"Don't let it end like this. Tell them I said something."
— *Pancho Villa, revolutionary*[30]

"What an artist dies in me! It is now too late."
— *Nero, Roman emperor*[31]

"Alas! I suppose I am turning into a god. An emperor should die standing" (And he stood.)
— *Vespasian, Roman emperor*[32]

"Read me something from the Bible, something brave and triumphant."
— *F. B. Meyer, pastor and author*[33]

First, God continually speaks an invitation to all who are thirsty: "Come!" The entire book of Revelation, in fact, can be regarded as a large invitation to separate oneself from the pollution of the world and its wickedness and to join God's eternal banquet. The Lord's ultimate reason for revealing future events is to draw people to Himself. The implied invitation woven throughout the book is made explicit in these last words.

In verse 17 the Spirit and the bride—speaking, as it were, in unison—mark the first invitation. The church, indwelt and empowered by the Holy Spirit, has been sent to bring the good news of the gospel to the ends of the earth (Acts 1:8). "The one who hears" may be John's own reference to himself—that is, John was the one who saw and heard the visions of this book. The invitation is made explicit in the rest of the verse: it is for anyone who thirsts for spiritual drink—the offer of living water is extended without cost . . . absolutely free! The image of thirst and water are favorites of the apostle John (see John 4:10–14; 7:37–39). Only Christ can quench the deepest needs and necessities of the human heart.

— 22:18–19 —

Following the general invitation, John includes a stern warning. There are two "if . . . then" conditions relating to altering words from the book of Revelation. *If* anybody, for whatever reason, adds to the words of the prophecy, *then* he or she will fall under the judgment of the plagues in the book. *If*, however, anybody removes words from the prophecy, *then* God will remove from him or her the eternal blessings described in the book. In other words, God is serious about His inspired words!

This warning is similar to the words God spoke to the people of Israel as they began to settle the Promised Land thousands of years ago. He said, "You shall not add to the word which I am commanding you, nor take away from it, that you may keep the commandments of the LORD your God which I command you" (Deut. 4:2). Even though it's inconceivable that believers would intentionally add to or subtract from God's inspired Scripture, there are other ways to accomplish the same thing without getting out the pen or eraser. Consider these more subtle ways of altering God's Word:

- *disobeying*—willfully rebelling against clear commands of Scripture
- *disregarding*—intentionally ignoring what is written
- *distorting*—purposely twisting the true meaning of God's Word to accommodate our opinions
- *diluting*—adding other traditions, texts, or teachers as "authoritative truth"

Some well-meaning theologians argue that certain versions or paraphrases of the Bible violate the parameters given in 22:18–19. Still others argue that accidental errors made by well-meaning students of Scriptures constitute "adding to" or "taking from" God's Word. While correctly handling Holy Scripture is vital to the health of the church, the warning of 22:18–19 addresses those who would intentionally, maliciously, and deceptively disobey, disregard, distort, or dilute God's authoritative Word. We keep the words of God by hearing, accepting, internalizing, and applying them to our daily lives.

—22:20-21—

The book of Revelation concludes with a benediction. The term *benediction* comes from the compound Latin word, *bene*, meaning "well," and *dicere*, meaning "to say."[34] It has been an ancient custom for leaders to dismiss a congregation or close a letter with a "good word," a blessing. Here, at the end of an often unsettling series of visions describing the eternal destinies of both believers and unbelievers, none other than the Lord Jesus Himself offers this "good word" of reassurance: "Yes, I am coming quickly" (22:20). Few promises offer more hope!

Speaking on behalf of us all, John adds his "Amen" to Jesus' words. The word *amēn* comes from a Hebrew exclamation based on a verb that means "to confirm, support, uphold; to be certain."[35] A literal rendering could be, "So be it!" John then added a personal prayer: "Come, Lord Jesus!" This last phrase may be derived from an Aramaic saying common among first-century Jewish Christians: *Maranatha*, or "Our Lord, come!" (1 Cor. 16:22). The Aramaic word *mare* was the word used to refer to YHWH—the divine name. So here, at the end of Revelation, John confesses Jesus as the God-Man who is coming soon.

Because this book takes the form of a letter, it closes with a blessing typical of Christian letters (Rom. 16:20; Gal. 6:18). The late pastor and author J. Vernon McGee noted that the Old Testament concluded by mentioning a curse (Mal. 4:4–6), while the New Testament ends with a blessing of grace (22:21).[36] This blessing is addressed to all, not just to the church. Indeed, the unbounded grace of God is offered to everyone.

It seems fitting that I end this commentary on Revelation—indeed, the entire series of New Testament Insights—with the final words of God's final book. Their simplicity and profundity speak for themselves, and I wouldn't presume to improve on them. Instead, I declare them as a prayer as I affirm them with my own "Amen!"

The grace of the Lord Jesus be with all.
Amen.

NOTES: Reign of the Coming King (Revelation 19:11—22:21)

1. Matthew Bridges, "Crown Him with Many Crowns," in *The Hymnal for Worship and Celebration*, no. 234.
2. Osborne, *Revelation*, 687.
3. Phillips, *Exploring Revelation*, 236.
4. Martin Luther, "A Mighty Fortress is Our God," in *The Hymnal for Worship and Celebration*, no 26.
5. Robert A. Pyne, *Humanity and Sin: The Creation, Fall, and Redemption of Humanity* (Swindoll Leadership Library; ed. Charles R. Swindoll; Nashville: Word, 1999), 223.
6. James Russell Lowell, "The Present Crisis," in *The Complete Poetical Works of James Russell Lowell* (ed. Horace E. Scudder; The Cambridge Edition of the Poets; Boston: Houghton Mifflin, 1897), 67.
7. Bauer and Danker, eds., *A Greek-English Lexicon of the New Testament*, 2.
8. Osborne, *Revelation*, 703.
9. For various views on the millennium, see Robert G. Clouse, ed., *The Meaning of the Millennium: Four Views* (Downers Grove, IL: InterVarsity Press, 1977).
10. Modern-day premillennialists often differ on the timing of the rapture in relationship to the seven-year tribulation that will precede the second coming of Christ. This feature of premillennialism is not reflected in this chart, which only compares the millennial views of the two major interpretations. A third view, similar in some ways to amillennialism, is postmillennialism. Proponents of this view hold that Christ will return *after* ("post") a golden age during which the world will be made just and beautiful through the Christianizing of all people. This necessitates the optimistic view that the world is improving as it moves into the future. For an overview of diverse millennial views, see Millard Erickson, *A Basic Guide to Eschatology: Making Sense of the Millennium* (Grand Rapids: Baker, 1998), 55–106.
11. For a defense of the literal view of the millennium, see John F. Walvoord, *End Times: Understanding Today's World Events in Biblical Prophecy* (Swindoll Leadership Library; ed. Charles R. Swindoll; Nashville: Word, 1998), 185–205.
12. Dante Alighieri, *Inferno*, Canto 3, translated from the Italian.
13. John MacArthur, *Revelation 12–22* (MacArthur New Testament Commentary; Chicago: Moody Press, 2000), 245.
14. Ibid., 245–46.
15. Gerhard Kittel, ed., *Theological Dictionary of the New Testament* (ed. and trans. Geoffrey W. Bromiley; Grand Rapids: Eerdmans, 1967), 3:447.
16. Bart Millard and MercyMe, "I Can Only Imagine," from *Almost There* (2001).
17. Thomas, *Revelation 8–22*, 433.
18. Ibid., 440.
19. Osborne, *Revelation*, 749.
20. MacArthur, *Revelation 12–22*, 279.
21. Johnson, "Revelation," 12:596.
22. Phillips, *Exploring Revelation*, 254.
23. Ps. 107:10–11; Prov. 2:13; 4:19; Isa. 5:20; 9:2; 42:6–7; Matt. 6:22–23; Luke 1:78–79; John 1:5; Rom. 2:17–21; Col. 1:13–14.
24. Ravi Zacharias, *Recapture the Wonder* (Brentwood, TN: Integrity, 2003), 27.

25. John MacArthur Jr., *The MacArthur Bible Commentary* (Nashville, TN: Nelson, 2005), 1993.

26. Herbert Lockyer, ed., *Last Words of Saints and Sinners* (Grand Rapids: Kregel, 1975), 117.

27. Ibid., 76.

28. Ibid., 56.

29. Roy Robinson, ed., *Famous Last Words: Fond Farewells, Deathbed Diatribes, and Exclamations upon Expiration* (New York: Workman, 2003), 1.

30. Ibid., 177.

31. Lockyer, *Last Words*, 75.

32. Ibid., 76.

33. Ibid., 72–73.

34. *Merriam-Webster's Collegiate Dictionary* (10th ed.; Springfield, MA: Merriam-Webster, 2000), s.v. "benediction."

35. R. Laird Harris, Gleason L. Archer Jr., and Bruce K. Waltke, eds., *Theological Wordbook of the Old Testament* (Chicago: Moody Press, 1980), 1:51.

36. J. Vernon McGee, *Thru the Bible with J. Vernon McGee*, vol. 5, *1 Corinthians–Revelation* (Nashville: Nelson, 1981), 1080.

Share Your Thoughts

With the Author: Your comments will be forwarded to the author when you send them to *zauthor@zondervan.com*.

With Zondervan: Submit your review of this book by writing to *zreview@zondervan.com*.

Free Online Resources at
www.zondervan.com

Zondervan AuthorTracker: Be notified whenever your favorite authors publish new books, go on tour, or post an update about what's happening in their lives at www.zondervan.com/authortracker.

Daily Bible Verses and Devotions: Enrich your life with daily Bible verses or devotions that help you start every morning focused on God. Visit www.zondervan.com/newsletters.

Free Email Publications: Sign up for newsletters on Christian living, academic resources, church ministry, fiction, children's resources, and more. Visit www.zondervan.com/newsletters.

Zondervan Bible Search: Find and compare Bible passages in a variety of translations at www.zondervanbiblesearch.com.

Other Benefits: Register yourself to receive online benefits like coupons and special offers, or to participate in research.

ZONDERVAN

ZONDERVAN.com/
AUTHORTRACKER
follow your favorite authors